S0-CPF-665

THE GREENHAVEN ENCYCLOPEDIA OF

The Civil War

Other books in the Greenhaven Encyclopedia series:

Ancient Egypt
Ancient Rome
Greek and Roman Mythology
The Middle Ages
The Vietnam War
Witchcraft

THE GREENHAVEN ENCYCLOPEDIA OF

THE CIVIL WAR

Patricia D. Netzley

Kenneth W. Osborne, *Consulting Editor*

Daniel Leone, *President*
Bonnie Szumski, *Publisher*
Scott Barbour, *Managing Editor*

San Diego • Detroit • New York • San Francisco • Cleveland • New Haven, Conn. • Waterville, Maine • London • Munich

For more information, contact
Greenhaven Press
27500 Drake Rd.
Farmington Hills, MI 48331-3535
Or you can visit our Internet site at http://www.gale.com

LIBRARY OF CONGRESS CATALOGING-IN-PUBLICATION DATA

Netzley, Patricia D.
The Civil War / by Patricia D. Netzley.
p. cm. — (The Greenhaven encyclopedia of series)
Summary: An alphabetical presentation of definitions and descriptions of terms, people, and events of the Civil War.
Includes bibliographical references and index.
ISBN 0-7377-0438-1 (Hardback : alk. paper)
1. United States—History—Civil War, 1861–1865—Encyclopedias, Juvenile.
[1. United States—History—Civil War, 1861–1865—Encyclopedias.] I. Title.
II. Greenhaven encyclopedias.
E468.N47 2004
973.7'03—dc22

2003011808

Printed in the United States of America

CONTENTS

PREFACE

In 1861, America was split when decades of disagreement between North and South over various issues, including states' rights in general and slavery in particular, culminated in the secession of eleven Southern states. These states went on to form a new nation, the Confederate States of America. To maintain its independence, the South was willing to fight. The North, particularly its president, Abraham Lincoln, was just as willing to fight to force the rebellious states back into the Union. The war that resulted was without precedent in terms of human and economic cost. By the time the Confederacy surrendered in 1865, between 620,000 and 1,095,000 people had been killed, much of the Southern countryside had been destroyed, and American society had suffered wounds that would take decades to heal. By virtually every measure, historians consider the Civil War one of the most pivotal events in American history.

The war was also unprecedented in its level of documentation, thanks to hundreds of photographs and eyewitness accounts. Though relatively new when the war broke out, photography was used extensively throughout the conflict. Moreover, a high literacy rate among the men involved in the fighting meant that direct accounts of battlefield experiences compose a huge body of literature. After the war, the number of works on the Civil War increased still further as people tried to make sense of the conflict. In fact, by some estimates, over seventy thousand books on the Civil War have been written since 1860. Many of these books are about a single aspect of the event, such as a battle, a general, a type of weaponry, or a political issue.

This wealth of information provides many details about the conflict, but it means that individuals seeking an introduction to the Civil War are often overwhelmed by the amount of material available. Any researcher can find it difficult to glean the most important facts from a mountain of sources. The *Greenhaven Encyclopedia of the Civil War* has therefore been written as a guide to the most significant facts about the Civil War, with 422 entries representing important battles, military equipment, people, places, and issues. While these entries are not intended to be exhaustive, they offer a solid overview of the subject and provide a starting point for readers embarking on an examination of the Civil War.

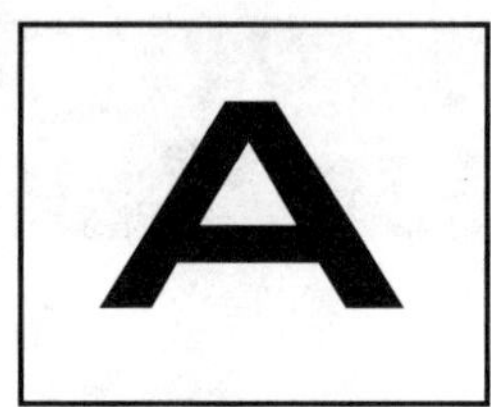

abolitionists

Abolitionists were people who actively advocated the abolishment of slavery. Among the first such people in America were members of a religious sect called the Society of Friends, commonly known as Quakers. Beginning in the eighteenth century, the Friends published numerous condemnations of slavery, including *A Serious Address to the Rulers of America, on the Inconsistency of Their Conduct Respecting Slavery* by Anthony Benezet (1783).

Such works typically framed their arguments in moral terms, taking the position that slavery was inherently evil. However, as abolitionism spread beyond religious organizations during the early nineteenth century, other arguments were used as well. For example, secular abolitionists often drew a parallel between slavery and the sort of oppression that America's founders rejected when they declared independence from England. Moreover, in 1846 radical abolitionists began to promote the idea that Southern slaveholders were plotting to take over the federal government so they could enslave poor whites as well as blacks. As this idea took hold, the abolitionist movement gained acceptance in the American mainstream, whereas previously it had been confined to isolated religious and secular groups.

Many of the groups that originally advocated slavery's abolition were allied with the American Anti-Slavery Society, an organization founded in 1833. This society included some of the most prominent abolitionists of its time, including Frederick Douglass, Sojourner Truth, Harriet Beecher Stowe, Julia Ward Howe, John Brown, Wendell Phillips, William Lloyd Garrison, Martin Delany, Henry Highland Garnet, William Still, and Thomas Morris Chester. Many of these individuals supported the society through antislavery writings and publications, such as Garrison's newspaper, the *Liberator.* In addition, the society published its own literature. For example, in 1835, it printed over a million antislavery pamphlets and sent them into the South hoping to influence opinion there.

Despite such efforts, abolitionism was largely based in the North, although there were many people in the South who shared the abolitionists' view that slavery was wrong. In fact, when the United States abolished the African slave trade in 1808, there were few protests from the South, and by the 1820s there were dozens of active antislavery groups in the region. However, after Northern slaves were emancipated in 1833 and radical abolitionists began to voice more extreme views, Southern abolitionists increasingly found themselves pressured to keep quiet. As a result, many abolitionists moved north and many abolitionist groups in the South dissolved.

Southern abolitionists often based their opposition on economics, arguing that the slave system was expensive to maintain and only benefited the relatively few individuals who could afford to own slaves.

Works arguing this position include the 1846 tract *Inquiry into the Causes Which Have Retarded the Accumulation of Wealth and Increase of Population in the Southern States: In Which the Question of Slavery Is Considered in a Politico-Economical Point of View,* by Daniel Reaves Goodloe; the 1849 pamphlet *A Sober View of the Slavery Question,* by school administrator Calvin Wiley; and the 1857 book *Crisis of the South,* by Hinton Rowan Helper.

During the 1850s, several people were arrested in the South for distributing such literature. At first, only visiting Northerners were targeted. For example, in 1850 two New York abolitionists, Adam Crooks and Jesse McBride, were arrested in North Carolina for passing out abolitionist literature. However, by 1859, Southerners were arrested for sharing such material as well. Among the most prominent was Daniel Worth, a relative of the governor of North Carolina.

Far more influential in popularizing abolitionism were newspapers and books by Northern opponents of slavery. Of these works, none was more influential than the 1852 antislavery novel *Uncle Tom's Cabin* by Harriet Beecher Stowe. This novel inflamed public sentiment in the North by portraying slaveholders as inhumane and evil. Thus demonized in the North, Southerners increasingly became angry and defensive. Consequently, by the time the Civil War broke out, Northern newspapers were blaming abolitionists for the conflict, saying that they had so inflamed passions on both sides that it was impossible for slaveholding states to stay in the Union.

See also Brown, John; Douglass, Frederick; Garrison, William Lloyd; Truth, Sojourner; *Uncle Tom's Cabin.*

Adams, Charles Francis (1807–1886)

The son of U.S. president John Quincy Adams and grandson of President John Adams, Charles Francis Adams worked abroad both before and during the Civil War to further the Union's war efforts through fund-raising and diplomacy. In 1861, under U.S. president Abraham Lincoln, Adams was appointed U.S. minister to Great Britain. As such, he officially protested the occasional British acquiescence in Confederate efforts to acquire ships and outfit them for war; specifically, he argued that such activities violated a May 1861 British proclamation that stated that Great Britain would remain neutral in America's Civil War and not provide weapons to either side in the conflict. Although Adams was unsuccessful in preventing British ships—particularly the raider *Alabama*—from being sold to the Confederacy, he did contribute to

The Liberator *was a popular abolitionist newspaper published by William Lloyd Garrison, a member of the American Anti-Slavery Society.*

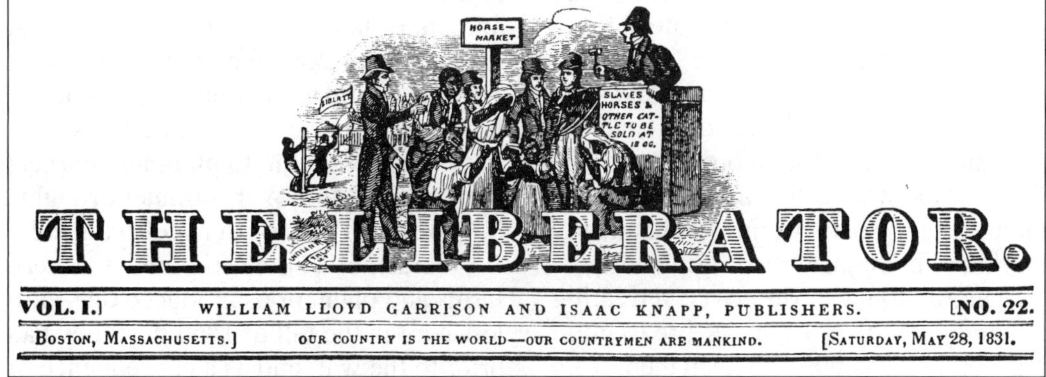

THE LIBERATOR.

VOL. I.] WILLIAM LLOYD GARRISON AND ISAAC KNAPP, PUBLISHERS. [NO. 22.

BOSTON, MASSACHUSETTS.] OUR COUNTRY IS THE WORLD—OUR COUNTRYMEN ARE MANKIND. [SATURDAY, MAY 28, 1831.

post–Civil War negotiations that resulted in Great Britain paying $15.5 million to the United States for damages caused during the war by the *Alabama* and two other Confederate ships with British origins.

Adams was also instrumental in keeping Great Britain from declaring war on the United States over a Civil War–related incident known as the *Trent* Affair, which took place in November 1861. At that time, soldiers on the U.S. frigate *San Jacinto* seized a London-bound British mail steamer, the *Trent,* at sea because it carried two prominent Confederate politicians. This seizure outraged the British, but Adams convinced them that the men who boarded the *Trent* had done so without orders; the British, once convinced that the seizure was not sanctioned by American officials, stopped talking of war with the United States. Adams also persuaded the British government not to recognize the Confederacy as a valid political entity, largely on the grounds that doing so would set a precedent that would encourage rebellions in other countries, perhaps even in British possessions. As a result of this lack of recognition, the Confederacy was prevented from receiving official aid from Britain. **See also** *Alabama,* CSS; foreign countries, involvement of; *Trent* Affair.

agriculture

The Civil War had long-term consequences for agriculture in both the North and the South. In the North, although thousands of Northern farmers (over 165,000 in the Midwestern states alone) left their land to fight in the Civil War, crop production actually increased as the government encouraged the conversion of idle land into farmland in order to provide food for the war effort. Meanwhile, agriculture in the South declined dramatically as Union invasions turned farmland there into battlegrounds. Moreover, retreating Confederate forces often set fire to grain and cotton storehouses to keep them from Union forces; attacking Union forces, meanwhile, burned Southern crops and houses to destroy their enemies' morale, livelihoods, and chances of survival.

Southern agriculture also suffered as a result of Northern blockades, which kept Southern agricultural products from reaching foreign markets and prevented some agricultural supplies, such as salt used for preserving pork, from reaching the South. In addition to shortages due to the blockades, from the outset of the war Southern banks typically refused to loan money to farmers, which meant that farmers often had difficulty buying seed and other supplies.

The Confederate government's policy of confiscating horses and other animals for the war effort further hampered farmers. Without enough animals to pull wagons, plows, and other farm implements, farms and plantations became less productive. Productivity was reduced still further by a Confederate law that required all able-bodied men except plantation owners (that is, owners of at least twenty slaves) to fight in the war.

As agricultural productivity declined and Northern blockades continued, food became scarce in the South. This was compounded by the fact that to stave off bankruptcy many farmers turned the corn and wheat they grew into alcohol, which they sold to the troops. As food supplies dwindled, the Confederate government passed laws to prohibit alcohol production and encourage farmers to increase the amount of land used to grow food crops. As a result, plantation owners shifted from growing cotton to growing corn. Nonetheless, food remained scarce because so few men were available to plant and harvest their crops. Moreover, summer droughts in 1862 and 1863 led to a reduced yield.

Overall, by some estimates Southern farms and plantations produced one-third less corn in the fall of 1863 than they had prior to the war, and as a consequence of such shortages crop prices rose dramatically. By the end of the war, corn had become very expensive; it was $30 a bushel in many places in the South, or around three times the average soldier's monthly pay. Other crops were expensive as well. Thus, even after the war ended many Southerners were unable to afford adequate food—a situation that persisted well into the Reconstruction period. **See also** cotton; plantations; Reconstruction.

Alabama

Also called the "Heart of Dixie" during the Civil War, the state of Alabama hosted the convention at which the nation called the Confederate States of America was created and Jefferson Davis was elected its president. This event took place in the state capital of Montgomery on February 4, 1861, approximately one month after Alabama seceded from the Union. Alabamans, however, were not unanimous in supporting the Confederacy, with the northern part of the state generally supporting the Union. This internal conflict continued throughout the Civil War, but Alabama's divisions did not affect its official commitment to the war effort. **See also** Confederate States of America; Davis, Jefferson.

Alabama, CSS

A thirty-two-foot-wide wooden sailing ship that was also equipped with a steam engine, the *Alabama* was the most successful Confederate raider of Union vessels of commerce. Commander James Dunwoody Bulloch of the Confederate navy ordered the construction of the vessel, originally called the *Enrica,* in a shipyard across the Mersey River from Liverpool, England. When the U.S. minister to Great Britain, Charles Adams, learned that the ship under construction was intended for the Confederacy, he protested to the British government, because Britain's Queen Victoria had earlier proclaimed that her country would remain neutral in regard to America's Civil War. After great debate, however, the British government decided that the *Enrica* was not a warship because it carried no weaponry.

Therefore British authorities allowed the *Enrica* to leave the shipyard under Bulloch's command, supposedly for a test sail on the Mersey River. Instead, Bulloch took it out to sea, and by August 1862 the ship was in the Azores being outfitted with seven smoothbore cannons, one rifled cannon, other weapons, and ample ammunition. Bulloch then transferred command of the ship—now renamed the *Alabama*—to Captain Raphael Semmes, who had orders from Confederate president Jefferson Davis to immediately begin attacking U.S. merchant vessels.

Over the next two years, without ever seeing a Confederate port, the *Alabama* attacked U.S. merchant ships and whalers in the Azores, and throughout the Atlantic, the Gulf of Mexico, and the Caribbean, sinking fifty-five ships worth $4.5 million and capturing ten ships worth approximately $500,000. The *Alabama*'s attacks ended in June 1864 just off the coast of Cherbourg, France, in the English Channel. There, the *Alabama* encountered the USS *Kearsarge,* one of several ships that had been hunting it. Captained by John A. Winslow, the *Kearsarge* sank the *Alabama* after a fierce seventy-minute gun battle that took place in full view of spectators both onshore and in neutral vessels. Most of the *Alabama*'s crewmen, including Captain Semmes, were rescued by a British yacht, the *Deerhound,* and taken to England, where British authorities refused to turn them over to Union authorities. **See also** Adams, Charles Francis; Semmes, Raphael.

alcoholism

Alcoholism was a major problem for both Union and Confederate forces. In particular, drunken brawls and alcohol-induced depression in military encampments threatened soldiers' morale and efficiency throughout the war. To combat this problem, enlisted men were not allowed to buy alcohol unless they had special permission for medical reasons, although Union soldiers were sometimes given small amounts of whiskey as rewards for exemplary behavior in camp or on the battlefield. Nonetheless, soldiers often smuggled whiskey into camp or made their own alcoholic beverages from ingredients they found in the area. Whether smuggled into camp or manufactured there, any alcohol was likely to be discovered by officers, who would then punish those in possession of it. Therefore soldiers tended to consume their alcohol as quickly as possible, and this binge drinking often made them ill.

While enlisted men were generally denied alcohol, officers in both armies were allowed to buy and consume as much whiskey as they wanted whenever they wanted. Consequently some officers, most notably Union general Ulysses S. Grant, became alcoholics. Such drunkenness sometimes led to battlefield command errors, as when one Confederate staff officer at the Battle of Ball's Bluff (in Virginia in 1861) accidentally ordered his men to attack troops that turned out to be from another Confederate unit. **See also** agriculture; Grant, Ulysses S.

Alexander, Edward Porter (1835–1910)

Georgia native Edward P. Alexander was a Confederate artillery expert who developed new weapons, including rockets, and innovative battle tactics. As an example of the latter, he built an observation tower that enabled him to monitor Union troop movements during battles in the Manassas, Virginia, area; during the Seven Days' Battles of June and July 1862 he employed an observation balloon for the same purpose. Alexander served the Confederacy as a captain in charge of the Confederate Signal Corps, first in Richmond, Virginia, and then in Manassas, Virginia, and as chief of ordnance, or artillery, for Confederate generals P.G.T. Beauregard, Joseph E. Johnston, and William N. Pendleton. He also trained artillery batteries under General Robert E. Lee and performed other duties related to the Confederate Ordnance Department. In late 1862 he was given command of an artillery battalion and immediately made changes in the unit's gun-positioning practices, thereby contributing to a Confederate victory at the Battle of Fredericksburg. In February 1864, as a brigadier general, Alexander was placed in charge of artillery in the First Corps, and in the final phase of the war he fortified Richmond, Virginia. After the war, Alexander wrote two books about his experiences, *Fighting for the Confederacy* (1889) and *Military Memoirs of a Confederate* (1907). **See also** artillery; balloons; Seven Days' Battles.

Alexandria, Virginia

Alexandria, Virginia, was the site of the first publicized fatality of the Civil War. On May 24, 1861, Colonel Elmer Ellsworth of the Eleventh New York Regiment, also known as the New York Fire Zouaves, led his men into the city in the first Federal invasion of Southern territory. There Ellsworth noticed a Confederate flag flying atop an inn and tavern called the Marshall House, and he forced his way inside to take the flag down. Ellsworth was shot by the innkeeper, James Jackson, who in turn was killed by one of Ellsworth's men. **See also** Ellsworth, Elmer E.

ammunition

Whether used in artillery (large weaponry such as cannons that took more than one man to operate) or small arms (weapons such as rifles that could be handled by an individual), Civil War ammunition amounted to a metal projectile hurled through a metal barrel by the explosion of a charge of gunpowder. However, ammunition varied depending on the peculiarities of the weapon, the intended target, and the availability of supplies.

The most basic type of small-arms ammunition was a metal ball, which was either provided ready-made or manufactured by the soldier himself by melting and molding metal while in camp. To use this bullet, a soldier would pour gunpowder into the bore of his rifle, or the tunnel within the barrel, from the muzzle, or discharging, end; then, using a pole called a ramrod, he would push the projectile deep into the gun. Since it was difficult to avoid using too much or too little powder during the chaos of battle, soldiers typically carried premeasured amounts of powder contained in paper- or linen-wrapped packets called cartridges. Thus, during gun loading, the soldier bit off the powder end of the cartridge, poured the powder into the gun barrel, inserted the bullet, and rammed it down into the gun with a rod.

Many cartridges contained not only the powder but the projectile as well. These cartridges were made by putting a small amount of gunpowder in the center of a scrap of paper or linen, placing a bullet on top of the mound, raising the edges of the paper or linen, and then wrapping and tying the packet with thread. Some cartridges contained more than one projectile, most commonly a collection of tiny metal balls called buckshot. As the war progressed, the North began to manufacture metal cartridges in which the projectile(s) sat in a metal base that held the gunpowder. These were typically used in rifles that loaded from the trigger end of the gun rather than the muzzle.

More advanced projectiles were also used during the war. Prior to the Civil War, soldiers relied on musket balls, which were smooth, solid, spherical pieces of metal named for the musket, a shoulder gun, that fired them. However, the shape of musket balls resulted in a rather slow and inaccurate projectile. To try to solve this problem, gun manufacturers created a new kind of gun called a musket-rifle, or rifle, which had spiral grooves cut inside its barrel (a process called rifling) in order to make the musket balls fit more tightly in the barrel and spin as they exited. (Not only do spinning balls fly straighter, but the greater the gap between the ball and the barrel interior wall, the less the ball's ultimate accuracy.) However, most musket balls did not fit tightly enough in these barrels to take full advantage of the grooves. Therefore for accuracy most Civil War soldiers chose the Minié ball, or "minnie" ball, instead.

Invented in 1848 by French army captain Claude Etienne Minié, minnie balls had been increasingly used in America during the early 1850s. The minnie ball was cylindroconical—cylinder shaped with a cone-shaped nose—and had a hollow base with a plug of wood or metal at the end. When impacted by the force of the gunpowder explosion, this plug would be driven into the ball's core, thereby expanding its sides and making it fit tightly in the gun barrel. As a result, minnie balls were so precise that the average soldier could hit his intended target from a distance of over 250 yards. (In contrast, musket balls were accurate to only 50 feet or less.) Minnie balls also flew faster than musket balls because their cone-shaped tips made them more aerodynamic. By some estimates, a minnie ball could travel more than a half-mile.

Just as small-arms ammunition varied, so too did artillery ammunition. Specifically, artillery projectiles came in many weights, such as twelve pounds, twenty-four pounds, and thirty-two pounds, and in several types, including solid shot, chain shot, grapeshot, canisters, and shells. Solid shot referred to solid balls of metal that were typically fired at distant, fixed targets. Shells, which were hollow and filled with explosives, were also fired at such targets.

Several men were needed to fire Civil War cannons. Some men loaded the shot while others primed the gunpowder and fired the ordnance.

Grapeshot and canisters were typically fired at moving targets because these projectiles exploded into many pieces; they were containers filled, respectively, with large metal balls and small metal balls. Canister containers were usually tin cans, while grapeshot containers were actually just tied wrappings of cloth or canvas. (Their name comes from the fact that the balls showed through the cloth, so they looked like a wrapped bunch of grapes.) Chain shot consisted of two balls linked by a chain; they were fired at ships because they could wrap around and break a mast or destroy rigging.

As with small arms, cannons typically used cartridges that combined shot and powder. Once the cartridge was in place, one of the gunners (it took several to man the cannon) jabbed a wire pick through a vent in the barrel to release the powder from the cartridge. Another gunner then put a primer into the vent hole, and a cord attached to the primer was jerked to ignite it. The resulting primer flame then detonated the main charge and fired the cannon. This process could be so coordinated that the cannon might be fired twice per minute, provided that there was enough ammunition. **See also** artillery; firearms; ordnance accidents; weapons.

Anaconda Plan

The Anaconda Plan was a name coined by the American press to refer to a military strategy recommended by the Union's general in chief, Winfield Scott, at the outset of the war. Scott proposed blockading the

Confederate coast and seizing the Mississippi River and its tributaries, thereby squeezing off the South's supplies the way an anaconda snake slowly suffocates its prey. But this strategy required time to work, and the Northern public wanted a quick end to the war. Consequently, Scott's recommendations were officially dismissed in favor of aggressive military attacks on Southern territory. By the end of 1861, Scott had been replaced as general in chief by Major General George B. McClellan. **See also** McClellan, George Brinton; Scott, Winfield.

Anderson, Robert H. (1805–1871)

Major Robert H. Anderson was the U.S. Army officer in charge of Fort Sumter (located on an island near Charleston Harbor in South Carolina) when, at 4:30 A.M. on April 12, 1861, the Civil War officially began with a shot fired on the fort from a battery located onshore. After more than fifty hours of bombardment, during which 3,341 Confederate shells were fired, Anderson surrendered Fort Sumter to Confederate general Pierre Beauregard.

Prior to the bombardment, Anderson and his men had been besieged since December 26, 1860. Approximately six thousand Confederate militiamen had prevented Anderson and his sixty-eight men from receiving supplies or reinforcements. Although running out of food, Anderson refused to surrender because he was under orders to hold the fort. Despite Anderson's dedication, though, historians believe that he was sympathetic to the Southern cause because he and his wife's relatives owned slaves in Kentucky and Georgia, respectively. **See also** Fort Sumter.

Anderson, William ("Bloody Bill") (1840–1864)

William "Bloody Bill" Anderson was the leader of a band of Confederate guerrillas known as bushwackers who repeatedly ambushed Union soldiers in Missouri. His nickname came from the brutality with which he treated his victims. For example, on September 27, 1864, Anderson captured twenty-four Union soldiers in Centralia, Missouri, and, despite the fact that these soldiers were unarmed, shot each of them in the head as they begged for their lives. Anderson then attacked 147 Union soldiers in the same area, killing 124 even though most had surrendered. He scalped some of his victims and beheaded others, urging his men to mutilate these and other corpses, and displayed a necklace of scalps around his horse's neck. Anderson's most infamous exploit, however, took place earlier, before he led his own guerrilla band. In 1863 he was part of a band of bushwackers led by William Quantrill that massacred at least 150 civilians in Lawrence, Kansas. Since the victims of this attack were unarmed, Quantrill, Anderson, and other participants were widely reviled in the North.

Because of his bloodthirsty behavior, many modern scholars believe that Anderson was mentally ill. However, his rage against Union soldiers was magnified by his belief that the U.S. government was responsible for the death and serious injury, respectively, of his sisters Josephine and Mary while they were in Federal custody. The two had been arrested for associating with Confederate guerrillas, and while in custody a wall collapsed on top of them; Anderson believed that this collapse had been purposely arranged, despite the government's insistence that it had been an accident.

Anderson's own death occurred during a fierce battle on October 26, 1864. At that time, Union forces surrounded him and seventy of his men near Richmond, Missouri. When Anderson attempted to ride through the line of militiamen, he was shot twice in the back of the head. **See also** guerrillas, partisan rangers, and irregulars; Kansas; Quantrill, William Clarke.

Andersonville

Located in Sumter County in southwest central Georgia, Andersonville was a Confederate military prison where captured Union soldiers were kept under inhumane conditions from February 1864 to May 1865. Officially the prison was called Camp Sumter, but it was more popularly known as Andersonville because it was located near the Andersonville Railroad Station. Andersonville was built to relieve the overcrowding of prisoners who were being held at various types of facilities in the Richmond, Virginia, area, but within a short time Andersonville too was overcrowded. Intended to hold ten thousand Union soldiers, it had approximately twelve thousand prisoners by May 1864 and by August 1864 it had approximately thirty-two thousand.

During this time, the prison stockade grew from 16.5 acres to 26 acres, part of which was swampland, but it lacked permanent structures. Inmates slept in sheds made from wood scraps, in tents made from blankets, or in pits dug in the ground. The main source of drinking water for the prisoners was a stream that quickly became polluted with human waste and garbage; in constructing the camp, the Confederates had located the guards' latrine and the cooking area upstream from the stockade. To obtain clean water, the prisoners dug their own wells, but these proved inadequate. In addition, the prisoners' waste fouled the swampland as well as the stream.

As a result of such living conditions, many prisoners suffered from dysentery and other ailments caused by poor sanitation. They also experienced starvation and malnutrition, because Andersonville had too little food for its growing population. Moreover, Andersonville had too few doctors as well as inadequate medical supplies. This contributed to the fact that, of the 49,485 prisoners who were held at the camp during the war, over 13,000 died, and most of the remainder developed serious illnesses. Although many deaths were due to malnutrition and disease, some inmates were executed for robbing and/or killing fellow prisoners.

When Union authorities heard about the horrible living conditions at Andersonville, they began to treat Confederate prisoners just as badly, reducing their allotments of food and supplies. In response to this, the Confederacy tried to improve conditions at Andersonville by erecting some permanent structures, which were intended as housing but were soon used as a makeshift hospital. In addition, shortly after the Union forces of General William T. Sherman occupied nearby Atlanta, Georgia, in September 1864, Confederate officials moved many of Andersonville's prisoners to other camps in Georgia and South Carolina. However, when Sherman removed his troops from Atlanta two months later, the Confederacy returned the relocated prisoners to Andersonville.

Because of the horrible conditions at the camp, Andersonville's commander, Captain Henry Wirz, was put on trial for war crimes as soon as the war ended. Wirz was found guilty, and on November 10, 1865, he was executed by hanging. No other soldier or officer, Confederate or Union, faced this type of postwar trial. **See also** prisons and prisoners of war; Wirz, Henry.

Antietam, Battle of (Battle of Sharpsburg)

The Battle of Antietam (called the Battle of Sharpsburg by the Confederacy) was the bloodiest battle of the Civil War. Fought along Antietam Creek near Sharpsburg, Maryland, on September 17, 1862, after Confederate general Robert E. Lee's Army of Northern Virginia marched into Maryland, the battle resulted in the deaths of 1,546 Confederate soldiers and 2,108 Union soldiers over just twelve hours of fighting; in addition, 7,754 Confederate and 9,549 Union men were

Confederate soldiers lie dead after the Battle of Antietam. Historians disagree over which side won the battle.

wounded and 1,018 Confederate and 753 Union men reported missing once the battle was over. In a cornfield where much of the initial fighting took place, more than 5,500 men were killed or wounded during less than an hour of heavy shell and musket fire. One Confederate general, John Bell Hood, lost 82 percent of his men during the Battle of Antietam.

Scholars disagree over whether the Battle of Antietam was a draw, a victory for the South, or a victory for the North. Those who call it a draw note that neither side prevailed on the battlefield. Those who call it a Southern victory do so on the basis of losses, because although the Confederate troops were severely outnumbered they lost over 10,000 men (killed, wounded, or missing) as opposed to the Union's loss of 12,410. Those who call the Battle of Antietam a Northern victory do so on the basis of politics. Because the battle was the Confederacy's first attempt to bring the war to Northern soil, the South's inability to prevail boosted Northern morale, and Great Britain later cited the Confederacy's failure to win on Northern soil as a reason not to officially recognize the Confederate government. In addition, U.S. president Abraham Lincoln used his announcement of the battle's outcome as an opportunity to release his Preliminary Emancipation Proclamation on September 22, 1862, declaring that as of January 1, 1863, all slaves in all states then in rebellion against the United States would be free. **See also** emancipation.

Appomattox Campaign

Also called Lee's Retreat, the Appomattox Campaign of March and April 1865 ended with the surrender of Confederate general Robert E. Lee to Union general Ulysses S. Grant, which in turn marked the beginning of the end of the Confederate States of America. At the outset of this campaign, Grant sent troops to the city of Petersburg, Virginia, to gain control of the Confederacy's South Side Railroad, and Lee sent Confederate general George E. Pickett to defend the railroad by holding off the Union forces at Five Forks, Virginia. On April 1, 1865, Pickett's roughly ten thousand Confederate infantry and cavalrymen fought against approximately twenty-two thousand Union infantry and cavalrymen. Pickett lost both the battle and the railroad, and the next day the fighting continued all around Petersburg and nearby Richmond. After suffering heavy losses, including the death of Confederate general A.P. Hill, Lee decided to abandon both cities.

Approximately fifty-eight thousand Confederate soldiers fled first to the town of Amelia Junction (also known as Amelia Court House) and then west to Farmville, pursued by about seventy-six thousand men from the Union's Army of the Potomac and the Army of the James. At Farmville, Lee's men crossed the Appomattox River, burning the bridges (four in all) behind them. After the Union armies saved one of the bridges and continued their pursuit, Lee took a stand just north of Farmville, but because he was low on supplies he abandoned his position when darkness fell and headed toward Appomattox Station, knowing that Confederate railcars filled with supplies waited there. Before his men could travel the thirty-eight miles, however, Union soldiers took the supplies and positioned themselves so that Lee's army was nearly surrounded. Seriously outnumbered and with no hope of either escaping or receiving supplies, Lee officially surrendered to Grant on April 9, 1865, in a private home in the town of Appomattox Courthouse.

During the Appomattox Campaign, Lee lost approximately twenty-eight thousand men, either to death or desertion, leaving about thirty thousand to be taken captive by the Union (although they were almost immediately set free). In contrast, the Union lost only about nine thousand men. With Lee's surrender, the Confederacy's Army of Northern Virginia ceased to exist; this loss meant that, although the Appomattox Campaign was not the final battle of the Civil War, the Confederacy was hard-pressed to continue the fight in the days that followed. In fact, after about another month the Confederacy officially ended. **See also** Grant, Ulysses S.; Lee, Robert Edward; Pickett, George Edward; Sheridan, Philip Henry.

Arkansas

Arkansas, a slaveholding state, seceded from the Union on May 6, 1861, and officially became part of the Confederate States of America on May 18, 1861. Less than three years later, pro-Union politicians took control of the Arkansas state government, and in January 1864 they voted to return their state to the Union. Nonetheless, some Confederate forces remained in Arkansas until May 1865. **See also** Confederate States of America.

armies, Confederate

When the Civil War began, the Confederacy had no standing army and had to raise one quickly. Therefore on February 28, 1861, the Confederate Congress authorized the creation of the Provisional Army of the Confederate States, a volunteer force of 100,000 men who would serve for a period of one year. In May the Congress increased this number by 400,000, with the term to be three years (or more if the war lasted longer). A year later, on April 16, 1862, the Confederate Congress passed a conscription act authorizing the drafting of men so that the army no longer had to rely on volunteers.

On March 6, 1861, the Confederate Congress also authorized the creation of a second force, the Army of the Confederate States of America. This was to be the Confederacy's standing army, called the Regular Army, and was intended to remain intact once the South won the war and its independence. Although the Regular Army was intended to have approximately fifteen thousand professional officers and soldiers, only about two thousand men joined this force, since few men wanted to make the military their profession. Nevertheless, altogether between 750,000 and 1.25 million men served in the Confederate armies during the Civil War.

The most experienced Confederate soldiers in the South were those who had once served in the U.S. Army. Approximately three hundred U.S. military officers who came from the South resigned their commissions at the outset of the war and returned home to organize volunteer armies for the Confederacy. Therefore a Northern officer and a Southern officer meeting in battle might have once served together in the U.S. Army or shared a classroom at the U.S. Military Academy at West Point.

Experienced officers were typically placed in charge of the volunteers in the provisional army, which was divided into units also known as armies. Most were named after the geographical areas in which they operated. Some of these many armies remained in existence for the duration of the war, while others were disbanded as new ones were formed. The three most notable Confederate forces within the provisional army were the Army of Northern Virginia, the Trans-Mississippi Army, and the Army of Tennessee.

Army of Northern Virginia. The largest and longest operating of the Confederate armies, this force had anywhere from thirty-five thousand to eighty-five thousand men at any one time. The Army of Northern Virginia operated exclusively in the eastern theater of the war under a series of commanders: Generals P.G.T. Beauregard, Joseph E. Johnston, and Robert E. Lee. Lee, who took command in May 1862, gave the army its name; previously it had been known as the Army of the Potomac, which was also the name of a Union army.

Most of the battles fought by the Army of Northern Virginia were in the Richmond area of Virginia. However, under Lee's command the army ventured into Maryland, where it fought in the Battle of Antietam (September 1862), and into Pennsylvania, where it fought in the Battle of Gettysburg (July 1863). The Army of Northern Virginia also participated in the First Battle of Bull Run (July 1861), the Battle of Seven Pines (May–June 1862), the Seven Days' Battles (June–July 1862), the Second Battle of Bull Run (August 1862), the Battle of Chancellorsville (May 1863), and the defenses of Petersburg, Virginia, and Richmond, Virginia (summer 1864). Associated with so many important battles, over time the Army of Northern Virginia became the army most strongly identified with the fortunes of the Confederacy. Therefore when General Lee surrendered the Army of Northern Virginia in April 1865, many Southerners considered the entire war to be over.

Trans-Mississippi Army. This army operated west of the Mississippi River. Prior to February 1863 it was known as the Southwest Army and was just one unit within a large military organization known as the Trans-Mississippi Department. The Confederacy created the Trans-Mississippi Department on May 26, 1862, as a territorial organization in charge of defending Texas, west Louisiana, Missouri, and Arkansas, as well as taking over Arizona Territory (which then included parts of present day Arizona and New Mexico) and Indian Territory. After February 1863, all units within the Trans-Mississippi Department were combined under one commander—briefly Thomas C. Hindman and then General Edmund Kirby Smith—as the Trans-Mississippi Army. This army consisted of over forty thousand men, although they were not concentrated in one place, and most were part of cavalry units because only on horseback could they cover the vast territories for which they were responsible. The Trans-Mississippi Army participated in fewer battles with Union troops than did other Confederate armies, although it had several confrontations with hostile Native Americans. The army did, however, achieve victory over the Union during its second Red River Campaign in 1864.

Army of Tennessee. This army engaged in many significant battles, including Murfreesboro and Chickamauga. In fact, it was the main Confederate army in the western theater, fighting in Tennessee, Mississippi, Alabama, Georgia, North Carolina, and South Carolina. However, although it was nearly as large as the Army of Northern Virginia, it was not very effective and had many internal problems, including a shortage of men—particularly those with military experience—and disagreements among its officers.

The greatest problem, however, was frequent changes in leadership. The army began in 1861 as a loose organization of western troops (although it was not named the Army of Tennessee until the end of 1862) under Albert Sidney Johnston, who led the force until he was killed in the Battle of Shiloh on April 6, 1862. President Jefferson Davis then gave command of the Army of Tennessee to P.G.T. Beauregard but removed him from the post after only a few months. The third commander, Braxton Bragg, asked to be relieved of his command in 1863. President Davis then gave command to Joseph E. Johnston, but removed him within a few months as well. John Bell Hood then took command. At the beginning of 1864, after a series of defeats, he joined his troops—then only eighteen thousand strong—with those of Lieutenant General Richard Taylor, who reassigned many of its soldiers to other areas. Those who remained were eventually again under the command of Joseph E. Johnston, who surrendered the army to the forces of Union general William T. Sherman on April 26, 1865. **See also** Johnston, Albert Sidney; Johnston, Joseph Eggleston; Lee, Robert Edward.

armies, Union

During the Civil War, over 2 million men served in the Union armies. Of these, fewer than twenty-five thousand were part of the professional military force known as the Regular Army—the U.S. Army as it existed prior to the war. The Union armies, then, consisted of volunteer forces whose basic units were organized at the local, state, or regional level. These units were often led by experienced officers drawn from the Regular Army. President Abraham Lincoln initially called for seventy-five thousand men to volunteer to fight for the Union for a period of ninety days, then asked for over forty thousand more to volunteer to fight for three years. After the First Battle of Bull Run in July 1861, however, it became obvious that the Union needed far more men: 1 million additional volunteers each serving for three years. Two years later, in March 1863, the U.S. Congress passed a conscription act under which the government drafted thousands more men into what were still called volunteer armies.

As the war progressed, the Union organized its armies by geographic department, with each army typically bearing the name of its department. For example, the Army of Northeastern Virginia was in the Department of Northeastern Virginia. These names were often derived from geographic regions, although many armies (such as the Army of the Ohio) took their name from a river within their geographical area. The most prominent of these forces were the Army of the Potomac, the Army of the James, and the Army of the Shenandoah, all in the war's eastern theater; the Army of the Frontier in the war's Trans-Mississippi theater, and the Army of the Mississippi, the Army of the Tennessee, the Army of the Cumberland, and the Army of the Ohio in the war's western theater. The areas of operation and primary commanders of these forces were as follows.

Army of the Potomac. Responsible for defending Washington, D.C., and trying to capture Richmond, Virginia, this army fought in many of the war's most violent battles, including Antietam (September 1862), Fredericksburg (December 1862), Chancellorsville (May 1863), and Gettysburg (July 1863), typically against the forces of Confederate general Robert E. Lee. The Army of the Potomac had a series of commanders. Over the first two years, George B. McClellan, Ambrose E. Burnside, and Joseph Hooker each held the position. In July 1863 George Meade took over and continued to lead until September 1865. However, from March 1864 until the end of the war, the head of all Union armies, General Ulysses S. Grant, accompanied the Army of the Potomac as well.

Army of the James. Under the command of Benjamin F. Butler, this force operated in Virginia and North Carolina from November 1863 to January 1865, at which point a substantial part of the Army of the James was incorporated into the Army of the Ohio. At full strength, the Army of the James had over fifty thousand men, including a number of black troops.

Army of the Shenandoah. Although an earlier army bearing the same name existed briefly in 1861, this army was formed in August 1864 specifically to drive the Confederates from Virginia's Shenandoah Valley. The valley was strategically important because it was a major source of food for the Confederacy as well

A group of Union officers from the Army of the Potomac poses in front of their headquarters in Cold Harbor, Virginia. The army fought in many of the Civil War's most violent battles.

as a launching point for invasions into the North led by Confederate general Jubal Early. Under the command of Philip H. Sheridan, the Army of the Shenandoah pursued and eventually defeated Early's forces and destroyed the valley's agricultural productivity. It then remained in the valley under the command of Alfred T.A. Torbert.

Army of the Frontier. Primarily commanded by John M. Schofield, this army was established in October 1862 to maintain the Union's control of Missouri (which had been gained the previous year by the Army of the Southwest, whose forces were then sent elsewhere). The Army of the Frontier also dealt with Confederate guerrillas in Missouri, and it fought Confederate forces in Arkansas as well as in Missouri.

Army of the Mississippi. Established in February 1862 to gain control of the Mississippi River, this army was led first by John Pope and then by William S. Rosecrans. At full strength it had approximately nineteen thousand men, as well as a fleet of ships and riverboats, and proved to be a highly successful force, capturing a long stretch of the river in Tennessee. Nonetheless, in October 1862 its forces were sent to serve elsewhere under General William T. Sherman. Shortly thereafter, President Abraham Lincoln decided that another Army of the Mississippi was needed to capture the Confederate city of Vicksburg, Mississippi; established on January 4, 1863, by General John A. McClernand, this army instead captured a Confederate fort at Arkansas Post, Arkansas, on January 10–11, 1863, after which its forces became part of Sherman's as well.

Army of the Tennessee. This army fought not only in Tennessee but in Georgia, Mississippi, and the Carolinas as well, participating in many battles and campaigns. Established on October 16, 1862, it had a series of commanders, including Ulysses S. Grant and William T. Sherman.

Army of the Cumberland. This army fought in eastern Tennessee, northern Alabama, and northern Georgia, first under General William S. Rosecrans and then under General George H. Thomas. At a peak strength of over seventy thousand men, the army participated in the Battles of Stones River and Chickamauga and defended Chattanooga, Tennessee, during a siege in September 1863. The army subsequently joined Sherman's Atlanta Campaign, and many of its troops accompanied Sherman on his march through Georgia to the sea; the remainder fought in the Battle of Nashville in Tennessee.

Army of the Ohio. This army existed in two forms. The first, under the command of Don Carlos Buell, operated in Kentucky and Tennessee from November 1861 to October 1862 and fought in several battles, including the Battle of Shiloh (April 1862). The second Army of the Ohio operated in east Tennessee from April 1863 to August 1865, commanded at first by Ambrose E. Burnside, then by John G. Foster, and then by John M. Schofield. Like its predecessor, this force also participated in many battles. For example, in Knoxville, Tennessee, when the Confederates laid siege to the city in November and December 1863, the Army of the Ohio distinguished itself by not only withstanding the siege but driving the attackers out of the area. **See also** Army, Regular (U.S.); conscription; Grant, Ulysses S.

Armistead, Lewis Addison (1817–1863)

Serving first as a colonel and then as a brigadier general, Lewis A. Armistead was one of the most respected Confederate officers. He fought in most major battles through the Battle of Gettysburg and was noted for remaining calm under fire. For example, in July 1863, as commander of an Army of Northern Virginia brigade consisting of the Ninth, Fourteenth, Thirty-eighth, Fifty-third, and Fifty-seventh Virginia regiments during the Battle of Gettysburg, he participated in a particularly courageous attack later known as Pickett's Charge. In this attack Armistead led 150 soldiers fourteen hundred yards across open ground under enemy fire, while holding his sword high with his hat atop the tip of the blade, and then climbed up and over a Union-built obstruction to approach the enemy's artillery. At this point he was wounded by cannon fire. Two days later he died in an enemy hospital, having willed his possessions to Union general Winfield Hancock, with whom he had become friends in the 1840s when the two were serving in the U.S. Army on the American frontier. **See also** Gettysburg, Battle of; Hancock, Winfield Scott; Pickett's Charge.

Army, Regular (U.S.)

Regular Army was the term used to differentiate the U.S. land force that existed prior to the Civil War from the Federal, or Union, armies established at the outset of the Civil War. Approximately sixteen thousand men were in the Regular Army at this time, stationed at various military bases across the country. The army maintained only 163 pieces of field artillery (cannons). A larger force was unnecessary before the war because the Regular Army shared responsibility for national defense with local militias. Once the war began, however, the United States increased the strength of the Regular Army to 22,714 men. This entity remained separate from the Union army throughout the war, although some Regular Army officers were reassigned to train the unskilled volunteers who made up the bulk of the Union's forces. **See also** armies, Union; artillery.

artillery

Also known as cannon, artillery is any kind of weapon that fires a projectile, takes more than one person to operate, and is too large to be carried by an individual. Many types of artillery were used during the Civil War, and each type could be classified in several ways, depending on its ease of use, type of barrel, weight of ammunition, method of loading, trajectory of ammunition fire, and type of deployment (i.e., whether it was best suited for attacking or defending troops on the battlefield, defending a seacoast or city, or laying siege to a town or fort).

When classified according to weight and typical use, artillery fell into two broad categories, field and heavy, with heavy artillery subdivided into siege artillery and coastal artillery. Field artillery was employed on the front lines because it was relatively easy to transport from battlefield to battlefield. Heavy artillery, as its name implies, was much more difficult to move, which meant that it was usually employed against permanent structures whose destruction required sustained bombardment or against ships approaching the shore. These two types of heavy artillery were called siege and coastal artillery, respectively. Of the two, the coastal weapons were the largest.

Artillery was also divided into two categories according to the type of barrel: smoothbore cannon and rifled cannon. The smoothbore cannon had a barrel that was smooth inside, while the rifled cannon had a barrel whose interior had been scored with grooves. This internal grooving, or rifling, made the weapon's ammunition spin as it exited the barrel, thereby increasing the projectile's accuracy, force, and range. For example, a smoothbore cannon might have a maximum range of seventeen hundred yards, whereas the same cannon with rifling might have a maximum range of twenty-three hundred yards. However, in many cases this increase in range did not result in greater accuracy because the soldiers firing the cannon often could not see their target clearly.

Smoothbore and rifled cannons differed in their composition. Smoothbore weapons were usually manufactured out of bronze, although as the war went on this material became unavailable in the South so they were made of cast iron. Rifled weapons, however, could be made only of wrought or cast iron because the grooves would quickly wear away in bronze, which is relatively soft. Nonetheless, sometimes old bronze weapons were later rifled in a temporary attempt to improve their accuracy.

Because rifling was a fairly recent innovation when the Civil War began, smoothbore cannons outnumbered rifled ones. As the war progressed, however, the number of rifled cannons increased. In fact, by the end of the war the rifled siege gun had largely replaced the smoothbore siege gun, because the former proved more effective in blasting through brick and stone fortifications.

Despite the advantages of rifling, the most commonly used field artillery for both the North and the South remained a smoothbore cannon known as the Napoleon. Named for French ruler Louis Napoleon, who first commissioned its creation, this relatively lightweight cannon was first employed by the U.S. Army in 1857. During the Civil War, the U.S. Army purchased 1,127 more of the weapons, and the South manufactured or purchased approximately 500. The Napoleon was popular because it was highly accurate at short range and very easy to transport. It was typically fired at targets less than 250 yards away, in either defense or offense. However, its effective firing range was nearly 2,000 yards. Moreover, the gun was easy to reload, making it possible for a seven-man team to fire two rounds of ammunition per minute.

Artillery was also classified according to the trajectory its projectile followed after firing. The three classifications were guns, howitzers, and mortars. Guns fired on a fairly straight trajectory. Howitzers, which had shorter barrels than guns, fired projectiles in an arching trajectory. Mortars, with an even shorter barrel, fired on a steep up-and-down trajectory. Some artillery pieces were hybrids of these basic types. The Napoleon, for example, was considered a gun-howitzer.

Artillery could be classified yet another way, according to whether the cannon was muzzle-loading, which meant that it was loaded from the barrel end of the weapon (the end where the ammunition exited upon firing), or breech-loading, which meant that it was loaded from the trigger end of the weapon. Most Civil War artillery, including the Napoleon, was muzzle-loading. The Confederate Army of Northern Virginia, however, used breech-loading artillery made by a British manufacturer, Whitworths. These cannons, known as Whitworths, had rifled barrels and an effective range of twenty-eight hundred yards.

In the armies of the Union, the men responsible for firing and maintaining artillery were part of a unit known as a battery. Each battery was typically assigned six pieces of artillery, six ammunition caissons (wagons), a commanding officer with the rank of captain, two other commissioned officers, fourteen noncommissioned officers, and 122 soldiers with the rank of private. In the armies of the Confederacy, the artillery battery was structured much the same, but after 1862 each battery had only four artillery pieces because of a shortage of weaponry. By this time, Southern batteries might also have to do with fewer soldiers because of a shortage of men. For example, some four-gun batteries had as few as forty-five men assigned to them.

That so many men were needed was due to the teamwork required to fire each gun. The firing process for most artillery pieces required one man to put a bag of gunpowder into the gun barrel, another to ram the projectile into the barrel, another to put a detonation device into the breech end of the gun, and another to ignite the detonation device, using either a lit fuse or a wire run through the device to create a spark. Other men were needed to steady the teams of artillery horses that hauled the weapons around while the gun was being fired, to prepare ammunition for each firing, and to clean the barrel of the gun after firing. **See also** ammunition; ordnance accidents.

artists and artwork

Artists created thousands of works depicting the most important people, places, and events of the Civil War. War correspondents sketched scenes of battlefield action and camp life that were then made into wooden engravings for printing in magazines and newspapers, which at the time lacked the ability to reproduce photographs. Meanwhile, painters produced artwork of popular subjects, such as portraits of Civil War heroes, that were put on display and/or made into prints and sold to the public.

Popular art was in great demand both during and after the war, and public displays attracted large crowds. In 1865, for example, hundreds of people lined up to see a portrait of Confederate general Robert E. Lee painted by deaf artist Edward Caledon Bruce, which was on display at the Confederate capitol in Richmond, Virginia. Other crowd-pleasers were large panoramic depictions of famous battles, some of which were painted by teams of artists working under a master who ensured a consistency of style in all sections of the work.

To feed the public's demand for artwork, some companies specialized in turning paintings into lithographic prints, which people in both the North and the South purchased to decorate their homes, hotels, shops, workplaces, bars, and similar places. Such companies might also commission artists to produce illustrations for reproduction. One of the most prominent popular art publishers was Currier and Ives, established in New York by lithographers

Currier and Ives turned paintings of battle scenes into lithograph prints like this one for sale to the public.

Nathaniel Currier and James Merritt Ives in 1857. While this company concentrated primarily on battle scenes and portraits, another popular art publisher in New York, Louis Prang and Company, published maps, battle plans, and war-related sheet music as well as images of Civil War battles and generals. Other notable popular art publishers who specialized in Civil War imagery were Kurz and Allison of Chicago, Illinois; Ayers and Wade of Richmond, Virginia; Blanton Duncan of Columbia, South Carolina; Blelock and Company of New Orleans, Louisiana; and Pessou and Simon of New Orleans. These companies might create lithographs of both Confederate and Union scenes, regardless of whether they were located in the North or the South.

Most of the Confederate etchings produced in the North were derived from the works of Bavarian artist Adalbert Volck (1828–1912), who lived in the Northern city of Baltimore, Maryland, but supported the South's cause. In addition to painting scenes of the South, he also produced cartoons and caricatures of Northerners, but few of these were printed during the war because Volck's Northern printers generally considered them Southern propaganda. Other prominent Civil War painters include Conrad Wise Chapman (1842–1910) and Julian Scott (1846–1901), both of whom made sketches while serving in the war (as a Confederate soldier and a Union drummer boy, respectively) and then turned them into paintings after the war; John Adams Elder (1833–1895), who painted portraits of many Confederate commanders, including Robert E. Lee and Stonewall Jackson, and produced a famous oil painting titled *The Battle of the Crater* in 1865; and Eastman Johnson (1824–1906), who concentrated on painting scenes of wartime home life and of African Americans.

Meanwhile, artist-correspondents provided depictions of action scenes for newspapers and periodicals, fulfilling the role that newspaper photographers perform today. These artists worked in the thick of the action while producing their pen-and-ink sketches, and many of them were wounded in the process. Artist Theodore R. Davis (1840–1894), for instance, was wounded twice on the battlefield. Hired in 1861 by the magazine *Harper's Weekly* to submit sketches that would be published as engravings in various editions, he traveled widely and reproduced numerous battle scenes, including the naval battle between the *Monitor* and the *Merrimack.* Davis also accompanied Union general William T. Sherman on his march from Atlanta, Georgia, to the sea. Other prominent artists making wartime sketches included Winslow Homer (1836–1910) and Edwin Forbes (1839–1895), who focused on camp life rather than battle scenes; Arthur Lumley (1837–1912), who produced drawings of army life in Washington, D.C., and of the First Bull Run battlefield; Alfred and William Waud (1828–1891; 1830–1878), who covered the war for *Harper's Weekly;* Thomas Nast (1840–1902), who did battlefield and camp-life sketches but was primarily known for his editorial cartoons and patriotic drawings supporting the Northern cause; and William Ludwell Sheppard (1833–1912), who drew sketches while serving as a Confederate soldier with the Army of Northern Virginia.

Like Sheppard, many of the most prominent Southern artists during the Civil War created their artwork while they were in the army, making hundreds of sketches that likely would not be shared, reproduced, or turned into paintings until the war was over. Because of a shortage of soldiers, the South could not afford to allow an able-bodied male to devote himself entirely to his artwork while the war was going on. In addition, many artists, both soldier and civilian, as well as printers in the South found it difficult to get the supplies they needed for their work because of Northern blockades. **See also** Forbes, Edwin; Homer, Winslow;

Nast, Thomas; Sheppard, William Ludwell; Waud, Alfred and William.

assassination of President Abraham Lincoln

In April 1865, a month after being inaugurated to his second term as U.S. president, Abraham Lincoln was assassinated by John Wilkes Booth, a stage actor and ardent Confederate. His plot to kill the president was originally designed as a kidnapping rather than an assassination. During the summer of 1864, just prior to Lincoln's reelection, Booth came to believe that the best way for him to aid the Confederate cause was to kidnap Lincoln, take him to the Confederate capital of Richmond, Virginia, and hold him hostage there until the Union released all Confederate prisoners of war. To this end, he recruited several coconspirators, including John H. Surratt, Michael O'Laughlin, Samuel Arnold, George Atzerodt, David Herold, and Lewis Paine (also known as Lewis Powell).

During the winter of 1864–1865, the conspirators met in Washington, D.C., in a boardinghouse owned by John Surratt's mother, Mary Surratt, to plot their crime. They made several attempts to carry out the kidnapping, but each of them failed for various reasons. For example, one attempt on March 17, 1865, was thwarted when Lincoln changed his plans at the last minute, with the result that he was not where the kidnappers expected him to be.

Booth's kidnapping plans became moot after Confederate general Robert E. Lee surrendered his Army of Northern Virginia, effectively ending the war. At this point, Booth's hatred of Lincoln, whom he blamed for destroying the South, led him to decide to assassinate the president. Booth further contended that Lincoln was planning to become a dictator. Booth saw his opportunity to strike when, on April 14, 1865, a friend told him that President Lincoln and General Ulysses S. Grant and their wives would be attending a performance at Ford's Theater that evening.

Booth further hoped that if Lincoln and other high-ranking U.S. government officials, such as Grant, were to die all at the same time, the Union would be thrown into chaos and the Confederacy might be able to snatch victory from defeat. Therefore, he told fellow conspirator George Atzerodt to kill Vice President Andrew Johnson, and instructed Lewis Paine and David Herold to kill Secretary of State William Seward. Both men were to be attacked in their Washington, D.C., homes, while Booth planned to kill Lincoln and Grant at the theater.

Booth, who often appeared in plays at Ford's Theater, was familiar with the play that was being staged—a British comedy called *Our American Cousin,* starring Laura Keene—and knew that a particular line during the third act would elicit a burst of laughter from the audience. He decided that the noise from the audience at this point would muffle the sound of a pistol shot, giving him time to escape before people realized that he had fired at the president. Thus, that evening he waited at a nearby bar, drinking brandy, until around 10 P.M. Booth then entered Ford's Theater through the front entrance and crept up to the president's private box, at the balcony level on stage left. Earlier in the day, he had studied the box and figured out a way to jam its outer door once he was inside so that he would have enough time to do his work without being interrupted.

Lincoln and his wife, Mary Todd Lincoln, had arrived at the theater shortly after the start of the play, whereupon the actors paused so the orchestra could play "Hail to the Chief" to welcome the president. As it happened, General Grant and his wife had not accompanied the Lincolns after all, having decided to go to Philadelphia instead. However, the Lincolns were accompanied by two other friends, Major Henry Rathbone and his fiancée, Clara Harris. Outside the presidential box was a police bodyguard, John Parker, who for reasons that remain unclear left his post around 10 P.M. (Parker's absence leads some historians to believe he was in on the plot, though there is no evidence of this.)

Booth went into the box at around 10:15 P.M., carrying a derringer pistol and a knife, and jammed the outer door closed as planned. He then opened the inner door, walked up behind Lincoln, and shot the president in the back of the head. At this point, Booth's plan went awry. Rathbone reacted quickly and grabbed Booth, the two struggled, and Booth stabbed Rathbone in the arm. Booth then climbed over the box railing and jumped to the stage below (a distance of roughly eleven feet), breaking his left leg just above the ankle when he landed, and shouted "Sic semper tyrannis!" (the Virginia state motto, which is Latin for "as always to tyrants"). According to some accounts, Booth also shouted "The South is avenged!" or "The South shall be free!" After this he hobbled from the stage and out of the theater through a door to the alley, where a young stage technician, with no idea of Booth's plan, was waiting with his horse.

Shortly after Booth made his escape, an unconscious Lincoln was carried to a boardinghouse across the street from the theater. The bullet had destroyed part of the president's brain and remained embedded there behind his right eye, so even though doctors tended to him throughout the night everyone knew he would not survive his injury. Lincoln's son Robert arrived to stay by his father's side, and crowds gathered outside the boarding-

This illustration depicts John Wilkes Booth firing a pistol into the back of President Lincoln's head at Ford's Theater.

house. The president died the next morning, April 15, 1865, at 7:22 A.M.

By this time Booth had escaped the capital and Secretary of War Edwin Stanton had launched a massive campaign to find him, as well as an unidentified man who had stabbed Secretary of State Seward. This man was Paine, who had carried out Booth's assignment. (George Atzerodt, who was given the task of assassinating the vice president, had lost his nerve and failed to act.)

After shooting Lincoln, Booth had met up with David Herold and the two men had ridden to the Maryland home of Dr. Samuel Mudd, whom Booth had met previously but by most accounts barely knew, so that Booth could get treatment for his broken leg. Booth and Herold then headed south into Virginia. On April 26, a Union cavalry troop learned that they were hiding in a tobacco barn at a farm near the Rappahannock River. After soldiers surrounded the barn, Herold surrendered. Booth, however, refused to leave the barn, so it was set on fire, and as it burned someone shot into the barn and killed Booth.

Soldiers searching Booth's clothing found his diary, which offered details about his plans and accomplices. As a result of this information, Booth's coconspirators were soon caught and put on trial in a military court. O'Laughlin and Arnold, who had not been involved in any murder attempts, were sentenced to life in prison; Arnold was later pardoned by President Andrew Johnson and released from prison in 1869, while O'Laughlin died in prison in 1867. Paine, Herold, and Atzerodt, who were all connected to assassination attempts, were hanged in 1865. Mary Surratt, who had allowed the conspirators to meet in her boardinghouse, was hanged as well, even though there was no evidence that she was directly involved in Booth's plans. Her son John Surratt, who was in Canada at the time of Lincoln's assassination, was released after a jury deadlocked on whether he was guilty or innocent. Dr. Mudd, who had treated Booth's injured leg, was sentenced to life in prison but was pardoned, along with Arnold, in 1869. The young stage technician who had held Booth's horse was sentenced to eight years in prison.

The executions of Paine, Herold, Atzerodt, and Mary Surratt were held on July 7, 1865, on the grounds of the Arsenal at the Old Penitentiary Building in Washington, D.C. Crowds gathered to witness the event, some of them upset that a woman was among the condemned. Paine was also upset over this; right before his death he cried out that Mrs. Surratt was innocent and begged for her to be spared. Nonetheless, the executions went forward as planned, overseen by Generals J.E. Hartranft and Winfield Scott Hancock. Five minutes after they dropped through the trapdoors, all of the condemned were pronounced dead.

In the months following her husband's assassination, Mary Todd Lincoln grew so mentally disturbed that she could barely function. Henry Rathbone, who had fought with Booth in the president's box, was similarly affected by Lincoln's death. Fraught with grief over what he saw as his failure to protect the president, Rathbone gradually lost his sanity. He eventually killed Clara, who by this time was his wife.

The assassination also took a toll on the nation, although many people in the South rejoiced over Lincoln's death. In addition to the trauma of losing Lincoln, America had to adjust to a new president, Andrew Johnson, who was in many people's minds ill equipped to take over the office. A Southerner himself, Johnson was lenient with the South in the aftermath of the war, quickly pardoning former Confederates for their misdeeds and easing the return of Confederate states to the Union. Some historians believe that Lincoln would have dealt with the South more harshly than Johnson did, but others believe that Lincoln would have been equally charitable and eager to reunite the country. **See also** Booth, John Wilkes; Johnson, Andrew; Lincoln, Abraham; Lincoln, Mary Todd.

Atlanta Campaign

Atlanta, Georgia, was a major industrial center for the South, but it was not until May 1864 that the North was able to launch a military campaign against the city. Led by Union general William Tecumseh Sherman, the campaign consisted of three armies: the Army of the Ohio with approximately 13,500 troops, headed by General John M. Schofield; the Army of the Cumberland with approximately 61,000 troops, headed by Major General George H. Thomas; and the Army of the Tennessee with 24,000 troops, headed by General James B. McPherson. Defending Atlanta and its environs was a force of approximately 43,000 Confederates, led first by General Joseph E. Johnston and then by General John B. Hood.

Sherman's assault began on May 9, 1864, when he moved into Georgia from Chattanooga, Tennessee. As his forces progressed toward Atlanta, several battles were fought at various points along the route, including the Battle of Peachtree Creek on July 20. This battle resulted in heavy Confederate losses—over 5,000 men, compared to fewer than 2,000 for the Union—and the Confederates fell back into Atlanta. The Confederates then counterattacked but experienced yet another serious defeat, with over one-fourth of their remaining force—roughly 10,000 men—killed during the Battle of Atlanta on July 22. (In comparison, only a few hundred Union soldiers were killed, although General McPherson was among them.) The remaining Confederate soldiers continued to defend Atlanta.

Meanwhile, for the next month Sherman tried to cut the railroad lines leading into Atlanta at several locations, and in mid-August he succeeded in cutting the lines south of the city. Now with no way of getting supplies and afraid of being trapped in Atlanta, the Confederates evacuated the city, after destroying all munitions and other military supplies to prevent the Union from using them. The city's mayor, James Calhoun, then had no choice but to officially surrender Atlanta to the Union on September 2, 1864, and five days later Sherman ordered all of Atlanta's residents out of the city. He then occupied the city for nearly two months, and when he abandoned it on November 15 he set it on fire.

In all, the Atlanta Campaign resulted in the deaths of 4,423 Union soldiers, with another 22,822 wounded and 4,442 missing or captured. The Confederates had 3,044 dead, with 18,952 wounded and 12,983 missing (many of them deserters) or captured. In addition to the human cost, the loss and subsequent burning of Atlanta was a serious psychological blow to the Confederacy. In the North, the taking of Atlanta gave a boost to the reelection campaign of Abraham Lincoln, who used this victory to enhance his image as commander in chief. **See also** Johnston, Joseph Eggleston; Sherman, William Tecumseh.

balloons

Large baskets suspended from hydrogen-filled balloons were used by Union and Confederate forces from 1862 to 1863 as observation posts to detect enemy troop movements. Soldiers were stationed aloft and equipped with flares, telegraph systems, or other means of sending messages to ground forces. The Confederacy apparently had only one such balloon, which was made of multicolored silk in Savannah, Georgia, and filled with gas at the Richmond Gas Works in Virginia. It was then tied to a railroad boxcar or a tugboat for observation purposes, under the direction of then Major (later Brigadier General) Edward Alexander of the Confederate Signal Corps. However, the balloon was used during only one campaign, the Seven Days' Battles (June 25–July 1, 1862) on the Virginia peninsula, because on July 4, 1862, the balloon was captured by Union forces after the tugboat to which it was tied ran aground.

The Union had at least seven balloons in its Balloon Corps, a division of the Union Signal Corps. Commanded by Colonel Thaddeus Lowe of the Army of the Potomac, who was given the title of chief of army aeronautics, these balloons were tied to riverboats that could move along key waterways. The balloons proved particularly valuable in detecting troop movements in Virginia and were used in the Battle of Chancellorsville. Nonetheless, they were difficult to maintain and maneuver, so when Lowe left the army in May 1863 the Union decided to disband the Balloon Corps. **See also** Alexander, Edward Porter.

Ball's Bluff, Battle of

The Battle of Ball's Bluff took place on October 21, 1861, after more than two thousand Union troops, led by Brigadier General Charles P. Stone, were ferried across the Potomac River at Ball's Bluff near Leesburg, Virginia. They were met by approximately sixteen hundred Confederate soldiers, who soon drove them back across the river. Before the Union soldiers could reach the opposite shore, however, their boats became swamped, and many drowned or were captured by Confederate soldiers. In all, approximately 700 Union men were taken prisoner and 921 were killed, including Colonel Edward D. Baker, who was also a U.S. senator, while only 149 Confederate soldiers were killed. Afterward, the U.S. government responded to the disaster by creating a joint congressional committee to investigate what happened; this committee held General Stone responsible for the deaths. He was imprisoned on charges of treason but later released to resume his military command. **See also** battles and campaigns.

Baltimore, Maryland

Baltimore, Maryland, was a site of citizen unrest after the Union established a military presence in the city shortly after the Civil War began. Prior to that time, Maryland had declared neutrality in the conflict because the state had both Northern and Southern sympathizers. The citizens of Baltimore had been among those siding with the South, and their opposition to the Union was problematic because Baltimore was on a railway line that routinely transported Union troops to Washington, D.C.

On April 19, 1861, a large group of Baltimore citizens threw rocks and other objects at soldiers from a Massachusetts regiment who were marching toward the railway station. A riot ensued during which four soldiers and twelve citizens were killed. That night, Baltimore's civic leaders decided to keep all other Union army personnel out of the city, and to this end they destroyed the rail line. Nonetheless, Union soldiers invaded the city and arrested its leaders, including the mayor and police chief. Once the Union had enough forces in and around the town to control it, the leaders were released from jail. **See also** Maryland.

Banks, Nathaniel Prentiss (1816–1894)

A native of Massachusetts, Nathaniel P. Banks was a powerful Republican politician who volunteered for military service in 1861. He immediately used his influence to be named a major general and was given a battlefield command. He then proceeded to lose almost every battle in which he led troops.

After suffering defeats in the Shenandoah Valley and at Winchester and Cedar Mountain in 1862, Banks was sent to New Orleans to replace Benjamin F. Butler as head of the Department of the Gulf. In this capacity in July 1863 Banks successfully captured the Confederate fortress of Port Hudson on the Mississippi River, but this occurred only after a costly forty-three-day siege. Moreover, his success was the direct result of the fall of Vicksburg upriver, because this prevented the besieged fortress from receiving supplies and reinforcements.

In 1864 Banks led the second Red River Campaign, which required him to take an expedition up the Red River to Shreveport, Louisiana. En route his force endured heavy casualties in several skirmishes, eventually retreating to Donaldsonville, Louisiana. After this failure Banks was relieved of his command, and he resigned from the army in August 1865. Historians say that his ouster might have happened earlier had his political connections to wealthy donors not made him so proficient at raising large amounts of money for the war effort.

Banks was ridiculed in the press for receiving no injuries during any of his campaigns. In fact, many reporters accused the general of riding behind his troops, using them as a shield rather than leading them into battle. But despite these criticisms, Banks remained a popular politician after leaving the military, serving in Congress from 1865 to 1878 and again from 1888 to 1891. **See also** Port Hudson, Louisiana; Red River Campaigns.

Barton, Clarissa (Clara) Harlowe (1821–1912)

The founder of the American Red Cross, Clara H. Barton began her humanitarian work during the Civil War. Prior to that time, she was a schoolteacher in Massachusetts and New Jersey and then a clerk in the U.S. patent office in Washington, D.C. Her first Civil War contribution was the nursing of injured soldiers sent to Washington, D.C., to recuperate. She also organized an agency whose purpose was to ensure that medical supplies reached wounded soldiers on the battlefield. As the war progressed, Barton became involved in fund-raising activities in New England that helped send nurses, including herself, to the front lines. In 1865, U.S. president Abraham Lincoln assigned her to establish an agency that would keep track of the men who were wounded, killed, or missing in action.

Clara Barton was a nurse during the Civil War. She went on to found the American Red Cross.

After the Civil War, Barton contributed to relief efforts, including those of the International Red Cross, related to medical care during the Franco-German War, the Spanish-American War, and various natural disasters such as floods and earthquakes. In 1881 she established the American National Red Cross and remained at its head until 1904. **See also** medical personnel and supplies.

Bates, Edward (1793–1869)

A native Virginian who had owned slaves while a lawyer in Missouri, Edward Bates served as the attorney general of the United States from March 5, 1861, to November 30, 1864. He received the appointment as part of a political deal during the 1860 presidential campaign; after Bates lost the Republican nomination to Abraham Lincoln, Lincoln offered him the cabinet position of his choice in exchange for his support, and Bates picked attorney general. From the beginning, however, there was friction between Bates and Lincoln. Bates agreed with Lincoln's decisions to suspend the writ of habeas corpus and blockade Southern ports, but he disagreed with nearly every other action of the president's. For example, Bates opposed mandatory emancipation in the states, believing that each slave owner should be able to decide whether to free his own slaves, as Bates had decided to free his. He also opposed the creation and admission to the Union of West Virginia. Eventually he decided to resign his cabinet position rather than continue arguing with Lincoln over various issues. He then returned to Missouri, where he led the opposition against Radical Republicans in his state. **See also** cabinet, U.S.; political parties; Radical Republicans.

Baton Rouge, Louisiana

Baton Rouge, Louisiana, was an integral part of Union plans to capture the town of Vicksburg, Mississippi, a Confederate stronghold controlling the central Mississippi River. As part of this campaign, in February 1863 Major General Nathaniel Banks established a Union base at Baton Rouge from which he attacked Port Hudson, downriver from Vicksburg. Two months later, to solidify the Union's hold on Baton Rouge, Union colonel Benjamin Grierson scourged six hundred miles of countryside from La Grange, Tennessee, to Baton Rouge over a sixteen-day period. This also served to divert Confederate attention from Union preparations to attack Vicksburg, which finally came under Union control in July 1863. **See also** Banks, Nathaniel Prentiss; Port Hudson, Louisiana; Vicksburg Campaign.

"Battle Hymn of the Republic"

The Civil War song "Battle Hymn of the Republic" was extremely popular with Union soldiers, who often sang it while rallying for battle. The tune, however, predates the Civil War as an 1856 Methodist camp-meeting hymn titled "Oh Brothers, Will You Meet Us on Canaan's Happy Shore?" by William Steffe of South Carolina. (It is not known whether he composed the lyrics as well as the tune.) Shortly after the war began, a group of Union soldiers in Boston, Massachusetts, composed new lyrics that referred to abolitionist John Brown, who had been hanged in Virginia in 1859 for trying to lead a slave rebellion. To many people in the North, John Brown was a hero, and the Union soldiers' lyrics called him "a soldier in the army of the Lord." This song, called "John Brown's Body," quickly became popular throughout the North.

In February 1862, poet Julia Ward Howe was visiting a Union army camp when a clergyman there suggested she write new lyrics for "John Brown's Body" that more closely reflected the moral underpinnings of the Civil War. According to Howe, it took her only one night to come up with the lyrics, which she then sent to the *Atlantic Monthly* magazine for publication as the "Battle Hymn of the Republic." It appeared in the magazine in February 1862, and Howe received $4 as compensation for her efforts. Shortly thereafter the song was adopted as a Union anthem. **See also** Brown, John.

battles and campaigns

There were approximately 10,450 military engagements during the Civil War, most of them in the South. Some of them were major battles, others minor skirmishes, and still others sieges on forts or cities that might last days, weeks, or months. In any case, they might be isolated events or they might be part of a series of military operations designed to achieve a specific, broader goal (such as the capture of an entire peninsula in a certain amount of time). Such operations, taken collectively, were called a campaign (e.g., the Peninsula Campaign).

Historians disagree somewhat on which battles should be included in a list of the most important Civil War conflicts. However, the most commonly cited major battles and campaigns are as follows:

The Attack on Fort Sumter. On April 12, 1861, the Confederates fired the first shots of the war when they attacked a federal garrison at Fort Sumter, located on a man-made island in the middle of Charleston Harbor in South Carolina; on April 14, after a seige of more than fifty hours, the fort fell into Confederate hands.

The First Battle of Bull Run (also known as the First Battle of Manassas). On July 21, 1861, near Centerville, Virginia, Confederate troops led by General Pierre Beauregard were victorious against Union troops led by General Irvin McDowell.

The Fort Henry and Fort Donelson Campaign (also known as the Henry and Donelson Campaign). On February 6 and February 14–16, 1862, Union general Ulysses S. Grant took two Confederate forts, Fort Henry and Fort Donelson, on the Tennessee and Cumberland Rivers, respectively, near Memphis, Tennessee.

The Battle of Shiloh (also known as the Battle of Pittsburg Landing). On April 6–7, 1862, on the west bank of the Tennessee River near Savannah, Tennessee, the Union's Army of the Tennessee and Army of the Ohio, led by Brigadier General Ulysses S. Grant and Major General Don Carlos Buell, respectively, were victorious against the Confederacy's Army of the Mississippi, led by Generals Albert Johnston and Pierre Beauregard.

Jackson's Valley Campaign. From March 23 to June 9, 1862, a series of battles took place in the Shenandoah Valley of Virginia between the Confederate forces of Major General Thomas J. "Stonewall"

Jackson and various Union commanders; the Confederates were ultimately victorious, despite the fact that Jackson's was by far the lesser force.

The Peninsula Campaign (also known as the Peninsular Campaign). From March to July 1862, Major General George B. McClellan led the Union's Army of the Potomac on a campaign across the southeastern Virginia peninsula in an attempt to capture the Confederate capital of Richmond, Virginia, but, after many victories, it was stopped by Confederate general Robert E. Lee and the Army of Northern Virginia. Among the most notable battles of this campaign were the Seven Days' Battles (from June 25 to July 1, 1862) and the Battle of Gaines' Mill (on June 27, 1862).

The Battle of Seven Pines (also known as the Battle of Fair Oaks). On May 31, 1862, Confederate troops led by General Joseph Johnston attacked Union troops led by General George McClellan near Seven Pines, Virginia, but were eventually forced back from the battlefield.

The Second Battle of Bull Run (also known as the Second Battle of Manassas). On August 28–30, 1862, at roughly the same place as the First Battle of Bull Run, Confederate troops led by General Robert E. Lee were victorious against Union troops led by General John Pope.

The Battle of Antietam (also known as the Battle of Sharpsburg). On September 17, 1862, Union troops led by General George McClellan met Confederate troops led by General Robert E. Lee at Antietam Creek near Sharpsburg, Maryland, with the result being a stalemate despite the loss of thousands of lives.

The Vicksburg Campaign. From November 1862 to July 1863 in western Mississippi, a series of Union attacks and sieges ultimately resulted in the fall of the city of Vicksburg, Mississippi.

The Battle of Fredericksburg. On December 13, 1862, at Fredericksburg, Virginia, Confederate troops led by General Robert E. Lee were victorious over the Union's Army of the Potomac, led by General Ambrose Burnside. Afterward there was an outcry in the North over the Union's sizable losses during the conflict (12,080 dead, 9,600 wounded, and 1,769 missing or taken prisoner).

The Battle of Stones River (also known as the Battle of Murfreesboro). From December 31, 1862, to January 2, 1863, the Union's Army of the Cumberland under Major General William S. Rosecrans battled the Confederacy's Army of Tennessee under General Braxton Bragg; the Union was ultimately victorious, but both sides had numerous casualties.

The Battle of Chancellorsville. On May 1, 1863, Confederate general Robert E. Lee sent General "Stonewall" Jackson to attack the right flank of the Union army, led by General Joseph Hooker, at Chancellorsville, Virginia, while Lee's remaining forces confronted the rest of Hooker's army—a strategy that resulted in a Confederate victory on May 4 and thousands of Union deaths.

The Battle of Gettysburg. On July 1–3, 1863, at Gettysburg, Pennsylvania, the Union's Army of the Potomac under General George Meade was attacked by the Confederate's Army of Northern Virginia under General Robert E. Lee as part of Lee's attempt to bring the Civil War to Northern soil. Lee was eventually defeated, but both sides had massive casualties.

The Battle of Chickamauga. On September 19–20, 1863, Confederate forces led by General Braxton Bragg attacked Union troops led by General William Rosecrans at Chickamauga Creek near Chattanooga, Tennessee, forcing Rosecrans to retreat.

The Battle of Chattanooga. On November 23–25, 1863, the Union's Army of the Cumberland, led by General George Thomas, continued an advance (apparently without authorization) on Missionary Ridge near Chattanooga, Tennessee, until it confronted the Confederate troops of General Braxton Bragg and forced them to retreat into Georgia.

The Battle of the Wilderness. On May 5–7, 1864, about fourteen miles west of Fredericksburg, Virginia, in thick woods, a series of battles took place between the Union's Army of the Potomac, under General Ulysses S. Grant, and the Confederacy's Army of Northern Virginia, under General Robert E. Lee, with no side victorious. Immediately afterward the two forces met again at the Battle of Spotsylvania.

Spotsylvania Campaign. On May 8–19, 1864, about ten miles southwest of Fredericksburg, Virginia, the combatants in the indecisive Battle of the Wilderness met again at a crossroads at Spotsylvania Court House, and ultimately the Union withdrew from the field.

Sheridan's Valley Campaign. From August 7, 1864, to March 2, 1865, Union major general Philip Sheridan, commanding the Army of the Shenandoah, embarked on a campaign through the Shenandoah Valley of Virginia to pursue and defeat Confederate general Jubal Early, whose corps of the Army of Northern Virginia had been raiding Union supplies. Sheridan defeated Early in several battles but failed to kill him, although he did destroy much of the valley to deprive the Confederacy of valuable crops.

The Atlanta Campaign. From May 9 to September 2, 1864, in northern Georgia, three Union armies (the Army of the Tennessee, the Army of the Ohio, and the Army of the Cumberland) participated in a campaign to fight their way to the city of Atlanta, which they captured on September 2. The commander in chief of these armies, Major General William T. Sherman of the Army of the Tennessee, subsequently left Atlanta to march to the Atlantic Ocean, leaving a path of destruction in his wake.

The Battle of Franklin. On November 30, 1864, near Franklin, Tennessee, Confederate troops under General John Bell

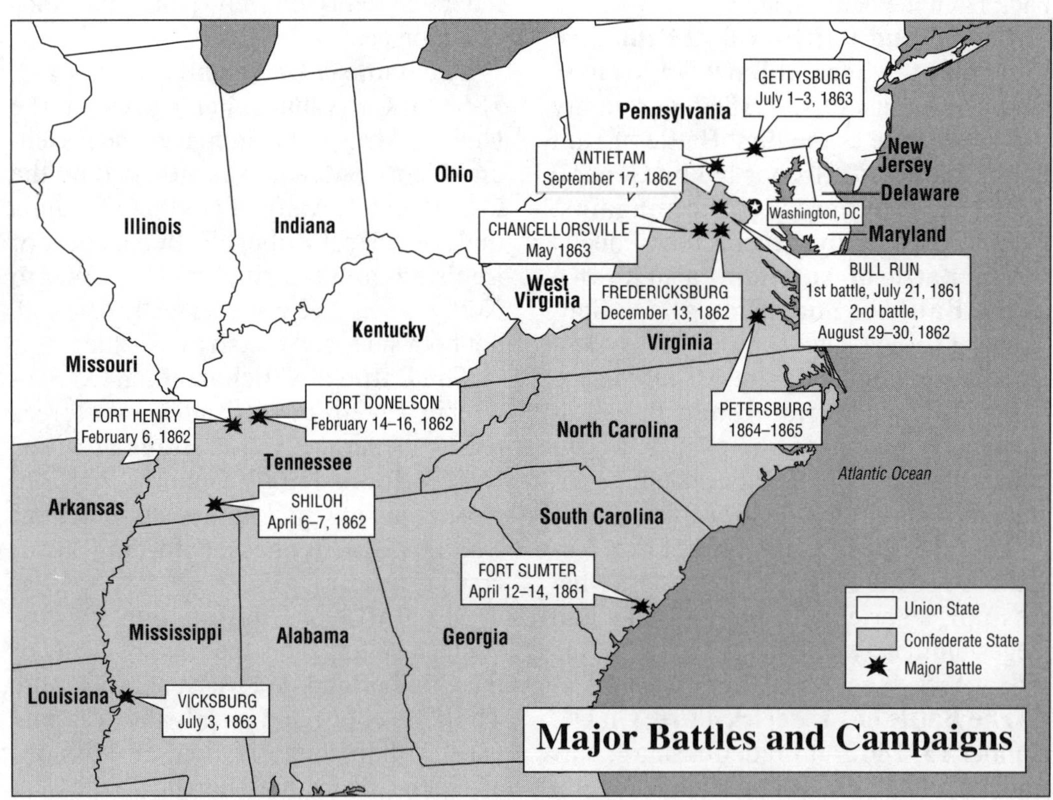

Major Battles and Campaigns

Hood experienced heavy losses while unsuccessfully trying to prevent Union general John M. Schofield's troops from joining those of Major General George Thomas in nearby Nashville, Tennessee. Together with the Battle of Nashville, this conflict is sometimes referred to as being part of the Franklin and Nashville Campaign.

The Battle of Nashville. On December 15–16, 1864, at Nashville, Tennessee, Union forces led by Major General George Thomas were victorious against Confederate forces led by General John Bell Hood.

The Petersburg Campaign. From June 15, 1864, to April 3, 1865, the Union launched several attacks on Petersburg, Virginia, attempting to take the city so that it would subsequently be easier to capture nearby Richmond, Virginia. One of these battles, the Battle of the Crater on July 30, 1864, resulted in the slaughter of hundreds of Union soldiers who had accidentally marched into a deep crater. The Union suffered other setbacks as well, but ultimately the Confederates abandoned Petersburg, largely due to a Confederate defeat in the nearby Battle of Five Forks.

The Battle of Five Forks. On April 1, 1865, Union forces led by General Philip Sheridan were victorious against the Confederate forces of General George Pickett at Five Forks, Virginia, about twelve miles southwest of Petersburg, Virginia.

Lesser but also significant battles include the Battle of Wilson's Creek on August 10, 1861; the Battle of Ball's Bluff on October 21, 1861; the Battle of Mill Springs on January 19, 1862; the Battle of Pea Ridge on March 7–8, 1862; the Battle of Drewry's Bluff on May 15, 1862; the Battle of Perryville on October 8, 1862; the Battle of Brandy Station on June 9, 1863; battles in Winchester, Virginia, in June and September 1863; and the Battle of Cold Harbor on June 3, 1864. **See also** *individual battle entries.*

Beauregard, Pierre Gustave Toutant (P.G.T.) (1818–1893)

P.G.T. Beauregard was one of only eight full generals in the Confederacy and as such was involved in several major battles (including the siege on Fort Sumter, which marked the start of the Civil War). Even before the war, though, Beauregard had extensive military experience, having fought with distinction in the Mexican-American War (1846–1848) at the battles at Veracruz, Contreras, and Mexico City. Following the Mexican-American War, Beauregard worked on a series of engineering and building projects for the U.S. Army, including supervising the construction of the Federal Customs House in New Orleans, Louisiana. In January 1861 he became the superintendent of West Point, but he was removed from the position after only five days for voicing support for Southern secession.

Beauregard then resigned from the U.S. Army to join the Orleans Guards in his home state of Louisiana. He had been part of this unit for only a week when Confederate president Jefferson Davis made him a brigadier general in the Confederate army and put him in charge of taking Fort Sumter. Beauregard's success in this endeavor made him a hero to the Confederacy. His reputation was further enhanced when he commanded thirty-five thousand men in the first Confederate victory of the war, at the First Battle of Bull Run in July 1861.

As a reward, Beauregard was promoted to full general, a position that intensified an arrogance he already possessed. He quarreled with other generals over battle tactics and grew angry when President Davis refused to implement his suggestions, which included crossing the Potomac River to launch an attack on Washington, D.C. By all accounts, however, Beauregard's battle plans were inferior to those of other commanders; his strength was his ability to make split-second decisions on the battlefield. Nonetheless, he viewed himself as a master military strategist akin to French emperor Napoléon Bonaparte, and indeed in 1862 he modeled his plans for the Battle of Shiloh after Napoléon's plan for the Battle of Waterloo.

At Shiloh, Beauregard was ordered to serve as second-in-command to Albert Sidney Johnston. When Johnston was killed on the first day of the two-day battle, Beauregard took over and gained ground until his men were too exhausted to continue. Beauregard was later criticized for allowing his soldiers to halt their progress, because the next day the Union gained reinforcements and drove the Confederates from the battlefield. Within a few weeks Beauregard had lost all of western Tennessee.

By this time Beauregard had developed a throat problem. Rather than follow military protocol by getting permission from Jefferson Davis to take sick leave, Beauregard simply left his troops in the care of his second-in-command, Braxton Bragg, and went to a nearby town for medical care. Davis responded by making Bragg's command permanent and giving Beauregard a less prestigious position, that of defending the port city of Charleston, South Carolina, and a stretch of Southern coastline. In 1863 in this capacity Beauregard fended off several Union attacks in the region.

In April 1864 Beauregard was given the task of similarly defending the southern approaches to Richmond, Virginia. There he commanded troops in opposition to the Union's Army of the James, which General Benjamin Butler led up the James River toward Richmond in May 1864. This second battle of Drewry's Bluff was a Confederate victory. However, Beauregard did not pursue the retreating Union army, a decision for which he was again criticized. Nonetheless, he remained in charge of defending the area, and shortly thereafter he prevented the forces of Union general Ulysses S. Grant from taking Petersburg, Virginia, holding the city until Confederate general Robert E. Lee could arrive with reinforcements (although later the Union succeeded in taking Petersburg).

After this, Beauregard was made the supervisor of two armies, those of General John Bell Hood and General Richard Taylor, in Georgia and Alabama, respectively. Shortly thereafter, Union general William T. Sherman began his march from Atlanta, Georgia, to the sea, and Beauregard proved unable to counter his movements. Eventually President Jefferson Davis demoted Beauregard, making him second-in-command under General Joseph Johnston in North Carolina; he remained in this position until the end of the war. In later years Beauregard was president of a railroad company and served the city of New Orleans as commissioner of public works. **See also** Bragg, Braxton; Bull Run, First Battle of; Sherman, William Tecumseh; Shiloh, Battle of.

Beecher, Henry Ward (1813–1887)

Born in Connecticut, Protestant minister Henry Ward Beecher was a passionate abolitionist who preached against slavery both before and during the Civil War in churches in Indianapolis and New York. He backed his words with actions, supporting antislavery political candidates prior to the war and funding the creation of a Northern regiment of soldiers during the war. Also during the war, Beecher sponsored a gun-smuggling ring whose aim was to arm abolitionists living in the South. These weapons were commonly called Beecher's Bibles. Beecher is also known for being the brother of Harriet Beecher Stowe, whose novel *Uncle Tom's Cabin* helped further the antislavery movement. **See also** Stowe, Harriet (Elizabeth) Beecher; *Uncle Tom's Cabin.*

Benjamin, Judah Philip (1811–1884)

Serving at various times as the Confederacy's attorney general, secretary of state, and secretary of war, Confederate politician Judah P. Benjamin was a leading proponent of secession. Once the Civil War began Benjamin became the Confederacy's secretary of war and adviser to Confederate president Jefferson Davis. However, within a year he had lost his position, having become extremely unpopular among his fellow Southerners. In part this unpopularity was due to the fact that the Confederacy lost several important battles under his watch, but it was even more the result of his outspoken belief that blacks would make good soldiers. His suggestion that blacks could be armed was highly unpopular in the South. At the war's end, Benjamin fled to England, where he practiced law and wrote about legal issues. **See also** cabinet, Confederate; Davis, Jefferson.

Bickerdyke, Mary Ann (1817–1901)

Also known as Mother Bickerdyke, Mary Ann Bickerdyke served under Union general Ulysses S. Grant as the head of nursing, hospital, and welfare services for his western armies during the Civil War. But hers was not strictly an administrative position. She worked tirelessly as a nurse on at least nineteen battlefields during the war, from the time she first became involved in the conflict in 1861.

At that time, a church group in Galesburg, Illinois, sent Bickerdyke, a widow who had established herself in the community as a "botanic physician" (that is, a doctor without formal training who treated illnesses with homegrown remedies), to Cairo, Illinois, to provide aid to an encampment of Federal soldiers. When she discovered that these men were living in filth and struggling with malnutrition, she worked to clean the camp and cook healthful meals for the soldiers, in addition to treating their illnesses.

The improvement in camp conditions attracted the attention of General Grant. He asked Bickerdyke to accompany his armies down the Mississippi River, establishing hospitals along the way and maintaining healthy conditions in his camps. Later she accompanied the soldiers on General William Tecumseh Sherman's famous march from Atlanta, Georgia, to the sea. By the end of the war, Bickerdyke had set up more than three hundred field hospitals, with the help of workers from the U.S. Sanitary Commission (the government agency then in charge of Federal hospitals).

Bickerdyke also changed government policy regarding the treatment of wounded soldiers. In particular, she ensured that marching armies were equipped to transport men who could not walk. She also insisted that men receive medical checkups regularly rather than just when they were injured. Noted for being stubborn, she argued with generals about what was in the best interests of their men, and she was known for taking wood from fortifications in order to feed campfires to keep her charges warm. After the Civil War ended, Bickerdyke became involved in efforts to help its veterans, and eventually she became an attorney who specialized in aiding veterans. **See also** Grant, Ulysses S.; medical facilities; medical personnel and supplies; Sherman, William Tecumseh; women, contributions of.

Bierce, Ambrose (1842–1914?)

Ambrose Bierce had a long career as a newspaperman, satirist, and short-story writer. In terms of the Civil War, however, he is renowned for using his experiences as a soldier in creating a number of works. These short pieces include the war memoirs "What I Saw of Shiloh," "A Little of Chickamauga," "The Crime at Pickett's Mill," and "A Bivouac of the Dead" and the short stories "A Son of the Gods," "The Coup de Grâce," "An Affair of Outposts," and "Two Military Executions."

Bierce enlisted for a three-month term in Company C of the Union's Ninth Indiana Volunteers in 1861 as a private and was sent to western Virginia. When the three months were up he went home, only to reenlist a month later. Promoted to sergeant and then sergeant major before again being sent to western Virginia, he fought in numerous engagements, including the Battles of Shiloh, Stones River, Chickamauga, Missionary Ridge, and Kennesaw Mountain, where he was wounded in the head in 1864. He went home to recover from his injury, but returned to the battlefield in time for the Franklin and Nashville Campaign. By this time he was a lieutenant, and he served one of the campaign's commanders, General Samuel Beatty, as a topographical engineer.

After the war Bierce moved to California and became a journalist. In subsequent years he produced numerous articles, short stories (primarily related to horror), and books, the latter of which include *The Fiend's Delight* (1872) and *Cobwebs from an Empty Skull* (1874). He also published a collection of twenty-six short stories titled *Tales of Soldiers and Civilians* in 1891. Most of his income, however, came from his work as a journalist and editor, which he continued until 1913. At that time Bierce decided to move to Mexico, telling friends that he was not at liberty to reveal why; shortly thereafter he disappeared. Bierce's fate is unknown, but some historians believe that he got caught up in Mexican politics and was killed by revolutionaries. **See also** literature, Civil War.

Black Codes

The term *Black Codes* refers to a group of laws enacted by local and state governments in the South immediately after the Civil War, supposedly to spell out rights for the newly emancipated blacks. In reality these laws included restrictions designed to maintain white supremacy. For example, although Black Codes gave blacks the right to marry, to sue in a court of law, and to own property, the laws made it illegal for blacks to marry whites or to testify against a white person in court and banned blacks from meeting in groups.

Black Codes varied from state to state, but blacks were generally not allowed to carry a weapon, assemble in large numbers, or behave in ways that whites considered disrespectful or indicative of laziness. Black Codes specifically made it illegal for blacks to remain unemployed. In general, any blacks who were unemployed were subject to arrest, and if they could not pay their fine they would be forced to work for someone who could. This involuntary servitude would continue until they had labored long enough to compensate for the amount of the fine. Black children were also forced to work if their parents were not able to support them adequately; it was often the same whites who had once owned these children as slaves who then became their employers.

Black Codes also allowed white Southerners to keep the wages of blacks low. Any black worker who asked to be paid more than what whites considered a fair wage was deemed a "vagrant" and subjected to the same penalties as the unemployed. Vagrancy laws were vaguely worded. In the state of South Carolina, for example, a vagrant was defined as a black who led a "disorderly" life, and in Alabama a vagrant was a black who was "stubborn." In Mississippi, blacks had to commit to jobs a year at a time, and if they quit before the year was up they would not get paid for any of the work they had already done. Moreover, if they quit they were subject to arrest, and once arrested they could be forced to work for their former employers.

Black Codes also were worded to keep blacks from working at anything other than the jobs they had held as slaves. In South Carolina, for example, if blacks wanted to work as anything other than a farm laborer or house servant they were taxed up to $100 per year. They also were not allowed to leave the plantation of their "master" without permission. In Texas, black women and children were required to work, and there was little else for them to do but farm and perform household tasks.

Under pressure from Northern politicians, some Southern states changed their Black Codes to make it sound as though these laws applied not only to blacks but to white vagrants. In practice, however, the racial discrimination that inspired the Black Codes continued until the U.S. Congress passed a series of bills in 1867–1868 that eliminated the South's freedom to treat its black citizens so poorly. **See also** Reconstruction.

black troops

Approximately 186,000 blacks, about 130,000 of them escaped slaves, served as Union soldiers during the Civil War. However, at the beginning of the Civil War, the Union did not particularly want black soldiers. Most of the blacks who enlisted were assigned to drive wagons or act as domestic servants for officers, and the few who joined white fighting units often faced discrimination. Therefore some blacks formed their own, all-black volunteer regiments, despite the fact that until the middle of 1862 the U.S. government refused to send them into combat.

Other blacks enlisted in the U.S. Navy, which allowed blacks to go into combat from the outset of the war. Still, racial stereotypes inspired the navy to adopt this different policy: The navy had no qualms about sending blacks into combat because individual sailors were not armed; the fact that every soldier was given a weapon was

Some blacks formed their own all-black volunteer regiments. In 1862 the U.S. government allowed these black regiments to join the fighting.

at the heart of the army's reluctance to send blacks into combat. Many whites argued that armed blacks would rise in rebellion against whites in general, both Northern and Southern. Others argued that arming blacks would endanger the success of military actions because black men were incapable of fighting effectively.

As the war progressed, however, and new recruits were desperately needed to replace soldiers who had died, been wounded, or deserted, abolitionists were able to convince the U.S. government to employ black troops. On July 17, 1862, the U.S. Congress approved the use of "soldiers of African descent," and on August 25, 1862, the U.S. War Department authorized the creation of five black regiments on the South Carolina Sea Islands. The first of these regiments to officially become part of the U.S. Army was the First Regiment of the Louisiana Native Guards (although it was not the first to be formed).

The organizer of the First Regiment, Major General Benjamin F. Butler, allowed black officers in all five regiments. However, his successor, Nathaniel Banks, believed that no black could be an officer in the U.S. Army and therefore used various tactics, such as intimidation and the filing of false charges, to force these officers to leave the military. The organizers of other black regiments often followed Banks's example, with the result that during the entire Civil War there were only thirty-two black officers, only ten of them field commanders. (The rest were chaplains and physicians).

President Abraham Lincoln's issuance of the Emancipation Proclamation in January 1863 did not improve the treatment of black officers. However, this act did lead to an increase in the number of black soldiers and regiments, and on May 22, 1863, the U.S. War Department created the Bureau of Colored Troops to deal with issues related to black recruitment and service. Meanwhile, the Confederacy decreed that, upon capture, all black soldiers and their commanding officers could be executed. In battles throughout the war, the Confederacy's attitude meant that Southern soldiers were more likely to shoot to kill a black soldier than a white one even if the man was trying to surrender. In at least one battle (the Battle of the Crater in July 1864), wounded black soldiers were bayoneted.

Black Union soldiers not only faced a greater danger of being killed than did their white counterparts, but they did so for less pay. When the first black regiments were formed, the War Department had officially stated that black and white soldiers would be paid the same amounts for their service. In June 1863 the department reversed this decision, saying that blacks would be paid less than whites. Specifically, whereas white soldiers were making \$13 a month, blacks were paid \$10. Moreover, white soldiers were given a clothing allowance, while black soldiers had to pay \$3 out of their \$10 per month as a clothing fee. This discrepancy so upset black soldiers that many of them wanted to leave the army, but they were not allowed to do so under the terms of their enlistment.

Meanwhile, black Union soldiers continued to protest the unfairness of being paid less than whites, as well as other inequities. One of these men was Sergeant William Walker, a member of the Twenty-first U.S. Colored Infantry who refused to perform his duties until he received his fair pay. The U.S. Army responded to his protest by finding him guilty of mutiny and executing him in January 1864. This act outraged many Northerners, and the public outcry eventually led Congress to grant black soldiers equal pay, retroactive to January 1864. However, this legislation did not apply to blacks who were freed after the war began; it was not until March 3, 1865, that a new law allowed blacks freed during the Civil War to receive their back pay.

Many white Northerners had also protested the inequality in pay, particularly after two well-publicized battles that proved that people's earlier fears about black soldiers' competency in battle were unfounded. The first occurred on June 7, 1863, at Milliken's Bend, Louisiana, where four regiments consisting of slaves who had been freed by Union soldiers fought with great bravery against a Confederate brigade, despite the fact that approximately 35 percent of them were killed. Black soldiers displayed equal bravery in the second battle, at Fort Wagner in South Carolina on July 18, 1863. At that time, a black corps, the Fifty-fourth Massachusetts Infantry, undertook the second of two attacks on the fort and almost succeeded in capturing it from the Confederacy despite extremely heavy fire. In the assault, nearly half of their number was lost, including their white commander, abolitionist Robert Gould Shaw.

By the last months of the war, the South had observed that blacks could perform well on the battlefield. This fact, combined with a desperate need for more soldiers, convinced the Confederacy to adopt General Patrick Cleburne's suggestion, made much earlier in the war, that slaves be given their freedom in exchange for enlisting in the Confederate army. However, by this time it was too late for any influx of black soldiers to prevent the South's defeat. **See also** abolitionists; Cleburne, Patrick Ronayne; pay, soldiers' and sailors'.

Blackwell, Elizabeth (1821–1910)

One of the first formally trained female physicians in America, Elizabeth Blackwell was instrumental in the creation of the U.S. Sanitary Commission, which oversaw the management of army hospitals during the Civil War. On April 15, 1861, she and her sister Emily held a meeting at the New York Infirmary, which they had established in 1857 with an all-woman staff, to discuss war-related medical issues. As part of this and subsequent meetings, they drafted a letter asking the government to create a soldiers' relief organization at the national level. Over ninety women, including the Blackwells, signed this letter, and these same women formed the Women's Central Association for Relief, an organization dedicated to lobbying politicians for their cause. Largely due to their efforts, on June 9, 1861, the secretary of war, Simon Cameron, established the U.S. Sanitary Commission.

Blackwell received her medical degree from the Geneva Medical College in New York (which later became Hobart College) in 1849, making her the first woman to get an M.D. degree from a U.S. medical school. Blackwell's efforts to be admitted to medical school were a testament to her persistence. Several schools rejected her application, so she studied privately with Samuel H. Dickson of the Charleston Medical College in South Carolina until she was admitted to Geneva College in 1847. Even then, the other students, all of them male, treated her with condescension.

After graduation Blackwell continued her studies at St. Bartholomew's Hospital in London, England, and at various hospitals in Europe. She began practicing medicine in a New York hospital before establishing her New York Infirmary. At first, this facility only treated patients, but later it also became a training center for women wishing to become physicians. In 1869 Blackwell returned to England to establish the London School of Medicine for Women. She remained there until her death in 1910. **See also** medical facilities; medical personnel and supplies; Sanitary Commission, U.S.; women, contributions of.

Blair, Francis Preston (1791–1876)

Missouri politician and political journalist Francis P. Blair was instrumental in arranging a peace meeting in Virginia between Federal and Confederate government officials—including U.S. president Abraham Lincoln and Confederate vice president Alexander H. Stephens—on February 3, 1865. Known as the Hampton Roads Conference, this meeting failed to resolve the conflict between North and South. Nonetheless, it was a historic event.

Prior to the Civil War, Blair had written newspaper editorials opposing the expansion of slavery into the territories acquired by the United States through the Louisiana Purchase, even though he himself owned slaves. When the Democratic Party adopted a platform in the 1848 presidential election that advocated the expansion of slavery, Blair transferred his support to its opposition, the Free-Soil Party; then in 1854 he helped establish the Republican Party. Six years later, with his son Francis Preston Blair Jr., Blair worked for the election of Republican presidential candidate Abraham Lincoln, and afterward the elder Blair became one of Lincoln's closest advisers. Both Blairs later supported the Reconstruction policies of Lincoln's successor, Andrew Johnson. The Blairs returned to the Democratic Party when the Radical Republicans opposed Johnson's policies. **See also** Blair, Francis Preston, Jr.; Hampton Roads; political parties.

Blair, Francis Preston, Jr. (1821–1875)

Missouri lawyer and politician Francis P. Blair Jr. fought for the Union in several major Civil War battles, first as a brigadier general and then as a major general. He also commanded some of the troops that accompanied General William Tecumseh Sherman in his 1864 march from Atlanta, Georgia, to the sea. However, Blair distinguished himself primarily in politics. He was appointed an interim attorney general of New Mexico Territory right after the United States acquired the region at the end of the Mexican-American War (1846–1848), and he helped establish the Missouri Free-Soil Party, which opposed the expansion of slavery into the new U.S. territories, even though he himself owned slaves. After serving two terms in the Missouri state legislature, in 1856 Blair became the only Free-Soil candidate to be elected to Congress from a slave state. In 1858, having lost his bid for reelection, he joined the Republican Party (which his father, politician Francis Preston Blair Sr., had helped form in 1854), worked for the party's establishment in Missouri, and was again elected to Congress in 1860.

As Southern states began seceding from the Union, Blair was instrumental in preventing Missouri from joining them. In 1862 he recruited enough Missouri soldiers to form seven regiments there. After his military service as their commander, he returned to politics. Elected to Congress in 1864, he often got into arguments with Radical Republicans, in large part over their insistence that blacks be given the right to vote. In 1865 Blair and his father both decided to abandon the Republican Party and become Democrats once more. Blair Jr. was the Democratic candidate for president in 1868 but lost to Ulysses S. Grant. In 1872, after serving briefly in the U.S. Senate, Blair fell ill and had to give up his political career. **See also** Blair, Francis Preston; Reconstruction.

blockades and blockade runners

From the beginning of the Civil War, the U.S. government recognized the damage that a naval blockade would inflict on the Confederacy. A blockade would keep Southerners from receiving goods, including military supplies, manufactured either in the North or abroad. The South would also be unable to export cotton and other products to foreign markets or to move troops and civilians by sea. Therefore on April 19, 1861, President Abraham Lincoln officially ordered a blockade on all ports in the Confederate states of South Carolina, Florida, Alabama, Georgia, Louisiana, and Texas, with North Carolina and Virginia added on April 27.

This encompassed roughly 3,550 miles of coastline.

To enforce the blockade, the Union needed to increase its number of ships. At the time the blockade was officially begun, the U.S. Navy had only 90 commissioned warships, and of these only 14 were immediately able to participate in the blockade. Of the remaining 76, 28 were either in foreign ports or far out at sea, 27 were under repair, and 21 were awaiting repair. Consequently the Union ordered the construction of additional ships, and in the meantime the U.S. government either bought or borrowed civilian vessels. One year later, it had increased the number of its warships to 390, and by the end of the war this number was 716. At the same time, the U.S. Navy increased the number of its sailors and officers approximately sevenfold, to about 51,000 and and 7,000, respectively.

Because of its shortage of vessels and crewmen, the Union early on did a poor job of blockading Southern ports. This enabled blockade runners—defined as either ships or captains dedicated to getting through the blockade—to bring supplies to the Confederacy with little trouble. By some estimates, between 1861 and 1863 blockade runners brought the South 60 percent of its weapons and 30 percent of its ammunition and most of its uniform cloth and shoe leather. In fact, even in the last year of the war some Confederate states were receiving a substantial portion of their food through blockade running.

Frustrated by the South's continuing ability to get war materials from abroad, Northern military planners worked to tighten up the blockade. To this end, the Union extended its blockade to include 180 inlets (harbors, bays, rivers, channels, lagoons, and swamps) that blockade runners were accessing in shallow-bottomed boats via inland waterways. The Union also made a priority of capturing a Southern harbor where ships could be stationed closer to the ports they were blockading. In November 1861 this goal was achieved by taking a Confederate-held sound in the Hilton Head–Port Royal area. This area, which was between Savannah, Georgia, and Charleston, South Carolina, then became a major base and supply station for Union blockade ships.

The Union also organized blockade forces into two squadrons to make their responsibilities easier to manage. The Gulf Blockading Squadron, based in Key West, Florida, covered the coastline of the Gulf of Mexico from Florida to Texas. The Atlantic Seaboard Squadron, based in Hampton Roads, Virginia, covered the Atlantic coast from Virginia down to the southern tip of Florida. However, by the end of 1861 the Union had further divided this squadron into the North Atlantic Blockading Squadron and the South Atlantic Blockading Squadron. The former, still based in Hampton Roads, was responsible for the Confederate coastline and inlets north of Wilmington, North Carolina. The latter, based in Port Royal, South Carolina, dealt with the coastline and inlets from this point to the southern tip of Florida. A few months later, the Gulf Blockading Squadron was also divided, into the West Gulf Blockading Squadron and the East Gulf Blockading Squadron, with the division being at Pensacola, Florida, and the bases being at Pensacola and Key West, respectively.

Meanwhile, blockade runners increasingly relied on North Carolina waterways, so in early 1862 the Union countered these efforts by attacking and capturing Roanoke Island, just off the northern coast of the state. This made it easier for the Union to prevent blockade runners from sailing into nearby Albemarle Sound and Pamlico Sound, but there were still vulnerable areas in the blockade farther south along the North Carolina coast. Wilmington, North Carolina—located on an inlet leading to the Atlantic—was particularly popular with blockade runners, because Confederate forts located in the area hampered blockade efforts until Union forces took them in 1865.

There were other weak spots in the Union blockade as well. The cities of Charleston, South Carolina; Savannah, Georgia; Fernandina, St. Augustine, and Pensacola, Florida; Mobile, Alabama; New Orleans, Louisiana; Galveston and Brazos Island in Texas; and Matamoros, Mexico (across the Rio Grande from Brownsville, Texas), were all used as blockade running ports during the Civil War. Blockade runners also used the foreign ports of Nassau, in the Bahamas, and Havana, Cuba. In both of these places, they would pick up various goods shipped from Britain, usually in exchange for cotton.

The willingness of the British to accept cotton, a bale of which was worth five times more in England than in the South, made blockade running a very profitable enterprise. In fact, ships with large cargo holds could make thousands of dollars for their owners in just one blockade run. Therefore many ships' captains were willing to risk having their vessels and cargoes confiscated should they be caught running the blockade.

Knowing the risks, blockade runners took measures to make capture less likely. By June 1862, blockade runners typically had steam engines to enable them to outrun Union warships despite their size. There were approximately three hundred steam-powered blockade runners operating during the Civil War, and they made at least one thousand successful trips. In addition, by the end of 1863, new blockade runners constructed abroad also had iron and steel hulls to protect them from Union attacks. However, even without such pro-

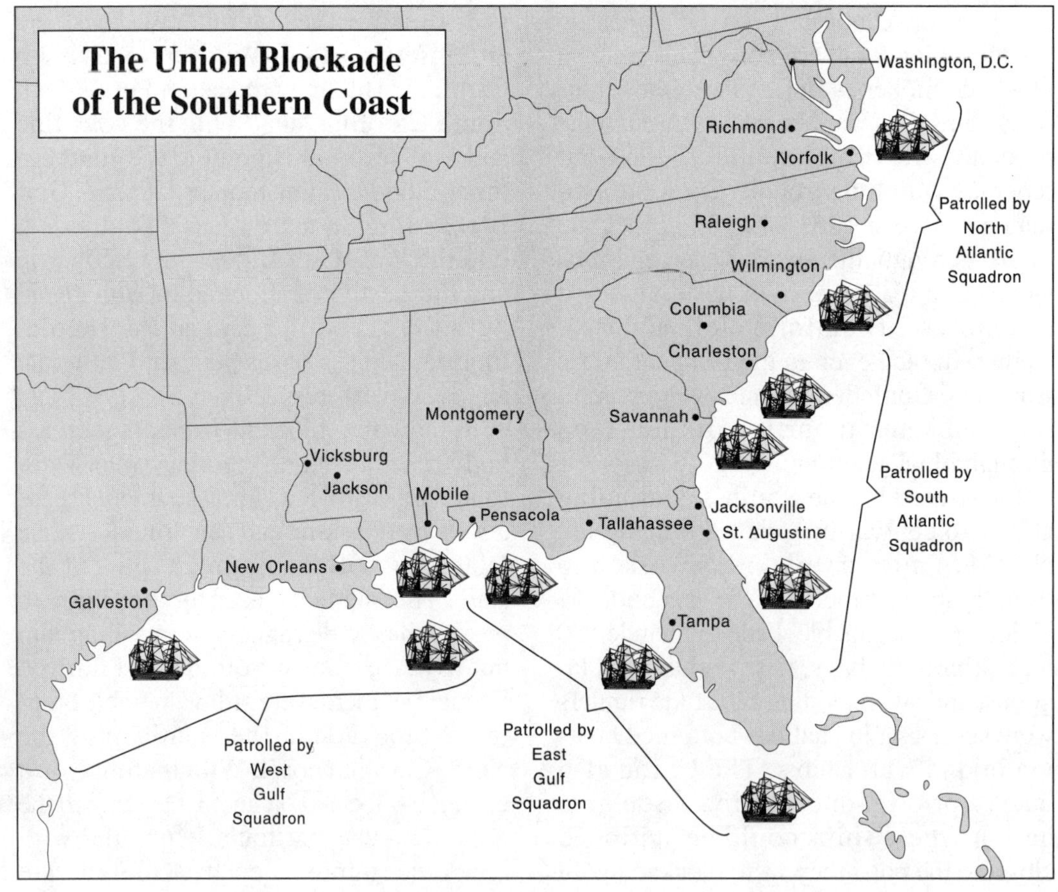

tection, most blockade runners did not sustain heavy damage when captured by the Union, because the U.S. Navy was careful not to sink blockade runners since doing so would result in losing the goods they carried and the Union wanted those items, too. Moreover, the Union often added captured ships to its blockade fleet. The Union captured about 140 blockade runners during the war, and an additional 85 were destroyed, either intentionally or accidentally.

Most ships made only a few trips before being captured, but some made dozens. The *Syren,* for example, made thirty-three voyages to the Atlantic coast, the *Denhigh* twenty-six to Gulf ports. Other successful ships included the *Kate,* captained by Thomas Lockwood, which made approximately twenty blockade runs along the Atlantic, and the *Alice,* captained by Robert Smith, which made eighteen trips in the Gulf. Lockwood, who was the premier captain among blockade runners, also helped design the *Colonel Lamb,* which is considered the best ship ever designed specifically for blockade running. Built for cargo space as well as speed, it could carry enough cotton to bring a profit of $100,000 per voyage.

Both Lockwood and Smith were entrepreneurs, and indeed until 1864 most blockade runners worked for private companies. Two such companies were operated by George Trenholm, who served as the Confederate secretary of the treasury in the last year of the war. Trenholm had over thirty ships, and he turned over much of the money he made—millions of dollars—to the Confederacy. A few companies were in partnership with the Confederate government, with the government paying a percentage of the expenses in exchange for a percentage of the profits. Although such agreements often benefited the blockade runner more than the government, the Confederacy accepted them because it needed military supplies so desperately. However, in 1864 the Confederacy implemented new regulations regarding blockade running that made it more difficult for blockade runners to profit at the expense of the Confederate government. For example, the Confederacy was allowed to claim as much as half of a ship's cargo space for its own use. In addition, the Confederate Ordnance Bureau went into the business of blockade running in its own right. Between 1862 and 1863, the bureau also had its own fleet of blockade runners, which exported government cotton out of Wilmington, North Carolina, in exchange for military and medical supplies from abroad.

Private blockade runners transported civilian goods as well as military and medical supplies, but they charged such high prices for these goods that few Southerners could afford them. For example, a ton of coffee could be purchased in Nassau for about $250 and sold at a Confederate port for $5,500, which meant that it cost $2.75 per pound, an exorbitant figure in those days. At first these high prices were simply a means of compensating blockade runners for the risks they incurred, but later such prices simply reflected the scarcity of goods. Once the Confederate government began to regulate blockade running, it placed a priority on the acquisition of war materials as opposed to goods intended solely for civilian use, and by the end of the war the average Southerner could not obtain even some of the most basic goods.

Because of such scarcities, many Southerners resorted to clever alternatives for common household items. For example, the Southern plant known as Spanish moss might be used to make rope, the thorns from hawthorn bushes to make needles, figs to make red dye, and raspberry leaves to make tea. Ground acorns, beets, chicory, corn, okra, peas, and pumpkin seeds might be ground to make a substitute for coffee. Eventually, however, even local foods became scarce, leading to widespread starvation and a few antiwar protests. **See also** cotton; navies, Confederate and Union; Trenholm, George Alfred.

Booth, John Wilkes (1838–1865)

John Wilkes Booth assassinated U.S. president Abraham Lincoln in April 1865. Booth came from a prominent family of stage actors and was himself a professional actor. His father was British-trained Shakespearean actor Junius Brutus Booth, who had moved to the United States from London, England, in 1821. John, the ninth of ten children, was born in Maryland in 1838. The family was wealthy enough to own slaves, and John Wilkes Booth grew up opposing abolitionism.

Booth made his theater debut in Baltimore, Maryland, in 1856, after which he performed in small roles in the Philadelphia, Pennsylvania, theater until 1859. He then joined a touring company based in Richmond, Virginia, and with them he performed throughout the South the following year. Still, he did not gain the acclaim that his older brother Edwin achieved on the stage.

Meanwhile, John Wilkes Booth's opposition to abolitionism increased. In 1859 he joined the Richmond volunteer militia and took part in its execution of abolitionist John Brown, who had been convicted of trying to start a slave rebellion. In 1860 Booth apparently began working as a Confederate spy in nearby Washington, D.C. By the summer of 1864, however, reasoning that should Lincoln be elected to a second term he would become a dictator, Booth decided he could help the South most by kidnapping him.

In the summer of 1864, Booth started to recruit former Confederate soldiers and Confederate spies who would help him achieve his objective. Booth's recruits included John H. Surratt, Michael O'Laughlin, George Atzerodt, Samuel Arnold, David Herold, and Lewis Paine (also known as Lewis Powell). During the winter of 1864–1865, the conspirators met in Washington, D.C., in the boardinghouse owned by John Surratt's mother, Mary

John Wilkes Booth, a Confederate sympathizer, assassinated President Lincoln.

Surratt, to develop various plans to kidnap the president. Once Lincoln won reelection and it became clear that the war was almost over, however, Booth decided to assassinate the president instead.

He struck on April 14, 1865, while Lincoln was attending a play at Ford's Theater in Washington, D.C. Booth entered the president's private box, on the second floor of the theater, and shot him in the back of the head with a derringer pistol, then jumped to the stage below, breaking his left leg in the process. He then shouted "Sic semper tyrannis!" (Latin for "as always to tyrants"). Some reports have him also saying "The South is avenged!" or

"The South shall be free!" before hobbling off the stage and through a door to where he had a horse waiting.

Lincoln died the next day. By that time, the government had launched a massive manhunt to find Booth. On April 26 Federal troops received word that he was hiding in a Virginia tobacco barn near the Rappahannock River. They surrounded the structure, and when Booth refused to come out they set it on fire. Shortly thereafter Booth was shot and mortally wounded. He was dragged from the barn to a nearby porch to die. (Initially most people believed that Booth had shot himself while in the barn, attempting to commit suicide rather than be taken alive. However, it now appears that a Union cavalryman, Sergeant Boston Corbett, acting against orders, fired the fatal shot into the barn.)

According to some reports, Booth was still able to talk despite his injury, and he asked the soldiers to tell his mother that he died for his country. Also according to these reports, Booth, who was paralyzed, asked that his hands be raised so he could see them, then called his hands useless and died. However, some people have questioned whether or not the man who died was actually Booth. Although a doctor who had treated Booth a year earlier positively identified the body, as did two other people who knew Booth, some believe that Booth actually escaped and that government officials conspired to cover up the fact. Since no evidence exists of Booth being alive after 1865, though, this theory appears highly unlikely. Such speculation was fueled by the fact that Booth was buried in a secret location, for fear that a marked grave would attract Confederate sympathizers who would turn Booth into a martyr for the Southern cause. Four years later, however, the government turned the body over to Booth's relatives for reburial in their family plot. **See also** assassination of President Abraham Lincoln.

border ruffians

In the years prior to the Civil War, antislavery forces began referring to Confederate guerrillas operating along the Kansas-Missouri border as "border ruffians." Later the term *bushwackers* was often substituted for such people, and the term *border ruffians* was sometimes used to refer not only to Confederate guerrillas but to Union guerrillas, who were also known as jayhawkers. In any case, border ruffians intimidated settlers in an attempt to influence their vote in elections that would determine whether Kansas would enter the Union as a free state or a slave state, often resorting to violence when lesser forms of intimidation failed to achieve the desired effect. **See also** bushwackers; guerrillas, partisan rangers, and irregulars; jayhawkers; Kansas; Missouri.

border states

Three slaveholding states on the border between the North and the South declared their neutrality once the Southern states had seceded from the Union: Maryland, Kentucky, and Missouri. (A fourth state, Delaware, also declared its neutrality, despite the fact that it allowed slavery, because it was geographically isolated from the Confederate states.) These states caused both the North and the South some concern because each side feared that the border states might suddenly join the opposition, bringing with them approximately 517,000 potential soldiers. In particular, U.S. president Abraham Lincoln worried that if he did anything to anger the people of Kentucky, that state would secede, and Maryland and Missouri would then follow. Therefore he took great pains not to call for the elimination of slavery in the border states, and he waited to send troops into Kentucky until the Confederacy had already done so. This meant that until September 1861, Kentucky served as a barrier between the

North and the Southern state of Tennessee. At that time, however, Kentucky did secede, after Confederate troops invaded it as part of an overall strategy to secure control of the Mississippi River Valley. Both Missouri and Maryland remained in the Union throughout the war (as did Delaware), despite the fact that these two states contributed soldiers to both sides in the conflict. **See also** Kentucky; Maryland; Missouri.

bounty system

In both the North and the South, the bounty system was a means for rewarding men who volunteered to serve in the army. Under this system, men were paid a bounty from the federal or Confederate government, and often from state and local governments as well, for enlisting. In many cases the total amount of each bounty exceeded $1,500 for a three-year enlistment and $500 for an enlistment of a year or less. This was a substantial sum given that the average yearly wage for most men of the period was $500. As a result, many men enlisted to get a bounty and then ran away from their regiment to reenlist for another bounty somewhere else. Such men, called "bounty jumpers," often became rich by repeating this scam multiple times. For example, one soldier admitted to bounty jumping a total of thirty-two times, and when he was finally caught he served four years in prison. There are no reliable records of how much money in bounties the South paid out during the war, but in the North the federal, state, and local governments spent over $600 million in bounties. **See also** desertion.

Boyd, Belle (1843–1900)

A Virginia native, Confederate spy Belle Boyd (also known by a nickname given to her by French newspapers, "La Belle Rebelle," or "the Beautiful Rebel") achieved notoriety during her lifetime for her extensive espionage activities. However, most reports of these activities come from Boyd herself, in the form of speeches, interviews, and autobiographical writings, which include *Belle Boyd in Camp and Prison* and *The Perils of a Spy;* the majority of her stories have not been independently corroborated, and historians therefore suspect that she embellished the facts.

According to Boyd, she began spying for the Confederate States of America at the age of seventeen. At first her approach to espionage was very unsophisticated: She would merely send notes to Confederate generals whenever she heard something that might be of use to them. Later, after the Union intercepted one of her notes, she developed more secretive means of passing information, hiding coded messages inside ordinary objects such as watches and rubber balls. She also used her beauty and flirtatiousness to trick Union soldiers and generals into believing she was harmless and not revealing important information.

Even when she was caught spying, she often talked her way out of punishment. Consequently, records indicate that although Boyd had been reported to authorities about thirty times before her twenty-first birthday, she had been arrested only six or seven times and imprisoned twice, spending only a few months in custody before being released. The first time Boyd went to prison was in July 1862; she spent a month in the Old Capitol Prison in Washington, D.C., before being released in a prisoner exchange between the North and the South. The second time, in 1863, she was released after about six months due to poor health.

Even in prison, Boyd managed to learn Union secrets and pass them to Confederate agents on the outside. When not in prison, she sometimes crossed battle lines to deliver messages. As a reward for such service, Boyd claimed, Confederate general "Stonewall" Jackson made her a captain as well as an honorary member of his staff.

After releasing Boyd from prison the second time, the Union sent her to England to recover her health. She attempted to return to the United States the following year aboard a blockade runner. The ship was captured, and Boyd convinced one of her captors, Ensign Samuel Hardinge, to leave his post so that the Confederate ship captain could escape. Hardinge was dismissed from the navy because of his neglect, and when Boyd was sent back to England by way of Canada he joined her. The two were married in London on August 25, 1864, in a ceremony reported in American, French, and British newspapers.

Shortly thereafter, Hardinge decided to join the Confederacy and left for the South. Boyd did not go with him, because the Union had warned her that the next time she was caught she would remain in prison until the war's end. Hardinge was captured and imprisoned soon after reaching America. The London press called for his release, but such pleas were ignored; Hardinge was held in a series of poor facilities, where he became ill and died. Now a widow, twenty-one-year-old Boyd became an actress, performing first in England and later in America as well. She packed theaters in both the North and the South, giving dramatic readings from *The Perils of a Spy* while wearing a Confederate gray uniform and a hat of a style that had been worn by Confederate general J.E.B. Stuart. **See also** spies.

Brady, Mathew (1823–1896)

Photographer Mathew Brady became famous for the work he did during the Civil War. At the beginning of the war he decided that he wanted to make a photographic record of the conflict, so he put together a staff of photographers, including Timothy O'Sullivan (ca. 1840–1882) and Alexander Gardner (1821–1882), and sent them to various locations to take pictures of soldiers in battle, at rest, or in death. Brady also took such pictures himself. His subjects included the battlefields at Gettysburg and Antietam, prominent Civil War generals such as Robert E. Lee, and U.S. president Abraham Lincoln. However, most of Brady's time was spent supervising the activities of his staff from an office in Washington, D.C. His expectation was that immediately after the war the U.S. government would buy his photographs, which had cost him over $100,000 to produce. However, the U.S. government waited to buy the photographs until after Brady went bankrupt in 1873, at which time they were purchased at a bankruptcy auction for only $2,840. Two years later, due to public pressure, Congress awarded Brady an additional $25,000 for his photographs, but by then he was so far in debt that the money did nothing to improve his circumstances. He died in 1896 in a New York hospital ward for the destitute after a long bout with alcoholism. **See also** artists and artwork; photography.

Bragg, Braxton (1817–1876)

Trained as an artillery officer prior to the Civil War, General Braxton Bragg was one of the least popular commanders of the Confederacy, hated not only by his own men but by many fellow officers as well. He drew his men's ire by being a strict disciplinarian in camp and an indecisive leader on the battlefield. Meanwhile, Confederate leaders found him argumentative and believed him to be incompetent in battle, although many reluctantly acknowledged that Bragg was a skilled military strategist. In particular, most Confederate soldiers considered Bragg's command of Confederate forces at the Battle of Chickamauga, which took place on September 19–20, 1863, to be inferior because, although he routed Union forces from the battleground, he failed to pursue them. Bragg's forces were subsequently defeated at the Battle of Chattanooga on November 23–25, 1863, and again at Missionary Ridge in 1864, whereupon he resigned as general to become an adviser to Confederate president Jefferson Davis. **See also** Chickamauga, Battle of; Davis, Jefferson.

Brandy Station, Battle of

Fought around the village of Brandy Station near Culpeper, Virginia, on June 9, 1863, the Battle of Brandy Station involved more cavalry—from both the North and the South—than did any other Civil War battle. On the Confederate side, General J.E.B. Stuart commanded six batteries of horse artillery and five brigades of cavalry, with approximately ten thousand men, as part of the Army of Northern Virginia. On the Union side, Major General Alfred Pleasonton led a cavalry unit from the Army of the Potomac that was eleven thousand men strong; it was accompanied by three thousand infantrymen.

Stuart was planning to take his men across the Rappahannock River to support Robert E. Lee's invasion of the Shenandoah Valley en route to Pennsylvania. Before Stuart's cavalrymen could leave camp, however, General Joseph Hooker sent Pleasonton and his forces into the area on a reconnaissance mission. Pleasonton's men crossed the Rappahannock River in two places, breaking into two columns and then reuniting at Brandy Station, where they encountered Stuart's force.

The battle there began shortly after 5 A.M. In the end, the Confederates drove the Union forces from the battlefield and suffered fewer casualties. The North lost 1,651 men, the South 51 (with an additional 132 missing). Nonetheless, Stuart's peers, the press, and the public criticized him for having been surprised by Pleasonton. **See also** cavalry; Hooker, Joseph; Lee, Robert Edward; Stuart, James Ewell Brown.

Breckinridge, John Cabell (1821–1875)

A Kentucky lawyer and a veteran of the Mexican-American War (1846–1848), John C. Breckinridge was a successful Confederate general. Prior to the war he served two terms as a U.S. congressman from 1851 to 1855, and he ran for U.S. president in 1860 as the Southern Democrats' candidate (while the Northern branch of the party nominated Stephen Douglas). At the same time, Breckinridge ran for the U.S. Senate; he was elected to that office but soon resigned to join the Confederacy. He commanded forces at Shiloh in April 1862, Stones River in December 1862–January 1863, Chancellorsville in May 1863, Chickamauga in September 1863, Chattanooga in November 1863, New Market in May 1864, and Cold Harbor in June 1864, and he participated in other offensive and defensive efforts as well. In February 1865 he became secretary of war for the Confederacy. As the war was ending in May 1865 Breckinridge sailed to Cuba and then to England, where he remained for three years. He then returned to Kentucky to reestablish his law practice. **See also** Douglas, Stephen Arnold.

bridges

Because most troops and military equipment during the Civil War had to travel overland, road and railway bridges over creeks and rivers featured prominently in the conflict. Existing bridges had to be considered in planning attacks, and temporary bridges sometimes had to be constructed to move troops and supplies into strategically important locations.

Temporary bridges constructed across waterways were typically pontoon bridges, wooden raftlike structures that floated on the surface of the water. The longest of these pontoon bridges was a 2,170-foot structure built across the James River in June 1864 by the U.S. Army Corps of Engineers. Bridges built across gullies and canyons were wooden trestles that often had to support railway cars filled with men and/or supplies. One such trestle, a 400-foot railroad bridge, was constructed

This pontoon bridge across the James River was the longest one constructed during the Civil War.

across Potomac Creek in only nine days. This bridge was a hodgepodge of lumber scraps and trunks of trees felled in the area and hewn by hand. In many cases, such structures were far from sturdy, and indeed some collapsed before they could be used.

Often bridges, either temporary or permanent, were intentionally destroyed for strategic reasons. For example, in the Vicksburg Campaign of 1863, retreating Confederate soldiers set fire to a railroad bridge and a pontoon bridge after crossing them. The Confederates tried to use the same strategy during the Appomattox Campaign of 1865, but Union forces crossed the Appomattox River Bridge and the High Bridge before the Confederates could burn these structures. **See also** Appomattox Campaign; Vicksburg Campaign.

Brown, John (1800–1859)

Connecticut schoolmaster John Brown was a leading abolitionist who advocated violence to end slavery. Specifically, he developed a plan to arm slaves by taking over a federal arsenal at Harpers Ferry, Virginia, with the idea that he would subsequently establish a colony of freed slaves there and use it as a base from which to launch other slave rebellions. Prior to developing his plan, Brown worked in Kansas in 1856 to prevent residents of that territory from voting to enter the Union as a slave state. At that time, pro-slavery forces were moving into Kansas to counter the abolitionists' efforts there, and in April 1856, these forces attacked the antislavery town of Lawrence, Kansas. Abolitionists retaliated four days later by massacring five pro-slavery settlers. John Brown was reportedly the leader of the abolitionist killers, although he was never charged with the crime.

In October 1859 Brown led a group of abolitionists in taking over the Harpers Ferry arsenal. Within a short time, however, Colonel Robert E. Lee and a group of U.S. Marines retook the town and captured Brown, who was soon tried and sentenced to hang for treason, among other charges. While awaiting execution, Brown wrote letters in defense of his actions and in support of abolitionism, and as a result some Northerners came to consider Brown a martyr. However, prior to Brown's execution, no Northern politician spoke out on his behalf or made any effort to stop his hanging, which took place on December 2, 1859. Meanwhile, Southerners not only reviled Brown but viewed his willingness to resort to violence to free slaves as typical of Northern attitudes. Consequently, many historians now believe that John Brown's actions added to Southern misperceptions about the mind-set of Northerners and made Southern secession more likely. **See also** Harpers Ferry; Kansas.

Brown, Joseph Emerson (1821–1894)

Joseph E. Brown served three terms as governor of Georgia, a position he held throughout the Civil War. As such, he was an outspoken opponent of efforts by Confederate president Jefferson Davis to centralize the power of the Confederate government. He also stockpiled weaponry for his state-controlled militia. In fact, he had so many of a certain type of pike that it was commonly called the Joe Brown pike. This weapon was a long staff consisting of two pieces of timber joined by an iron band and capped by a fifteen-inch-long blade. **See also** weapons.

Buchanan, Franklin (1800–1874)

Franklin Buchanan was a Confederate naval officer who held several key positions during the Civil War. Prior to the war he was a lieutenant (1825–1841) and then a commander (1841–1845) in the U.S. Navy before being appointed the first superintendent of the U.S. Naval Academy in Annapolis, Maryland. He returned to active duty as a ship commander during the Mexican-American War (1846–1848) and continued to command ships until 1855, when he was put in charge of the Washington, D.C., Navy Yard.

After the Civil War broke out, Buchanan joined the Confederacy as a captain and became an adviser to the Confederate secretary of the navy, Stephen R. Mallory. In February 1862 Buchanan was given command of the Confederate fleet protecting Norfolk, Virginia, and the James River. In discharging this duty, he personally captained the CSS *Virginia,* an ironclad warship equipped with a ram. Buchanan used this ram during the Battle of Hampton Roads in March 1862 to sink the USS *Cumberland.* He also tried to ram the USS *Congress* but instead ran it aground and fired at it until it caught fire and its captain surrendered. Buchanan was shot in the thigh during this battle and had to spend several weeks recovering from the wound.

In August 1862 Buchanan was made an admiral, and the following month he was charged with defending Mobile Bay, Alabama. To this end, the Confederacy provided him with several new ships, including ironclads and wooden gunboats. Buchanan chose one of the ironclads, the *Tennessee,* to captain himself, and he was at its helm during the Battle of Mobile Bay on August 5, 1864. A decisive Union victory, this conflict resulted in the destruction of many of Buchanan's ships, as well as another injury for Buchanan; he broke his leg when a piece of the *Tennessee* struck him. After this incident, he surrendered the fleet and remained in the custody of the Union until a prisoner exchange in February 1865. **See also** ironclads; navies, Confederate and Union.

Buchanan, James (1791–1868)

The fifteenth president of the United States, Democrat James Buchanan completed his term of office in 1861, the year the Civil War broke out. Throughout his life he spoke out against the evils of slavery, although he supported Southerners' constitutional right to own slaves. Therefore as a U.S. senator (from 1834 to 1845) and secretary of state (1845 to 1849) he opposed laws and bills that infringed on that right, and he backed the Compromise of 1850, which ensured that the balance between slave states and free states was maintained as western U.S. territories achieved statehood.

When Buchanan became president of the United States in 1857, he faced several crises related to slavery, including abolitionist John Brown's attack on the federal arsenal at Harpers Ferry, Virginia, and violence in Kansas between abolitionists and pro-slavery forces. Buchanan was still president when seven states seceded from the Union in response to Abraham Lincoln's election to the presidency. Buchanan did nothing substantial to address this crisis, although he did reinforce federal forts in the South, including Fort Sumter (the bombardment of which later officially began the Civil War). After leaving office, Buchanan went into retirement in Lancaster, Pennsylvania. **See also** Brown, John; Compromise of 1850; Harpers Ferry; Kansas.

James Buchanan supported the constitutional right of Southerners to own slaves.

Buckner, Simon Bolivar (1823–1914)

An experienced military officer and former instructor at the U.S. Military Academy at West Point, Simon B. Buckner was offered a position as brigadier general by both U.S. president Abraham Lincoln and Confederate president Jefferson Davis when the Civil War began. He chose to support the Confederacy, and in February 1862 was at Fort Donelson on the Cumberland River when it was attacked by Union forces. During this attack, the Confederate forces were under the command of Generals Gideon J. Pillow and John B. Floyd. Soon, however, Pillow and Floyd fled, leaving Buckner to surrender to General Ulysses S. Grant.

Buckner was then taken to a prison at Fort Warren in Massachusetts, but he was soon sent back to his own forces as part of an exchange of prisoners. He subsequently fought at Perryville, Chickamauga, and Knoxville and served under General Edmund Kirby Smith along the Mississippi. In May 1865, he was in New Orleans, Louisiana, when he was once again left to surrender his army because his superiors made themselves unavailable. Shortly thereafter the war ended, by which time Buckner was a lieutenant general. In the years after the Civil War, Buckner became a newspaper editor in Kentucky while investing in real estate. He then turned to politics, serving as the governor of Kentucky from 1887 to 1891, and in 1896 he ran as the Democratic candidate for U.S. vice president (with John M. Palmer as the presidential candidate). After losing his election bid, he returned to his business concerns. **See also** Fort Henry and Fort Donelson Campaign; Grant, Ulysses S.

Buell, Don Carlos (1818–1898)

A graduate of West Point and a veteran of Florida's Seminole Wars and the Mexican-American War, Don C. Buell served the Union as a brigadier general under General George McClellan from October to

November 1861, when he helped establish the Army of the Potomac. He was then placed in charge of the Army of the Ohio. After attacking and taking the city of Nashville, Tennessee, he provided valuable reinforcements to General Ulysses S. Grant at a critical point in the Battle of Shiloh in April 1862 and was therefore credited with ensuring the Union's victory there. Later, however, following the Battle of Perryville in October 1862, Buell's superiors criticized him for failing to pursue retreating Confederate forces. Buell was therefore relieved of his command, and in June 1864 he resigned his commission. After the war, he went into business in Kentucky. **See also** armies, Union; Shiloh, Battle of; West Point.

Bull Run, First Battle of (First Manassas)

Called the First Battle of Manassas or First Manassas by Confederates, the First Battle of Bull Run took place on July 21, 1861, near Bull Run Creek at Manassas, Virginia, roughly thirty miles west of Washington, D.C. It was the first major battle of the Civil War and part of a series of Union military maneuvers known as the Bull Run Campaign, which was designed to repel Confederate troops threatening the U.S. capital. The Union infantry troops at Bull Run, attached to the Army of the Potomac and led by Brigadier General Irvin McDowell, numbered approximately 18,500. On the Confederate side there were approximately 18,000 infantry and cavalrymen led by Brigadier General Pierre Beauregard and Brigadier General Joseph E. Johnston.

The Union expected to win this battle handily, despite the fact that the two sides were of roughly the same fighting strength. However, the Union made several serious mistakes during the battle. For example, at one point Union artillery forces were holding a key position atop a slope when an infantry regiment came toward them from the nearby woods. The Union soldiers thought that this regiment was a Union one and ignored it—until its members, all Confederates, began firing on them. As a result of this error, most of the artillerymen were killed, and the rest were forced to abandon the slope. Immediately thereafter, General McDowell went up the slope, expecting his men to be supported by artillery fire. Instead he found himself fired upon by Confederates.

Eventually McDowell's troops began to abandon the battlefield, despite his calls for them to stay and fight. As the men retreated, they became entangled with dignitaries and other civilians from nearby Washington, D.C., who had come to watch the battle. A sudden burst of heavy Confederate fire caused soldiers and civilians alike to panic, and the result was complete mayhem. Military historians have long disagreed on why Confederate forces failed to pursue the retreating Northerners, since doing so might have given the South a chance to take Washington, D.C. In any case, the First Battle of Bull Run was a crushing defeat for the Union, in terms of both morale and casualties. After the battle the North counted 460 dead, 1,124 wounded, and 1,312 missing, while the Confederates had 387 dead, 1,582 wounded, and 13 missing. **See also** Beauregard, Pierre Gustave Toutant; Johnston, Joseph Eggleston; McDowell, Irvin.

Bull Run, Second Battle of (Second Manassas)

Part of the Second Bull Run Campaign, which lasted from August 9 to September 1, 1862, the Second Battle of Bull Run (called the Second Battle of Manassas by Confederates) took place on August 28–30, 1862, at Manassas, Virginia, near Bull Run Creek. The main commander on the Union side was Major General John Pope, who led the newly created Army of Virginia and also had certain units of the Army of the Potomac at his command, for a total strength of about seventy thousand men. His opponent at the start of the battle was General Thomas J. "Stonewall" Jackson, who had led about twenty thousand men on what is considered one of the most impressive marches of the war, covering over fifty miles on August 25–26, in order to take a position between Pope's troops and the Confederate capital of Richmond, Virginia.

Pope was convinced that he would defeat Jackson's troops, so much so that on the third day of the battle he sent a victory telegram to Washington, D.C. Pope's confidence was understandable given that many of Jackson's men had run out of ammunition and resorted to throwing stones. However, on August 30 Generals Robert E. Lee and James Longstreet arrived on the battlefield with an additional thirty thousand Confederate soldiers, and the situation quickly changed. Lee's artillery began firing on the Union forces, and the newly combined Confederate armies attacked Pope's forces in the largest such assault (i.e., involving several units striking at once) of the war. By the end of the day, Pope had decided to retreat to Centerville, Virginia, and he retreated still farther the next day despite Lee's attempts to prevent this. In all, about 1,750 Union soldiers and 1,500 Confederate soldiers were killed during the battle, and another 20,000 men from both sides were wounded, missing, or captured. The Union also suffered a serious crisis of confidence after this battle, and Pope received much of the blame—although he in turn blamed another Union general, George McClellan, for arriving in the area with reinforcements too late to affect the battle's outcome. Meanwhile, Southern leaders were disappointed that Lee had not pursued Pope more aggressively after the battle, but were still pleased at having nearly destroyed a powerful Union army. **See also** Bull Run, First Battle of; Jackson, Thomas Jonathan; McClellan, George Brinton; Pope, John.

Bureau of Refugees, Freedmen, and Abandoned Lands

Also known as the Freedmen's Bureau, the Bureau of Refugees, Freedmen, and Abandoned Lands was established by an act of Congress on March 3, 1865, to provide food, clothing, medicine, and fuel to war refugees and freed slaves. Rumor had it that every freed slave would also get forty acres and a mule from the bureau, but in actuality the land—which had been seized from Confederate owners—was only rented to former slaves for a three-year period. Moreover, there were not enough of the available tracts to go around, so many former slaves went without. The bureau was more successful, however, in its distribution of food and clothing. Thanks to donations from the U.S. Army, by the end of 1865 the bureau was regularly providing meat, bread, and coffee to fifty thousand people.

As more and more of the basic needs of the freedmen were being met, the bureau began to address the social problems facing black Americans. Under the direction of bureau commissioner General Oliver Otis Howard, the bureau worked to create schools, colleges, and universities exclusively for blacks, and its legal representatives argued in court on behalf of former slaves, trying to get them the same rights that whites were accorded during trials. The bureau also kept records of incidents of abuse, or "outrages," by whites against blacks.

In 1866, the bureau started fighting to improve working conditions for black laborers, supporting the routine use of contracts between white employers and black employees to establish work duties, length of employment, and pay. However, when some freedmen refused to sign these contracts, the bureau often curtailed their benefits and threatened to remove them from their land. Many freedmen also lost their land after President Abraham Lincoln's successor, Andrew Johnson, decreed that all lands confiscated during the Civil War had to be returned to their original owners.

The bureau was originally intended to exist for only a year, to supplement the relief efforts of private agencies such as the Freedmen's Aid Society and the Free African Society. Instead, this agency lasted seven years, providing food and supplies to approximately 21 million former slaves and poor whites. The bureau also operated forty-two hospitals, treating approximately 1 million people.

The bureau was shut down on June 20, 1872, after Congress decided that new laws it had passed to protect blacks made the organization unnecessary. By that time, most people considered the Bureau of Refugees, Freedmen, and Abandoned Lands a success, but there were some who considered it a disappointment because it had not done more to help former slaves. Today, however, most historians believe that any ineffectiveness on the part of the bureau was due to the obstruction of its efforts by Southern racists, rather than to any lack of effort by the bureau's agents. **See also** Howard, Oliver Otis; Johnson, Andrew; Reconstruction.

Burnside, Ambrose Everett (1824–1881)

A former U.S. Army officer and gun manufacturer prior to the Civil War, Union general Ambrose E. Burnside (who was so famous for his abundance of facial hair that whiskers like his became known as "sideburns") led troops in several battles, including the First Battle of Bull Run, the Battle of Antietam, and the Battle of Fredericksburg. At the outset of the war he organized a Rhode Island regiment and served as its colonel at the First Battle of Bull Run, after which he was promoted to brigadier general of volunteers. Burnside was promoted to major general after the North Carolina coast campaign in early 1862, then commanded troops in Virginia and Maryland. In September 1862 he took part in the Battle of Antietam, but his performance was ineffective, his troops got lost on their way to a strategically important bridge, and then, once there, were trapped and largely destroyed by artillery and musket fire. Nonetheless, when George McClellan—under whom Burnside had commanded troops at Antietam—was removed as commander of the Army of the Potomac, Burnside was asked to take his place. Although reluctant to accept, Burnside eventually led this army at the Battle of Fredericksburg (December 1862), where he experienced a crushing defeat that was later blamed on his battlefield tactics. As a result, he too was removed as commander of the Army of the Potomac.

General Ambrose Burnside is best remembered for how he wore his facial hair, a style that became known as sideburns.

Burnside was next sent to command troops in Ohio, where he effectively dealt with a Confederate raid. After this he marched into Tennessee and took the city of Knoxville, successfully fighting off a subsequent siege there by Confederate general James Longstreet. In 1864, however, he was given an assignment in Virginia, leading troops under Ulysses S. Grant. In this capacity, Burnside participated in the Overland Campaign, the Wilderness Campaign, and the Petersburg Campaign, the latter of which led to his undoing. During a battle at Petersburg, Virginia, on July 30, 1864, Burnside ordered a mine to be exploded under Confederate troops. The resulting explosion killed approximately three hundred Confederate soldiers, but it also left a crater in the ground that was approximately 170 feet long, 70 feet wide, and 30 feet deep. Not taking this crater into account, Burnside then ordered his men forward. They fell into the crater and were slaughtered by Confederates as they scrambled to get out. After this massacre, which became known as the Battle of the Crater, a military court of inquiry blamed Burnside and two other generals, Edward Ferrero and James H. Ledlie, for these deaths, and Burnside resigned from the military. Despite the taint left by this blunder, in 1866 he was elected governor of Rhode Island and served until 1869. In 1875 he was elected U.S. senator, and he remained in this office until his death in 1881. **See also** Crater, Battle of the.

bushwackers

The term *bushwackers* was applied to Confederate guerrillas (unofficial or civilian soldiers) who attacked Union troops and antislavery civilians along the Kansas-Missouri border, although they made forays into other nearby antislavery territories as well. Most bushwackers, such as William Quantrill and "Bloody Bill" Anderson, had a reputation for being extremely violent. However, they were no more violent than their Union counterparts, guerrillas known as jayhawkers who lived in Kansas and operated in Missouri.

But whereas the federal government did little to stop the jayhawkers, it was determined to end "bushwacking" (bushwacker attacks) in Kansas. The bushwackers were difficult to find, so during the summer of 1863 Union general Thomas Ewing Jr. tried to flush them out of hiding by arresting women—their wives, girlfriends, and sisters—who provided them with food and supplies. Four days later Ewing issued an order, General Order Number 10, decreeing that all women known to associate with guerrillas had to leave the district of the border and the state of Missouri immediately. In response, the bushwackers attacked the antislavery town of Lawrence, Kansas, which was a center of abolitionist sentiment, on August 21, 1863, slaughtering at least 150 unarmed civilians and several unarmed Union soldiers camped nearby.

Four days later, Ewing responded to this attack by issuing General Order Number 11, which decreed that everyone except for military personnel had to leave certain parts of Missouri immediately. Specifically, three and a half counties along the Missouri-Kansas border, all areas known to be largely sympathetic to bushwackers, were to be cleared of civilians within fifteen days, with no exceptions being made for those who swore their loyalty to the Union. Ewing deployed soldiers to defend the civilians as they evacuated, but his defenses were inadequate to prevent people from being robbed or harassed by jayhawkers as they traveled. Moreover, the jayhawkers burned the homes of known bushwacker sympathizers once the region was emptied.

This did not end bushwacking, however. In fact, it increased the bushwackers' determination to attack anyone allied with the Union, and for a short time they continued to operate, though not in Kansas. Eventually, however, the federal government was able to break up the bushwackers' bands and kill many of their leaders, including Quantrill and Anderson. **See also** Anderson,

William; border ruffians; Ewing, Thomas, Jr.; guerrillas, partisan rangers, and irregulars; jayhawkers; Kansas; Quantrill, William Clarke.

Butler, Benjamin Franklin (1818–1893)

Union major general Benjamin F. Butler is most remembered for his cruel treatment of Southerners after he was made military governor of New Orleans, Louisiana, in May 1862. So harsh was this treatment that he was nicknamed "Beast." As an example of his cruelty, he executed a Southerner who damaged a U.S. flag and punished those who refused to pledge allegiance to the flag by transferring ownership of their land and personal possessions to the U.S. government.

A politician in Massachusetts prior to the war, Butler served in the military as the commander of troops in Baltimore, Maryland, in early 1861, followed by the command of Fort Monroe, Virginia. While at Fort Monroe he refused to return escaped slaves to their owners. Perhaps because of the acrimony this caused, he was rumored to be a thief who headed a corrupt administration. In 1862 he lost his position after numerous complaints were lodged with the U.S. government regarding his claims on property. Nonetheless, in November 1863 he was given command of the Army of the James in Virginia, but he was relieved of this command in January 1865 after a string of military failures attributable to his incompetence. **See also** armies, Union; Fort Monroe.

cabinet, Confederate

The Confederate States of America modeled its government after that of the United States, choosing to have a cabinet consisting of the president, the vice president, and the men who headed each department of the executive branch of government. These departments were the same as those in the United States (except that there was no Department of the Interior): the Departments of State, War, Justice, the Treasury, the Navy, and the Post Office. The heads of the Departments of State, War, the Treasury, and the Navy were called secretaries; the head of the Department of Justice was called the attorney general; and the head of the Post Office was called the postmaster general. Although the president, the vice president, the secretary of the navy, and the postmaster general (Jefferson Davis, Alexander H. Stephens, Stephen R. Mallory, and John H. Reagan, respectively) remained in their positions throughout the war, the other cabinet members often changed. Some men left the cabinet because they had difficulty getting along with Davis, who often interfered in their efforts to do their jobs. Others left their cabinet positions to take battlefield commands. Still others left due to political pressures. For example, former U.S. congressman James A. Seddon abandoned his position as the Confederate secretary of war after the Confederate Congress blamed him for every Confederate military defeat.

Turnover in the Confederate cabinet was considerable. In all, six men served as secretary of war for the Confederacy: Seddon, John C. Breckinridge, Leroy Pope Walker, Judah P. Benjamin, George Wythe Randolph, and Gustavus Woodson Smith. There were five attorneys general during the course of the Confederacy (Judah P. Benjamin, Thomas Bragg, Thomas H. Watts, Wade Keyes, and George Davis); four men who held the position of secretary of state (Robert Toombs, Robert M.T. Hunter, William M. Browne, and Judah P. Benjamin); and two men who held the post of secretary of the treasury (Christopher G. Memminger and George Trenholm). **See also** Benjamin, Judah Philip; Davis, Jefferson; Mallory, Stephen R.; Memminger, Christopher Gustavus; Reagan, John H.; Toombs, Robert A.

cabinet, U.S.

During the Civil War, the U.S. cabinet consisted of President Abraham Lincoln, his vice president, Hannibal Hamlin (replaced by Andrew Johnson in March 1865), and the heads of the departments making up the executive branch of government: the Departments of State, War, Justice, the Treasury, the Navy, the Interior, and the Post Office. The heads of the Departments of State, War, the Treasury, the Navy, and the Interior (which was then primarily responsible for the American frontier) were called secretaries. The head of the Department of Justice was called the attorney general, while the head of the Post Office was called the postmaster general.

Members of the U.S. cabinet frequently received their positions for political reasons rather than because of their leadership ability. For example, the secretary of war during the first year of the war, Simon Cameron, was named to the cabinet as part of a political deal in which he agreed to end his own candidacy for U.S. president in 1860 to support Lincoln's. Similarly, cabinet members often left their posts for political reasons. For example, Salmon P. Chase resigned as secretary of the treasury to run unsuccessfully for U.S. president in 1864, and Postmaster General Montgomery Blair resigned his position in September 1864 over a political dispute within the Republican Party.

However, resignations were far less common in the U.S. cabinet than in the Confederate cabinet, where a succession of as many as six men might hold one position. By contrast, Lincoln had the same secretary of state and secretary of the navy throughout the war—William H. Seward and Gideon Welles, respectively—and after Simon Cameron resigned amid charges of bribery, Edwin M. Stanton took over and remained the U.S. secretary of war for the duration of the war and beyond. There were also only two U.S. attorneys general during the Civil War, Edward Bates and James Speed; two U.S. postmasters general, Montgomery Blair and William Dennison; three secretaries of the treasury, Salmon P. Chase, William P. Fessenden, and Hugh McCulloch; and two secretaries of the interior, Caleb B. Smith and John P. Usher. **See also** cabinet, Confederate; Cameron, Simon; Chase, Salmon Portland; Seward, William Henry; Stanton, Edwin McMasters; Welles, Gideon.

Calhoun, John Caldwell (1782–1850)

Prominent South Carolina politician John C. Calhoun was one of the foremost advocates of states' rights and therefore argued that slavery should not be a concern of the federal government. A wealthy lawyer, he was elected to the South Carolina legislature in 1808 and to the U.S. House of Representatives in 1811. While in the House he headed the Foreign Relations Committee and supported a war against Great Britain, and in 1817 U.S. president James Monroe appointed him secretary of war. Calhoun subsequently ran for U.S president three times. He never achieved this office, but in 1824 he was elected U.S. vice president (under John Quincy Adams) and in 1828 was reelected (under Andrew Jackson).

In 1831 Calhoun vigorously supported a concept known as nullification, according to which a state could declare that an act of Congress was not constitutional and therefore could be put into place only through a constitutional amendment. Since a constitutional amendment required the approval of both houses of Congress as well as two-thirds of the states, nullification would have given states more power, and Calhoun believed that such power would help preserve slavery. Nonetheless, most Southerners, including the future president of the Confederate States of America, Jefferson Davis, did not support states having the right to nullify acts of Congress.

In 1832, following a personal disagreement with President Jackson, Calhoun resigned as U.S. vice president. He was then elected to the U.S. Senate, where he served for nearly twenty years. During this time he passionately defended slavery but also worked to preserve the Union. Calhoun did not want any states to secede; nonetheless, shortly before his death in 1850 he correctly predicted that the South would separate from the Union within twelve years. **See also** Jackson, Andrew.

California

Because of its geographical isolation from where the bulk of the fighting took place, California had little direct impact on the course of the Civil War, though it did declare its support for the Union early on.

However, the state was of crucial importance in the political jockeying that led up to the conflict. When California applied for statehood after an influx of new settlers in 1849, the majority of its residents opposed slavery. Therefore California declared that it would be a free state. This threatened the existing balance between the number of free states and the number of slave states represented in Congress, which led the Southerners in Congress to oppose California's admission into the Union unless slavery was permitted in at least part of the state. Some suggested that the southern half of California be declared a slave area while the northern half remain free; others proposed that California be admitted as two states, a northern free one and a southern slaveholding one. There was a movement in California that favored the latter idea as well. In the end, however, California was admitted to the Union as a free state as part of an act of Congress called the Compromise of 1850, which allowed western territories to vote on whether they would permit slavery within their borders. In return, Southern congressmen got passage of the Fugitive Slave Act of 1850, according to which slaves who escaped to the North were supposed to be returned to the South. **See also** Compromise of 1850.

Cameron, Simon (1799–1889)

Pennsylvania politician Simon Cameron was the U.S. secretary of war at the beginning of the Civil War. However, in running the War Department he showed favoritism in selecting and dealing with subordinates, accepted bribes in awarding army contracts, and publicly advocated arming slaves to perpetrate violence against Southern civilians. As a result, in January 1862 President Abraham Lincoln removed Cameron from the cabinet and made him the U.S. minister to Russia. He was unhappy with this post, though, and by the end of the year he had resigned.

In 1867 Cameron was elected to the Senate. This was his third term, having previously served from 1845 to 1849 and 1857 to 1861. In 1872 he was given the chairmanship of the Foreign Relations Committee, a position he held until he retired midterm in 1877. At that time, on his request, his Senate seat was turned over to his son, James Donald Cameron (1833–1918), who had served President Ulysses S. Grant as secretary of war. **See also** Lincoln, Abraham.

camps and camp life

Civil War camps were places where soldiers were lodged temporarily, usually in tents that were made to hold anywhere from four to twenty men who were grouped together according to military unit and rank. Life in these camps, which were typically overcrowded and unsanitary, filled with foul odors, annoying insects, and life-threatening diseases such as typhus, cholera, and typhoid fever, was anything but pleasant. As a result of such conditions, one of the most common topics in soldiers' letters home was how miserable their living conditions were.

Due in part to the poor living conditions and in part to soldiers' own unsanitary practices, disease was an everyday fact of camp life. Water sources near camp were often polluted with human waste and garbage, and men often washed themselves and their horses in the same water they relied on for drinking. Consequently, many men in camp became sick from ingesting contaminated water, and diseases spread rapidly among the soldiers, as did pests like lice and fleas.

Adding to the misery of camp life, in the summer the soldiers were tormented by mosquitoes, heat, and humidity; for Southerners this was nothing unusual, but Northerners often had difficulty adjusting to the climate and many experienced heatstroke and dehydration. Even Southern soldiers, however, could suffer from these given the lack of shade in many camps. At other times of the year, both Union and Confederate soldiers suffered from bitter cold, for which they were often ill equipped.

Soldiers also had to cope with preparing their own food. In the first months of the war, all camps had mess tents where food was prepared in enormous batches by regimental cooks, and when it was time to eat, the soldiers would simply line up to receive their meals. Within a year, however, most commanders decided that it was more practical for men to prepare their own meals. Since many soldiers did not know how to cook, this change brought numerous complaints, and soldiers often teamed up in small groups to share food supplies and culinary knowledge. To make their own meals, soldiers used rations they received every few days. They typically supplemented these rations with nuts, berries, game, and whatever else they found near camp. In the latter half of the war, however, Confederate soldiers suffered from scarcities in food supplies, and both the North and the South often had problems with food spoilage.

Along with these difficulties, soldiers had to deal with many hours of boredom. The daily routine in camp rarely varied, and much of what happened during an ordinary day was unexciting. Every morning at 5 A.M. in the summer or 6 A.M. in the winter, the soldiers were roused from their sleep, usually by a bugler blowing a tune known as reveille but sometimes by the sound of fifes and/or the beating of drums. This meant it was time for roll call, the taking of attendance to make sure that no one had deserted camp or died during the night. During roll call, the men of each company would line up and their company's sergeant would mark them present. After this, on some days soldiers were allowed to go back to sleep. On others, they were required to stay up and eat breakfast. Cavalrymen, however, had to feed their horses before getting their own breakfast.

After breakfast, which usually lasted no more than an hour, the day's routine varied according to camp needs and officers' wishes, with camp musicians signaling through different tunes or drum cadences what was to come next. Generally, though, the soldiers had to clean their tents and wash their breakfast dishes, after which those who had guard duty or picket duty would go to their assigned posts. Told of their duties the night before, guards would be positioned at various strategic points to protect the camp, while pickets would walk the camp perimeter and sound an alert if the enemy seemed about to attack.

At around 8 A.M. the camp musicians sounded sick call, the time when anyone who was ill could visit the camp physician. Then came water call, the time to lead horses and other animals to nearby water sources so they could drink, and fatigue call, the time to do various chores either in camp or in the surrounding area for the benefit of an upcoming military campaign. Assigned tasks might include the building of roads, bridges, and fortifications. Typical in-camp chores included cleaning guns, boots, saddles, and other items; gathering wood for campfires; and digging new latrines.

This initial period for performing chores typically lasted two hours, but there were other, perhaps shorter such periods of activity during the day. These came in between drill sessions, when soldiers practiced military maneuvers over and over again. There might be as many as five drill calls in a day, with each session lasting about two hours. Soldiers frequently complained that these sessions were the most boring part of camp life. After the last drill session, animals were watered and fed again.

The men usually ate what they called dinner at around noon or 1 P.M. and supper at around 6 P.M. Before supper, however, was a period known as dress parade, when the men wore their full uniforms to listen

Soldiers of an infantry regiment participate in a drill at their camp. Camp life revolved around chores, drills, and mealtimes.

to lectures given by their commanding officers. After supper was another roll call, sometimes called the tattoo call, to make sure that no soldiers had disappeared from camp during the day. This usually took place at around 8 or 8:30 P.M., and lights had to be out all over camp at around 9 or 9:30. Once the camp musicians had sounded taps—the signal for lights out—no one in camp was allowed to talk until morning.

Between supper and lights out, as well as on days when the weather made drilling and doing outdoor chores impossible, soldiers entertained themselves in a variety of ways. These included singing and playing musical instruments, carving objects from wood or soapstone, sewing, playing baseball, bowling (using cannonballs), and playing cards, often for money though gambling was technically against military rules. Soldiers might also gamble on races, whether between men or between various animals, ranging in size from horses down to cockroaches. Sometimes a camp had organized entertainments, such as theatrical performances, band concerts, and debates. In addition, from the huge volume of letters and diaries that were produced during the Civil War, it is clear that soldiers spent a great deal of their leisure time writing, with those who were illiterate dictating to those who could read and write. **See also** cards and card playing; food; letters and diaries; tents.

Canada

At the time of the Civil War, Canada was under the control of Great Britain, which had declared itself neutral in the conflict. Because of this neutrality, Canada gave asylum to Confederate and Union deserters. Canada also served as a haven for Confederate agents who wanted to operate near Union territory in safety. In fact, on February 15, 1864, the Confederate

Congress met in a secret session to approve the expenditure of $5 million to establish a Confederate spying operation in Canada. Its purpose was not only to gather information about the North but also to meet with Northerners interested in pressuring their government to make peace with the South. After the war, Canada was also a refuge for former officials of the Confederate States of America who were fleeing arrest and prosecution by the U.S. government. **See also** spies.

cards and card playing

Card playing was extremely popular among Civil War troops from both sides. In fact, some men played cards at nearly every free moment. Among the most common card games played were poker, twenty-one, faro, euchre, and whist. In most cases the players bet money in such games, even though both the Union and Confederate militaries had regulations prohibiting gambling.

Because of the popularity of card playing, some card manufacturers made decks specifically for men in the military. For example, one New York company created a card deck for Union soldiers in 1862. Rather than using red hearts, red diamonds, black spades, and black clubs as the card suits, this company used red stars, red flags, blue eagles, and blue Federal shields, respectively. In place of jacks, queens, kings, and aces, the decks had cards with the faces of Union officers and Lady Liberty, a woman draped in the U.S. flag, symbolizing freedom. **See also** camps and camp life.

Carolinas Campaign

Initiated by Union general William T. Sherman, the Carolinas Campaign was a series of battles in North and South Carolina that lasted from January to April 1865. It began when Sherman decided to take his army (which had recently completed its famous march from Atlanta to the sea) from Savannah, Georgia, north through the Carolinas to Virginia, to confront the Confederacy's Army of Northern Virginia under Robert E. Lee. As Sherman's soldiers marched, they burned and pillaged various cities and engaged in several battles, none of which presented much risk of defeat. These included the Battle of Rivers Bridge (February 2–3, 1865), the Cheraw Skirmish (March 3), the Battle of Monroe's Cross Roads (March 10), the Battle of Averasborough (March 16), and the Battle of Bentonville (March 19–21). At Bentonville, Confederate general Joseph Johnston, commanding twenty thousand soldiers, held his position for a time against thirty thousand Union soldiers, but eventually he was forced to retreat, and the following month he surrendered to Sherman. **See also** Johnston, Joseph Eggleston; North Carolina; Sherman, William Tecumseh; South Carolina.

carpetbaggers

During the postwar period called Reconstruction, some Northerners traveled south to take advantage of the political, social, and economic conditions there. Southerners called such people carpetbaggers, referring to the suitcases that many of these individuals carried—bags literally made out of carpet material. Carpetbaggers entered the South for a variety of reasons. Some did so to take a political office, buying or influencing the votes of newly freed slaves. Others sought to capitalize on the fact that Reconstruction laws prohibited some Southerners from running some types of businesses, so Northerners started commercial ventures and exploited the lack of competition by demanding high prices for the goods and services they offered. Still others manipulated tax laws or terms of loan agreements to gain title to large tracts of real estate. Although the term *carpetbagger* was usually derogatory, a few such individuals made their money honestly and fairly, helping rebuild the South's economy rather than exploiting it. **See also** Reconstruction.

Carroll, Anna Ella (1815–1893)

Author Anna Ella Carroll claimed to have given President Abraham Lincoln the idea of attacking the South via the Tennessee and Cumberland Rivers, a military strategy known as the Tennessee Plan. She met the president in 1861, after writing pamphlets in support of his decisions at the outset of the war, which included the suspension of the writ of habeas corpus. Around the same time, the U.S. Congress and the War Department started distributing Carroll's pamphlets as propaganda. However, although Carroll did suggest the Tennessee Plan in her writings, Union military planners maintained that they already had the idea long before she mentioned it. Therefore in the years after the war, the U.S. Congress refused to honor Carroll's requests for official recognition for her contributions to the war effort. **See also** habeas corpus; propaganda.

casualties

In military parlance, *casualties* may be either deaths in battle or combatants who are suddenly rendered unable to fight—whether killed, injured, missing, or taken ill. Estimates of the number of deaths during the Civil War range between 618,000 and 1,095,000, with the former being the most quoted number. Disease was by far the deadliest foe in the war. Of those who died, at least twice as many succumbed to disease as to battle wounds. According to the most common calculations, the Union armies had between 2.5 and 2.7 million men and lost 360,222, with 110,070 dying from battlefield injuries and 250,152 from disease. The Confederates had between 750,000 and 1.25 million men and lost 258,000, with 94,000 dying from battlefield injuries and 164,000 from disease. One example of disease's devastation on Civil War troops was the case of the Twelfth Connecticut Regiment, which had 1,000 men at the start of the war. Before ever seeing a battle, this regiment lost 400 soldiers due to disease.

Using the broader definition to calculate Civil War casualties is far more difficult, because Confederate records of men who became disabled due to illness or wounds or were simply missing in action were often destroyed as Confederate government installations were burned near the war's end. Nonetheless, military historians have based estimates of Confederate casualties for certain battles on their knowledge of troop strength, eyewitness accounts, and other means. From these sources they have determined that some military units suffered a disproportionately large number of casualties, sometimes in a very short time. For example, the First Maine Heavy Artillery suffered the death of 635 of its 900 men in a seven-minute period at Petersburg. More than 6,000 men of the Union's Irish Brigade were killed during the war, with the Sixty-ninth New York Regiment of the Irish Brigade having a 75 percent casualty (death) rate. The Twenty-sixth North Carolina lost 714 of its 800 men at Gettysburg, with 584 being killed during the first day alone.

Determining which was the costliest battle in terms of casualties is highly subjective. Gettysburg was particularly lethal for the Union army as a whole, with 3,070 men and 3,000 horses killed during the battle. However, Antietam is often called the bloodiest battle of the Civil War because more men were killed there in a single day than in any other battle. On September 17, 1862, the Union lost 12,410 and the Confederates over 10,000, with neither side gaining a decisive victory.

Many soldiers died not on the battlefield but as prisoners of war. The Union kept statistics for such deaths, as well as for deaths due to murder, execution, and other means. Records indicate that 24,866 Union soldiers died in prison, 4,944 died of drowning, 4,144 were killed in accidents unrelated to combat, 520 were murdered, 391 committed suicide, 313 expired from sunstroke, 267 were executed by the Union military, 64 were executed by the Confederate military, and 104 were killed right after being captured by the enemy.

In the first months of the war, the bodies of slain soldiers were routinely taken by train to various cemeteries and buried with honors. As casualties mounted, however, burials became more casual—if they were done at all. By the end of the war, bodies were often buried or left where they had fallen. This increased the risk that streams would be contaminated by bacteria that would then cause surviving soldiers to become sick after a battle. **See also** Appendix: Casualty Figures; diseases, dietary illnesses, and infections.

causes of the war

During the Civil War, most people blamed the war on disagreements surrounding the issue of slavery. However, slavery was only a point of focus for more complex political, economic, and cultural conflicts between North and South. Among these was the fact that Northerners and Southerners held different views on how the framers of the U.S. Constitution intended the nation to be governed.

In essence, Northerners believed that the United States should be truly united, so the federal government had the absolute right to establish laws to which the citizens of all states had to adhere. Southerners, by contrast, believed that each state should have the right to establish its own laws for its own citizens, under the assumption that a true democracy would not allow a few federal representatives to regulate behavior throughout the country. Moreover, Southerners feared that a centralized government would quickly lead to tyranny; therefore when Abraham Lincoln, whose Republican Party was in favor of restricting states' rights, was elected U.S. president, many Southerners supported secession because they were convinced that Lincoln would rule as a tyrant.

Economic concerns also contributed to Southern secession. In the decades prior to the war, the federal government adopted economic policies that favored the industrialists and other businessmen of the North, often at the expense of Southern farmers. For example, after the South began buying certain goods abroad because it was cheaper than buying them from the North, the federal government imposed tariffs on any imported goods that were also available from Northern suppliers. When in 1832 South Carolina refused to collect these tariffs, the federal government sent soldiers in to force compliance with the law. With such policies in place, the South had economic incentives to secede from the Union. Conversely, the North had incentives to fight to keep the South in the Union because as a separate nation the South would most likely have formed commercial alliances with various European countries and enacted economic policies that would disadvantage the North economically. In particular, the textile industry, which at the time was primarily situated in New England, would have been particularly hard hit because it was dependent on Southern cotton.

Economic concerns also underlay Southern fears that Lincoln intended to emancipate the slaves immediately after he took office. (Though Lincoln stressed in his inauguration speech that he had no such intentions, many Southerners were convinced he did.) In the South's view, ending slavery meant economic ruin for plantations, which depended on the low-cost labor slaves provided. (In contrast, the North did not need slaves because it had an ample number of immigrants who provided low-cost labor. Between 1840 and 1860, approximately 4.3 million immigrants arrived in the United States, and of these nearly 90 percent settled in the North.)

Some historians, however, have suggested that the Civil War was more about a clash of cultures than about concerns related to the economy and emancipation. They have noted that the leaders of the South could be categorized as Southern gentlemen—rich, white aristocrats reminiscent of those in England's feudal class—while Northern leaders typically had their roots in the working class. Therefore, such historians argue, the two sides simply could not relate to each other and war was inevitable, regardless of what issues became the ultimate points of contention. Similarly, some historians argue that the North and the South were doomed to break apart because whereas Northerners eagerly embraced new inventions and technology, Southerners resisted innovation.

Whatever the roots of their differences, the schism between Northerners and Southerners was made wider by abolitionists, who demonized Southerners and characterized slaves as Christian martyrs. (One of the best-selling American novels in the decade prior to the war, abolitionist Harriet Beecher Stowe's novel *Uncle Tom's Cabin,* features a Christian slave who, while being beaten to death, prays that his evil master will be forgiven by God.) Using such characterizations, abolitionists argued that no Christian country could allow slavery to exist within its boundaries, thereby raising the fight against slavery to the level of a religious crusade. As a result, it became more difficult for politicians to strike compromises that could have averted the war. **See also** abolitionists; economy, Southern vs. Northern; *Uncle Tom's Cabin.*

cavalry

Both the Union and the Confederate armies had cavalrymen, soldiers who fought on horseback, but for the first three years of the war those from the South were far superior to their Northern counterparts. One of the most important reasons for this was that Southern horses were generally faster and more agile than Northern ones, because Southerners had long bred horses for racing and jumping. In contrast, most Northern horses were heavy-boned animals bred for working, and were therefore more suited for pulling wagons and plowing than for riding.

Northern and Southern riders likewise came from different traditions. In the prewar South, where there were few roads suitable for buggies or wagons, most men learned to ride at a young age. Moreover, horsemanship was not just a means of getting around but a social activity, and a man was in part judged according to his riding skill. This meant that a majority of Southern men not only rode but rode well. In the North, however, few young men rode horses, and instead traveled by wagon, carriage, coach, or other wheeled vehicle. Those who did ride tended to care less about technique, and their poor form made it more difficult for them to stay on their horses during a cavalry engagement. Still another difference between Northern and Southern cavalrymen was that Northerners were issued their mounts by the military, whereas Southerners brought their own horses with them into the war. This meant that at least at the beginning of the war, Northern cavalrymen were unfamiliar with their mounts, while Southern cavalrymen generally knew their horses well.

Beyond the differing traditions between North and South, there was also a difference in attitude toward the importance of the cavalry. Many Union commanders felt that advances in weaponry had made the cavalry obsolete; no longer did a man have to charge up to the enemy on horseback in order to kill him since rifles and artillery were capable of hitting targets from quite far away. Therefore, in the first year of the war, the Union primarily used its cavalry for reconnaissance and scouting missions rather than on the battlefield. In contrast, Southern commanders believed that cavalry was vital to the prosecution of the war,

The Union relied on cavalrymen to conduct reconnaissance missions, while Confederate cavalry fought on the battlefield.

because cavalrymen could cover ground more quickly and quietly than infantrymen. A skilled Southern cavalry commander could lead his forces completely around a camped enemy army without detection, either to cut off a Union retreat or to raid Union supplies. Indeed, Confederate cavalry commander J.E.B. Stuart did this on many occasions during the first years of the war.

Because of such successful attacks, Northern commanders eventually became convinced of the need for cavalry and therefore began to increase their number of mounted troops. At the beginning of the war, the U.S. Army had only eight mounted cavalry troops (with a troop being the equivalent of an infantry company, with approximately eighty men each), but the number of troops increased as the army trained additional horses for cavalry work. By 1863, there were forty Union cavalry regiments (each made of twelve troops) organized into three divisions in the Army of the Potomac alone. Volunteer and state militia cavalry units were also created during the war. There were eventually 258 such Union cavalry regiments as well as 170 independent cavalry troops, all of them primarily used to guard the supply centers and communication systems of Union states. Theoretically, each Union regiment was supposed to have around a thousand troopers, but due to a lack of trained horses the average number was actually closer to four hundred.

The Confederacy also suffered from a shortage of trained horses. As the war progressed it became increasingly difficult to replace the many riders and mounts killed in battle, and the number of mounted cavalrymen decreased accordingly. Whereas in 1861 most regiments had nearly eight hundred men, by the end of 1863 most regiments had fewer than six hundred men and about a third of them lacked horses. In

1864, the number of men dropped to fewer than four hundred, with only about half having horses.

By the middle of 1863, the Union cavalry rivaled the Confederate cavalry in competence when the two sides met on the battlefield. This was first demonstrated at the Battle of Brandy Station, the biggest cavalry battle of the war. Although in the end the Confederate cavalry drove the Union cavalry from the field, the Union cavalry managed to stay in the fight for three hours and many Confederate cavalrymen were unhorsed. In several subsequent cavalry battles, the Union army was equally successful in challenging the Confederacy's mounted forces, although in part this was due to the South's limited resources. By the end of the war, many of the Confederacy's cavalry units were completely without horses, and those few mounted units that remained were seriously outnumbered. **See also** artillery; Brandy Station, Battle of; infantry, Confederate and Union; Stuart, James Ewell Brown.

Chamberlain, Joshua Lawrence (1828–1914)

Union general Joshua L. Chamberlain is perhaps best known for his book on the Appomattox Campaign titled *The Passing of the Armies: The Last Campaign of the Armies.* However, Chamberlain also distinguished himself on the battlefield. As a colonel he commanded a regiment at the Battle of Gettysburg in 1863 and performed so admirably, despite being wounded, that he was subsequently awarded the Congressional Medal of Honor. Chamberlain was also wounded at the 1862 Battle of Fredericksburg and at the first assault on Petersburg, Virginia, in 1864. His injuries at Petersburg were so severe that doctors there erroneously announced that he was going to die, and in response General Ulysses S. Grant promoted him to the rank of brigadier general as a way to honor him.

After recovering from this wound and spending a few months away from the battlefield, Chamberlain was again wounded at the second assault on Petersburg. He also participated in the Battles of Antietam, Chancellorsville, Cold Harbor, and Appomattox, among others, and was present at the final Confederate surrender. After the war he served one term as the governor of Maine and later became president of that state's Bowdoin College, where he had been a professor prior to volunteering for the war in 1862. In 1912 Chamberlain wrote an article about the Battle of Fredericksburg, which was published in *Cosmopolitan Magazine,* and shortly thereafter he began working on *The Passing of the Armies.* **See also** Appomattox Campaign; Fredericksburg, Battle of; Gettysburg, Battle of; Petersburg Campaign.

Chambersburg, Pennsylvania

Chambersburg, Pennsylvania, was the only Northern city to be burned by the Confederates during the Civil War. The town's destruction was ordered by General John McCausland on July 30, 1864, after his cavalry unit had been sent into the area by General Jubal Early (then commander of the Confederate's Army of the Shenandoah). McCausland demanded that the town pay a $100,000 ransom to the Confederacy, and when its leaders refused he set Chambersburg ablaze. Later the Confederacy justified this act, saying it was revenge for the Union's burning of the Virginia Military Institute the previous month, on June 12, 1864. **See also** Early, Jubal; Virginia Military Institute.

Chancellorsville, Battle of

The Battle of Chancellorsville took place nine miles west of Fredericksburg, Virginia, on May 1–4, 1863, as part of the Chancellorsville Campaign of April–May 1863. Led by Major General Joseph Hooker, this Union campaign was an attempt to surround the Confederate forces of the Army of Northern Virginia, led by Robert E. Lee. However, Hooker made several mistakes during the battle and never gained an advantage over the enemy, despite having a force of approximately 134,000 men as opposed to the Confederacy's 57,000. On the fourth day of fighting, Hooker, outmaneuvered and with Union casualties mounting, ordered a retreat across the Rappahannock River. Union losses totaled over 17,000, while the Confederate losses were fewer than 13,000. Consequently, the Battle of Chancellorsville is considered Lee's greatest victory of the war. However, it also included a serious loss for the South: the death of General "Stonewall" Jackson, who was mistakenly shot by one of his own men and later died from complications of this wound. **See also** Hooker, Joseph; Jackson, Thomas Jonathan; Lee, Robert Edward.

chaplains, army

The issue of whether an army should be served by a clergyman, or chaplain, was a matter of controversy during the Civil War because of the strongly held belief in a clear separation between church and state. Confederate president Jefferson Davis, in fact, decreed at the war's outset that no Confederate army should have a chaplain. However, within a few months he reversed his position when both soldiers and civilians demanded that wounded and dying men be allowed the comfort of a clergyman's presence. Davis then told battlefield commanders to find chaplains, by either choosing them themselves or allowing their men to choose their own chaplain by popular vote. Eventually, over six hundred men served as Confederate army chaplains.

As for the U.S. government, Congress had enacted a law in 1859 that greatly reduced the number of chaplains serving the army. Therefore when the Civil War began there were only thirty chaplains attached to the Regular Army. This number was obviously inadequate to serve the thousands of men who joined the volunteer army in the first months of the war, so the Union encouraged its regiments to find their own chaplains, and eventually there were approximately twenty-three hundred, all of them male. One regiment, the First Wisconsin Heavy Artillery, chose a woman pastor, the Reverend Ella E. Gibson of the Religio-Philosophical Society of St. Charles, Illinois, as its chaplain, but Secretary of War Edwin Stanton refused to allow her to serve.

Blacks were not allowed to be Union chaplains either, until the enactment of the Emancipation Proclamation in January 1863. At that time, fourteen black clergymen petitioned for acceptance as army chaplains. The first to be appointed to a regiment, in September 1863, was Henry McNeal Turner of the Israel African Methodist Episcopal Church in Washington, D.C. He and all other black chaplains were only allowed to serve black troops, however.

Another requirement for Union army chaplains in the first year of the war was that they be Christian. (Most were Methodist, followed by Episcopalians, although other Christian denominations were represented as well.) By the second year of the war, however, Congress decreed that chaplains could be of any religion to allow for the fact that some soldiers were Jewish, but there was still only one Jewish chaplain during the war: Rabbi Ferdinand L. Sarner, who served a New York regiment. In the South, there were no Jewish chaplains, although there was never a law or policy prohibiting their service.

The South also did not specifically define the duties of its army chaplains, although most used a treatise, *Letter to the Chaplains in the Army* by Methodist bishop James O. Andrews, as a guide. In the North, chaplains relied on *The Army Chaplain, His Office, Duties, and Responsibilities, and the Means of Aiding Him* by the Reverend William Young Brown for guidance, but they also had some specific directives from the Union army. Their main task was to improve the soldiers' morality and "social happiness" and to report on the religious condition of the men if asked. How they were to make these improvements, however, was largely left up to them.

In general, most Union and Confederate chaplains spent their time comforting soldiers, particularly the frightened, the wounded, and the dying, and leading prayer meetings. Furthermore, when a soldier died, it was often his regimental chaplain who wrote the letter to his family informing them of his death. Chaplains might also maintain a camp library and teach soldiers how to read and write. On a few occasions, chaplains went out onto the battlefield to rescue wounded men, even under heavy fire. Three Union chaplains were awarded the Congressional Medal of Honor for such heroism: Francis B. Hall, Milton L. Haney, and John M. Whitehead.

Both armies paid chaplains for their service. In the Confederacy, chaplains earned $85 a month in the first months of the war. This amount was later reduced to $50 as a cost-cutting measure, but after some complaints from Southern churches the pay was raised to $80 for the remainder of the war. In addition, some churches supplemented this amount. In the North, chaplains were paid $120 a month. **See also** black troops; Congressional Medal of Honor.

Chapman, Maria Weston (1806–1885)

Massachusetts abolitionist Maria W. Chapman organized fund-raisers for antislavery groups and in 1832 helped create and run one such group, the Boston Female Anti-Slavery Society. She also helped abolitionist William Lloyd Garrison run the Massachusetts Anti-Slavery Society and edited various abolitionist publications for him.

A direct descendant of the Pilgrims, Chapman came from a socially prominent family and married a wealthy Boston merchant, Henry Grafton Chapman, in 1830. She became involved in the abolitionist movement shortly after her marriage. In 1835, during a meeting of her Boston Female Anti-Slavery Society, pro-slavery men threatening violence surrounded the building where the meeting was being held. Chapman, fearing that her black members would be attacked, suggested that each black woman link arms with a white woman—who, because of the social mores of the time, was unlikely to be harmed in public by a white man—and walk from the meeting hall. As the women did this, the mob expressed its outrage but did not touch the women, who reconvened their meeting at Chapman's house.

After this incident, Chapman became William Lloyd Garrison's principal assistant, and whenever he was out of Boston on a lecture tour she would edit his abolitionist newspaper, the *Liberator.* From 1839 to 1842, she also edited another of Garrison's publications, the *Non-Resistant,* which represented the views of the abolitionist New England Non-Resistant Society. In 1839, Chapman, concerned that divisions over the issue of women's rights were weakening the abolitionist movement, wrote a pamphlet, *Right and Wrong in Massachusetts,* arguing that abolitionists needed to be just as united in their support of women's rights as they were in support of blacks' freedom. **See also** Garrison, William Lloyd.

Charleston, South Carolina

In addition to being the location of Fort Sumter, which was the target of the first shots of the Civil War, Charleston was significant as a site of weapons manufacturing and ship construction. At a former federal arsenal located on the outskirts of the city, the Confederacy manufactured artillery shells and cartridges. At the city's shipyards, three warships were built: the

150-foot *Palmetto State,* the six-gun iron-armored *Chicora,* and the ironclad *Charleston.* In addition, the port was routinely used by blockade runners seeking to get goods into the South.

With the onset of the war, Union warships moved to blockade Charleston, and its citizens feared that their city would soon be attacked. Instead, it took a year for the Union to launch an assault on Charleston. When the assault finally came, in June 1862, it employed over six thousand Federal troops, which were brought by ship to a point just southeast of the city. This attack failed, but in April 1863 another was launched, this time using nine ironclads, which bombarded Fort Sumter. Again the Union attack failed, largely because the Confederates were defending their waters with explosive mines.

A third Union attack on Charleston began in July 1863. It was intended to be a joint land-sea operation; the plan was that a force of six thousand men would land on Morris Island, where a Confederate fort, Fort Wagner, protected Charleston Harbor, and then capture the fort to allow Union warships to enter the harbor. The landing was accomplished, but the Union soldiers were unable to take the fort, which meant that the Union warships could not participate in the attack. Nonetheless, the commander of the troops, General Quincy A. Gillmore, occupied Morris Island and erected long-range guns that he trained on nearby Fort Sumter and Charleston itself. On August 22, 1863, after giving the Confederates a chance to surrender, Gillmore began to bombard Charleston.

Charleston, South Carolina, lies in ruins in 1865 after a series of devastating Union attacks.

In response, the citizens of Charleston moved their major services, such as banks and hospitals, to places out of range of Gillmore's artillery, and those people who could afford to leave the city did so. Those who remained endured great stress, although the shelling was sporadic. On some days, very few shells struck the city, while on others there might be dozens. Among the heaviest days was October 10, 1864, when 165 shells struck the city, killing several citizens. Another time of heavy shelling was a nine-day period in January 1864, when fifteen hundred shells hit the city, many of them starting fires. Meanwhile, the Confederacy sent thousands of soldiers into the Charleston area to shore up its defenses, but by January 1865 it decided that the city was no longer worth defending. On the night of February 17, 1865, Charleston was evacuated, and approximately ten thousand Confederate troops left the region. The next day the Union took over the city. **See also** Fort Sumter; Fort Wagner; South Carolina.

Chase, Salmon Portland (1808–1873)

Prominent Ohio politician Salmon P. Chase was outspoken in his opposition to slavery both before and during the Civil War. He began his involvement with the antislavery movement as a lawyer defending runaway slaves and their supporters during the 1830s. During the 1840s he led the antislavery Liberty Party in Ohio, and in 1848 he helped found a similar political party, the Free-Soil Party. In 1854 he was involved in the formation of the Republican Party, and in 1855 Chase became Ohio's first Republican governor. From 1849 to 1855, and again from 1860 to 1861, he served as a U.S. senator.

From 1861 to 1864 Chase served in the cabinet of President Abraham Lincoln as secretary of the treasury, a position that carried with it responsibility for finding ways to finance the Union's war effort. Chase received this appointment because, during the 1860 Republican Convention, at which he was vying for the presidential nomination, he stepped aside to allow Lincoln to achieve the candidacy. In 1864 Lincoln appointed Chase chief justice of the U.S. Supreme Court. In this capacity Chase dealt with many legal issues related to Reconstruction and presided over the Senate's trial of the impeached president Andrew Johnson in 1868. **See also** Johnson, Andrew; Reconstruction.

Chattanooga, Battle of

The Battle of Chattanooga took place on November 23–25, 1863, after a two-month siege of the Union-held city by the Confederates. The first Union forces arrived in Chattanooga after retreating from the nearby Battle of Chickamauga (September 19–20, 1863). Once in the city they dug trenches and built other fortifications to protect themselves from an expected frontal Confederate assault, and they received supplies and over thirty-six thousand reinforcements from across the Tennessee River at their rear. Because of this supply line the siege was ineffective, and the Confederate Army of Tennessee, led by General Braxton Bragg, eventually decided to attack the city.

Several Union commanders were involved in this battle, including Major Generals Ulysses S. Grant, George Thomas, and William T. Sherman. They coordinated their efforts to attack the Confederates at various high points around the city, including Lookout Mountain and Missionary Ridge, and eventually forced the Confederates to retreat. In achieving this victory, the Union had approximately 5,800 casualties (about 750 dead, 4,700 wounded, and 350 missing or taken prisoner) among its roughly 70,000 men, and of the Confederacy's approximately 50,000 men there were about 360 dead, 2,180 wounded, and 4,200 missing or taken prisoner. **See also** Chickamauga, Battle of; Grant, Ulysses S.; Sherman, William Tecumseh; Thomas, George Henry.

Cheatham, Benjamin Franklin (1820–1886)

Active in the Tennessee state militia prior to the Civil War, Confederate officer Benjamin F. Cheatham served in the Army of Tennessee and the Army of Mississippi as a brigadier general before being promoted to major general in the Confederate army. He fought in every major Confederate military action except for the Battle of Chattanooga and was known for his bravery. However, he was severely criticized (as were other officers) for his actions at Spring Hill, Tennessee, where, during the Franklin and Nashville Campaign, disorganization in the Confederate camps allowed thousands of Union soldiers to march from the area unhindered. After the war, Cheatham returned to farming in Tennessee. Later Cheatham became a prison official and then a postmaster. **See also** Franklin and Nashville Campaign.

Chesnut, Mary Boykin (1823–1886)

South Carolina military wife Mary B. Chesnut was the author of *A Diary from Dixie,* one of the most important sources of Southern observations on life during the Civil War. Published posthumously in 1905, this 400,000-word diary originally consisted of fifty notebooks covering the period between February 15, 1861, to August 2, 1865.

Chesnut was the daughter of Stephen D. Miller, a politician who had served as governor of South Carolina and U.S. senator. In 1840, when she was seventeen years old, she married James Chesnut Jr., who was a U.S. senator as well. Mary Chesnut's diary spans the period when she accompanied her husband to various military camps, battlefields, and battlefield hospitals as he served as an officer in the Confederate army. In addition to describing these places, the diary speaks of Chesnut's hatred for abolitionists, whom she viewed as hypocrites because they called blacks their equals but did not live with them in their homes. Although she was a slave owner herself, Chesnut expressed outrage over some aspects of slavery—in particular, slave auctions—and also expressed affection for one of her slaves, Nancy. In addition, Chesnut's diary entries chronicle the emotions that the typical Southerner felt as the war progressed: patriotic elation at the war's beginning, followed by increasing horror and sadness as more and more soldiers were wounded and killed. By the end of the war, Chesnut was wondering whether the Confederate cause had been worth all of the misery she had witnessed, yet she still spoke of her extreme hatred for the North. **See also** letters and diaries; literature, Civil War.

Chester, Thomas Morris (1834–1892)

Born in Pennsylvania, Thomas Morris Chester was the only black journalist to report on the Civil War for a major newspaper. Hired as a war correspondent for the *Philadelphia Press* in 1864, he covered only the last year of the conflict, but his reports were unique in that he told about the activities of both white and black troops. Chester reported from several battlefields, as well as from Richmond, Virginia, after the Union captured the city. Prior to the war, he helped recruit black soldiers, and in 1863 he spent some time in England giving lectures about the lives of blacks in America. After the war he returned to England and studied law; he then returned to the United States to practice. In 1873 he became the first black attorney in Louisiana. **See also** newspapers.

Chickamauga, Battle of

The Battle of Chickamauga resulted in the largest number of casualties of any battle in the western theater, leaving approximately 16,200 Union and 18,500 Confederate soldiers dead, wounded, or missing. The confrontation took place on a heavily wooded battlefield at Chickamauga, Georgia, just south of Chattanooga, Tennessee, on September 19–20, 1863, after a Union brigade from the Army of the Cumberland ran into a Confederate cavalry brigade and two Confederate infantry brigades from the Army of Tennessee. Soon additional forces from both armies became involved in the fight, amid a great deal of chaos due to the difficult terrain. Once darkness fell, the soldiers' confusion worsened, but the fighting continued until around midnight.

At dawn on the second day of the battle, the Confederates launched an assault that eventually split the Union's Army of the Cumberland in two. The Union soldiers then panicked and began to retreat under heavy fire. Only one of the Union generals, George Thomas, stayed firm, earning himself the nickname "the Rock of Chickamauga." He and his brigade inflicted heavy casualties on the Confederates and provided cover for retreating Union soldiers, but by nightfall Thomas's forces retreated as well. The Union forces then took a defensive position in Chattanooga, where Confederate general Braxton Bragg's forces immediately placed them under siege, a situation that lasted until the Battle of Chattanooga. **See also** Chattanooga, Battle of; Thomas, George Henry.

children in the Civil War

Children were often victims of the war, as were many adults, when cities were shelled or burned or when guerrillas attacked innocent civilians. For example, several children were among the civilians massacred in Lawrence, Kansas, by Confederate guerrillas in August 1863. But many boys as young as nine also fought in the Civil War, despite the fact that both the Union and the Confederacy required that their soldiers be over eighteen.

Many young boys, like John L. Clem, were members of Civil War regiments.

Statistics vary on just how many boys became soldiers. According to some historians, in the two armies there were between 250,000 and 420,000 boy soldiers. According to others, there were 1 million such soldiers in the Union alone. Estimates vary so widely because the only way a boy could enlist was to lie about his age. (Many did so while standing on a piece of paper on which the number eighteen had been written so that they could literally say they were "over eighteen.") Thus officially there were no underage recruits.

A recruiter who thought that a would-be enlistee was lying about his age might turn the boy away, but many simply let such boys join the army anyway. Either at this point or once part of a regiment, the youngest-looking boys were typically assigned to be musicians, because they would not have to fight in battles. The most famous boy to go to war as a musician was John L. Clem, who joined the Twenty-second Michigan Infantry at the age of ten and was immediately given the position of drummer boy.

According to newspaper reports of the period, Clem's drum was smashed by a shell at the Battle of Shiloh in April 1862, earning him the nickname "Johnny Shiloh," and at the Battle of Chickamauga in September 1863 he was said to have picked up a gun and shot a colonel off his horse. It is unclear whether these incidents really happened or whether they were an invention of the Northern press. In any case, after the war the young man tried to join the U.S. Military Academy. He was refused entrance, but the president of the United States, by then Ulysses S. Grant, made him a second lieutenant in the U.S. Army. Clem remained in the army until 1916, when he retired as a major general.

Whereas Clem served in the Civil War as a musician, a few boy soldiers served in combat. For example, George S. Lamkin of Mississippi joined an artillery battery at the age of eleven and was seriously wounded at Shiloh. Michael Dougherty of Pennsylvania joined the cavalry when the war broke out; in October 1863, at the age of sixteen, he was captured by Confederates and sent to the Andersonville prison camp. In 1906 he published an account of his time there as *Prison Diary,* in which he described the suffering he saw all around him.

Boy soldiers lost their childhoods to the war, but even children who did not enlist in the military had to grow up quickly in the Civil War years, particularly in the South. Southern children had to deal with many physical hardships as their homelands were turned into battlefields. In addition, both Southern and Northern children had to take on more work and responsibilities when their fathers and older brothers went to war. **See also** Andersonville; civilians, war's impact on; conscription.

civilians, war's impact on

In both the North and the South, civilians were immediately affected as men left homes, farms, and businesses to enter the military. Women and children were forced to take on duties for which they were sometimes unsuited and often unprepared, such as plowing and harvesting crops. In the South, moreover, because most battles were fought on Confederate soil, people saw their livelihoods destroyed as farms became battlegrounds and their homes, crops, and towns were destroyed. Invading troops often stole civilians' property, and even the Confederate government could and did confiscate livestock, food, and other items for the war effort. In addition, as the war progressed many Southerners faced starvation due to massive food shortages, the high price of food, and declining wages. In February 1863, for example, a machinist in Richmond, Virginia, earned $5 a day and a carpenter $2 a day, yet a pound of beef cost $1 and a pound of butter $3. By January 1865, incomes had risen to about $10 a day, but by then a pound of beef was $8 and a pound of butter $15. **See also** economy, Southern vs. Northern; food.

civil rights, black

Even after slavery ended, blacks were denied many civil rights. In fact, during Reconstruction, Southern states were allowed to enact laws, known collectively as the Black Codes, that ensured blacks would have no civil rights, thereby effectively continuing their subservience to whites. However, these Black Codes so inflamed former abolitionists that many lobbied the federal government to enact civil rights laws. In 1866, Congress passed a law (over the veto of President Andrew Johnson) that gave every person born in the United States (except Native Americans) certain rights related to contracts and the ownership of property. The following year, Congress gave black men living in the District of Columbia and all U.S. territories the right to vote, and in the Reconstruction Act of 1867 it decreed that no Southern state could be readmitted to the Union until its constitution gave black men the right to vote. However, this right was sometimes ignored in practice, so the following year Congress passed the Fourteenth Amendment to the U.S. Constitution. The amendment made blacks U.S. citizens and promoted black suffrage by basing the number of representatives in Congress on the percentage of adult males in a state that were allowed to vote. This gave states an incentive to allow blacks to vote, and those that did not would suffer politically. Despite such an inducement, some states continued to deny the vote to their black citizens through various legal loopholes and manipulations, such as literacy tests and poll taxes. Moreover, although the Fourteenth Amendment allowed blacks to sue in a court of law and enjoy certain other legal protections, as a practical matter they continued to be denied equal treatment. **See also** Black Codes.

Clay, Henry (1777–1852)

Known as the Great Compromiser or the Great Pacificator, politician Henry Clay supported both the Missouri Compromise (1820) and the Compromise of 1850 out of his conviction that the United States should be kept together. Clay began his career as a lawyer in Virginia in 1797 but soon moved to Kentucky to establish his own practice. There he married a wealthy woman, Lucretia Hart, became a plantation owner, and entered Kentucky politics. Though he owned slaves and saw them as necessary if his plantation was to be profitable, Clay opposed slavery in principle and suggested that all Southern plantations adopt a paid labor system instead. Once he determined that his opinions on this issue were unpopular, however, he stopped arguing in favor of emancipation. Clay subsequently served as a U.S. congressman (1811–1814, 1815–1821, and 1823–1825) and senator (1831–1842 and 1849–1852). His last major political act was his support of the Compromise of 1850, the details of which he helped shape. However, experts disagree on just how much influence Clay had on the construction and passage of this act. Clay died from tuberculosis in 1852, just two years after the compromise went into effect. **See also** Compromise of 1850; Jackson, Andrew.

Cleburne, Patrick Ronayne (1828–1864)

An Irish immigrant who had once served in the British army, Confederate officer Patrick R. Cleburne is credited with the idea of giving slaves their freedom in exchange for their enlistment in the Confederate army, although his suggestion was not implemented until late in the war. By then, Cleburne was dead, having been killed in the Battle of Franklin on November 30, 1864. Cleburne was also noted for being a commander who was both highly skilled and extremely popular with his troops. He worked his way up through the Confederate ranks from captain to major general and fought in many important Confederate campaigns, including the Kentucky Campaign, the Atlanta Campaign, and the Franklin and Nashville Campaign. During his military career he served with the Arkansas State Troops, the Army of Central Kentucky, the Army of the Mississippi, and the Army of Tennessee, and he was wounded in battles in Richmond, Virginia, and

Perryville, Kentucky. Cleburne was also instrumental in protecting retreating Confederate soldiers at the 1863 Battle of Chickamauga in Georgia, during which he defended Tunnel Hill. **See also** armies, Confederate; black troops; Franklin and Nashville Campaign.

Cobb, Howell (1815–1868)

A Georgia lawyer and politician, Howell Cobb served the Confederate States of America first as a political leader and then as a military commander. Prior to the Civil War, he had served as governor of Georgia (1851–1854) and as a U.S. congressman (1842–1851, 1855–1857). He also held the position of U.S. secretary of the treasury under President James Buchanan. During this period Cobb, a plantation owner with many slaves, supported Unionism (i.e., the South remaining in the Union) while working for compromises that would maintain slavery. However, when Abraham Lincoln was elected president in 1860 Cobb began to promote secession, believing as many Southerners did that Lincoln was the puppet of abolitionists.

After Georgia seceded, Cobb was one of ten men chosen to represent his state at a convention in Montgomery, Alabama, to establish thc Confederate States of America. There he was selected to lead the Provisional Congress, the temporary governing body of the Confederacy, until congressional elections could be held. As the first leader of the Confederacy, he administered the oath of office to the Confederate States of America president Jefferson Davis.

Long before the Provisional Congress gave way to an elected one (in February 1862), Cobb served as a military commander, splitting his time between the battlefield and the Confederate capital of Richmond, Virginia. During the summer of 1861 he organized his own Georgia regiment and led it as a colonel, but by the end of the war he was a major general, having fought in several battles. He also formed the Georgia State Guard, which helped defend Georgia from August 1863 to February 1864.

In 1864 Cobb established the headquarters of the Georgia Reserve Force in Macon, Georgia, and oversaw the defense of the city. In September 1864 he was given command of a new military district, the District of Georgia, which encompassed the cities of Macon, Augusta, and Columbus and was under the supervision of the Army of Tennessee. These forces, however, were no match for the troops of General William Tecumseh Sherman, who burned Atlanta in November 1864; one of Cobb's plantations was destroyed during Sherman's subsequent march from Atlanta to the sea.

In January 1865 Cobb headed to southwest Georgia to defend it against another Union army, led by Major General John H. Wilson. Although Cobb's men fought well, they were seriously outnumbered and undersupplied, and by April they had no choice but to surrender to Wilson. After the war ended, Cobb returned to practicing law in Macon, Georgia. **See also** Atlanta Campaign; Georgia.

codes and ciphers

During the Civil War, both the North and the South used both simple and complex codes and ciphers to communicate without alerting the enemy as to military plans or moves. A code is a system in which number groups, nonsense words, or actual words can be translated into other words according to a prearranged system. For example, the message "attack tonight" might be written as "7538 899," "skeyx grmol," or "pick apples." During the Civil War, code translations were typically written down in a dictionary known as a code book, but since such books were difficult to use on the battlefield and could fall into enemy hands, most spies and officers preferred to rely on ciphers instead.

A cipher is a system in which a grid or chart equates individual letters of the alphabet with other letters or numbers. For example, Union spy Elizabeth Van Lew used a grid with a horizontal and a vertical row of single-digit numbers that, when matched up, equaled a letter. Thus if she wanted to indicate the letter R, for instance, she would find R on her grid, see that it was in vertical row 6 and horizontal row 1, and write the letter as 61. Van Lew's grid was difficult to memorize, so she kept a copy hidden within her watch, where it was found after her death. Most Civil War ciphers, however, had grids that were easily remembered or reproduced using a particular system. For example, a grid might have several lines of letters written in alphabetical order alternating with lines of letters written in the reverse order. Ciphers created using the most popular Confederate cipher grid, the Virgenere Table (named after its eighteenth-century French inventor), also required a key phrase for deciphering. The letters within this phrase told decipherers how to line up the rows of the grid in order to be able to figure out the message.

During the course of the war, the Confederacy changed its key phrase only twice, so only three were ever used. This made it easier for experts in the U.S. War Department to figure out the cipher about midway through the war. The Confederacy, however, did not know that this cipher had been broken, so many of its spies continued to use it, thereby providing the Union with valuable information whenever messages were intercepted. Meanwhile, the Confederates were apparently unable to crack any Union codes or ciphers. Therefore Northern generals could send coded or ciphered messages to one another, either via couriers or telegraph, asking that reinforcements or supplies be sent to a particular location without fear of the South learning their troop movements and battle plans. **See also** communication systems; spies.

colonization movement

More than forty years before the Civil War, abolitionists began to propose that free American blacks establish their own colonies abroad in order to avoid the indignities they were suffering due to racism. However, few free blacks were interested in the colonization movement until the 1850s, when it became apparent that the U.S. government was not interested in protecting them from being kidnapped and sent south to be sold as slaves. (Both an 1842 U.S. Supreme Court decision, in the case of *Prigg v. Pennsylvania,* and the Fugitive Slave Act of 1850 made it extremely difficult for anyone to interfere with the capture of a fugitive slave, even in an attempt to determine whether the captive was an escaped slave or a free man.) The colonization movement also gained the support of many Southern slave owners, who wanted to rid the United States of free blacks under the belief that such people encouraged slave rebellions and furthered the abolitionist movement.

Consequently, various abolitionist groups developed to support efforts to establish colonies of free American blacks abroad. Among the most prominent of these groups was the American Colonization Society, founded in Washington, D.C., in 1817. In 1822, this group purchased land in Africa and created a colony of American blacks in Liberia; in 1847 this colony became the independent Republic of Liberia. By 1860, thanks to the support of such prominent abolitionists as William Lloyd Garrison, the society had helped send approximately ten thousand American blacks to Liberia.

In 1862, the U.S. government contributed $100,000 to further these colonization efforts, out of a total of $600,000 allocated that year for such projects. (President Abraham Lincoln had requested this funding after signing a bill in April 1862 that abolished slavery in the District of Columbia out of concern over how these former slaves were going to earn a living.) The U.S. government also supported colonization efforts in Haiti, where by December 1862 approximately two thousand American blacks had been relocated. However, living conditions there were so harsh that by the following year almost all of the colonists had either died or returned to the United States.

Meanwhile, U.S. officials and abolitionists continued to suggest other possible locations for colonization efforts. For example, in August 1862 President Lincoln proposed sending former slaves to Central America, where, he suggested, they could work in coal mines. Black leaders rejected this idea, arguing that such labor would be no better than what the colonists had experienced as slaves.

By this point, a majority of free blacks had decided that they would rather remain in the United States, both because it was their home and because it finally looked as if all American blacks would one day be emancipated. Nonetheless, in 1863 the U.S. government sent a group of over five hundred free blacks to Ile à Vache, an island south of Haiti, hoping they would have success establishing a colony there. Instead, many of them died under harsh living conditions similar to those that had earlier plagued the Haiti colony, and the remainder were so miserable that within a few months they asked the government to bring them home. The following year, in July 1864, Congress ended all government funding for colonization, and when the Civil War ended the colonization movement effectively died—although during Reconstruction some political leaders suggested that black colonies be established in U.S. territories. **See also** Fugitive Slave Acts; Garrison, William Lloyd; Reconstruction.

Colorado

Colorado was a U.S. territory during the Civil War years, having officially gained that status on February 26, 1861. As such, it had no state militia and remained officially neutral throughout the conflict. However, because the U.S. Army units that had protected settlers and stagecoaches from Indian attacks were battling the Confederates, Colorado had to create volunteer militias to take up the slack. Men who wanted to fight in the Civil War also created their own volunteer regiments and headed east to aid the Union effort in the war's Western Theater. **See also** West, the.

Colt, Samuel (1814–1862)

Gunmaker Samuel Colt manufactured the majority of the handguns used during the Civil War. Colt patented the first handgun with a revolving cartridge cylinder—a weapon that became known as a revolver—in 1835, and later extended this technology to rifles. However, between 1842 and 1847 no Colt firearms were manufactured due to lack of demand, a situation that changed after the U.S. government ordered one thousand handguns for use in the Mexican-American War. In 1855 Colt built a major manufacturing plant and an armory for his weapons in Hartford, Connecticut, where he developed new technologies that included interchangeable parts and an assembly line. These technologies enabled him to mass-produce his weapons, thereby ensuring that Civil War soldiers had an ample number of guns. **See also** ammunition; weapons.

Columbia, South Carolina

The capital of South Carolina, Columbia was home to factories and mills that provided many supplies to the South, most importantly gunpowder used by the Confederate navy. For this reason, Union general William Tecumseh Sherman targeted Columbia for destruction. He attacked the city, in February 1865, shortly after burning Atlanta and Savannah, Georgia, and Columbia was soon in flames. However, it is unclear whether Sherman was responsible for the fire that ultimately destroyed the city or whether Confederate authorities set Columbia on fire to keep its valuable supplies from falling into Union hands. **See also** Sherman, William Tecumseh.

commerce raiding

The Confederacy extensively practiced commerce raiding (the capture and/or destruction of ships carrying merchant goods) during the Civil War. Specifically, the Confederate navy attacked merchant ships to disrupt U.S. trade and force the Union navy to expend resources in defending commercial shipping. Private vessels engaged in commerce raiding as well, under the authorization of the Confederate government. The crews of these ships, known as privateers, were allowed to keep part of the cargo they captured.

During the course of the war, commerce raiders destroyed approximately two hundred U.S. merchant vessels, resulting in millions of dollars in losses. The most successful Confederate naval ship engaged in such activities was the CSS *Alabama,* which captured and/or destroyed sixty-five Union merchant ships in just two years. Other commerce raiders included the *Florida* and the *Tallahassee,* which each took thirty-eight enemy ships and their cargo; the *Shenandoah,* which took thirty-seven vessels; the *Tacony,* which took fifteen; and the *Georgia,* which took nine. While some of these vessels, such as the *Alabama,* were specially built for commerce raiding, others were ships whose purpose had been changed. For example, the steam cruiser *Tallahassee* was formerly the *Atlanta,* a blockade runner. **See also** *Alabama,* CSS; blockades and blockade runners; navies, Confederate and Union.

communication systems

There were three main systems of communication during the Civil War. The most basic system was couriers, people who hand-delivered messages, verbal or written and possibly in code. This method was extremely slow, taking hours or even days. The other two systems were more sophisticated and nearly instantaneous: the telegraph and a signaling system commonly known as wigwag signaling.

Developed in 1856 and patented two years later by a U.S. Army surgeon, Albert J. Myer, wigwag signaling used the movements of a handheld flag or, at night, a torch (a hollow metal cylinder filled with liquid fuel) to signal messages using a code based on the changing position of the flag or torch. By moving the flag or torch in various ways, the signaler could indicate any letter of the alphabet in order to spell out words. However, as it became obvious that spelling out words was a slow process, Myer added signals for more than two hundred commonly used words and abbreviations. He also created standardized square-shaped signal flags that were white with a red square in the middle. However, sometimes to improve visibility a red flag with a white square was used or, whenever there was snow on the ground, a black flag with a white square. In any case, flags were attached to a sixteen-foot pole that was put together in the field from four-foot sections.

In 1860 Myer was made the head of the new Signal Corps of the United States and began training soldiers as signalers. Meanwhile, one of the men who had helped Myer perfect his system, Edward Porter Alexander, began training men for a Confederate Signal Service. Although this entity was not officially established by the Confederacy until April 1862, Confederates began using wigwag signaling on the battlefield months before the Union did. Its first use was at the First Battle of Bull Run (July 21, 1861), when a Confederate signalman contributed to the Confederate victory by warning Colonel Nathan Evans that Union troops were approaching from the colonel's left.

The main duty of both the Union Signal Corps and the Confederate Signal Service was to enable military units to communicate with one another whenever a telegraph system was unavailable. Therefore many naval vessels and every infantry division and cavalry brigade had signalmen. When army signalmen could not pass messages via signaling, because of bad weather or difficult terrain, they might be used as couriers or scouts. When it was possible to signal, the signalman sending the message would station himself on high ground, atop a tall building, or on a signal tower constructed specifically for his use. Meanwhile, the signalman reading the message would be in a similar location, using field glasses or a telescope to make out the signals from a distance. Signal towers were typically constructed at varying intervals (with the distance depending on terrain) along a line stretching from a command position or military headquarters to a military camp or outpost. Meanwhile, the enemy would station sharpshooters near these stations in an attempt to take out the signalmen.

The messages sent by signalmen were typically in code to prevent the enemy from being able to understand them. Because of their knowledge of codes and ciphers, as well as the fact that their tendency to work on high ground made them aware of the landscape and troop positioning, some signalmen became involved in spy activities, reporting their observations or picking up and delivering messages as part of their courier duties. In fact, Major William Norris, who took over the Confederate Signal Service when Alexander was reassigned, not only supervised signalmen but also ran a network of spies known as the Secret Line out of his Signal Service offices.

Despite this side benefit of signaling, the telegraph was still the preferred method of communication during the war because of the speed with which it could transmit messages over great distances. At the beginning of the Civil War, there were approximately fifty thousand miles of telegraph wires in the United States and roughly fifteen hundred stations where messages were being received and sent by trained telegraph operators. The bulk of this system, however, was located in the North. During the war, the Union added another fifteen thousand miles of line and the Confederacy one thousand. The Confederacy wanted to add more to its system, but it had difficulty getting the necessary supplies due to the Northern blockade. The head of military telegraph communications in the South, Dr. William S. Morris, eventually built a wire factory in Richmond, Virginia, to try to solve this problem, but the Confederacy still struggled to obtain the battery material, bluestone (copper sulphate), needed to power the telegraph system. Without a steady supply of batteries, the Southern telegraph system was often unreliable.

The South actually had two separate telegraph systems, one military and one civilian. The Confederate government was reluctant to seize commercial stations and therefore established its own separate telegraph lines. However, the military was sometimes forced to use commercial lines because the civilian system was more extensive. When this occurred, the civilian operators, who were primarily women (although male operators were exempted from the draft), sometimes walked off the job over disagreements with military commanders. One of the most common points of contention was how many hours and under what conditions an operator could be expected to work; military telegraph operators were often forced to remain at their post for twenty-four hours or more, sometimes under heavy fire, but civilian opera-

At a makeshift telegraph station in the field, men stand atop tree trunks being used as telegraph poles. The North had a better telegraph system than the South.

tors were typically unwilling to do this. When such refusals occurred, the military had no choice but to put up with them, and throughout the war the South suffered from a shortage of skilled telegraph personnel.

In contrast, the North had an ample supply of telegraph operators. However, all of them were civilian, even those who worked for the U.S. Military Telegraph Service of the U.S. Army Quartermaster Corps (an exception was a small group that was part of a branch of the Signal Corps known as the Field Telegraph Service, which in 1863 was placed under the control of the U.S. Military Telegraph Service as well). Because of friction between civilian operators and military commanders, General John Frémont formed his own telegraph battalion in the West in 1861, but he was forced to disband it after commercial companies insisted that the only way they would cooperate with the U.S. Army's use of their lines was if all telegraph stations continued to be manned by civilians.

As in the South, the civilian telegraph system in the North sent both civilian and military messages. In fact, in the first year of the war, most Union military messages were sent via commercial companies. However, the U.S. War Department had no qualms about seizing some commercial telegraph lines for use by the military. This was the case with all commercial lines in Washington, D.C., in 1861.

Regardless of what lines were used, both Northern and Southern generals had difficulty keeping their telegraphed messages secure. To prevent enemy spies from acquiring important military information, some generals traveled with their own personal telegraph officers, and some of them became skilled at intercepting enemy transmissions. For example, Confederate general Robert E. Lee's telegraph operator, C.A. Gaston, often tapped Union telegraph lines to gather information from and send false messages to Union generals. (Someone who has tapped into a telegraph line can transmit messages that appear to have been generated by a telegraph station within the system.) To try to prevent such tricks, each side began transmitting its messages in codes or ciphers. **See also** codes and ciphers; spies.

Compromise of 1850

The Compromise of 1850 was a package of laws passed by Congress designed to address the question of slavery in territories acquired by the United States after the Mexican-American War (1846–1848), lands that eventually became the states of California, Nevada, Utah, and Arizona and parts of what became New Mexico, Colorado, and Wyoming. Antislavery groups argued that American settlers moving into these territories should immediately be allowed to prohibit slavery, while slavery advocates argued that settlers had the right to bring all their possessions—including slaves—with them when they moved into new lands.

Eventually three congressmen—Henry Clay of Kentucky, Daniel Webster of Massachusetts, and Stephen Douglas of Illinois—developed a piece of compromise legislation that seemed to satisfy all parties in the debate. Their legislation had five parts, known collectively as the Compromise of 1850. Essentially, the five components of the compromise were as follows: California would be admitted into the Union as a free state; the territories of New Mexico and Utah would be considered neutral until they applied for statehood, whereupon their citizens would decide whether each state would support slavery; Texas, which had been admitted earlier as a slave state but was trying to enlarge its territory, would keep its existing boundaries in exchange for some financial aid from the government; the District of Columbia, the site of the nation's capital, would no longer allow the slave trade within its boundaries; and the federal government would assist slave owners in recovering runaway slaves. This last part of the compromise, known as the Fugitive Slave Act, denied any black accused of being a runaway slave the right to a hearing, and in fact many free blacks were enslaved as a result.

The Compromise of 1850 did not, however, settle the slavery issue, since the second component of the compromise (regarding New Mexico and Utah) was interpreted differently by pro- and antislavery forces. Pro-slavery forces believed that it meant that any individual within one of these territories could decide to own slaves, while antislavery forces believed it meant that the citizens of these territories could vote to prohibit slavery. For this reason, many historians say that the Compromise of 1850 merely delayed the ultimate confrontation between North and South. **See also** California; Clay, Henry; Douglas, Stephen Arnold; Fugitive Slave Acts; New Mexico.

Confederate States of America

The entity known as the Confederate States of America, or CSA, was formed in 1861 and eventually consisted of eleven Southern states and a total of about 9 million people (3.5 million of them slaves). The CSA began with seven Southern states: South Carolina, Mississippi, Florida, Alabama, Georgia, Louisiana, and Texas. On February 4, 1861, representatives from these states met in Montgomery, Alabama (except for the Texas representatives, who were late in arriving), to establish the CSA, organize a provisional Confederate government, and adopt a constitution. At this time, Montgomery was named the provisional capital city of the new nation and Jefferson Davis was named the provisional president. On February 18, 1861, the CSA inaugurated Jefferson Davis into office.

On May 11, 1861, the permanent CSA Constitution was signed, and on May 17–21, 1861, four more states joined the CSA: Virginia, Arkansas, Tennessee, and North Carolina. (However, a portion of Virginia later rejoined the Union.) In addition, the CSA claimed two border states, Kentucky and Missouri, as its own, even though the Union claimed them as well, and allowed representatives of these state governments to participate in the Confederate Congress.

The CSA's constitution in many ways resembled that of the United States. Overall, most of the differences in the CSA's constitution were designed to give individual states greater power at the expense of the central government. For example, whereas the U.S. Constitution allowed its president and vice president to run for an unlimited number of four-year terms (the two-term restriction would not be added until 1951), the Confederate Constitution mandated that they were each to be elected for a single six-year term. Moreover, constitutional amendments did not first require a vote in Congress to be sent to the states for ratification. Instead, an amendment could pass into law if two-thirds of the Confederate states voted in favor of it. The Confederate Constitution also allowed the ownership of slaves, although it forbade its citizens from importing them from abroad.

The Confederate States of America officially ceased to exist with the end of the war in 1865. By 1870 all of the former Confederate states had been readmitted to the Union. **See also** border states; cabinet, Confederate; Congress, Confederate.

Congress, Confederate

The legislative branch of the Confederate States of America (CSA), like that of the United States, was bicameral—that is, the Congress consisted of two legislative bodies, the House of Representatives and the Senate. Moreover, the Confederate Congress operated under essentially the same rules and procedures as the U.S. Congress did. However, the CSA began with a Provisional Congress (which convened on February 18, 1862) and only later elected a permanent Congress (which convened on May 2, 1864). The CSA also allowed representatives from five tribes of Native

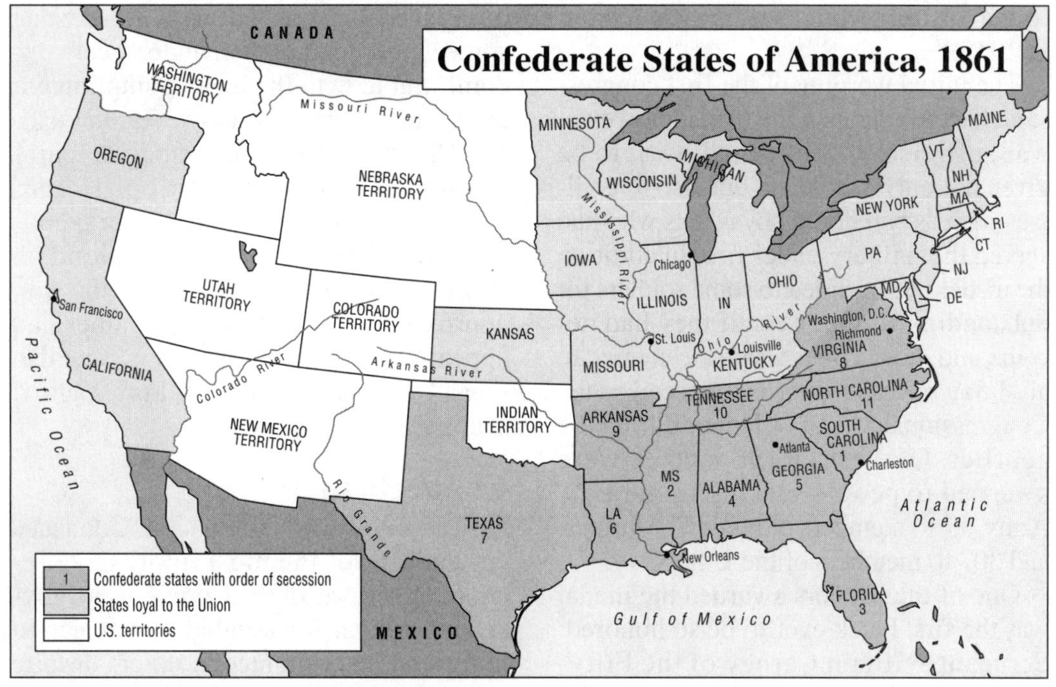

Americans (Creek, Choctaw, Cherokee, Chickasaw, and Seminole) to participate in debates in the Confederate Congress, although these representatives had no power to vote. **See also** cabinet, Confederate; cabinet, U.S.; Confederate States of America; Native American soldiers; Union.

Congressional Medal of Honor

In December 1861, U.S. senator James W. Grimes of Iowa proposed and achieved the passage of an act of Congress creating a medal of honor that could be awarded to sailors who had displayed bravery under fire. Under the act, only enlisted men (not officers, who were expected to display bravery as a matter of course) from the U.S. Navy or Marine Corps were eligible for the Congressional Medal of Honor. In February 1862, Senator Henry Wilson of Massachusetts proposed and Congress passed an extension of the act to include U.S. Army enlisted men, with recognition for their bravery to include actions that had taken place from the beginning of the Civil War. On March 3, 1863, another act of Congress made army officers eligible for the Congressional Medal of Honor. (Naval officers would not be included until 1915.)

The initial wording of the first congressional act to establish the medal, however, was sufficiently vague to allow it to be given not only to soldiers but also to civilians such as battlefield physicians who had served the military under fire. In addition the medal was awarded to some soldiers for outstanding service even if they had not come into direct contact with the enemy. In all, 1,519 men and one woman received the Congressional Medal of Honor during the conflict. Of these, 1,196 medals were awarded to people serving in the U.S. Army, 17 to members of the U.S. Marines, and 307 to members of the U.S. Navy.

One of the soldiers awarded the medal was the first black ever to be so honored: Sergeant William Carney of the Fifty-fourth Massachusetts Regiment, who was involved in an attack on Fort Wagner in South Carolina. Although all of the members of this all-black regiment exhibited bravery during the attack, Carney received particular attention because he saved a U.S. flag from being captured by the Confederates. The sole female recipient of the medal, Mary Walker, received the honor because she was a battlefield physician. However, she was among over nine hundred honorees asked to return their medals in 1917 after a military board decreed that the Medal of Honor could be given only to members of the U.S. military who had come into direct contact with the enemy and performed above and beyond the call of duty despite great personal risk. (Walker refused to give the medal back, and in 1975 Congress posthumously reinstated her award.)

The Confederacy awarded no equivalent to the Congressional Medal of Honor, although as of October 1862 the Confederate Congress decreed that President Jefferson Davis could bestow such a medal. The reason for this had to do with difficulties the Confederacy had in manufacturing medals, as well as with the fact that some Confederate commanders were uncomfortable with the idea of singling out individuals for honor. However, in October 1863 the Confederacy began maintaining a Confederate Roll of Honor, where names of particularly courageous men would be listed and read aloud on special occasions. By the end of the war, approximately two thousand names had appeared on the Roll of Honor. **See also** flags, U.S. and Confederate; Fort Wagner; Walker, Mary Edwards.

Connecticut

Among the states of the Union, Connecticut had one of the most impressive recruitment efforts of the Civil War. Its governor, William Buckingham, managed to recruit 54,882 volunteer soldiers despite the fact that his state had only 461,000 residents. **See also** conscription.

conscientious objectors

During the Civil War, conscientious objectors (people who object to the war on moral principles and therefore refuse to fight) typically came from certain religious groups, most notably the Society of Friends (Quakers), Shakers, Mennonites, Dunkards (or Tunkards), and Nazarines. Both before and during the conflict, these groups publicized their views on war. In addition, Quakers and Mennonites, who together numbered over 200,000 members in the first year of the war, engaged in political activism to try to force both the North and the South to grant their members blanket exemptions from military service.

As a result of such efforts, in October 1862 the Confederacy officially exempted the members of four groups—Quakers, Mennonites, Dunkards, and Nazarines—from military service, provided that individuals paid a fee of $500 or provided someone else to serve in their place. But as the war progressed and soldiers were desperately needed, this exemption was often ignored and conscientious objectors were forced into service through threats of violence, large fines, or arrest. However, a few Confederate generals—most notably Thomas "Stonewall" Jackson—recognized the futility of trying to make such individuals fight and instead assigned them to noncombat duties.

In the North there was no draft exemption based on religious grounds. However, in February 1864 the United States decreed, through a new version of the Conscription Act, that members of certain religious groups could substitute hospital duty for combat duty. Theoretically, this same act also allowed such a person to avoid service by paying $300, but military commanders usually ignored this provision and forced conscientious objectors to fight anyway. Moreover, any objector who complained about the situation risked being beaten or otherwise mistreated. Prior to 1864, a conscientious objector in the Union army who refused to fight or even practice military drills might be tortured and/or court-martialed and imprisoned.

Meanwhile, pacifists who were ineligible for service (because of their age, gender, health, or occupation) expressed their religious views by refusing to pay taxes that would support the war effort—a stand that often resulted in their property being seized. They also participated in fund-raising activities that provided the money to those who needed to pay other people to fight in their place, and they provided "safe houses" for soldiers who fled the battlefield because of conscientious objection. In Kentucky, for instance, the Shakers estimated that they provided food and shelter to at least fifty thousand conscientious objectors, both Northerners and Southerners, fleeing duty. **See also** conscription; desertion; peace movements and societies; Quakers.

conscription

Also known as the draft, conscription is the practice of forcing individuals into military service. The first conscription act in America was passed by the Confederate Congress on April 16, 1862, although the law provided many exemptions from service that favored the wealthy. For example, it allowed men to pay others to serve in their place, either directly or through a $500 fee given to the government, and it excluded from service men who supervised twenty or more slaves, whether as plantation owners or overseers (although the exemption for overseers was eliminated at the end of 1863).

Other Confederate conscription acts were passed in September and October 1862, May 1863, and March 1864 to redefine who would serve and to transfer certain numbers of men from one type of service to another. For example, the General Conscription Law of 1864 stated that the Confederate army was to give twelve hundred men to the Confederate navy. In all, between April 1864 and April 1865, conscripts made up approximately 25 to 35 percent of the Southern armies.

The Union draft began with the U.S. Conscription Act of March 3, 1863. Signed into law by President Abraham Lincoln, it required all able-bodied men between the ages of eighteen and forty-five to register and make themselves available to serve when called, although it exempted people of certain occupations. For example, railroad engineers and telegraph operators were not required to become soldiers because their services were valuable to the war effort. However, able-bodied men whose jobs were not exempted could, as in the South, pay someone else to serve in their place. A Northerner could also get out of having to serve by paying a $300 fee. Because of these two options of getting out of service, of the nearly 250,000 men who were drafted, only about 6 percent actually served. Still others got out of service because of some physical or mental disability.

Although the federal government mandated conscription, the states were in charge of overseeing the process and calling up men to serve. Most states used a lottery system to make their selections, with the number of men that would be called at any given time determined by the federal government based on each state's population. The number of men a state was required to draft could be reduced by volunteerism, and indeed many men volunteered rather than waiting to be drafted.

There were two reasons that men preferred to volunteer rather than be drafted. First, once they became soldiers, men who had volunteered generally received more respect from officers than conscripts did. Second, men who volunteered received a bounty, an amount of money to reward them for coming forward. Both the North and the South used the bounty system, with the bounty payment varying from state to state and community to community.

Conscription was highly unpopular, and in the North protests against the draft sometimes turned into riots. The worst of these riots occurred in New York City from July 13 to 17, 1863, after free blacks had been hired to replace striking Irish American dockworkers. When these dockworkers learned that they were being drafted to replace Union soldiers killed at the Battle of Gettysburg, they became outraged at being called on to fight in a war that, if won, would free more blacks who could serve as strikebreakers. In the resulting riot, the striking workers attacked blacks and abolitionists and destroyed the buildings of organizations dedicated to freeing the slaves, and more than one hundred people were killed. **See also** bounty system; riots.

contrabands of war

Contrabands of war were goods prohibited in trade during the war, but the term was generally used to refer to fugitive slaves who sought protection behind Union lines. Union general Benjamin Butler was the first to classify fugitive slaves as contraband, under the argument that because the Confederacy sometimes pressed fugitive slaves into service to build fortifications, refusing to return them to the South served a military purpose.

At the beginning of the war, Union military leaders often returned fugitives because they did not have enough food and supplies to care for them. In August 1861, however, the federal government passed the Confiscation Act, which decreed that any fugitive slave who had been used, with his owner's knowledge, to support the Confederate war effort (such as by building fortifications) was to be claimed by the Union as a war prize and given freedom. However, some of these freed slaves were then hired out to farmers or set to work in army camps, albeit for pay. Others were housed in contraband camps, many of

Contraband, or Southern slaves who escaped to the North, were hired to work for pay or were sent to live in camps.

which were overcrowded and rife with disease. In December 1862, the commander of the Union's Department of the South, Brigadier General Rufus Saxton, tried to solve the overcrowding problem in contraband camps by giving some of the freed slaves in his jurisdiction two acres of land each, along with the tools necessary for them to grow cotton for the Union.

Nonetheless, many of the contraband camps remained so unpleasant that some of the freedmen who lived in them eventually decided to return to their former owners. Others enlisted in the Union army, once the federal government decided to allow black troops; approximately 130,000 freed slaves became Union soldiers during the war. Freedmen who did not enlist might follow along with Union armies anyway, in hopes of receiving food and supplies. Only toward the end of the war, in March 1865, did the U.S. Congress form an organization, the Freedmen's Bureau, specifically designed to deal with the problems related to freed slaves. **See also** Bureau of Refugees, Freedmen, and Abandoned Lands; Butler, Benjamin Franklin.

Corinth, Mississippi

The city of Corinth, Mississippi, was the point where two major Confederate railroad lines, the Mobile and Ohio Railroad and the Memphis and Charleston Railroad, met. During the Civil War, these lines were vital to the movement of supplies and troops to various parts of the South, and they were the primary means of bringing ammunition and other materials from Southern factories to the battlefield. Consequently, the North made capturing the city a high priority.

In March 1862, after the Union captured parts of middle and western Tennessee, Union general Henry W. Halleck (then in command of all Union forces in the region) sent Brigadier General Ulysses S. Grant's Army of the Tennessee—roughly thirty-seven thousand men—to destroy the Corinth railroad lines. Before these troops could reach the site, however, they were ordered to wait at Pittsburg Landing on the Tennessee River for the arrival of twenty-five thousand additional troops. Meanwhile, as part of a plan to regain lost territory, the Confederacy started massing forces in the town, using it as the staging ground for an attack on Grant's army. Ultimately over forty-four thousand Confederate soldiers were sent to Corinth, under the command of Generals Albert Sidney Johnston and P.G.T. Beauregard, and on the morning of April 3, 1862, they began to march toward Pittsburg Landing. The resulting battle, known as the Battle of Shiloh, took place on April 6 and 7.

The Battle of Shiloh ended in a Confederate defeat, after which the Confederates retreated to Corinth. Shortly thereafter, after bringing even more reinforcements into the area, the Union began advancing on the city. However, as General Halleck approached Corinth on May 30, he discovered that the Confederates had already abandoned it.

Roughly five months later, the Confederates attempted to retake the city, with a force of twenty-two thousand men under General Earl Van Dorn. Known as the Corinth Campaign, this military action included a battle on October 3 and 4 in which approximately twenty-two thousand Union soldiers, commanded by Major General William Rosecrans, defended Corinth against Van Dorn's troops. At first it seemed as though the Confederates were going to win the battle, but by the second morning, under heavy fire, they gave up. In all, the Confederates lost 4,838 men in the conflict, while the Union lost 2,359, and afterward Corinth remained in Union hands until the war's end. **See also** Halleck, Henry Wager; Shiloh, Battle of.

cost of the war

In January 1863, the U.S. government estimated that the Civil War was costing it $2.5 million daily. In 1879 the government made a final estimate of the war's cost to the Union as $6,190,000,000, and the Confederate cost was estimated to be $2,099,808,707. By 1906 the U.S. government determined that it had spent an additional $3.3 billion on pensions and other benefits for Federal soldiers. All of this is aside from the economic costs related to rebuilding infrastructure, such as bridges and buildings; restoring agricultural productivity; and dealing with the problems associated with the loss of over 600,000 men. **See also** casualties; economy, Southern vs. Northern; taxation.

cotton

By the time of the Civil War, cotton was the dominant crop in the South. As such, it encouraged the continuance of slavery, because planting and harvesting the crop required a large number of laborers. Moreover, cotton was a key component not only in the Southern economy but in the European economy as well. By 1860 at least 85 percent of Europe's cotton came from the American South, including three-fourths of the cotton used by the British and French textile mills.

Because of Europe's reliance on its cotton, the South felt that it had the upper hand in international relations. Specifically, the South believed that if it chose to cut off Europe's supply of cotton, so many foreign textile mills would have to close that Europe would suffer an economic crisis accompanied by massive unemployment and civil and political unrest. This scenario was often called "King Cotton," based on an 1855 book by economist David Christy, *Cotton Is King,* that emphasized the importance of cotton in the world economy. In 1858, South Carolina senator James Hammond used this phrase in a rousing speech before the U.S. Congress in which he suggested that the South could bring the world economy to its knees simply by withholding its cotton.

Southern cotton growers had King Cotton in mind when they voluntarily ended the exportation of cotton as soon as the war began. However, their cotton embargo failed to have the intended results because the previous year, due to particularly good growing conditions, Southern cotton had been so plentiful and so cheap that foreign mill owners had bought extra, and this oversupply kept them in operation throughout 1861 and 1862. (After that, mills were able to make up any shortfall by purchasing cotton from India, Brazil, and Egypt.) Within a few weeks of enacting their embargo, moreover, Southern cotton growers recognized the folly of the King Cotton theory and began exporting cotton again, and the Confederacy obtained foreign loans based on the money that future sales of cotton abroad would provide. Nonetheless, the South still did not ship much cotton to Europe because of a Northern blockade of Southern ports, and the Southern economy suffered as a result.

Although the Southern economy depended on cotton sales, in May 1861 the Confederate government decreed that no Southern cotton could be sold to Northern buyers. In March 1862 the government further decreed that a state government could burn any cotton at risk of falling into enemy hands. Despite such laws, however, as the war progressed many Southern growers secretly met with Northerners to sell their cotton or offer it in trade.

To address this problem, all Confederate states eventually adopted some type of restriction regarding the amount of land a planter could devote to cotton as opposed to food crops. Most planters complied with these restrictions, reducing their cotton yield by as much as half in order to produce more food. This, combined with decreases in crop production brought on by wartime conditions (specifically, a loss

Slaves harvest cotton on a Southern plantation. Cotton production in the South depended on slave labor.

of manpower as farmers became soldiers and a loss of croplands as fields became battlegrounds), reduced the amount of cotton grown in the South. As a consequence, whereas in 1816 approximately 4.5 million bales of cotton were produced in the South, this number dropped to 1.5 million in 1862, 500,000 in 1863, and 300,000 in 1864.

After the war, the South continued to experience a decrease in cotton production. This was due not only to the physical and economic destruction the region had experienced during the war but also to the fact that Southerners had abused their soil for many years. Specifically, in the prewar South, cotton growers had failed to allow their fields to "rest" periodically so that the soil could recover from the cotton plants' depletion of its vital nutrients. Instead, plantation owners relied on the fact that when one field was exhausted they had enough means to acquire another one—an approach to farming that could not be maintained in the poverty-stricken postwar South. **See also** economy, Southern vs. Northern; plantations.

Cox, Jacob Dolson (1828–1900)

Although born in Canada, Jacob D. Cox was a prominent U.S. politician who became a Union general during the Civil War. Unlike many politicians of the period who joined the military, Cox was a competent and well-respected commander. His first connection to the war effort occurred in 1861 when, while serving in the Ohio state senate, the governor appointed him a general of the state militia. During this period Cox began studying military strategy and history, and he soon became an expert in the subjects. In 1861 Cox contributed to recruitment efforts for the Union army, which rewarded him with the rank of brigadier general in charge of volunteers. In this capacity he led troops in Virginia from 1861 to 1862, fought in the Battle of Antietam in 1862, and was part of the Union's Atlanta Campaign in 1864.

After the war, Cox practiced law in Ohio and continued to be active in politics, serving as governor of Ohio (1866), U.S. secretary of the interior (1869–1870), and a U.S. congressman (1876–1880). In addition, throughout his postwar years he was a military historian, teaching and writing books on a variety of military topics but particularly the Civil War. His best-known work is the two-volume *Military Reminiscences of the Civil War,* published in 1900, the year Cox died. **See also** Antietam, Battle of; Atlanta Campaign.

Crater, Battle of the

The Battle of the Crater was a major disaster for the Union. Part of the Petersburg Campaign (June 15, 1864–April 3, 1865), this battle took place at Petersburg, Virginia, on July 30, 1864. Roughly a month earlier, the Union had devised a plan to destroy a line of Confederate soldiers defending Petersburg. Following this plan, a Pennsylvania regiment consisting primarily of former coal miners dug a tunnel from the Union camp to a point about five hundred feet away, then created two seventy-five-foot chambers beneath where the enemy soldiers were standing. On July 23, when this excavation project was completed, Union forces put eight thousand pounds of gunpowder in the chambers, and at around dawn on July 30 they detonated the explosives.

The resulting blast killed approximately three hundred Confederate soldiers and created a crater in the earth approximately thirty feet deep, with a length of about 170 feet and a width of about 70 feet. The blast also left an opening in the Confederate line, and Union general Ambrose Burnside ordered his troops to charge toward it—forgetting that there was now a hole in the earth between them and the Confederate lines. As the Union soldiers fell into the crater, Confederates who had survived the explosion ran up to the crater's rim and fired their weapons down at the enemy. The Confederates ignored many of the Union soldiers' attempts to surrender, particularly those of black troops, and continued to shoot until they were driven back by Union soldiers who had not fallen into the crater. By the end of this battle, nearly four thousand Union soldiers had been killed, along with about fifteen hundred Confederates. The North was outraged not just over the behavior of the Confederate soldiers but over what many observers considered to be Burnside's blunder. **See also** Burnside, Ambrose Everett; Petersburg Campaign.

Crittenden Compromise

The Crittenden Compromise was a collection of six constitutional amendments proposed to Congress in December 1860 by U.S. senator John J. Crittenden (1787–1863) of Kentucky as a way to prevent the Civil War. Specifically, the Crittenden Compromise would have restored and extended a dividing line established in 1820 through legislation known as the Missouri Compromise so that it went all the way across the continent to the Pacific Ocean. States south of this line, which was located at latitude 39°43', would have been required to support slavery, while those to the north would not. However, territories would be allowed to decide whether or not they would support slavery until their admission to the Union. The Crittenden Compromise would also have maintained slavery in the District of Columbia and prohibited Congress from ending slavery on government lands in certain slavery-protected areas. In addition, it would have protected slave owners' right to transport slaves from state to state and ensured that slave owners were compensated for the loss of slaves who ran away to the North. The last amendment in the compromise prohibited the compromise's amendments from ever being overturned. The Senate rejected the Crittenden Compromise by a vote of 25 to 23, whereupon Crittenden officially called for a national referendum on his measures. The Civil War broke out, however, before any action was taken on this matter. **See also** Compromise of 1850; Missouri Compromise.

Crook, George (1829–1890)

A major general who commanded Union troops during battles in Virginia, Tennessee, and Georgia, George Crook participated in the Shenandoah Valley and Chickamauga Campaigns, the Battle of Antietam, the Second Battle of Bull Run, and other conflicts. However, he is best known to history for his later activities as an Indian fighter. In 1871 he was assigned to fight the Apache in Arizona, and in 1875 he became involved in a military campaign against the Sioux. By 1882 he was back in Arizona to participate in a campaign to force the Apache onto reservations. In his later years, however, Crook spoke out against the poor treatment of the Apache and became an advocate for Indian causes. **See also** Antietam, Battle of; Bull Run, Second Battle of; Chickamauga, Battle of; Shenandoah Valley Campaigns.

Custer, George Armstrong (1839–1876)

Although most famous for his 1876 death at the hands of the Sioux Indians at the Battle of the Little Bighorn, George A. Custer also had a role in the Civil War. Serving under Union general George B. McClellan as the brigadier general of a cavalry brigade, Custer fought in several major battles, including the First Battle of Bull Run in 1861, the Peninsula Campaign of 1862, the Battle of Gettysburg in 1863, and the battles leading up to the surrender of General Robert E. Lee in 1865.

Only twenty-three years old when he first took command, Custer had the distinction of being the youngest Union general of the Civil War.

After the war, Custer was sent to Kansas in 1866 to assist General Winfield Hancock in a campaign against the Plains Indians. He was court-martialed there after leaving camp to visit his wife rather than perform a routine duty. However, within a year he was reinstated because the U.S. Army was short-handed, and in November 1868 he led a successful attack against a Cheyenne Indian village. In 1874 he joined a military campaign to eliminate Indians from the Black Hills of South Dakota and was later killed, along with more than 260 of his men, when he led them into an ambush on the Little Bighorn River in Montana. **See also** Hancock, Winfield Scott; Lee, Robert Edward.

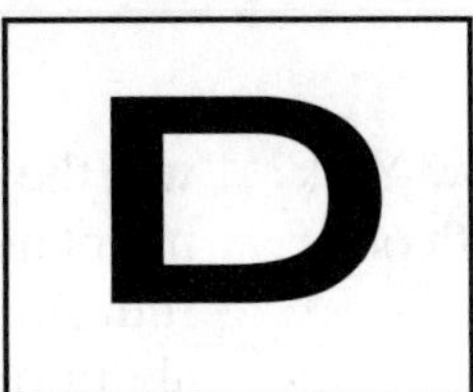

Dahlgren Papers

The Dahlgren Papers were papers found in the pockets of a Union officer, Colonel Ulric Dahlgren, who had been killed during a Union cavalry raid on Richmond, Virginia, in March 1864. In the papers were references to a plan to assassinate the members of the Confederate cabinet, including President Jefferson Davis, and burn the Confederate capital. It is unclear who wrote the papers Dahlgren carried and why. U.S. government officials denied authorizing any assassinations, and the leader of the cavalry raid, General Judson Kilpatrick, insisted that his raiders had never intended to burn Richmond or attack Confederate officials there. Because of these denials, some Northerners suggested that the papers were forgeries planted on the body by Southerners wanting to keep anti-Union sentiments burning, but before the original documents could be more closely examined they mysteriously disappeared. Nonetheless, from studying other documents and letters, most military historians believe that the papers were genuine and that some Union generals must have been involved in plots to assassinate Confederate leaders.

Historians also believe that the discovery of the Dahlgren Papers and the subsequent publication of their text in Confederate newspapers inspired corresponding Confederate attempts during the Civil War to kidnap or kill U.S. president Abraham Lincoln. Various historians have attributed such plots to Confederate generals Bradley T. Johnson, Wade Hampton, Jubal Early, Thomas Nelson Conrad, and John Singleton Mosby, but there is much disagreement over how much credence should be given to any of these connections. In addition, some historians have suggested a link between the Dahlgren Papers and John Wilkes Booth's attempts to kidnap the president, because although his hatred for Lincoln dated from the beginning of the war his kidnapping plans were developed after the discovery of the papers. **See also** Booth, John Wilkes; Early, Jubal A.; Hampton, Wade; Mosby, John Singleton.

Dana, Charles Anderson (1819–1897)

American journalist Charles A. Dana wrote numerous influential antislavery pieces prior to and during the Civil War. Dana also served as an assistant secretary of war for the U.S. government from 1864 to 1865. During the war, he created the popular slogan "Forward to Richmond," which encouraged Union forces to redouble their efforts to win the war, presumably by taking the Confederate capital. Dana's career as a journalist began in the late 1840s, when he worked first for the Boston *Weekly Chronotype* and then for the *New York Tribune*. In 1849 he became the managing editor of the *Tribune* and began writing editorials that promoted the abolition of slavery. In 1862 Dana left the paper and went to work for the U.S. War Department, sending reports to Washington, D.C., from the front lines; two years later he was named second assistant secretary of war.

After the war, Dana edited the New York *Sun,* which he also owned along with other investors. **See also** newspapers.

Davis, Jefferson (1808–1889)

Jefferson Davis was the president of the Confederate States of America (CSA) throughout the Civil War. Born in Kentucky, Davis grew up on a plantation in Mississippi and attended school in both Kentucky and Mississippi before entering the U.S. Military Academy in 1824. He graduated in 1828 with the infantry rank of brevet (that is, temporary) second lieutenant. For the next seven years, Davis fought Indians on the American frontier, particularly in Wisconsin, but in 1835 he left the army to marry and establish a plantation in Mississippi. His wife, Sarah Knox Taylor, fell ill and died three months after their wedding; ten years later, at the age of thirty-seven, Davis married nineteen-year-old Varina Howell.

Shortly thereafter, Davis was elected to Congress but left his position to serve in the Mexican-American War (1846–1848) as a colonel in a Mississippi regiment. Following his return from the war—with serious war wounds and military honors, both of which were due to his conduct at the Battle of Buena Vista—he was elected to the U.S. Senate, and within a short time he had become the chairman of the Military Affairs Committee. In 1850 he quit the Senate to run for governor of Mississippi but lost to Henry S. Foote.

In 1853 Davis was named secretary of war under President Franklin Pierce. He used his position to encourage the military to adopt new weaponry and ammunition—including the Minié ball—strengthen forts, and build new railroad lines. In 1857 he was again elected senator, and he remained in this office until Mississippi seceded from the Union in January 1861. Davis had initially argued against secession, though he supported slavery. By 1860, however, he had decided that secession was the only way for the Southern states to maintain their rights, since in his view the federal government was dominated by abolitionists.

Upon the establishment of the Confederate States of America, Davis was elected president and took up residence in the Confederacy's capital city of Richmond, Virginia. After that city fell into Union hands in April 1865, he ran his government from Danville, Virginia. The following month, having been forced to relocate his government again, he was captured in Irwinville, Georgia. Davis spent the next two years in prison at Fort Monroe, Vir-

Jefferson Davis was the president of the Confederate States of America.

ginia, awaiting trial for treason, but eventually he was released on bail and in the end the federal government decided that the nation would be better healed if it did not put him on trial.

Now in poor health due to his long confinement, Davis traveled to Canada and Europe to recover, but he never did become truly well. He also suffered from poverty in his later years, going from job to job and investment to investment, never making much money. In 1877 he stopped trying to find work and retired to an estate near Biloxi, Mississippi, to write a book, *The Rise and Fall of the Confederate Government.* Meanwhile, Varina Davis supported the family through savings she had accumulated prior to the war and a variety of odd jobs, and they lived meagerly. Jefferson Davis died in May 1889 of a lung ailment. **See also** Confederate States of America; Davis, Varina Banks Howell.

Davis, Sam (1842–1863)

Confederate soldier Sam Davis was executed by the Union as a spy on November 27, 1863, thereby becoming a hero and martyr among Southerners. Davis had enlisted as a private in the First Tennessee Infantry, and after being wounded at the Battle of Shiloh he became part of a company of scouts under the command of Captain H.B. Shaw. In November 1863, Shaw ordered Davis to carry a packet of information on Union troop movements through enemy territory to another Confederate commander. Federal soldiers caught Davis, and although he explained that he was a messenger rather than a spy, he was put on trial, found guilty, and hanged. **See also** spies.

Davis, Varina Banks Howell (1826–1906)

Wife of Confederate president Jefferson Davis, Varina H. Davis was known as the "First Lady of the Confederacy." Convinced from the beginning that the Confederacy would fail, she firmly believed that the Southern states should stay with the Union. For this reason, she was not well liked by the Southern press.

Married when she was nineteen and her husband in his midthirties, Davis was a well-educated planter's daughter, but her husband failed to recognize her intelligence. He controlled all family finances, made decisions without consulting her, and ordered her about. Despite this treatment, however, Varina remained a strong supporter of her husband long after the outcome of the war had robbed him of his position and income.

By the time the Civil War ended, Varina Davis had begun selling possessions, including slaves and horses, to support her family and was hoarding any excess money because she believed that she would be impoverished after the war. Her prediction proved correct, since Jefferson Davis was imprisoned for two years after the Confederacy surrendered and after his release was unable to find meaningful work. Varina Davis therefore took on the financial responsibility for her family and barely kept her children from poverty. (Davis had six children, four of whom died before the end of the Civil War; her firstborn son, Samuel, died of measles in 1852 at the age of two, and seven-year-old Joseph was killed when he fell twenty feet out of a Confederate White House balcony or a window on April 30, 1862.) After her husband's death in 1889 she moved to New York to work as a writer for newspapers and magazines. **See also** Davis, Jefferson.

De Forest, John William (1826–1906)

John W. De Forest wrote a major Civil War novel, *Miss Ravenel's Conversion from Secession to Loyalty* (1867), based on his own experiences as a Civil War soldier in the Union army. The son of a

Connecticut textile manufacturer, he lived in Europe as a young man, traveled extensively, and wrote books on history and travel—*History of the Indians in Connecticut* (1851), *Oriental Acquaintance* (1856), and *European Acquaintance* (1858)—before returning to the United States shortly before the Civil War broke out. He then helped recruit and organize a New Haven, Connecticut, volunteer regiment and served as its captain in several battles in Louisiana and the Shenandoah Valley.

After the war De Forest was appointed to supervise the activities of the Freedmen's Bureau in Greenville, South Carolina, serving from 1866 to 1867. During this period, he wrote *Miss Ravenel's Conversion,* which is about a New Orleans physician who moves to Boston, Massachusetts, rather than support the Confederate war effort. This novel was unique for its time in that it contained many realistic battle scenes, which was in keeping with De Forest's beliefs about how novels should be written. In January 1869 he wrote an article titled "The Great American Novel" for the *Nation* in which he argued that novels should be as realistic as possible.

De Forest subsequently wrote several other novels: *Kate Beaumont* (1872) and *The Bloody Chasm* (1881), which describe life in South Carolina before and after the war, respectively; *Honest John Vane* (1875) and *Playing the Mischief* (1875), which focus on government corruption under President Ulysses S. Grant; and *A Lover's Revolt* (1898), a romance set during the time of the American Revolution. In addition, the letters that De Forest wrote to his wife during and after the war were published posthumously, along with some of his magazine articles, as *A Volunteer's Adventures* (1946) and *A Union Officer in the Reconstruction* (1948). **See also** literature, Civil War.

Delany, Martin Robinson (1812–1885)

Abolitionist Martin R. Delany was involved in the first efforts to bring black soldiers into the U.S. Army and served in the Civil War, first as a physician and then as a soldier. During Reconstruction he was a member of South Carolina's Freedmen's Bureau, helping former slaves adjust to freedom. Delany had become involved in the antislavery movement in the 1830s, when he belonged to several groups dedicated to caring for former slaves. At the same time, two white physicians took Delany on as their student, training him as a physician's assistant and dentist. In 1839 Delany traveled through the South and Southwest as a physician caring for blacks. He then settled in Pittsburgh, Pennsylvania, and established a newspaper, the *Mystery,* which ran articles concerning blacks' civil rights and women's rights. In 1846 he was also involved in the publication of abolitionist Frederick Douglass's newspaper, the *North Star.* In 1849 Delany decided to get a medical degree, becoming the first black to be admitted to Harvard Medical School. However, violent student protests against the presence of a black student forced him to leave school early.

In 1852 Delany wrote a book titled *The Condition, Elevation, Emigration, and Destiny of the Colored People of the United States Politically Considered,* which discussed the condition of blacks in America and the idea that they should be sent to Africa to create colonies of African Americans there. By this time, Delany had grown tired of American racism, and in 1856 he moved to Canada, where he established a medical practice. He also became involved in the African American colonization movement, and in 1859 he and several other people who shared his views traveled to West Africa, where they spent a year studying possible settlement sites in the Niger River Delta.

Delany returned to the United States in 1861 to help with the war effort by recruiting black troops and soon became the physician for the all-black Fifty-fourth Massachusetts Volunteers. He served with this unit until February 1865, at which time he enlisted as a soldier in the U.S. Army. Given the rank of major, he was the first black to receive a Regular Army commission. However, he did not go into combat; instead, he spent his time recruiting Union soldiers from among former slaves in South Carolina. **See also** abolitionists; Army, Regular; black troops; Douglass, Frederick.

Delaware

Delaware was a slave state at the time the Civil War began. However, slavery had greatly decreased in the state, and by this point there were only about eighteen hundred slaves in Delaware, down from a high of eighty-nine hundred in 1790. This decreasing reliance on slavery, coupled with the fact that Delaware had strong economic ties with the North, resulted in Delaware's refusal to secede from the Union.

Nonetheless, U.S. president Abraham Lincoln feared that Delaware and other slave states remaining in the Union might one day join the Confederacy. Therefore when he drafted his Emancipation Proclamation he limited the mandatory freeing of slaves to states and regions in rebellion against the United States as of January 1, 1863. In other words, Delaware and other slave states loyal to the Union were exempt from the ruling. Despite this concession, Delaware's voters did not support Lincoln's reelection as president in 1864, and they largely opposed his ideas related to Reconstruction. **See also** emancipation; Reconstruction.

dentists

During the Civil War, dentists had very limited procedures and tools at their disposal, and the anesthetics they had available were few. This was particularly true in the South, where Union blockades made it difficult for dentists to acquire supplies. Nonetheless, they fulfilled their main duties: pulling teeth, filling cavities, and mending broken jaws. In the South, a separate corps within the Confederate Medical Department consisted entirely of dentists. In the Union, however, men who practiced dentistry were part of the U.S. Army Medical Department's staff of surgeons and assistant surgeons. **See also** medical personnel and supplies.

depots, supply

Supply depots were caches of supplies (food, ammunition, and so forth) established in the field. Both the Confederate and the Union quartermaster corps set up supply depots within easy reach of their respective armies' defensive positions, as well as near locations that these armies intended to reach as part of offensive campaigns. Supplies required in each location depended on the size of the armies that would be using them; thus in planning large campaigns, a general often tried to position his troops so that they could receive supplies from depots located near waterways or rail lines. In this way, access to supplies sometimes determined where battles were fought. **See also** railroads; rivers, significant.

desertion

According to some estimates, well over 300,000 soldiers—more than 65 percent of them Union—deserted, or abandoned their duties, during the Civil War, sometimes at a rate of five thousand per month. The largest number of desertions would take place right before a battle that promised to be bloody. For example, Union records suggest that more than eight thousand soldiers and three hundred officers deserted just prior to the Battle of Antietam.

Not all of these soldiers deserted permanently, however. Some only wanted to take time off from their battlefield duties to attend to their farms, families, or other matters. In addition, some men deserted and reenlisted over and over again, in order to receive the bounties, or monetary rewards, that the Union and Confederate armies offered to volunteers. Still others deserted from one army unit to switch, through reenlistment, to another when they were unable to receive an official transfer.

The penalties for desertion ranged from mild to severe and depended on whether a commanding officer wanted to make an example of a particular deserter. The mildest punishments involved marking the deserter in some way, such as shaving the man's head, making him wear certain clothes, or branding him. More serious penalties were prison terms and, in the South, flogging. (The Union army outlawed flogging as a punishment in 1861.) As the war progressed, however, executions increasingly became the penalty for desertion. No information is available on how many Confederate soldiers were executed for desertion, but the Union executed over 140 men between 1863 and the end of the war, usually by firing squad.

In addition to imposing harsher punishments for desertion, as the war progressed both the Union and the Confederacy began fining or imprisoning civilians caught helping soldiers who deserted. Consequently it became more and more difficult for deserters to find safe places to wait out the war, particularly since forces were sometimes sent to round them up. As a result, approximately ten thousand to fifteen thousand deserters fled to Canada; others chose places in the United States that were far from civilization, sometimes joining up with other deserters so that they would be better able to fight off anyone who came to arrest them. Still, some deserters simply went home, hoping that Confederate and Union authorities would be too busy on the battlefield to send someone to get them. **See also** bounty system; executions.

diseases, dietary illnesses, and infections

Approximately 620,000 soldiers died during the Civil War. Of these, at least 415,000 died of diseases, dietary illnesses, and infections as opposed to being killed in battle. Tens of thousands more soldiers became sick and survived their ailments only to become sick again. (More precise numbers are unavailable because the Confederacy's medical records were destroyed in a fire in Richmond, Virginia, in 1865.) This prevalence of illness was due to the conditions under which Civil War soldiers lived, to the fact that medical knowledge of the day was limited, and to a shortage of trained physicians.

The most serious illnesses of the war were caused by bad hygiene, particularly careless disposal of human waste. Army regulations called for each camp to have an eight-foot-deep latrine, with a six-inch layer of fresh dirt shoveled over their waste each day, but because the smell of these facilities was usually unbearable some soldiers would instead defecate elsewhere. Rain would then carry human waste into streams that supplied drinking water, contaminating it with bacteria that caused illness. In addition, both human and animal waste—produced by the many horses and mules that typically traveled with armies—was a breeding ground for disease-carrying flies.

Soldiers were even more careless when it came to washing clothes, animals, food, and themselves in rivers or streams that supplied drinking water. Civil War–era physicians did know that if this water was boiled it was somehow less likely to cause disease, even if it was subsequently cooled, but most soldiers did not bother to follow such basic procedures. Historians note that water-borne illnesses might have been far worse save for the fact that most soldiers preferred to drink hot coffee rather than water, with the result that many disease-causing organisms were killed in the brewing process.

The most deadly water-borne disease was typhoid fever, also known as camp fever, caused by a bacterium known as *Salmonella typhosa.* From 1861 to 1866, there were nearly 150,000 reported cases of typhoid fever or typhoidlike fever in the Union army, and of these at least 30,000 resulted in death. Even a soldier who was not visibly ill could be a carrier of the disease, perhaps by failing to wash his hands after using the latrine and then preparing food that was shared with others. Overcrowding was also a major contributor to the spread of the disease; for this reason, it was particularly prevalent on naval vessels, where it was typically called ship fever.

Typhoid fever usually spread quickly through a ship or military camp in large part because the disease causes diarrhea, thereby increasing the opportunities for contamination. Civil War physicians—most of whom thought that typhoid fever was caused by bad air rather than bad water—made the situation worse since they treated sufferers with laxatives in the mistaken belief that the disease needed to be purged from the body. In the most severe cases, they bled the patient or gave him turpentine to drink so that he would throw up, again to force the supposed "poison" from the body. Such treatments typically increased the severity of the dehydration caused by the disease's symptoms, and as a result most soldiers died within two weeks of contracting typhoid fever.

Two other potentially deadly diseases were yellow fever and typhus, which combined killed about three thousand soldiers in the Union army alone (although some of the deaths attributed to typhus might have been caused by typhoid fever instead). Yellow fever is a viral infection carried by mosquitoes, while typhus is caused by a microorganism (rickettsia) carried on fleas and body lice. These diseases have symptoms similar to typhoid fever and were treated by Civil War physicians in the same way, without anyone realizing that the insects so prevalent in military camps were responsible for spreading disease. Both yellow fever and typhus primarily showed up as small, localized outbreaks, with the result that they killed relatively few soldiers. These diseases could spread quickly on board naval vessels, however, where close quarters made transmission easy. Therefore, on some ships the mortality rate from yellow fever was over 10 percent.

Another common but less deadly mosquito-borne illness was malaria, which was caused by a parasitic organism called a plasmodium. Victims of this disease experienced high fevers, chills, headaches, and profuse sweating, which Civil War physicians treated by giving the patient quinine (a substance produced in a certain kind of tree bark) dissolved in water or whiskey. However, because this treatment could not eliminate the presence of the organism from the bloodstream, the symptoms could reoccur months or even years later. There were at least 1.3 million cases of malaria among Union soldiers, causing about thirteen thousand deaths.

A much larger number of deaths were caused by diarrhea and dysentery, both of which caused increased defecation resulting in severe dehydration and malnutrition. There were over 1.7 million cases of severe dysentery and diarrhea (not including those cases caused by other diseases such as typhoid fever) in the Union army alone, and records indicate that 995 out of every 1,000 Union soldiers had some degree of diarrhea and dysentery each year. Over 45,000 Union soldiers died from dysentery and diarrhea without the presence of other diseases.

A soldier generally developed dysentery after consuming food or water that had been contaminated by the feces of infected men or by their dead bodies, while diarrhea was caused by eating undercooked or spoiled food or by having an inadequate diet. Civil War physicians often treated both conditions by giving the patient something to make him vomit, since as with typhoid fever they believed that this would expel the "poisons" causing the symptoms. Unfortunately for the patients, this treatment typically made the men sicker yet.

However, physicians did recognize that diarrhea and dysentery could be the result of poor sanitary conditions and bad food (although they also mistakenly thought that diarrhea could also be caused by exposure to extreme cold). Consequently, by the second year of the war, the Union army had instituted a system in which the U.S. Sanitary Commission inspected camps and tried to improve living conditions there. This commission also provided officers and military physicians with a variety of pamphlets on health-related matters to educate them on how to prevent and treat diseases. Their advice included admonitions to bathe once a week whenever conditions allowed and to wash hands once a day. However, soap was not always made available to the men.

Little was done to improve the soldiers' food, though. The men rarely received an ample amount of food rations, particularly in the South, and what little they did receive was often of poor quality. Cooking and storage techniques were usually inadequate as well, which in turn led to spoilage and an increased risk of disease. Malnutrition and scurvy (a disease caused by a lack of vitamin C) were common, which meant that most soldiers were in poor physical condition.

Because of the generally weakened condition of most Civil War soldiers, when they contracted a disease they had little

Camp soldiers prepare a meal. Because of bad food and unsanitary conditions, disease was rampant throughout the camps.

strength to fight it. This was particularly true of pneumonia, which could occur as a complication of a variety of other illnesses. Pneumonia was typically brought on by a sick soldier's repeated exposure to heat and cold due to inadequate clothes, shoes, and tents, along with a lack of fresh air due to overcrowding and poor ventilation in tents and barracks and on board ships. About seventy-five thousand Union soldiers suffered from pneumonia during the war, and about eighteen thousand died from it.

Being in generally poor health also increased the likelihood that a soldier who was wounded on the battlefield would subsequently develop a life-threatening infection. This risk was even further increased by the fact that Civil War physicians did not understand the connection between cleanliness and the prevention of wound infection. In fact, many of the deaths attributed to battlefield injuries were actually due to infections. Statistics indicating just how many casualties were due to infection are unavailable, but out of 29,980 reported Union amputations—a surgery on wounded soldiers that was typically performed under extremely unsanitary conditions—over 7,400 resulted in death.

Additional deaths were occasionally caused by illnesses like measles. Although many had had measles as children and were therefore immune, men who had grown up in relative isolation on farms and in small towns would suddenly find themselves thrown into the close quarters of military life, and there they easily contracted such viruses. As a result, approximately seventy-six thousand cases of measles occurred in the Union army, along with a similar number of chicken pox cases. Even when no disease-related deaths occurred, an epidemic could still debilitate an entire army. For example, in 1861 one Union regiment reported that an outbreak of measles and chicken pox sickened 960 of its 1,150 men. **See also** casualties; drugs, medical; medical facilities; medical personnel and supplies; Sanitary Commission, U.S.; surgery.

Dix, Dorothea Lynde (1802–1887)

Massachusetts social reformer Dorothea L. Dix is best known for her work during the 1840s and 1850s to improve conditions in facilities that housed the mentally ill. However, she also made significant contributions to efforts to improve the treatment of injured soldiers during the Civil War. In May 1861 in Boston, Massachusetts, Dix called for female volunteers to sew hospital shirts for Federal soldiers, and as a result received five hundred such shirts within thirty-six hours. Shortly thereafter, the U.S. Sanitary Commission, which oversaw army hospitals, placed Dix in charge of all female nurses associated with the Federal army. She immediately instituted rules related to the appearance of her charges, requiring them to dress only in brown or black dresses—with no hoop skirts allowed—and to wear neither jewelry nor fancy hairstyles. She also refused to allow any woman under the age of thirty to work as a nurse in a government hospital.

Dix had become involved in social work after working as a teacher for many years in Boston. In 1841, while leading Bible studies in a Cambridge, Massachusetts, jail, she became concerned with how mentally ill prison inmates were being treated. Consequently, she began visiting prisons and hospitals throughout the state to learn more about the conditions under which the mentally ill were housed, and in 1843 she reported on the issue to the Massachusetts state legislature. Her work led to changes in the housing and treatment of the mentally ill, first in Massachusetts and then, after she became an advocate for the mentally ill in other locations as well, in other states, Canada, and Europe. **See also** medical facilities; medical personnel and supplies; Sanitary Commission, U.S.

"Dixie"

The Confederate Civil War song "Dixie," also known by its opening line, "I Wish I Was in Dixie's Land," was popular throughout the South during the war. In fact, it was played at the ceremony establishing the Confederate government, at the inauguration of its president, Jefferson Davis, and at many other official events as well. Written by Ohio songwriter, minstrel singer, and musician Daniel Decatur Emmett, "Dixie" was intended as an expression of longing and love for home rather than as a call to arms. However, from its first performances the public associated the song with the Southern cause because of a line in the chorus: "In Dixie land, I'll take my stand to lib [live] and die in Dixie."

In 1859 Emmett received $500 for the song from a New York company, Peters, which required him to give the company all publication rights. However, once the war broke out a publisher in New Orleans, P.P. Werlein, began to publish "Dixie" as well. As a result of Werlein's efforts, thousands of copies were distributed throughout the South during the war years. Meanwhile, Northerners created parodies of "Dixie," inventing new lyrics for Emmett's tune. The most popular of these parodies was "Away Down South in the Land of Traitors," whose chorus says, "Each Dixie boy must understand/That he must mind his Uncle Sam" (a personification of the federal government). **See also** songs.

Dodge, Grenville Mellen (1831–1916)

Union brigadier general Grenville M. Dodge contributed greatly to the U.S. war effort, not only as the commander of the Sixteenth Army Corps during the Atlanta Campaign but also as a military engineer and a spymaster. His involvement with intelligence work began in 1862 when he was a division commander with the Army of the Southwest in Missouri. At that time, he created the Corps of Scouts, an intelligence-gathering unit consisting of men from the Twenty-fourth and Twenty-fifth Missouri Regiments. Dodge trained these men himself, teaching them how to spy on enemy troops, make accurate calculations regarding enemy troop strength, and carry or pass on messages without being caught. Dodge was such a successful spymaster that his superior officer, Ulysses S. Grant (then a major general), asked him to create a broader intelligence-gathering agency to serve him in the Western Theater. This agency ultimately had more than one hundred spies—many of them Southerners sympathetic to the Union cause—who relied on a network of couriers, rather than the more risky telegraph, to send coded messages that were destroyed as soon as they were received and read.

Dodge proved equally valuable as an engineer. He had graduated from Norwich University in Vermont in 1851 with a degree in military and civil engineering, and after the war broke out he offered the U.S. Army his expertise in building bridges and railroad lines. One of his most impressive projects was the construction of a bridge needed to move Union troops across the Chattahoochee River; pressed to complete it as quickly as possible, men reporting to Dodge built the 14-foot-high, 710-foot-long bridge in only three days. After the war, Dodge worked on a variety of railroad construction projects throughout the western and southwestern United States, including the Transcontinental Railroad. By some estimates, between 1874 and 1884 Dodge was responsible for building roughly nine thousand miles of railroad track. **See also** Atlanta Campaign; bridges; railroads; spies.

Doubleday, Abner (1819–1893)

Abner Doubleday is best known for inventing baseball (although not all sports historians agree that he actually deserves this credit). However, he also made a significant contribution to the Civil War. As the commander of the U.S. Army's gunners at Fort Sumter, South Carolina, Doubleday was present when the South fired the first shot of the war, and in response he ordered the first Northern shots of the war. A veteran of the Mexican-American and Seminole Wars, Doubleday fought at the Second Battle of Bull Run and the Battles of Antietam, Fredericksburg, and Gettysburg. From 1863 to 1864 he was temporarily made the major general of volunteers for the North, and in 1867 he was given the permanent rank of colonel, which he held until he left the army in 1873. **See also** Fort Sumter.

Douglas, Stephen Arnold (1813–1861)

As a U.S. senator from 1847 to 1861, Stephen A. Douglas worked to preserve the Union through political means. Douglas, who was only five feet, four inches tall, was a powerful orator and extraordinarily persuasive; consequently he was nicknamed the "Little Giant." After the South seceded, he visited the border states to encourage them to remain in the Union. Many of the bills he drafted and/or supported related to his belief that, in order to keep the Union whole, slavery had to be allowed in certain parts of the country. For example, he was instrumental in securing the passage of the Compromise of 1850, which maintained a balance between the number of slave states and free states, and in 1854 he wrote the Kansas-Nebraska Act, which permitted people living in territories to decide the slavery issue for themselves by popular vote. When this bill passed, Southern Democrats, who were passionately pro-slavery, blamed Douglas for Kansas becoming a free state.

During his 1858 campaign for reelection to the Senate, Democrat Douglas engaged in a series of debates with his Republican opponent, Abraham Lincoln, during which he made a statement that angered some of his Southern supporters. Douglas said that, although the U.S. Supreme Court in the *Dred Scott* decision had held that slavery could not be prohibited in a U.S. territory, there were still ways that the government and legal authorities could maintain such a prohibition. Some Southern Democrats mistakenly took this to mean that Douglas favored the abolition of slavery, so when Douglas ran for U.S. president against Lincoln in 1860 they broke from their party to put forth their own candidate, John C. Breckinridge. As a result, Douglas failed to garner enough votes to beat Lincoln in the election. Following his defeat, Douglas returned to the Senate, where he unsuccessfully urged the South not to secede. **See also** Breckinridge, John Cabell; Compromise of 1850; *Dred Scott* decision; Kansas-Nebraska Act; political parties.

Douglass, Frederick (ca. 1817–1895)

Frederick Douglass was a leader of the abolitionist movement, although he had been born a slave. Originally known as Frederick Augustus Washington Bailey, Douglass lived on a Maryland plantation until the age of eight, whereupon he became a house servant for Baltimore businessman Hugh Auld. Auld's wife began teaching Douglass to read and write, despite laws forbidding her to do so, but when Auld found out he made her stop. Douglass then continued his education in secret, teaching himself with the help of white schoolboys in his neighborhood.

At the age of sixteen, Douglass was forced to return to the plantation to work in its fields. A short while later, his owner sent him back to Baltimore to work for a shipbuilder. In 1833 he tried to escape but failed; he tried again in 1838 and succeeded, making his way to New York City.

Frederick Douglass was an escaped slave who became a prominent abolitionist leader.

There he changed his last name to Douglass to avoid being found by slave hunters.

After spending a short time in New York, Douglass moved to New Bedford, Massachusetts, where he became acquainted with local abolitionists. In 1841 they invited him to speak about his experiences as a slave at a convention of the Massachusetts Anti-Slavery Society in Nantucket, Massachusetts. His address went so well that the society arranged for him to speak at more meetings, and soon he was famous throughout New England. Douglass's fame spread throughout the United States in 1845 when he published his autobiography, *Narrative of the Life of Frederick Douglass, an American Slave, Written by Himself,* in order to counter accusations that he spoke too well to have ever really been a slave. Because the book revealed the name of his former owner, Douglass feared that he might be captured and returned to slavery. To prevent this, he went on a speaking tour of Great Britain; by the time he returned to the United States in 1847 his supporters had bought his freedom. They also provided him with the funds to start an abolitionist newspaper, the *North Star,* aimed primarily at black readers. (This name was based on the fact that slaves escaping north would typically use the North Star by night to guide them, but Douglass later renamed it *Frederick Douglass's Paper.*)

Douglass continued to publish his newspaper until 1860. During this time, he sometimes disagreed with other abolitionists, particularly in regard to the use of violence. For example, Douglass voiced his disapproval of abolitionist John Brown's attack on the federal arsenal at Harpers Ferry, Virginia. Douglass supported the Republican Party, and when the Civil War broke out he became an adviser to President Abraham Lincoln. In this capacity, Douglass pressed for the recruitment of black soldiers and, once this began, argued that they should be treated the same as white soldiers. During the postwar Reconstruction era, he fought for civil rights for both blacks and women, and he continued to be involved in these causes for the rest of his life. In fact, on the day he died he attended a women's rights meeting. **See also** abolitionists; Brown, John.

Dred Scott decision

The *Dred Scott* decision was the opinion handed down by the U.S. Supreme Court in the case known as *Dred Scott v. Sanford,* which had far-reaching effects on the issue of slavery. Dred Scott was a Missouri slave who traveled with his master, army surgeon John Emerson, to various military camps, including Fort Snelling in the Wisconsin Territory. According to legislation known as the Missouri Compromise, this territory prohibited slavery, and Scott decided that even temporarily living in this territory made him a free man. He therefore decided to sue Emerson for his freedom.

In 1850 a court in St. Louis, Missouri, declared that Scott had become a free man by virtue of having lived part time in the Wisconsin Territory, and further declared that this freedom could not be taken away when Scott returned to Missouri. Two years later the Missouri Supreme Court reversed this decision. Scott then brought his lawsuit to the U.S. District Court; by this time Emerson had died, so Scott sued the executor of Emerson's estate, John F.A. Sanford. Sanford argued that Scott had no right to sue for his freedom because blacks did not have the right to sue whites in a federal court. The central focus of the trial then became whether Scott was a U.S. citizen, which would have given him the right to sue. In the end the court decided that Scott was a slave, not a citizen.

Scott's case against Sanford then went to the U.S. Supreme Court. This court chose to focus on two issues: whether a black man could be considered a U.S. citizen, and whether a territory had the right to prevent a slave owner from keeping his property (i.e., his slaves). Led by a proslavery chief justice, Roger B. Taney, the Court ultimately decided that no black man or woman could be a U.S. citizen, although an antislavery state had the right to declare blacks to be state citizens. Moreover, the Court declared that the Missouri Compromise had been unconstitutional because it had violated the Fifth Amendment of the U.S. Constitution, which stated that no one could have his property taken from him without due process of the law.

Far from settling the issue of slavery, the *Dred Scott* decision deepened the divisions in the United States. During his 1860 campaign for U.S. president, Abraham Lincoln argued that the decision meant that the U.S. Supreme Court would eventually declare that free states as well as territories had to allow slavery. Abolitionists therefore voted for Lincoln, whom they believed would appoint antislavery justices to the Court if any of the current justices died or retired. Thus, although Taney and others in favor of slavery assumed that the *Dred Scott* decision would help their cause, instead it led to the election of an antislavery president. **See also** Lincoln, Abraham; Missouri Compromise; Taney, Roger Brooke.

drugs, medical

At the beginning of the war, Union and Confederate physicians relied heavily on several classes of drugs: anesthetics, antiseptics, stimulants, and narcotics. Physicians also used drugs that were believed to expel poisons from the body, generally by irritating the skin, making the patient sweat excessively, or causing vomiting or diarrhea. The most popular vomit-inducing, or cathartic, drug was tartar emetic, while the most popular diarrhea-inducing, or purgative, drug was calomel. Both of these drugs came with the risk of serious side effects, including tooth loss and mercury poisoning, so the U.S. surgeon general, William Hammond, banned their use in May 1863, but many Union battlefield doctors continued to employ them anyway.

By 1863, Confederate physicians were having a difficult time getting drugs of any kind because of Union blockades, since most drug manufacturers were in the North. As a result, the Confederate surgeon general, Samuel P. Moore, ordered the creation of a book, *Resources of Southern Fields and Forests, Medical, Economical, and Agricultural* by Dr. Francis P. Porcher (published in 1863), that contained instructions Confederate physicians could use to create their own medicines from plants available in the South. The Confederacy also established its own drug laboratories, but the chemists who ran them had to rely primarily on native plants as well. However, they were sometimes able to get drugs that had been smuggled from the North by Confederate sympathizers and drug manufacturers seeking to make a hefty profit from such illicit trade. **See also** medical facilities; medical personnel and supplies; surgery.

Du Pont, Samuel Francis (1803–1865)

A member of a family that became wealthy through the manufacture of explosives, U.S. naval officer Samuel F. Du Pont helped to establish the curriculum of the U.S. Naval Academy at Annapolis, Maryland, in 1842, and during the Civil War he commanded squadrons and fleets as part of the U.S. blockade of Southern ports. On November 7, 1861, as captain of a fleet, Du Pont led a successful naval attack on Port Royal Sound, South Carolina, in concert with a land attack by Union troops led by Brigadier General Thomas W. Sherman. Beginning in April 1863, Du Pont commanded nine ironclads in a series of assaults on the defenses of Charleston, South Carolina, having by then achieved the rank of rear admiral. One of these attacks—on July 18 at Morris Island—resulted in a major defeat for the Union. Blamed for this defeat, Du Pont was relieved of his command and did not receive another. **See also** blockades and blockade runners; navies, Confederate and Union.

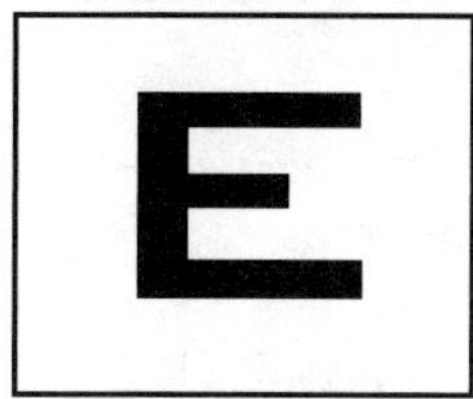

Early, Jubal A. (1816–1894)

A Virginia lawyer who had spoken out against secession prior to the war, Confederate general Jubal ("Old Jube") Early commanded troops in many major battles, including the First Battle of Bull Run, the Virginia Campaigns of 1862–1863, the Battle of Fredericksburg, the Battle of Gettysburg, and the Wilderness Campaign. Some of his most significant battles occurred during the summer of 1864, when he commanded 8,000 to 14,500 men in the Confederate Army of the Valley. At that time, having moved quickly up the Confederate ranks from colonel to lieutenant general, Early fought in a series of campaigns in both the Shenandoah Valley and the Potomac Valley and conducted numerous raids there.

The most notable raid occurred in July 1864, during which Early led approximately fourteen thousand men from a point near Richmond, Virginia, through the Shenandoah Valley into Maryland and threatened to enter Washington, D.C. Early's progress forced the Union to divert key forces from a pending confrontation with the Army of Northern Virginia, and when this force battled Early's beside the Monocacy River on July 9 the Union lost approximately thirteen hundred soldiers while Early lost only seven hundred.

Between June and November 1864, Early's Army of the Valley fought in approximately seventy-five battles in Virginia and Maryland, over an area of roughly sixteen hundred miles. During this time Early had several victories, including a raid on the environs of Washington, D.C., that resulted in the burning of Chambersburg, Pennsylvania. However, in October 1864 he lost three important battles—at Winchester, Fisher's Hill, and Cedar Creek—against General Philip Sheridan, thereby losing control of the Shenandoah Valley. Many Confederates severely criticized Early for these losses, in part because he had made serious errors in troop placement during his battles. However, Early was also the target of criticism because he was not well liked. Throughout his military career he had been outspoken and difficult, sometimes refusing to carry out orders with which he disagreed. Consequently, he had few supporters in the Confederate military, and when he again suffered serious losses at Waynesboro in March 1865 General Robert E. Lee relieved him of his command.

When the war ended, Early went west to Texas, then to Mexico, and finally to Canada, returning to the United States only after U.S. president Andrew Johnson issued a pardon to all former Confederates in 1869. Early then returned to practicing law and wrote articles about the Civil War. In the 1870s he founded and supported—along with a few other former Confederate leaders—the Southern Historical Society (SHS), which promoted certain views after the war that collectively were known as the Lost Cause. Specifically, the SHS published and promoted materials suggesting that the South seceded from the Union not to preserve slavery but to protect the freedom of state governments to enact and administer their own laws. Lost Cause proponents also argued that the Confederacy made no strategic errors during the war and therefore never technically lost a battle. According to this reading of events, whenever Confederate troops retreated, they did so deliberately and for sound military reasons. As the main spokesperson of the SHS, Early promoted the view that a lack of manpower and resources rather than tactical mistakes had cost the Confederacy the war, and he often stated that Confederate generals Robert E. Lee and Thomas J. "Stonewall" Jackson were among the greatest American heroes. Until his death from medical complications resulting from injuries sustained in a fall in early 1894, Early remained at the forefront of the SHS and always wore the color gray as a way to honor the lost Confederate cause. **See also** Chambersburg, Pennsylvania; Shenandoah Valley Campaigns; Sheridan, Philip Henry.

economy, Southern vs. Northern

Although few historians blame economic differences alone for the South's defeat, most agree that the differences between the Northern and Southern economies gave the Union distinct advantages in the Civil War. In particular, because the South was agrarian, its economy suffered from the fact that most of the war's battles were fought on Southern soil, destroying numerous crops and farms. Meanwhile, the North, being industrial, experienced economic growth as its factories worked overtime to provide materials for the war effort.

At the outset of the war, the Confederacy also lacked the money to buy necessary war supplies. Consequently, Confederate secretary of the treasury Christopher Memminger sold government bonds and raised taxes to boost government funds. At first, only a small property tax was imposed: half of 1 percent of a property's value, with no one being taxed who owned less than $500 worth of property. However, if a state paid the taxes for all of its citizens at once, it received a 10 percent discount from the Confederate government, giving the state a profit when it later received the money from its citizens. Unfortunately, states often had problems collecting the money they were owed, and this resulted in large state debts.

By 1863, the Confederate government realized that if it did not find a way to raise more money it would soon lose the war by virtue of bankruptcy. Therefore the Confederacy tried various means to increase revenue, including taxing income, goods, and services as well as property and selling additional bonds (backed by cotton). The government also tried to acquire foreign loans, but many investors were leery of supporting the South.

The South also printed a great deal of paper money, over $1.6 billion by the end of the war. Each bill was backed by a promise that it would be worth its face value plus interest six months after a permanent peace was declared between the North and South. However, as more bills were printed, the Confederate dollar was worth less. At the end of 1861, a dollar was worth approximately 80 cents in gold, less than two years later it was worth only 20 cents, and about two years after that it was worth less than 2 cents. Meanwhile, given the Northern blockade of the South, the demand for goods far exceeded the supply, leading to inflated prices. This added to the Confederacy's problems in buying necessary war supplies.

As a result of these problems, in March 1863 the Confederate government began confiscating goods from private citizens under what was known as an act of impressment. This meant that farmers and others were required to turn any goods (which included slaves) needed by the

Confederacy over to their government in exchange for currency or an I.O.U., with the value of each item being set by the government. (Citizens were typically not compensated nearly enough for their goods, and politically prominent citizens or those with connections to the military were often unfairly spared impressment.) But because of the Northern blockade and the devastation caused by various battles, by the last year of the war there was not much left in the South worth confiscating. This situation, combined with the Confederacy's lack of money, meant that Confederate soldiers often had to do without vital supplies like tents and meat; ammunition was rationed, if it was available at all, and most cavalry units lacked horses.

Meanwhile, the North had no problems buying military supplies, although it sometimes experienced logistical problems in getting them to battlefields. Northern businesses boomed during the war, particularly in the areas of manufacturing and mining, and unemployment was low. In addition, between 1862 and 1864 stocks greatly increased in value. However, there was a high national debt due to a dramatic increase in military spending, and this debt load sometimes triggered financial panics among investors.

Like the Confederacy, the U.S. government provided additional money for the war effort by printing more paper dollars, called greenbacks for their green writing. Approximately $432 million were printed during the war, but unlike the Confederate dollar, the U.S. currency was backed with gold rather than promises of future interest payments. As a result, the dollar's value held up well. In 1862 it was worth 91 cents, and except for a few momentary drops when a particular battle or campaign went badly, it remained at least this high throughout the war.

The U.S. government also raised money by instituting a tax collection system, beginning with an income tax in August 1861 and including other types of taxes as the war continued. Most of the financing for the war, however, came from bonds that the U.S. government marketed to its citizens. By 1862, approximately $550 million worth of bonds had been sold, with the majority of the money from these sales being spent on the war effort. **See also** blockades and blockade runners; food; Memminger, Christopher Gustavus; taxation.

Edmonds, Sarah Emma (aka Franklin Thompson) (1842–1898)

During the Civil War, Sarah Emma Edmonds enlisted in the Union army disguised as a man and calling herself Franklin Thompson. After her enlistment she worked as a male nurse and a male spy. In the course of her espionage work, Edmonds became a master of disguises. Her identities included the woman she actually was, a black man named Cuff (whom she created in part by coloring her skin with silver nitrate and wearing a black wig), an old black woman who was a laundress or a nursemaid, an overweight Irishwoman who peddled goods in Confederate army camps, and a young Southern white man.

An immigrant from Nova Scotia, Edmonds had begun dressing as a boy while a child in order to please an abusive father who had wanted a son instead of a daughter. When the Civil War broke out, she cut her hair short and donned men's clothing to join the Second Michigan Volunteers as a male nurse. Her unit was soon sent to serve under General George B. McClellan of the Army of the Potomac, who had recently assigned the well-known detective Allan Pinkerton the task of creating a network of spies. Edmonds heard about Pinkerton's need for agents and volunteered for the job.

On her first assignment, Edmonds disguised herself as the black slave Cuff and showed up as one of the workers building a fort for the Confederacy. After a day she found the work too physically demanding, but she managed to get herself reassigned to kitchen work. She spent a day listening to soldiers talk about their unit's plans, then returned to the North to report on their weaponry, number, and tactics. She then went back to her job as a male nurse.

Edmonds went on eleven spy missions in all, returning to her nursing job in between each one. Whenever her unit was transferred, she continued her duties for her new commander. Therefore in addition to spying for McClellan she also spied for General Philip Sheridan and General Ambrose Burnside as well. Her last spy mission for Burnside took place at the end of 1862, when she went to Louisville, Kentucky, disguised as a young white man named Charles Mayberry to uncover a spy network there. Edmonds's unit was then transferred to serve under General Ulysses S. Grant.

Shortly after this, while serving in her capacity as a male nurse, Edmonds fell ill with malaria. Afraid that if she were treated in camp her true gender would be discovered, she sneaked away to a hospital in nearby Cairo, Illinois, and was admitted as a patient under her real name. She planned to return to her unit once she was cured. Before she could do so, however, she learned that she had been listed as a deserter and would be punished if the Union caught her. Consequently, she traveled to Washington, D.C., and took a job as a female nurse.

For many years thereafter, Edmonds felt bad about being listed as a deserter. She eventually asked the War Department to correct the public record and give her an honorable discharge from the U.S. Army, providing them with evidence to back her claims. By this time she had also written a book about her experiences, *Nurse and Spy in the Union Army.* (Another, titled *Unsexed, or the Female Soldier,* was to follow.) In July 1884, after a debate in the House of Representatives, her request was granted, and she was additionally awarded back pay and a $12 monthly veteran's pension. She also became the only woman ever admitted to the Union veterans group known as the Grand Army of the Republic.

By this time Edmonds was married and had three sons. From 1867, the year of her wedding, until her death in 1898, she lived as a woman. During this period she donated much of the money she earned from her best-selling books to war relief efforts. **See also** Pinkerton, Allan; spies.

education

During the Civil War, education in the North remained virtually unaffected by the conflict, but this was not the case in the South. In the first months of the war, most Southern colleges were closed because the majority of their students had enlisted in the Confederate army. The few colleges that remained open were either women's colleges or colleges that began allowing female students as a way to make ends meet during the war. Even then, colleges had to increase their tuition in order to compensate for the decreased number of students, although students were increasingly allowed to pay in goods as the value of the Confederate dollar dropped.

As for lower education during the war, again the North saw few changes. School textbooks and curricula were the same, with students continuing to learn only the basics of reading, writing, grammar, and arithmetic. (Few students went on to high schools, whose purpose was to teach geometry, algebra, history, and surveying, and in any case such schools were rare.) One noticeable change was that the number of female teachers increased because many male teachers joined the army. The South also experienced this shift in gender among its teachers during the war, but to an even greater degree: By the end of the war, almost all Southern teachers were female. The few that were male were typically clergymen who entered the classroom because of severe shortages of teachers in the South.

There were shortages of teaching supplies in the South as well, despite the fact that schools charged tuition. Paper, pencils, and chalk were difficult to obtain during the war, and schools did not always have the money for them because students were allowed to pay their tuition in goods instead of currency. Books also caused some measure of concern among Confederate teachers. The reading and spelling books they had employed before the war had been printed in the North, and many Southern parents were offended by the idea of their continued use. Therefore, various groups supported the publication and distribution of Southern versions of these texts. These included the *Dixie Primer* (1863), the *Dixie Speller* (1864), and *The Geographical Reader for the Dixie Children* (1863) by Marinda Branson Moore, the latter of which blamed abolitionists and President Abraham Lincoln (in Moore's view, a weak man controlled by abolitionists) for the war, and *Elementary Arithmetic* by Professor L. Johnson (1864), which had sample problems that asked how many Union soldiers a Confederate soldier could kill in a given amount of time. Some of these books could still be found in Southern schoolrooms after the war.

During Reconstruction, the focus of education in the South was the black student. However, poor white students benefited from this focus as well, because all Southern states were required by the federal government to establish public education

Schools like this one were built in the South specifically for freed slaves after the Civil War.

systems for both blacks and whites. These public schools, however, were usually segregated. Except for Louisiana and South Carolina, which officially allowed black and white students to study in the same school, Southern state constitutions did not address the issue of integrated versus segregated schools. Nonetheless, segregation was the norm, even in Louisiana and South Carolina. (After Reconstruction, segregation became mandated by law in the South.) Southern blacks took advantage of their new access to education (albeit segregated). By 1870, their literacy rate had risen from 5 percent to 20 percent. **See also** children in the Civil War; Reconstruction.

elections, Civil War

During the Civil War, the two national elections held in the South and the one held in the North suggest that voters on both sides were dissatisfied with their respective leader's handling of the war. For example, the 1862 midterm election in the North resulted in a gain for Democrats in Congress as well as an increase in Democratic governors. Furthermore, Republican candidates who advocated harsh antislavery measures more often than not lost to Democrats who took a more moderate stance.

Nonetheless, the Republicans managed to retain their control of both the U.S. House of Representatives and the Senate, and by 1864, when President Abraham Lincoln ran for reelection against Democrat George McClellan, public sentiment had once again swung in favor of Republicans. Lincoln received 55 percent of the popular vote and every state's electoral votes except those of Kentucky, New Jersey, and Delaware. At the same time, the Republicans increased their majority in Congress.

The 1863 Confederate election, which took place over the course of six months in order to give all soldiers a chance to vote, was also considered a referendum on the war. Congressional candidates who promoted peace did well among civilians, but due to public apathy, far fewer civilians voted than soldiers—who, like their counterparts in the North, considered a vote against their existing government to be unpatriotic. Therefore, President Jefferson Davis and his associates remained in control of the Confederate government, although about 40 percent of the members of the Confederate Congress were voted out of office. **See also** cabinet, Confederate; cabinet, U.S.; Congress, Confederate.

Ellet, Charles, Jr. (1810–1862)

Engineer Charles Ellet Jr. was the inventor of the "ram-boat," a ship with an iron ram protruding from its prow, which enabled it to sink enemy ships by piercing them below the waterline. Ellet had already thought of adding rams to warships when the Confederate navy developed a type of vessel known as an ironclad, whose sides were plated with iron above the waterline. Consequently when the U.S. Navy commissioned Ellet to create a ship that could sink these ironclads, he immediately began to transform nine steamers into ram-boats. These ships were victorious in their first battle (which also involved five new Union ironclads), in which they fought against a Confederate fleet near Memphis, Tennessee, on June 6, 1862. Ellet died from wounds received during the battle. **See also** ironclads; navies, Confederate and Union.

Ellsworth, Elmer E. (1837–1861)

At age twenty-four, Union colonel Elmer E. Ellsworth became the first military officer to be killed during the Civil War. Moreover, after his death he became a symbol of patriotism for Northerners, many of whom idolized him.

Ellsworth was famous even before his death. Prior to the war, he commanded the

U.S. Zouave Cadets, a group of volunteer soldiers from Chicago, Illinois, that performed showy military drills. During the summer of 1860, Ellsworth and his Zouaves toured the eastern United States, visiting twenty cities to great acclaim. That same year, Ellsworth campaigned for Abraham Lincoln during the presidential election; when Lincoln was elected, Ellsworth became his bodyguard as well as a close friend of the Lincoln family.

As soon as the Civil War began, Ellsworth formed a new group of Zouaves from among members of the New York City Fire Department. Called the New York Fire Zouaves, this regiment was the first to invade Southern territory—an honor that Ellsworth requested from Lincoln. On May 24, 1861, the regiment crossed the Potomac River into Virginia, which had seceded from the Union only the day before, and attacked the port city of Alexandria. The Zouaves had an easy victory there after the militiamen guarding the town abandoned their posts. Then Ellsworth noted a Confederate flag flying atop an inn and tavern known as the Marshall House, and he went upstairs to remove it. On his way back down the three-story staircase he was shot dead by innkeeper James Jackson, who in turn was shot dead by one of Ellsworth's men, Corporal Francis E. Brownell.

President Lincoln and his family were grief-stricken over the news of Ellsworth's death, and Lincoln's wife, Mary Todd Lincoln, subsequently refused to accept as a keepsake the flag that Ellsworth had died trying to capture. On the president's orders, an honor guard brought Ellsworth's body back to the White House, where it lay in state on May 25, 1861, and all U.S. flags were flown at half-mast. Then a memorial service was held, after which the body was taken to New York City for a public viewing at City Hall. Ellsworth was buried along the Hudson River in Mechanicville, New York, where he had been born.

In the months following his death, Ellsworth was memorialized in a variety of ways. He became the subject of poems, songs, newspaper articles, and paintings. Envelopes bearing his likeness, some including a message he had written to his parents on the night before his death, were distributed throughout the North, and photographs of him became a popular collectible. His uniform jacket, complete with the hole made by the fatal bullet, was put on display, as was the blood-stained Confederate flag. Corporal Brownell, who had avenged Ellsworth's death, was also treated like a hero, and photographs of him were sold as well; he was soon promoted to the rank of second lieutenant in the Regular Army. In addition, Zouave units modeled after Ellsworth's regiment were formed in many cities, and his name was often used as part of efforts to recruit volunteers for the Union army. **See also** Alexandria, Virginia; Zouaves.

emancipation

At the outset of the Civil War, President Abraham Lincoln was reluctant to promote emancipation of the slaves for fear that slave states that had remained loyal to the Union would secede. For this reason, he continually stressed his position that it was up to the states to decide whether or not to eliminate slavery. Moreover, when two of his generals took it upon themselves to emancipate slaves in Missouri (General John C. Frémont in August 1861), Florida, Georgia, and South Carolina (General David Hunter in May 1862), Lincoln rebuked them both and countermanded their acts of emancipation.

Finally, though, Lincoln decided that the Union would benefit if its cause became the abolition of slavery, a moral imperative, rather than the maintenance of the Union, a political imperative. This shift in purpose also was intended to dissuade the British, who had long opposed slavery on moral grounds, from siding

This illustration depicts President Lincoln at the signing of the Emancipation Proclamation, the document that ultimately ended the institution of slavery in the United States.

with the South, with which it had long enjoyed a good relationship through the cotton trade. However, Lincoln still could not afford to alienate the slave states that had remained in the Union (i.e., the border states). Therefore he decided to limit the emancipation of slaves to those states that had officially seceded from the Union.

Lincoln drafted his Emancipation Proclamation in June 1862, but he waited until the Union had won a major battlefield victory before making it public so that the order would appear to carry some authority. The opportunity Lincoln sought came on September 17, 1862, when the Union thwarted the Confederates' attempt to bring the war to Northern soil, at the Battle of Antietam. Five days later, Lincoln issued the Preliminary Emancipation Proclamation, which decreed that if the Confederate states did not rejoin the Union within one hundred days their slaves would be declared emancipated. After this deadline passed, Lincoln issued another version of this document, the official Emancipation Proclamation, which he signed on January 1, 1863. It emancipated all slaves in the Confederacy, but still specifically excluded those slaves living in areas held by the Union; therefore, since federal authorities still could not enforce orders in Confederate-held territory, the decree resulted in the wartime freeing of fewer than 200,000 slaves. However, the Emancipation Proclamation also meant that any slave who escaped to the North or who was captured by Union soldiers in the South would be considered free and could enlist in the Union army—a fact that added to the imbalance in manpower between the North and the South. **See also** Antietam, Battle of; Lincoln, Abraham.

engineers

During the Civil War, engineers were military officers who planned and oversaw the building of bridges, pontoons, and fortifications and the destruction of such structures in enemy territory. Many of these officers had been trained at the U.S. Military Academy, which was originally founded as a school for army engineers, in classes specializing in this aspect of war. Most military units had at least one engineer, and there were also engineering units made up of engineers and their assistants. For example, the U.S. Army Corps of Engineers, which had existed before the war, served with the Army of the Potomac both as engineers and as a fighting unit. At the beginning of the war there were also two Union regiments from New York and one from Michigan composed entirely of engineers and their assistants, and many additional engineering companies formed as the war progressed.

The Union also had another type of engineer corps at the beginning of the war, the Corps of Topographical Engineers. These men were specialists in surveying and geography, and they were sent on reconnaissance missions to explore uncharted areas and study the terrain for possible defensive sites. They also created and distributed maps. Eventually this corps was placed within the U.S. Army Corps of Engineers.

The Confederacy created its own Confederate Corps of Engineers at the beginning of the war. Unlike Union engineer corps, which relied on military personnel for labor, the Confederate Corps of Engineers used slaves and civilians as well as enlisted men to build the many fortifications it needed. Throughout the war, Confederate engineers suffered from a lack of surveying and other equipment, although they were able to acquire some of this material from foreign sources or capture it from the enemy. The Confederacy also lacked reliable maps at the beginning of the war, so one of the main duties of its Corps of Engineers was to make maps or steal them from the enemy. **See also** bridges; maps.

Ewell, Richard Stoddert (1817–1872)

Confederate lieutenant general Richard S. Ewell, a Virginia native, is best known for leading the Second Corps of the Army of Northern Virginia under General Robert E. Lee during the Battle of Gettysburg (1863) and at Spotsylvania (1864). Ewell took command of the corps after the death of its previous leader, General Thomas "Stonewall" Jackson, and at age forty-seven was the oldest commander to serve General Lee.

A veteran of the Mexican-American War, Ewell was an experienced cavalry officer when the Civil War began. Therefore the Confederacy made him a cavalry instructor, but during the First Battle of Bull Run in 1861 Ewell was given command of an infantry brigade, although the unit saw no action. The following year he took charge of a division under Stonewall Jackson. After several more battles Ewell was seriously wounded at the Second Battle of Bull Run (August 1862); shot in the right knee, he had to have his leg amputated.

In May 1863, after spending several months in Richmond, Virginia, recuperating from his injury, Ewell took command of the Second Corps in the Shenandoah Valley of Virginia. There he engaged in several battles before heading to Pennsylvania for the Battle of Gettysburg. During this battle he refused to obey an order to attack a particular group of Union troops because he thought it unwise, and later Ewell was severely criticized for this decision (although military historians now agree that Ewell made the right choice). Ewell was also justifiably criticized for a delayed and scattered charge against the North on the third day of the battle.

After the Confederate defeat at Gettysburg, Ewell spoke of giving up his command, complaining that he was suffering anew the effects of his amputation. After resting in a camp along the Rappahannock River during the winter, however, he decided to return to the battlefield. In May 1864, he fought in the Wilderness Campaign, where due to a tactical error by General Robert E. Lee he was without his artillery when the Union attacked. As a result, Ewell lost over half of his troops. Guilt-ridden over this failure, he took a leave of absence and was replaced by his major general, Jubal Early. Before Ewell could return to the battlefield, General Lee made this replacement permanent. Ewell was then given command of some of the defenses at Richmond, Virginia, a position he considered a demotion. Meanwhile, Ewell's wife, a nurse who had previously supported Ewell's military career, abandoned the Confederate cause, took an oath to support the Union, and moved to Louisiana, where she remained until the war ended.

Richard Stoddert Ewell led the Second Corps of the Army of Northern Virginia in the Battle of Gettysburg.

Ewell stayed in Richmond until the city was evacuated on April 2, 1865. Four days later he was captured by Union forces during the Battle of Sayler's Creek. He spent the next three months as a prisoner at Fort Warren in Boston Harbor, after which he joined his wife. They lived on her Tennessee plantation until January 1872, when both succumbed to pneumonia. **See also** Early, Jubal A.

Ewing, Thomas, Jr. (1829–1896)

As the commander of the District of the Border (which encompassed the area along the Kansas-Missouri border) in 1862–1863, Union brigadier general Thomas Ewing Jr. used particularly harsh measures to deal with the activities of Confederate guerrillas known as bushwackers. His district was the site of numerous bushwacker raids by a band that eluded capture for months. Finally, during the summer of 1863, Ewing decided to flush the guerrillas out of hiding by arresting their wives, girlfriends, and sisters, who provided them with food and supplies. While in custody, five of these women were killed when the wall of a Kansas City building collapsed on top of them, and several others were seriously wounded. The bushwackers, led by William Quantrill, blamed Ewing for these deaths, believing that he had orchestrated the collapse to kill the women and make it look like an accident, and they vowed revenge.

Nonetheless, four days later Ewing issued an order, General Order Number 10, decreeing that all women known to associate with Confederate guerrillas had to leave the District of the Border and the state of Missouri immediately. Hearing of this order while they were still in mourning for their loved ones, the bushwackers became so enraged that they decided to attack the antislavery town of Lawrence, Kansas, on August 21, 1863. There they slaughtered at least 150 defenseless citizens, as well as several unarmed Union soldiers who were camped nearby.

Ewing responded to this attack four days later by issuing General Order Number 11, according to which civilians in three and a half counties along the Missouri-Kansas border had to leave within fifteen days, and no exceptions would be made for anyone who swore loyalty to the Union. Ewing deployed soldiers to defend the civilians as they evacuated. However, his defenses could not prevent people from being robbed or harassed, usually by Union guerrillas (known as jayhawkers), as they traveled. In addition, once the region was cleared, Union guerrillas burned the homes of known bushwacker sympathizers. Southerners, as well as some Northerners, later blamed Ewing for the poor treatment of the evacuating civilians. **See also** Anderson, William; bushwackers; jayhawkers; Kansas; Quantrill, William Clarke.

executions

Both the North and the South executed military personnel for certain types of crimes, although the death penalty was applied inconsistently. In general, however, men were executed for committing murder or rape, assaulting a superior officer, deserting their post, or committing treason (including the act of intentionally damaging a flag). Captured spies were also typically executed, although some of the most notorious female spies escaped this fate again and again.

The chosen method for execution depended on the severity of the crime. Death by firing squad was considered a humane method of execution because it was, in theory, relatively quick and painless, so it was employed for deserters (who were viewed as being cowardly rather than evil). Individuals who were viewed as having committed a particularly brutal crime were hanged. However, Union statistics indicate that black soldiers were hanged more often than white soldiers who had committed the same crime, suggesting that racial prejudice governed the decisions of those determining punishments. **See also** punishments.

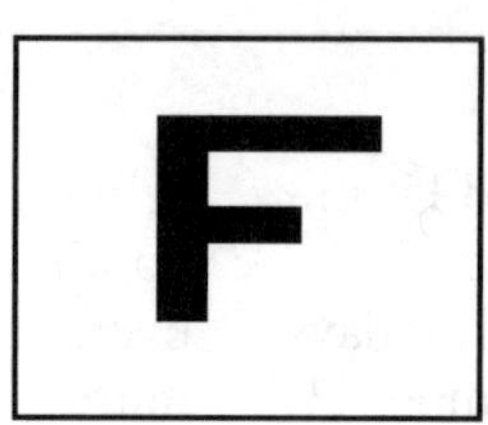

Farragut, David Glasgow (1801–1870)

An admiral in the Union navy, David G. Farragut was one of the North's most effective commanders. He began serving in the U.S. Navy as a midshipman shortly before the age of ten under the direction of his adoptive father, David Porter, a U.S. Navy captain who later became a commodore. At age twelve, Farragut served under Porter on the frigate *Essex* during the War of 1812 and was temporarily allowed to captain one of the many British ships captured by the *Essex*. In 1823 Farragut again assisted Porter in the capture of ships, this time while fighting pirates in the Caribbean Sea. In 1824 Farragut received command of the USS *Ferret*.

In December 1861 Farragut was put in charge of the West Gulf Blockading Squadron (a naval unit consisting of warships). The following April, he was ordered to sail up the Mississippi River to capture New Orleans. To avoid facing heavy fire from two Confederate forts prior to reaching the city, Farragut took his fleet past them in the dead of night, navigating in darkness despite the risk posed by unseen obstacles. This enabled him to surprise a Confederate squadron protecting New Orleans, and he easily defeated it before landing Union troops that took the city. This victory earned him a promotion to rear admiral.

In 1863 Farragut earned more acclaim by providing naval support for Union general Ulysses S. Grant's successful land assault on Vicksburg, Mississippi. Specifically, Farragut managed to get his squadron past the Confederates' defenses at Port Hudson, Louisiana, on the Red River, a tributary of the Mississippi, and establish a blockade there so that the Confederates could not use the Red River to provide Vicksburg with reinforcements.

The following year, Farragut displayed even greater heroics in sailing his fleet, which included both wooden and armored vessels, past several Confederate forts defending Mobile Bay, Alabama. The largest of these forts, Fort Morgan, was on one side of a channel leading into the bay, and on the other side was a line of mines (known then as torpedoes). On August 5, 1864, Farragut was leading his ships past this fort under heavy firing when one of them, the ironclad *Tecumseh,* was destroyed by a mine. Seeing the panic of his men, he exhorted his other ships to continue by shouting, "Damn the torpedoes! Full speed ahead!" and then put his own ship, the *Hartford,* in the lead, courageously plowing through the minefield. The remainder of his ships followed, none sustaining any serious damage. Farragut was honored for his heroism with a promotion to vice admiral. Because he was in poor health, however, the Battle of Mobile Bay was his last active duty, though he remained in the navy. In 1866 he was promoted to full admiral, and in his later years he toured naval ports abroad. **See also** navies, Confederate and Union; Porter, David Dixon.

field defenses

The accuracy of Civil War weapons resulted in numerous casualties if commanders sent their men out to battle on open ground. Therefore, an important part of both Northern and Southern military strategy was the use of elements of the landscape to create shelters against attack on the battlefield. Also known as field defenses, these shelters were used not only by defending armies, whose soldiers wanted to protect themselves from attack, but by attacking armies, whose soldiers wanted to be safe while firing at the enemy. The most common field defenses were those that were already in place as a battle ensued, such as deep woods, ravines and gullies, boulders, railroad embankments, and fences. However, soldiers also created their own field defenses prior to or during a military engagement. For example, they might dig holes or trenches to protect themselves, although because they lacked the proper tools, such indentations in the ground were usually quite shallow. Alternatively, given enough time, they might use logs and bushes to create shielded areas or even to build temporary walls. **See also** fortifications.

firearms

The firearms that troops carried changed over the course of the Civil War. In the beginning, volunteer soldiers used firearms they brought from home; these were typically smoothbore, long-barreled shoulder guns called muskets, outdated weapons that had been passed down from fathers or grandfathers. U.S. Army soldiers, however, had rifle-muskets or rifles, shoulder guns with rifled bores that enabled projectiles to fly farther. (Rifle-muskets had longer, thinner barrels than rifles.)

Within a short time, many volunteer soldiers had traded their muskets in for rifle-muskets. Consequently, about 85 percent of all battlefield casualties in the Civil War were caused by shoulder-fired rifle-muskets. Of these, the most common and second most common Union rifle-muskets were the Springfield and the Enfield, respectively. (Figures on Southern weaponry are unreliable, but because Springfields were manufactured in the North the Confederates probably used Enfields, which came from Great Britain.) Springfields were four and a half to five feet long (or longer with a bayonet—a knife twelve to eighteen inches long—attached to the end) and weighed about nine pounds, while Enfields were slightly shorter and heavier. Both were muzzle-loading, which means that their ammunition had to be pushed down the barrel with a ramrod. Because of this, Springfields and Enfields could fire only a single shot before needing to be reloaded.

As the war continued, gun manufacturers developed weapons that could fire several shots in succession before needing to be reloaded. Known as repeating rifles and loaded from the trigger, or breech, end, these weapons allowed a soldier to lay down a barrage of fire, but they also tended to waste ammunition. Therefore they were more popular in the North than in the South, because the Confederacy had difficulty getting sufficient ammunition due to the Northern blockade.

Several types of repeating rifles existed, but the most common in the Eastern Theater was the Spencer. This weapon held seven bullets, or rounds of ammunition, and in skilled hands could fire these rounds in less than a minute. In the Western Theater, the most popular repeating rifle was the Henry rifle, invented in 1860 by B. Tyler Henry of the Winchester Arms Company in New Haven, Connecticut. The Henry rifle could fire sixteen shots before it needed to be reloaded.

For some purposes, a carbine was more practical than a rifle. Carbines were lighter in weight than a rifle, but the barrel was shorter and therefore a bullet only carried about 450 to 600 feet. Their lightness, however, made them the firearm of choice for the cavalry, because a horseman found it difficult to ride and shoot with a long-barreled, heavy rifle. (However, when cavalrymen fought on foot, as they often did after a charge into battle, they might use a rifle.) An older version of the carbine was the musketoon, a short musket. The Spencer carbine was only three feet long and could fire five times faster than a Springfield. There were other types of carbines as well, including the Enfield and the Burnside, which was designed by Union general Ambrose E. Burnside during the war. Another carbine was the Sharps, manufactured in the North but soon copied by the Robinson Arms Manufacturer in Richmond, Virginia. The Sharps could fire three times faster than the Springfield.

Two other types of firearms were the pistol and the revolver, which were typically carried by officers, artillerymen, and, by the end of the war, many cavalrymen as well. (Artillerymen primarily used the weapon to shoot wounded draft horses when the animals had injuries that were judged unable to heal.) Pistols were single-shot handguns, while revolvers were repeating handguns. As with rifles and carbines, there were many versions of these guns. The most popular was the Colt revolver, named for its manufacturer, Samuel Colt. There were two models of Colt revolvers, one called the Army Colt and the other the Navy Colt. The Army Colt took a bigger cartridge of ammunition than the Navy Colt, but otherwise the revolvers were similar, with both able to fire six shots before needing to be reloaded. **See also** ammunition; swords, sabers, and bayonets; weapons.

fire-eater

In the years leading up to the Civil War, the term *fire-eater* was used to label Southern politicians who were particularly outspoken and passionate in arguing among Southerners that the South had the right to secede from the Union. The most famous fire-eaters were Edmund Ruffin, Robert B. Rhett Sr., and William Yancey. All of them framed the debate over slavery in terms of states' rights, characterizing the dispute between North and South as a legal issue rather than a moral one. **See also** Ruffin, Edmund; Yancey, William Lowndes.

Five Forks, Battle of

The Battle of Five Forks at Five Forks, Virginia, on April 1, 1865, was one of a series of battles in the Union's June 1864–April 1865 campaign to take the city of Petersburg, Virginia. This battle holds particular significance, however, because it was such an overwhelming victory for the Union that it led Confederate general Robert E. Lee to abandon Petersburg (about twelve miles northeast of Five Forks) after sundown on the following day. Major Generals Philip Sheridan of the cavalry and Gouverneur Warren of the infantry led the Union attack at Five Forks against Confederate major general George Pickett, who had retreated to the town after being defeated in a battle at nearby Dinwiddle Courthouse the previous day. Sheridan's cavalrymen fought a particularly fierce battle, laying down heavy fire and riding their horses through difficult terrain to confront the enemy. When this battle began, Pickett was about two miles away, enjoying a meal with other generals, but even after he reached the battlefield there was little he could do to achieve a victory; he had only about seven thousand men, while the Union had about four times that number. As a result, the Confederates lost approximately five thousand men, about one thousand of which had been taken prisoner. **See also** Petersburg Campaign; Pickett, George Edward; Sheridan, Philip Henry.

flags, U.S. and Confederate

During the Civil War, the United States was represented by a flag consisting of thirteen

A Union soldier holds a war-torn flag with thirteen stripes and a star for each state.

stripes of red alternating with white, representing the original colonies, and a blue field in the upper left-hand corner bearing white stars equal to the number of states (including those that had seceded). As states were added, the number of stars increased; there were thirty-three in early 1861, thirty-four in mid-1861 (after Kansas was added to the Union), and thirty-five in 1863 (after West Virginia became a state); after the war, in July 1865, a thirty-sixth star was added for Nevada, which had become a state the previous year.

The Confederacy had three different flags during the war. The first, known as the "Stars and Bars," was similar to the U.S. flag, or the "Stars and Stripes." It had two wide horizontal red bars separated by a horizontal white bar, and a blue field with white stars representing the Confederate states in its upper left corner. As more states joined the Confederacy, the number of stars increased. Eventually this number reached thirteen, even though only eleven states had officially seceded from the Union; the Confederacy's leaders believed that Missouri and Kentucky were actually on their side despite their reluctance to secede. In May 1863, however, the Confederate Congress decided that it wanted the Confederate flag to be substantially different from the U.S. flag and therefore adopted a new one. Known as the "Stainless Banner," this flag was white with a red field in the upper left corner, inside of which was a blue, star-covered cross that came to be called the "Southern Cross." Within a short time, however, the Confederate Congress decided that having a primarily white flag was unwise, given that an all-white flag was the symbol of truce or surrender. Therefore in March 1865 the Confederacy added a thick red bar to the fly end of the white flag.

That so much care was given to the design of the Confederate flag is indicative of how important flags were to people of the Civil War era. Most Civil War soldiers believed that physically protecting actual flags was worth the risk of death—and indeed, some did die trying to keep the flag belonging to their regiment from being captured by the enemy. Moreover, someone caught intentionally damaging a flag was charged with treason and often executed. **See also** executions.

Florida

Florida seceded from the Union and joined the Confederate States of America on February 1, 1861. When this occurred, the U.S. Army immediately strengthened its hold on two coastal Florida forts, Fort Pickens near Pensacola and Fort Jefferson in the Dry Tortugas (a string of islands and sandbars near Key West), by sending additional troops there from other parts of Florida. In April, when the Civil War officially began, the Union sent still more troops to these forts by sea. These forces eventually enabled the army to take other coastal forts, as well as coastal cities and islands. By May 1862, the Confederacy had abandoned much of the Florida coast to the Union. The Confederacy surrendered the entire state in May 1865. **See also** fortifications.

food

For troops in the first months of the Civil War, food was fairly plentiful, if not always palatable. In ideal circumstances, a Union soldier received twenty ounces or more of fresh or salt beef or twelve ounces of salt pork per day. The salt preserved the meat but made it so leathery that it was difficult to chew. To improve the texture of salt meats, soldiers often soaked them overnight in fresh water to soften them. For fresh meat, armies typically relied on butchers who traveled with them and slaughtered cows and pigs, when available, within a few hours of mealtime. The most common way to cook fresh meat was to boil it in a pot, although it could also be cooked on a skewer over an open fire or pan-fried with pork or bacon fat.

Confederate soldiers preferred their beef cooked in a stew, with cornbread or biscuits crumbled over the top. If bread was not available, they would mix flour, water, and bacon grease together in a pan to make a pastelike substance, which they called slosh, and then add the meat. When there was no meat, they would eat the slosh without it. By the winter of 1863–1864, meat was so scarce in some Southern armies that some soldiers reported eating rats or living entirely on cornmeal.

Soldiers received flour and cornmeal on a daily basis, if possible. In fact, U.S. Army regulations required that Union soldiers receive over a pound of flour a day. Cornmeal and water could be mixed together, then shaped and fried with animal fat to make a type of skillet bread. With a bit more effort, either cornmeal or flour could be used to make something similar to a pancake. Flour could also be used to thicken gravy or to make dumplings or biscuits.

At the beginning of the war, however, both the Union and the Confederacy gave soldiers a daily ration of bread, with Federal bakeries in Washington producing 16,000 loaves a day and a Confederate bakery in Petersburg, Virginia, producing 123,000 loaves a day (working around the clock). However, the North soon found that it was too difficult to keep bread fresh on its way to the troops, so the Union began providing its soldiers with hardtack, a sort of thick, hard cracker made from flour and water and baked. Although hardtack, as well as flour and cornmeal, could become moldy or infested with bugs, even then it remained edible and it was easier to store and transport than bread.

Like flour alone, hardtack could be used to thicken gravy (usually by being dropped or crumbled into stew and left to soak). It could also be smashed and mixed with water and then fried with animal fat to create a dish called skillygalee. Hardtack, which was generally impossible to eat when dry, could also be eaten plain after being soaked in water, but then it was not only gummy but extremely bland.

In addition to meat and flour, soldiers were typically provided with salt, pepper, sugar, vinegar, and beans. In the best of times, soldiers were each given one peck (a quarter-bushel) of dried beans about every one hundred days, and it was up to them to make this supply last. Soldiers would usually bake the beans, sometimes with pork and sugar or molasses. Both the North and the South recognized that the soldiers needed other vegetables as well, so they tried to send such foods to their troops via railroad or wagon. However, eventually this became so difficult that the North developed a dehydrated vegetable product made with turnips, parsnips, cabbages, onions, and possibly other greens as well. Called desiccated vegetables, this product—which in many people's opinion tasted terrible—was delivered to the soldiers as one-ounce, three-inch cubes that would expand when soaked in water.

Potatoes were also sometimes available to Union and Confederate soldiers, as were peas, rice, and hominy. When rice was available it was a popular food to take on a march, because it was lightweight to carry yet filling when eaten. In such cases, rice was commonly boiled with molasses and spread over hardtack. Another popular food for soldiers on the march was a soup made by boiling dried peas in water with salt pork.

Whether on the march or in camp, the soldier's beverage of choice was always coffee (since drinking alcohol was typically forbidden). Union soldiers received ten pounds of unroasted coffee beans or eight pounds of roasted ones. Unroasted beans had to be roasted overnight in pits in the ground, and both unroasted and roasted beans had to be crushed—usually between rocks or with an object like a rifle butt—before they could be boiled to make coffee. As the war progressed, however, Confederate soldiers sometimes had no coffee beans, and instead would substitute concoctions made with chicory, peanuts, acorns, sweet potatoes, dandelion root, cotton seed, okra seeds, or other items.

Confederate soldiers often got ideas for such substitutions from Southern housewives, who were also dealing with food shortages. One of the most popular books published in the South in 1863 was the *Confederate Receipt Book,* a cookbook that had such recipes as "Apple Pie Without Apples," the main ingredient of which was crackers soaked in water. Confederate soldiers either cooked such foods themselves while in camp or received them from patriotic Southern civilians while

Soldiers line up to purchase food from a sutler. Sutlers usually charged very high prices for their goods.

passing through a town. Union soldiers rarely received such gifts, although they might steal or buy food from civilians even though most Union commanders forbade their men from such pillaging.

Confederate and Union soldiers also lived off the land whenever they could. They fished, trapped, or hunted for meat; picked berries and fruit, looking particularly for citrus fruit, which could prevent a nutritional ailment known as scurvy; harvested wild honey; and took eggs and milk from chickens and cows that might be wandering loose. In addition, traveling salesmen called sutlers followed regiments in order to sell goods to troops, albeit at very high prices. Condensed milk, for example, was 75 cents a can, yet many soldiers wanted it because it could be combined with hardtack to make milk toast.

By the end of the war, however, the South was short of so many goods that even a sutler or foraging soldier could not find them. Therefore, unless they could raid Union supplies, Confederate soldiers often had to survive on extremely short rations. For example, during the Battle of Chancellorsville in 1863, Confederate soldiers were given only four ounces of bacon and eighteen ounces of flour a day, although some also had a bit of rice. Later, Confederate soldiers were reduced to eating items barely fit for humans, including corn cobs; soups made of tree roots, weeds, and grass; and a variety of bugs. By this point, such items were all that was available, since all livestock, and even dogs and cats, had already been eaten. **See also** camps and camp life; economy, Southern vs. Northern; sutlers.

Foote, Andrew Hull (1806–1863)

The son of a U.S. senator, Andrew H. Foote was a successful Union naval commander. He joined the U.S. Navy in 1822 as a midshipman and was eventually given command of the USS *Perry,* charged with patrolling the African coast to prevent illegal slave trading. In 1854 he published a book about his experiences, *Africa and the American Flag,* that was a powerful condemnation of slavery. Two years later Foote was given command of the USS *Portsmouth* and sent to the China coast, where he offered support to British ships then involved in a war with China. When Chinese forts began firing on Foote's vessel, he destroyed them.

In August 1861, the U.S. secretary of the navy, Gideon Welles, put Foote in charge of the Union naval forces defending the upper Mississippi River. In this capacity he established a flotilla of well over a dozen gunboats, seven of them new ironclads. In February 1862 this force offered support to a land attack in Tennessee led by Union general Ulysses S. Grant, sailing first on the Tennessee River to take Fort Henry on February 6 and then down the Cumberland River to attack Fort Donelson from February 14 to 16. During the latter attack, Foote was wounded in the leg; nonetheless, he continued on to the Mississippi River and went downriver to Island Number 10, a Confederate stronghold on the Kentucky-Tennessee border (about fifty-five miles below Cairo, Illinois). There he again offered support to land forces attacking the area, and as a result the Union finally captured the island on April 7.

In July 1862 Foote was honored for his courage with a promotion to rear admiral. He was then placed in charge of the Bureau of Equipment and Recruiting, with the idea that this desk job would make it easier for him to recover from the injury he had received during the attack on Fort Donelson. In June 1863, Foote appeared to be well enough to be made the commander of the South Atlantic Blockading Squadron, but he took a turn for the worse and died before he could assume his new post. **See also** Fort Henry and Fort Donelson Campaign; navies, Confederate and Union.

Forbes, Edwin (1839–1895)

Trained in fine arts at the National Academy of Design, Civil War artist Edwin Forbes sketched numerous scenes of camp life for *Frank Leslie's Illustrated News,* a popular newspaper of the period. While working as an artist-correspondent, Forbes was present at many major battles between 1862 and 1865, including the Shenandoah Valley Campaign, the Second Battle of Bull Run, the Battle of Antietam, the Battle of Chancellorsville, the Battle of Gettysburg, and the Wilderness Campaign. After the war, Forbes published his works in two books, *Life Studies of the Great Army* (1876) and the two-volume *Thirty Years After: An Artist's Story of the Great War* (1890s). **See also** artists and artwork.

foreign countries, involvement of

Foreign countries had virtually no involvement in the Civil War, though the Confederacy actively courted the leaders of Mexico, Great Britain, and France, trying in various ways to get them to declare war on the United States, fund the Confederate war effort, or at the very least recognize the Confederacy as a valid government. The South's efforts in Mexico were futile, since Mexico was a poor nation and its leader, Benito Juarez, opposed slavery, but similar efforts in Europe had some chance of succeeding.

The South's diplomatic prospects in France were bright, because French emperor Napoléon III wanted a Southern victory in the Civil War. His reasons for this were twofold. First, France had long had an affinity for the South because its leaders were aristocratic in manner and therefore, in French eyes, superior to the leaders of the North, who seemed uncultured by comparison. Second, in 1863 France had established a puppet regime in Mexico, and Napoléon believed that a victorious South would allow him to maintain control there. The South, in fact, told France that it would not oppose French control of Mexico in exchange for French recognition of the Confederacy and trade through Mexico. Mexico's puppet government, however, balked at the idea of such an arrangement, and France did not force the issue, although it did later provide the Confederacy with a loan equivalent to $8 million in gold.

In Great Britain, the South came closer to getting what it wanted. In large part this was because Britain's textile mills relied on cotton supplied by the South. In the first months of the war, the Confederacy tried to coerce Britain by withholding cotton shipments, but the British government was still reluctant to openly side with the Confederacy. For one thing, Britain was not inclined to support any kind of independence movement, for fear that it might encourage rebellions within the British Empire. For another thing, the British public was already opposed to slavery, and once the Union cast the Civil War as a fight to emancipate the slaves (a characterization that did not occur until the end of 1862), support for the South among the British people eroded even more. Also by this time, Europe had begun to experience a shortage of wheat and was turning to Northern grain exports to make up the shortfall. Therefore neither Britain nor France could afford to recognize the Confederacy after 1862.

Britain and France, then, remained officially neutral, although one incident nearly brought Britain into the war. In the fall of 1861, a U.S. naval vessel seized a British mail steamer, the *Trent,* because it was carrying Confederate diplomats to England. This act outraged the British, who felt that the seizure violated their neutrality; Great Britain therefore prepared for war, sending eleven thousand soldiers to Canada to prepare for an attack on the North, notifying its warships to stand ready, and demanding an apology and return of the prisoners. At this point, many Northerners spoke out in favor of going to war with the British, but eventually President Lincoln decided to issue an official apology instead. As a result, Britain maintained its position of neutrality, but it also subsequently allowed Confederate agents to arrange private loans and buy supplies and ships in Great Britain. **See also** cotton; economy, Southern vs. Northern; *Trent* Affair.

Forrest, Nathan Bedford (1821–1877)

Confederate lieutenant general Nathan B. Forrest led numerous cavalry raids in Tennessee, often behind enemy lines, to disrupt the Union's ability to get supplies to its garrisons and battlefield troops. He was also known for being one of the fiercest fighters of the war. Forrest claimed to have killed thirty soldiers in direct hand-to-hand combat, and according to some reports he ordered his troops to show less mercy to blacks than to whites during attacks.

Having been born into a poor family and with little education, Forrest struggled to make a living until the early 1850s, when he became a slave trader in Memphis, Tennessee. Profits from this business enabled him to buy his own plantation in Mississippi, where he served in law enforcement and the militia and dabbled in local politics. When the Civil War broke out, Forrest enlisted as a private in a Tennessee cavalry unit, but because he was a rich man the governor of Tennessee asked him to leave that unit to form his own. Forrest complied, using his own money to equip his troops, and was made the lieutenant colonel of the unit.

Forrest fought in several battles before distinguishing himself during a Union attack on Fort Donelson in February 1862. At that time, after defending the fort during a siege, he managed to evacuate his men from the area prior to its surrender, slipping through enemy lines undetected. Subsequently made a full colonel, Forrest fought and was wounded at the Battle of Shiloh, then became the brigadier general of a cavalry brigade and began making his Tennessee raids. One of these raids, in December 1862, made it impossible for Union general Ulysses S. Grant to get the supplies he needed to complete his first attack on Vicksburg, Mississippi.

Nathan Bedford Forrest led many successful cavalry raids in Tennessee.

In 1863, Forrest's cavalry supported the evacuation of Chattanooga, Tennessee, and participated in the Battle of

Chickamauga in Georgia. However, after a dispute with his superior officer, Braxton Bragg, Forrest asked for and received a transfer to Mississippi, though he continued to conduct raids into Tennessee as well as in Mississippi and Alabama. One of these raids, in April 1864, resulted in a massacre at Fort Pillow, Tennessee, in which many Union soldiers (a disproportionate number of them black) were shot while trying to surrender. A year later Forrest failed to defend Selma, Alabama, against a Union takeover, and the following month he surrendered his cavalry to the Union at Gainesville, Alabama.

After the war, Forrest became the first grand wizard, or head, of a secret racist organization known as the Ku Klux Klan. He also supported politicians whose goal was to prevent blacks from achieving social or political equality with whites. **See also** cavalry; Fort Pillow massacre; Ku Klux Klan.

Fort Fisher

Located on a peninsula at the headwaters of the Cape Fear River near Wilmington, North Carolina, Fort Fisher was the site of the largest land-sea assault of the Civil War, which took place in February 1865. At that time, it was the most heavily fortified defensive position in the Confederacy, containing forty-four heavy guns and surrounded by minefields and trenches. Such fortifications were needed because Wilmington was not only the port most used by the South's blockade runners but also the site of vital shipyards and railroad yards.

On December 7, 1864, General Ulysses S. Grant initiated a Union attack on both Fort Fisher and Wilmington by sending Major General Benjamin F. Butler to assault these locations by land while Rear Admiral David D. Porter led a corresponding sea assault. Both failed due to bad weather and other problems, including Butler's poor command skills. Grant then replaced Butler with Brigadier General Alfred Terry, and in February another land-sea assault took place, with Terry commanding nearly ten thousand men and Porter over sixty vessels. The fort was soon taken, and the Confederacy evacuated both Fort Fisher and Wilmington on February 22. **See also** Butler, Benjamin Franklin; fortifications; Grant, Ulysses S.; Porter, David Dixon.

Fort Henry and Fort Donelson Campaign

The Fort Henry and Fort Donelson Campaign was a successful Union attempt in early 1862 to take two Confederate forts on the Tennessee and Cumberland Rivers, respectively. The Confederacy had built these forts in 1861 on sites where the two rivers were only twelve miles apart in an attempt to protect these waterways from falling into enemy hands. This was critical because the Tennessee River traveled deep into Confederate territory, and the Cumberland went past two key cities: Clarksville, Tennessee, where the South had its second largest ironworks, and Nashville, Tennessee, which was a supply center for Confederate armies. However, Fort Henry had been mistakenly built on ground that was subject to flooding, and it was during one of these floods on February 6, 1862, that a Union fleet of ironclads, under the command of Flag Officer Andrew Foote, managed to capture the fort. Foote then led his fleet in an attack on nearby Fort Donelson, but after a long artillery battle the Confederates managed to retain control of the fort. This victory was reversed, however, by the arrival of Union land forces under the command of Ulysses S. Grant. His infantry captured Fort Donelson on February 16, 1862. **See also** Foote, Andrew Hull.

fortifications

In terms of Civil War military defenses, fortifications were protective structures intended to last for the duration of the war—as opposed to field defenses, which were built to protect soldiers during combat on a specific battlefield. Some fortifications had been built prior to the war to defend strategically significant locations, such as the headwaters of an important river, against all potential adversaries. The most common such fortification was the fort, which consisted of a high surrounding wall or stockade (a barrier of timbers) with openings through which soldiers could shoot at approaching enemies using a variety of weapons that often included cannons. Newer forts of the period had walls of masonry, while older ones were made of earth and wood. In the West, most forts were constructed from logs.

Another type of fortification was constructed during the war as part of an extensive military campaign: walls and batteries built to shelter troops and artillery pieces during long engagements and sieges. These earthenwork structures were made by digging wide ditches and then piling up and sloping the earth next to them to create defensive walls. Often these structures had different levels, with higher platforms where infantry troops could stand and lower ones for artillery pieces. Logs might also be incorporated into the structures to give the walls additional strength. In addition, an army might build several rows of these structures around an area to be defended so that the enemy would have to fight its way through many layers of fortifications. Similarly, troops might construct additional fortifications—in the form of earth, log, or masonry walls—around a fort to provide it with additional protection; Southern cities were typically reinforced in this way in the first months of the war. **See also** field defenses.

Fort Monroe

Located on the James River in Virginia, the Union's Fort Monroe was the base for General George McClellan's successful assault on Yorktown, Virginia, in May 1862. The previous month, McClellan had sent his troops by riverboat to take the fort from the Confederates, and shortly after the battle President Abraham Lincoln visited Fort Monroe to observe its gunboat operations. Even after it became a Union stronghold, however, the fort allowed peaceful, or "flag of truce," boats to travel past it en route to and from the Confederate capital of Richmond, Virginia. **See also** fortifications; Yorktown, Battle of.

Fort Pillow massacre

The Battle of Fort Pillow in Tennessee on April 12, 1864, was subsequently called the Fort Pillow massacre in the North because when Union soldiers tried to surrender they were shot by Confederates. An earthenwork fort on the Mississippi River, Fort Pillow held 285 white Union soldiers and 295 black soldiers, commanded by Major William Bradford, when it was attacked by 1,500 Confederate soldiers led by Major General Nathan Forrest. During this battle, not only did the Confederates continue shooting and killing soldiers even after they had surrendered, but they primarily targeted the black soldiers. As a result, of the 231 Union soldiers killed and 100 wounded, about 65 percent were black. In 1864, a U.S. congressional committee investigated the incident and found Forrest responsible for the massacre, although he never accepted blame. **See also** Forrest, Nathan Bedford.

Fort Sumter

Located on a man-made island in the middle of Charleston Harbor in South Carolina, Fort Sumter is famous for being the place where the first shot of the Civil War was fired; this first volley came from the Confederates on April 12, 1861. The attack on the fort had actually been planned since January 1861, when troops from a Federal garrison at nearby Fort Moultrie joined the forces at Fort Sumter because Fort Moultrie's fortifications were inadequate against a Confederate assault. Shortly thereafter,

The Confederates bombarded Fort Sumter from April 12 to April 14, 1861. These sieges marked the beginning of the Civil War.

Confederate brigadier general P.G.T. Beauregard demanded that all of the soldiers at Fort Sumter surrender, and when they refused he blocked supplies from reaching the fort. Eventually the Union commander, Major Robert Anderson, asked President Abraham Lincoln for help, but although the president said he would find a way to get supplies to the fort, he refused to send in additional soldiers to reinforce its defenses. Once the Confederates learned this, they began firing on Fort Sumter. Their siege lasted for more than fifty hours, after which Anderson—whose men were by then almost out of food—finally surrendered the fort. None of Anderson's men were killed during the siege, but one, U.S. private Daniel Hough, was killed accidentally in an explosion just after the surrender. Shortly thereafter the fort's soldiers and officers were sent by ship to New York, taking with them the American flag—now torn—that had flown above the fort. **See also** Anderson, Robert H.; Charleston, South Carolina.

Fort Wagner

Located at Charleston Harbor in South Carolina, Fort Wagner was the site of a battle that proved the bravery of black soldiers and increased their acceptance in the U.S. military as a result. On July 18, 1863, a Union corps composed of black soldiers, the Fifty-fourth Massachusetts

Infantry, undertook the second of two attacks on the fort and almost succeeded in capturing it. During their assault, nearly half of their number was lost, and their white commander, abolitionist Robert Gould Shaw, was killed. **See also** black troops.

Fox, Gustavus Vasa (1821–1883)

As the U.S. assistant secretary to the navy during the Civil War, Gustavus V. Fox encouraged the production of new types of ironclad warships. He was also responsible for David Farragut's assignment to command the West Gulf Blockading Squadron, which ultimately resulted in the Union's capture of New Orleans, Louisiana, from the Confederacy in April 1862. After the war, Fox worked to rebuild the U.S. Navy, again encouraging the creation of new and better ships. **See also** Farragut, David Glasgow; navies, Confederate and Union.

Franklin and Nashville Campaign

Also called Hood's Tennessee Campaign, the Franklin and Nashville Campaign was a series of battles in Tennessee instigated by Confederate general John B. Hood between November 29 and December 27, 1864. By this time, Union general William T. Sherman had driven Hood's Army of Tennessee from Atlanta, Georgia, and sent troops into Nashville, Tennessee, as support for his Atlanta operations. Hood decided to attack these Tennessee troops as a way to strike back at Sherman. However, before they could reach Nashville, Hood's infantry forces, along with a Confederate cavalry led by Nathan Forrest, encountered a Union army led by Major General John M. Schofield on November 30 at Franklin, Tennessee. Unfortunately for Hood, Schofield's men were well protected by entrenchments, and sixty-two hundred Confederates were killed in the ensuing battle. Afterward, Schofield's forces went into Nashville and Hood followed. The Confederates surrounded the city in anticipation of a long siege, but after two weeks, on December 15, 1864, Union troops led by Major General George H. Thomas poured out of Nashville in an attack that nearly wiped out the Confederate Army of Tennessee. Hood then retreated to Tupelo, Mississippi, and on January 13, 1865, he resigned his command. **See also** armies, Confederate; Hood, John Bell; Sherman, William Tecumseh; Tennessee; Thomas, George Henry.

Fredericksburg, Battle of

The result of a December 13, 1862, Union attack on Confederate troops stationed on the Rappahannock River at Fredericksburg, Virginia, the Battle of Fredericksburg brought criticism to both the Union commander, General Ambrose Burnside, and the Confederate commander, General Robert E. Lee, from Northerners and Southerners, respectively. The previous month, Burnside had received permission from President Abraham Lincoln to lead the 120,000-man Army of the Potomac in capturing Fredericksburg from the Confederates, because the city was on the road to the Confederate capital of Richmond, Virginia. At that time, Lee's Army of Northern Virginia, with 78,000 men, was scattered along the Rappahannock River and therefore in no position to protect Fredericksburg. However, Burnside had to cross the river in order to reach the city, and due to bad weather and a delay in receiving proper equipment (pontoon boats and bridging materials), he was held up in reaching his destination. As a result of Burnside's slow progress, Lee had time to bring his troops together and move them into a defensive position. By taking advantage of high ground and other aspects of the terrain, the Confederate army was subsequently able to kill or seriously injure over twelve thousand Union soldiers while losing fewer than fifty-five hundred, though the town of Fredericksburg suffered serious damage.

The next morning, Burnside wanted to attack the Confederates again, but given the number of Union casualties, the generals under his command balked. After some debate Burnside backed down, at least for the moment, and declared a truce so that both sides could bury their dead. Since the weather was still bad this took a few days, by which time the Confederates had moved to a position that made another attack impossible. Specifically, in the middle of the night on December 15 they crossed the river on pontoon boats so that by morning they could be seen but were not within firing range. After this, neither side made a move to continue the engagement. Some Southerners later called Lee's decision to sneak away dishonorable, while Burnside's superiors blamed him for the battle's high casualties and relieved him of his command. **See also** Burnside, Ambrose Everett; Lee, Robert Edward.

Freedman's Village

In December 1863, Freedman's Village was established near Arlington, Virginia, by the U.S. government to house freed slaves and their families. It was considered a model of its kind, with a hospital, nursing home, school, and one hundred duplexes that could each be rented for $3 a month. The village also held workshops in order to teach men in the village a trade. Located on land that was once owned by Confederate general Robert E. Lee, Freedman's Village was closed in 1882, whereupon this land became part of Arlington National Cemetery. **See also** Lee, Robert Edward.

Frémont, John Charles (1813–1890)

When California became a state in 1850, explorer John C. Frémont was elected one of its first two senators, and he immediately became one of the most outspoken abolitionists in Congress. In fact, he was such a devout abolitionist that when he ran for U.S. president in 1856 Southern states threatened to secede immediately if he was elected. Meanwhile, in the North Frémont was a national hero because of his earlier exploits in surveying the American West. He was also notorious for being difficult, particularly because while serving in the Mexican-American War (1846–1848) as a battalion major he had been court-martialed and dismissed from the U.S. Army for disobedience. (Later, President James K. Polk reinstated Frémont, who promptly resigned his commission.)

Shortly after the Civil War broke out, President Abraham Lincoln gave Frémont command of the Western Department, which included Missouri. Frémont subsequently took it upon himself to free Missouri's slaves. This caused an uproar not only in Missouri but in other slave states that had remained loyal to the Union. Lincoln responded by reversing Frémont's emancipation order, rebuking him for acting without authority, and eventually transferring him to another command, the Mountain Division. The following year, Frémont resigned from the army after being replaced as the commander of the Mountain Division. In 1864, after deciding not to run for president, he retired from public life until 1878, when he was elected governor of the Arizona Territory; he held this office until 1883. **See also** Missouri.

Fugitive Slave Acts

The U.S. government passed several acts designed to deal with fugitive slaves. The first, in 1787, prohibited slaves from gaining freedom by fleeing from a slave state to a free state; fugitive slaves therefore had to be returned to their owners immediately. In 1850, as part of compromise legislation proposed by Senator Henry Clay, Congress passed another Fugitive

Slave Act that imposed penalties on people who helped fugitive slaves and authorized federal marshals to capture such fugitives. Under such laws, little evidence was required to prove ownership of a purported slave. Furthermore, the U.S. Supreme Court, in the 1842 case *Prigg v. Pennsylvania,* had declared that no state could interfere with the capture of a fugitive slave, even in an attempt to determine whether the purported slave was actually a free man. As a result, many free blacks living in the North were kidnapped and sent south as slaves.

This practice continued even after the Civil War began, and the U.S. government did little to stop it. In fact, President Abraham Lincoln decreed that runaway slaves from states that were loyal to the Union still had to be returned to their owners. Moreover, an April 1862 act abolishing slavery in the District of Columbia also mandated that slave owners be compensated for their loss in the amount of $300 per slave. It was not until June 28, 1864, that Congress repealed all fugitive slave laws. **See also** Clay, Henry; Compromise of 1850.

Garfield, James Abram (1831–1881)

Although perhaps best known for being the twentieth president of the United States, James A. Garfield also served as a general in the Civil War. When the war began he was involved in recruitment efforts for the Forty-second Ohio Volunteer Infantry and was eventually made its colonel. In April 1862 he participated in the Battle of Shiloh, and afterward he became chief of staff of the Army of the Cumberland. By this time a brigadier general, Garfield coordinated Union espionage activities and trained his spies to accurately estimate troop size and location. In fact, he earned the reputation of being one of the best spymasters in the Union. In September 1863 he fought in the Battle of Chickamauga and shortly thereafter was promoted to major general.

After the war, as a member of the U.S. House of Representatives, Garfield was a Radical Republican—that is, a member of the branch of the Republican Party that advocated harsh treatment of the South during Reconstruction. Garfield served in the U.S. House of Representatives until 1880, when he was elected president. Garfield had been in office for only four months when he was assassinated. **See also** Pinkerton, Allan; political parties.

Garrison, William Lloyd (1805–1879)

Journalist William Lloyd Garrison was one of the leading abolitionists of his time. Garrison first became involved in journalism as a boy, when he was apprenticed to a Vermont newspaper printer. He became involved in the abolitionist movement in 1830 at the age of twenty-five. By this time he had already worked as an editor on two newspapers, *National Philanthropist* (in Boston, Massachusetts, in 1828) and *Journal of the Times* (in Bennington, Vermont, from 1828 to 1829), both of which promoted social reforms. In 1829 he became an editor of the antislavery paper *Genius of Universal Emancipation.* In this position he worked in Baltimore, Maryland, with a leading abolitionist, Benjamin Lundy, and became deeply involved in the abolitionist cause. As a result of his beliefs, Garrison wrote an unflattering article about a slave trader, and the man had him arrested for libel. The few months that Garrison spent in jail left him even more committed to abolitionism. In 1831 he established his own newspaper, the *Liberator,* which soon became the most prominent abolitionist periodical in the United States. In it Garrison advocated immediate emancipation of all slaves and their integration into American society. This position represented a change of heart; in his first years as an abolitionist, Garrison believed that, upon emancipation, all blacks should be sent to Africa.

In 1832 Garrison helped establish the New England Anti-Slavery Society, the first abolitionist group to advocate the immediate emancipation and integration of

Journalist William Lloyd Garrison was a leading abolitionist.

all blacks. In 1833 he helped establish the American Anti-Slavery Society, which held to the same position. By this time Garrison was also an advocate of women's rights, so he allowed women to participate in his organizations. This angered many male members of the American Anti-Slavery Society, who in 1840 decided to leave the group to establish the all-male American and Foreign Anti-Slavery Society.

Another unpopular Garrison position was the idea that organized religion should be shunned because leaders of the established faiths were immoral for failing to work to end slavery. For the same reason, he believed that the U.S. government did not deserve its citizens' support if it supported slavery in any fashion. In fact, he proposed that the North secede from the Union and form a new antislavery nation; his slogan was "No Union with Slaveholders." However, Garrison was also a pacifist, so he felt that such a secession had to be accomplished peacefully.

During the 1850s, Garrison used the *Liberator* as a way to voice his opposition to the Compromise of 1850, the Kansas-Nebraska Act, and the *Dred Scott* decision. Once the government outlawed slavery by adopting the Thirteenth Amendment to the Constitution (December 1865) Garrison stopped publishing the *Liberator* and retired from public life, although he did quietly continue to support the Republican Party, women's rights, and pacifist groups. **See also** abolitionists; colonization movement.

generals, Confederate and Union

During the Civil War, the Union had 583 generals, with another 1,367 individuals achieving the rank as a brevet (a temporary honor); the Confederacy had 425 generals, none brevet. These generals had different levels of responsibility depending on grade (i.e., whether they were major generals, brigadier generals, and so on), but many shared a common experience: prewar military training at the U.S. Military Academy at West Point, the foremost institution of its kind. Thus it was not uncommon for two opposing generals to have once been schoolmates, or for a former West Point teacher to find himself fighting against one of his former students. It was also not uncommon for opposing generals to know what maneuvers to expect from one another, since everyone who had gone to West Point had essentially learned the same military tactics and strategies. In fact, even generals who had attended a different military school often shared this common knowledge, since such schools typically used the same instructional materials and methods as West Point.

Of the few generals who lacked a military-school education, many received their rank and their command positions because of wealth and/or political connections. For example, Union general Nathaniel P. Banks, a powerful Republican politician, used his influence at the outset of the war to be named a major general. (Banks then proceeded to lose almost every battle he commanded.)

The Union had many such difficulties with incompetent generals at the beginning of the war, in large part because Northerners did not put much value on formal military training when selecting commanders. In fact, many Northern political leaders were biased against men who had gone to military school, arguing that formal training stifled creativity in regard to battlefield tactics. The leaders of the Confederacy, however, believed that generals who had received formal military training were superior, which was understandable given that Confederate president Jefferson Davis had attended West Point. (U.S. president Abraham Lincoln had no formal military training whatsoever.) In part because of the greater level of experience and training of its generals, the Confederacy enjoyed considerable success early in the war. **See also** armies, Confederate; armies, Union; infantry, Confederate and Union; military schools, bias against.

Georgia

On January 19, 1861, Georgia became the fifth state to secede from the Union, at which point it became an important source of troops and supplies for the Confederacy. In fact, the city of Atlanta, Georgia, was one of the most significant Confederate supply depots, as well as a key industrial center. For this reason, Union general William Tecumseh Sherman targeted Atlanta as part of an aggressive 1864 campaign to bring down the Confederacy. Beginning in July, he marched on Atlanta, took over the city, evacuated its citizens, and burned it to the ground. He then marched fifty miles to Savannah, Georgia, leaving destruction in his wake, and took that city as well.

The state suffered many other hardships during the war. Because of Northern blockades and the lack of manpower on its farms and plantations, Georgia's citizens were often deprived of food and goods. In addition, its production and sale of cotton, a vital part of the state economy, dropped so dramatically that by 1865 Georgia was in financial ruin. **See also** Atlanta Campaign; Sherman, William Tecumseh.

Gettysburg, Battle of

The Battle of Gettysburg, from July 1 to 3, 1863, at Gettysburg, Pennsylvania, was a major defeat for the Confederacy, which had instigated the battle in an attempt to bring the Civil War to Northern soil. In addition, the defeat seriously impacted both Southern and Northern morale. Roughly forty Northern reporters had been present at Gettysburg during the fighting, and they made much of the South's loss in subsequent newspaper articles and editorials, thereby increasing support for the war effort in the North while demoralizing the South.

In the days leading up to the battle, Confederate general Robert E. Lee had brought his Army of Northern Virginia, with about seventy-five thousand men, north through the Shenandoah Valley to Pennsylvania's Cumberland Valley. Shortly after these troops set out, their movements were detected by the Union, which then sent the Army of the Potomac, with about ninety-five thousand men, to meet them.

The battle began around dawn on July 1 with the Confederate forces coming from the north and west into Gettysburg, where Lee knew that a Federal cavalry division was stationed. After a day of fighting, the Union retreated to an area of high ground

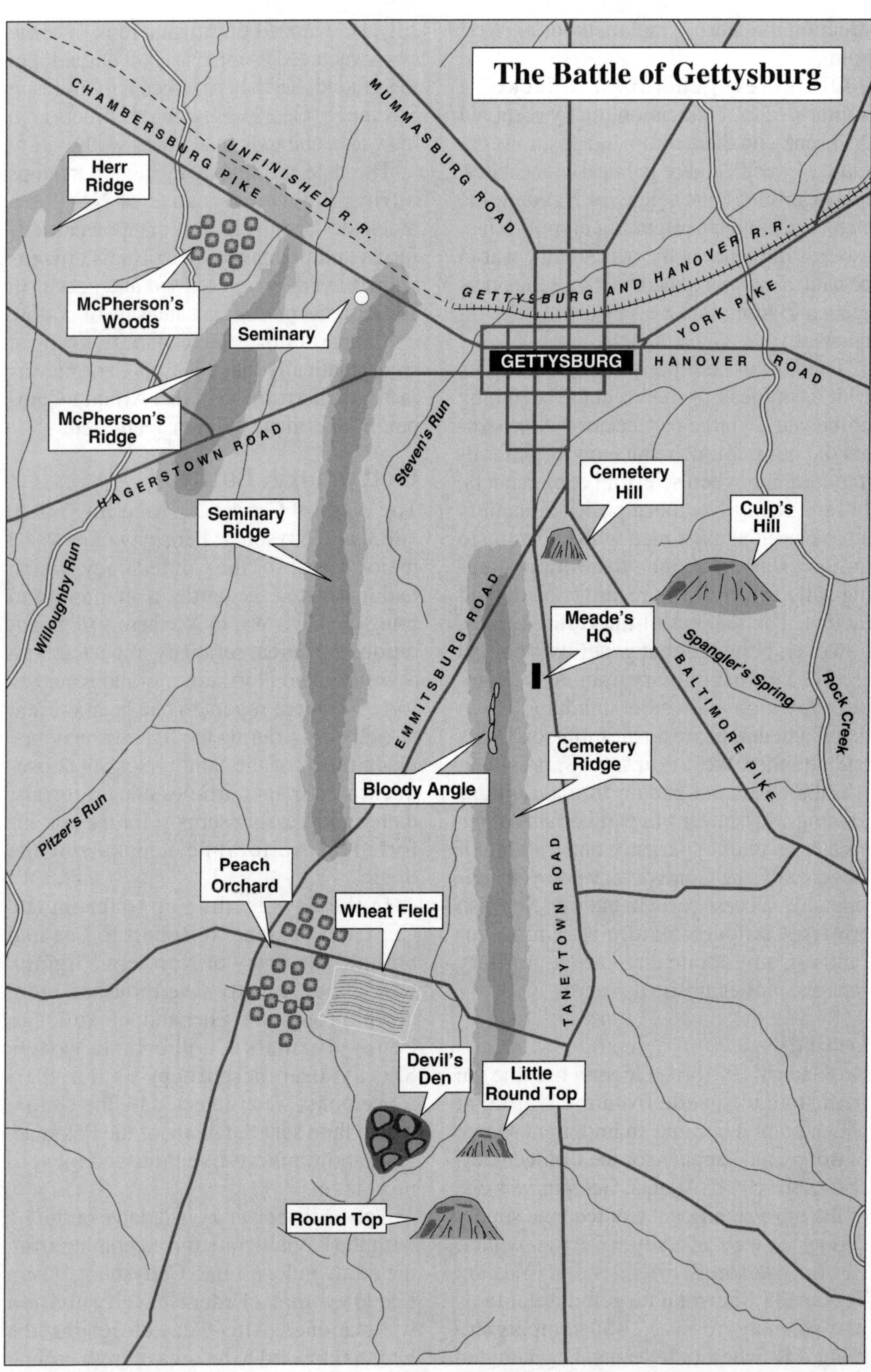
The Battle of Gettysburg
CHAMBERSBURG PIKE
UNFINISHED R.R.
MUMMASBURG ROAD
GETTYSBURG AND HANOVER R.R.
YORK PIKE
HANOVER ROAD
GETTYSBURG
Herr Ridge
McPherson's Woods
Seminary
McPherson's Ridge
HAGERSTOWN ROAD
Steven's Run
Cemetery Hill
Culp's Hill
Seminary Ridge
Willoughby Run
EMMITSBURG ROAD
Meade's HQ
Spangler's Spring
BALTIMORE PIKE
Rock Creek
Cemetery Ridge
Bloody Angle
Pitzer's Run
Peach Orchard
Wheat Field
TANEYTOWN ROAD
Devil's Den
Little Round Top
Round Top

just south of Gettysburg known as Cemetery Hill. By dawn of the next day, both sides had received reinforcements and strategically positioned their troops. Lee's men attacked the Union at various locations, including Cemetery Hill, Culp's Hill (just to the east of Cemetery Hill), Cemetery Ridge (a strip of high ground running south from Cemetery Hill), Round Top, and Little Round Top, but by the end of the day the Confederates had failed to push the Union from any of its main positions.

On the third day, Lee tried once more to rout the Union, this time with the help of a cavalry unit led by General J.E.B. Stuart, who had ridden for days to position his forces at the Union's rear. As before, various Confederate units struck the Union at various locations, but each assault failed. Moreover, the Confederacy suffered serious casualties during a full frontal attack that later became known as Pickett's Charge, when three brigades from the division of Confederate major general George Pickett lost about two-thirds of their forty-three hundred men.

Because of this and other failures, General Lee decided to withdraw his forces from the battlefield the following morning. In all, he had lost about twenty-eight thousand of his men, with the Union losing about twenty-three thousand. Lee later blamed himself for these losses and offered to resign, but Confederate president Jefferson Davis refused to accept his offer. Meanwhile, the Southern press blamed Davis as well as his generals for the defeat, suggesting that the Confederacy had underestimated the advantage an enemy gained, both physically and psychologically, from fighting on home soil. **See also** Brandy Station, Battle of; Pickett's Charge.

Gettysburg Address

Delivered by President Abraham Lincoln on November 19, 1863, as part of the dedication ceremonies for a national soldiers' cemetery at the site of the Battle of Gettysburg, the Gettysburg Address is one of the most famous speeches in American history. In powerful language, Lincoln offered a brief justification for the war, beginning with the words "Four score and seven years ago our fathers brought forth on this continent a new nation, conceived in liberty and dedicated to the proposition that all men are created equal."

On the day the Gettysburg Address was delivered, however, the audience was less than enthusiastic about it, not through any fault of its content but because the speech was so short and Lincoln's speaking style so understated in comparison with the previous offering, a two-hour account of the events of the Battle of Gettysburg and their significance by orator Edward Everett. Consequently, after delivering the Gettysburg Address, Lincoln thought that he had failed in his purpose: to make Northerners feel as though Union soldiers who had been killed in the war had died while supporting a noble cause. But over the next few days, as Northern newspapers printed and reprinted the speech, public response indicated that Lincoln had achieved his goal. Nonetheless, some Northern editorials did criticize various aspects of the speech's content and/or the president's decision to be present at a cemetery dedication when he had so many more important responsibilities to deal with. **See also** Gettysburg, Battle of.

Gordon, John B. (1832–1904)

Confederate major general John B. Gordon was known for his heroism as well as his military skill. Having worked in Georgia as a lawyer, political reporter, and manager of coal mines prior to the war, Gordon's first military position was as a major in a regiment formed by his older brother. Known as the Sixth Alabama Infantry Regiment even though its soldiers came from not only Alabama but also Georgia and Tennessee, the Sixth Alabama came under the command of General P.G.T. Beauregard at the First Battle of Bull Run in July 1861, but the infantry unit was never sent into the action.

Roughly a year later Gordon, by then a colonel, saw heavy combat at the Battle of Seven Pines in Virginia, where over half of his men were killed. He was then given temporary command of a brigade whose officer, Robert Rodes, had been injured, and led his men into battle at South Mountain, Maryland, and Sharpsburg, Virginia, in September 1862. At Sharpsburg Gordon nearly died from a battle wound but soon recovered and fought as a brigadier general in the Battles of Chancellorsville (May 1863), Gettysburg (July 1863), and Spotsylvania (May 1864). Promoted to major general, he then helped General Robert E. Lee defend Petersburg, Virginia, in June 1864 and participated in the Shenandoah Valley Campaign (August 1864) and the Battles of Third Winchester (September 1864), Fisher's Hill (September 1864), and Cedar Creek (October 1864). He participated in several more military actions in 1865 before surrendering along with Lee at Appomattox in April.

After the war, Gordon practiced law in Atlanta, Georgia, until 1873, when he was elected to the U.S. Senate. From 1886 to 1890 he was the governor of Georgia, and in 1891 he returned to the Senate for another term. He also served as the head of the United Confederate Veterans from 1890 to 1904. **See also** Beauregard, Pierre Gustave Toutant; Seven Pines, Battle of.

Gorgas, Josiah (1818–1883)

Josiah Gorgas established and served as the chief of the Confederate Bureau of Ordnance, which was responsible for acquiring and distributing military weapons, ammunition, and equipment. To accomplish this task, he had to buy some of the weapons and supplies in Europe and supervise the manufacture of others by Southern factories. The rest came from Confederate donors or were taken from Union soldiers.

Gorgas had experience in weaponry before joining the Confederate army, having served in the U.S. Army and overseen the activities of its Mount Venice Arsenal in Alabama. When Alabama seceded, Gorgas left the U.S. Army to support the Confederate cause. **See also** weapons.

Grant, Ulysses S. (1822–1885)

As the commander in chief of all Union armies in the last year of the war, General Ulysses S. Grant developed an aggressive military strategy that ultimately led to the surrender of the Confederate armies. Grant served as commander in chief from March 1864 to March 1869. He then served as president of the United States for two terms.

Grant's given name was Hiram Ulysses Grant, but when he was enrolled at the U.S. Military Academy at West Point in 1839 he was accidentally listed as Ulysses S. Grant, a name he ultimately decided to keep—continually insisting, however, that the middle initial "S" did not stand for anything. After graduating from West Point in 1843, Grant served as a second and then a first lieutenant with the Fourth U.S. Infantry, which by July 1854 was stationed on the Pacific Coast. By this time, though, he had a wife, Julia, and four children and did not like being separated from them, so he resigned from the military and settled on his wife's family estate in Missouri, working as a farmer and investing in real estate. In 1860 he joined his father and brothers in a business selling leather goods in Galena, Illinois.

Grant did not enjoy being a businessman, however, so the following year, when the Civil War broke out, he immediately got involved in the recruitment and training of Union volunteer troops in Illinois. In June 1861 he was made a colonel and the commander of the Twenty-first Illinois Volunteers. Without even seeing

General Ulysses S. Grant was an extremely aggressive military leader.

battle, he was soon made a brigadier general due to the political influence of a family friend, U.S. congressman Elihu B. Washburne, from Galena. By the end of the year Grant was stationed in Cairo, Illinois, as the head of the U.S. Army's District of Southeast Missouri.

Grant chafed at not being involved in frontline fighting, however, so in January 1862 he asked for and received permission from the Union army to lead forces in an attack in Tennessee. Known as the Fort Henry and Fort Donelson Campaign, this February 1862 series of military actions led to the capture of two Confederate forts on the Cumberland and Tennessee Rivers. As the first major Union success of the war, the campaign enhanced Grant's reputation and earned him both a promotion to major general of volunteers and the command of the Army of the Mississippi. Grant's reputation was somewhat tarnished, however, at the Battle of Shiloh in April 1862, because although it was another victory for the Union it also resulted in heavy Union casualties. As a result, Grant temporarily lost command of his army to General Henry Halleck, but he regained it in time to capture Vicksburg, Mississippi, from the Confederates in July 1863 after a long and difficult campaign. Grant was subsequently promoted to lieutenant general.

In March 1864 President Lincoln gave Grant command of all Union armies, largely because of Grant's successful Vicksburg Campaign. Shortly after being named to this position, Grant devised a plan in which he would lead troops against Confederate general Robert E. Lee in Virginia while a Union force led by General William T. Sherman would march through Georgia to prevent Lee's escape. Meanwhile, the Union cavalry, led by Philip Sheridan, was assigned the job of destroying Virginia railroad lines so that Lee could not receive supplies. Grant's strategy was successful; on April 9, 1865, Lee was finally forced to surrender to Grant at Appomattox Courthouse. After the war, Grant was hailed in the North as a hero, and in 1866 he was given a new official rank: general of the armies of the United States.

Grant's war successes translated into political popularity, and he was elected president of the United States in 1868. He won reelection in 1872. However, his second term was marred by financial scandals, although Grant himself was not accused of misdoings.

Throughout his presidency, Grant was at the forefront of efforts to ensure that blacks enjoyed civil rights; at the same time, he pushed for giving amnesty to former Confederates. After leaving the presidency, Grant made several bad investments that resulted in the bankruptcy of his family. He then began writing magazine articles about the war to raise money, and eventually wrote his memoirs. They were published posthumously after Grant died of throat cancer in 1885. **See also** armies, Union; Fort Henry and Fort Donelson Campaign; Lee, Robert Edward; Shiloh, Battle of; Vicksburg Campaign.

Greeley, Horace (1811–1872)

Prior to and during the Civil War, newspaper editor Horace Greeley wrote numerous antislavery articles that influenced public opinion in the North. Apprenticed to a Vermont newspaper publisher as a boy, Greeley first worked as an editor in 1834, when he joined the staff of the New York–based literary magazine the *New Yorker.* This job led to work as a political writer for the Whig Party in 1838 and 1840. It also led to a close relationship between Greeley and New York governor William H. Seward, who later became President Abraham Lincoln's secretary of state.

In 1841 Greeley established his own newspaper, the *New York Tribune,* which espoused Whig views. As such, it promoted a variety of social reforms, including abolition, although it opposed giving women the vote. Greeley saw to it that his paper's articles reflected sound reporting and disdain for sensationalism. As a result, by the 1850s the *Tribune* was widely respected and had the largest circulation of any newspaper in the United States.

By this point Greeley had become disenchanted with the Whigs because he did not believe that they opposed slavery strongly enough. Therefore he switched his support to the newly formed Republican Party. Greeley's editorials during this period opposed every attempt by the U.S. government to strike a compromise on the slavery issue, such as the Kansas-Nebraska Act, and he particularly opposed laws that supported the returning of runaway slaves to their masters. After the Civil War began, he argued in favor of the immediate emancipation of all slaves, and once the war was over and emancipation had been achieved, he became an outspoken advocate of civil rights.

By 1872, however, he had become so dissatisfied with the Republican Party—largely because of corruption in the administration of President Ulysses S. Grant—that he helped create a new political party, the Liberal Republican Party, and was immediately selected as its candidate for U.S. president. After a brutal campaign during which he suffered numerous attacks on his character, he received 40 percent of the popular vote and eighty-six electoral votes, which went to four other candidates when he died suddenly before the electoral college could meet. **See also** Kansas-Nebraska Act; political parties.

Greenhow, Rose O'Neal ("Wild Rose") (1815?–1864)

Rose O'Neal Greenhow, nicknamed "Wild Rose," was a Washington, D.C., socialite who spied for the Confederacy. She also led a vast ring of Confederate espionage agents under the supervision of Confederate general P.G.T. Beauregard's adjutant general, Colonel Thomas Jordan. Jordan had recruited Greenhow, an ardent secessionist, to spy for the South even before the war officially began.

Making Greenhow particularly valuable was the fact that, as the widow of a U.S. State Department official, she had many prominent friends in the U.S. government. In fact, she was acquainted with two U.S. presidents, James Buchanan and Abraham Lincoln. Members of her spy ring also included many prominent government officials, including members of the War Department, Navy Department, Provost Marshal's Office (ironically, a government agency that tried to catch spies), Adjutant General's Office, and Military Affairs Committee. In addition, Greenhow gleaned information from conversations with unwitting politicians and military officers who succumbed to her charms.

Because of her connections, Greenhow had many successes as a spy. Her greatest success, however, was related to the First Battle of Bull Run in July 1861. Just prior to this conflict, she found out that the Union had thirty-five thousand soldiers in Washington, D.C., and another eighteen thousand in Harpers Ferry, whereas the Confederacy had only twenty-two thousand men nearby to combat them. She relayed this information, written in code, to General Beauregard via a courier, and he in turn passed it on to Confederate president Jefferson Davis. On the basis of Greenhow's message, Davis then sent additional troops, commanded by General Joseph E. Johnston, to support Beauregard, resulting in a Confederate victory.

Rose O'Neal Greenhow poses with her daughter at the Old Capitol Prison in Washington, D.C.

By August 1861, however, the head of a Union spy network, Allan Pinkerton, had started to suspect that Greenhow was a Confederate agent. He had noticed mysterious men, some of them suspected spies, visiting Greenhow's home at night, and on one occasion he saw her receiving a packet of letters from one of them. Consequently, Pinkerton arrested Greenhow on August 23. However, he allowed her to remain in her home, which proved to be a serious mistake. In the first hours after her arrest, she destroyed all evidence of her espionage activity. Later, she sent her twelve-year-old daughter to warn certain members of her spy network of her capture. She also continued to receive visitors from among her most upstanding Union friends. Since many of these individuals were also actually Confederate agents, she was able to use them to pass along information she had obtained from her Union guards. She also transmitted information by placing coded messages inside her daughter's toy rubber balls, which she then bounced out of a window to a waiting Confederate agent.

In January 1862, Greenhow was transferred to Old Capitol Prison along with her daughter Rose. While there, she continued to receive visitors who were actually spies and pass messages via rubber balls. In June 1862, she and her daughter were released from prison in a prisoner exchange with the South, with the proviso that they were to leave the North and not return until the end of the war.

Greenhow then went to Richmond, Virginia, where she was hailed as a Southern hero. The following year, in August 1863, President Davis sent her to England and France on an informal diplomatic mission to garner support abroad for the Confederate cause. She remained there for a year, during which she wrote a memoir, *My Imprisonment and the First Year of Abolition*

Rule at Washington, that was published in London, England, in late 1863.

In September 1864, Greenhow embarked for home on the British steamship *Condor,* hoping to get through a Northern blockade of Southern ports. Off the coast of North Carolina on October 1, the *Condor* was forced to run aground by a Union warship. When Greenhow attempted to reach shore in a rowboat, it capsized and she drowned. She was buried the following day in Wilmington, North Carolina, with military honors. **See also** Beauregard, Pierre Gustave Toutant; Pinkerton, Allan; spies; women, contributions of.

grenades and rockets

Both sides in the Civil War employed grenades and rockets as a way to kill enemy troops. Rockets, most commonly used by sailors engaged in close ship-to-ship combat, were less than a foot long and fired from a long metal tube angled into the air. Grenades were tossed by hand, generally by soldiers in trenches. Some rockets and grenades had a plunger-and-detonator mechanism that caused them to explode when the plunger hit the ground; others had fuses that were lit before they were fired or thrown. **See also** ammunition.

guerrillas, partisan rangers, and irregulars

Guerrillas were members of bands that typically operated as unofficial military units both before and during the Civil War. Prior to the war, Kansas was the primary site of guerrilla attacks because of conflicts between pro- and antislavery forces there over whether the state would support slavery when it joined the Union. In fact, so many Kansas citizens were murdered by bands of guerrillas (variously called border ruffians, bushwackers, or jayhawkers) that during the late 1850s the state became known as Bleeding Kansas. During the Civil War, however, guerrilla attacks occurred in many other places as well, including Tennessee, Kentucky, Arkansas, and Louisiana, with the number of such attacks increasing after the Confederacy passed the Partisan Ranger Act on April 21, 1862.

The Partisan Ranger Act gave the Confederate president the authority to commission officers for the purpose of establishing regiments that used unconventional tactics (i.e., other than direct battlefield confrontations) to attack Union troops and raid Union supplies. Under this law, guerrillas became commissioned Confederate officers by registering with the Confederate government, whereby they were called partisan rangers or irregulars (for their use of irregular tactics), as were the members of their bands. The Northern guerrillas were also called irregulars, but the Union had few such soldiers because the U.S. government never passed a law giving official sanction to their activities.

Because guerrilla warfare relied on hit-and-run tactics and ignored concerns regarding how prisoners should be treated, it attracted men who had little patience with military rules and discipline. As a result, clashes with guerrillas were usually violent and bloody and often resulted in the death of innocent civilians and unarmed soldiers. Two guerrilla commanders operating near the Missouri-Kansas border both before and during the war were particularly notorious for their viciousness: William Quantrill and William Anderson, the latter of whom earned the nickname "Bloody Bill" because he often mutilated his victims' bodies.

By the summer of 1862, such activities prompted the Union to develop an official policy for dealing with guerrillas that depended on their government status. Guerrillas whose bands had been formed under the Partisan Ranger Act and truly represented the Confederate army, though using irregular tactics, would be treated as military prisoners when caught. Those whose activities were not officially sanctioned by the Confederate government—which included many of the most violent Confederate guerrillas—would be treated as unredeemable outlaws and executed immediately upon being caught.

However, this policy was not an effective deterrent, given that the Union rarely captured either kind of Confederate guerrilla. Such men were highly skilled at inflicting serious damage without getting caught, largely because of the efforts of civilians sympathetic to their cause. Consequently in the summer of 1863, after a particularly brutal guerrilla attack in Kansas in which 150 defenseless citizens were killed, Union general Thomas Ewing Jr. issued an order decreeing that everyone except for military personnel had to leave those parts of Missouri where Confederate guerrillas like Anderson and Quantrill were known to hide. This evacuation did decrease guerrilla activity in Kansas, but did not directly lead to the death of any important Confederate guerrillas. (Union forces did not kill Anderson until October 1864, Quantrill until June 1865.) Moreover, the Union could not use such an approach on guerrillas operating in other places because, outside of the Missouri border region, their sympathizers were not just difficult to identify but widely scattered. **See also** bushwackers; Ewing, Thomas, Jr.; jayhawkers; Kansas; Missouri.

gunpowder

At the war's onset, the Union had far more mills where gunpowder was made than did the Confederacy. The Confederacy therefore placed a priority on building gunpowder mills and obtaining the raw materials—sulfur, charcoal, and saltpeter (potassium nitrate)—necessary to make gunpowder. All three of these materials were available in both the North and the South, but both sides, particularly the South, had to import saltpeter in order to have enough for gunpowder manufacturing. Because of the Northern blockade on Southern ports, however, the Confederacy was chronically short of saltpeter and therefore gunpowder as well. This shortage affected the Confederates' battlefield tactics, as generals struggled to decide where best to use the little gunpowder they had, and in some cases it also led to an increase in battlefield errors and accidents, because Confederate soldiers could not afford to practice with live ammunition as much as Union soldiers did. **See also** ammunition; industry and technology.

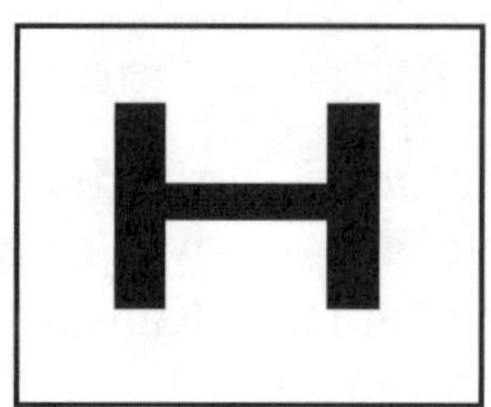

habeas corpus

Under the U.S. Constitution, all criminal defendants are entitled to demand a writ of habeas corpus, a legal document that requires prosecutors to either charge a suspect with a crime or release the accused. However, the U.S. Constitution allows suspension of this privilege "when in cases of rebellion or invasion the public safety may require it." When the writ of habeas corpus is suspended, a person can be held in custody indefinitely.

On April 27, 1861, U.S. president Abraham Lincoln suspended the writ of habeas corpus from Philadelphia to Washington, D.C.—a region that included the state of Maryland—in response to rioting by Confederate sympathizers in Baltimore, Maryland, eight days earlier. Federal authorities were therefore able to lock up many of the city's citizens, including the mayor, without charging them with a crime. They also arrested John Merryman just outside of Baltimore for trying to destroy the rail line that connected Baltimore with Washington, D.C.

Merryman's arrest set up a confrontation between Lincoln and Supreme Court chief justice Roger Taney, who issued a writ of habeas corpus to secure Merryman's release on the grounds that only Congress, not the president, had the power to suspend the writ of habeas corpus. The other Supreme Court justices, however, sided with Lincoln, and the military officers holding Merryman at Fort McHenry refused to comply with Taney's writ. Therefore Merryman remained in jail (although he was released some weeks later without being charged), and Lincoln's suspension of the writ of habeas corpus stood. Moreover, in March 1863 Congress passed the Habeas Corpus Act, which stipulated that the president did have the authority to suspend habeas corpus (though after the war the U.S. Supreme Court limited the circumstances under which the president would be allowed to take this action). By the end of the war, approximately eighteen thousand civilians had been imprisoned without being charged with a crime.

In 1861 Confederate president Jefferson Davis severely criticized Lincoln for suspending the writ of habeas corpus, but later he tried to convince the Confederate Congress to grant him the same power. The Confederate Congress several times gave Davis limited power in this regard, but each time public outrage forced the lawmakers to rescind the authority. However, the Confederate Congress did allow agents of the War Department to detain treasonous citizens with the idea that these people would eventually be taken before a judge. By delaying court appearances for such prisoners, the Confederacy effectively suspended the writ of habeas corpus without formally doing so. **See also** Baltimore, Maryland; conscription.

Halleck, Henry Wager (1815–1872)

From 1862 to 1864, Union general Henry W. Halleck served as the general in chief of all Union armies. At the outset of the war he was considered an expert on military strategy, having lectured on the subject while a U.S. Army engineer during the 1840s and having authored a book, *Elements of Military Art and Science* (1846), that was subsequently used as a textbook at the U.S. Military Academy. However, by the time the war was over, many people were criticizing Halleck for "sticking to the book," or not being more flexible in his approach to battlefield tactics.

A veteran of the Mexican-American War (1846–1848), during which he served as secretary of state under California's military government, Halleck was a civilian lawyer when the Civil War broke out. After he reenlisted in the army as a major general, Halleck was placed in charge of the western theater. He immediately proved to be a skilled administrator who excelled in organizing volunteer armies, but his battlefield skills were so weak that he had to rely on subordinates, such as General Ulysses S. Grant, to make decisions in combat. When these men were successful, Halleck received the credit; when Halleck made a mistake, he blamed someone else. This strategy allowed him to gain command of all Union armies in 1862, even though he was not up to the job. As general in chief, Halleck had difficulty developing an effective military strategy for the war as a whole, and he quarreled with subordinates and with Secretary of War Edwin M. Stanton. As a result, in March 1864 he was relieved of his command and replaced by General Ulysses S. Grant. Halleck was then sent to Washington, D.C., to serve as chief of staff, an administrative position. **See also** Grant, Ulysses S.

Hamlin, Hannibal (1809–1891)

Hannibal Hamlin was the vice president of the United States from March 4, 1861, to March 4, 1865, under President Abraham Lincoln. Lincoln chose him as a running mate because he had a lot of experience with political campaigns, having already served as the governor of Maine and as a U.S. senator. However, Hamlin and Lincoln soon parted ways over the slavery issue; Hamlin believed that Lincoln should move more quickly to emancipate slaves not just in the Confederacy but in the still-loyal slave states. As a result of this disagreement, when Lincoln ran for reelection in 1864, the president chose Andrew Johnson, who was far more moderate on the slavery issue, as his running mate. **See also** Johnson, Andrew; Lincoln, Abraham.

Hampton, Wade (1818–1902)

South Carolina aristocrat Wade Hampton was an influential Southern politician both before and after the Civil War, and during the war he became a Southern hero through his exploits as a Confederate cavalry commander. Hampton was also one of only three men without professional military training to achieve the rank of lieutenant general in the Confederacy.

The son of a wealthy planter who owned many slaves, Hampton managed his family's lands in both South Carolina and Mississippi while serving first in the South Carolina House of Representatives and then in the state senate during the 1850s. Although he initially argued in favor of remaining with the Union, by 1859 Hampton had decided that the federal government was making it nearly impossible for the South to avoid secession. In 1861 he resigned from public office to volunteer as an ordinary Confederate soldier, but the governor of South Carolina, Francis W. Pickens, convinced Hampton instead to use his vast wealth and political connections to create his own private army, Hampton's Legion. There were only ten legions in the Confederacy (largely because the Confederacy soon banned their creation, uncomfortable with the idea of having a large number of independent armies). Of these ten, Hampton's Legion was the best trained and best equipped, primarily thanks to Hampton's enormous financial resources. This legion was also among the largest; within weeks of asking for volunteers, Hampton had approximately six hundred men, enough to create six infantry units, four cavalry units, and an artillery unit with six new guns. Many of these men came from the most socially prominent families in South Carolina. Therefore the legion traveled with dozens of slaves who tended to soldiers' personal needs.

Hampton commanded his legion himself, initially as a colonel with no military experience. Due to his own lack of training, in the legion's first battle, the First Battle of Bull Run, Hampton was wounded and his second-in-command and most experienced officer, Colonel Benjamin J. Johnson, was killed, along with 120 soldiers. In 1862 Hampton's Legion was placed under the command of James Longstreet, although Hampton became its brigadier general, and by the end of the year the legion as a distinct unit ceased to exist. Hampton fought in several more battles, and after a brief period of recuperation from a wound suffered during the Battle of Seven Pines (May 1862) he was made senior brigadier in General J.E.B. Stuart's cavalry corps. In this capacity, he fought in several major battles, becoming known for his courage and skill as a cavalry commander.

In 1863, after being wounded in the Battle of Gettysburg, Hampton was promoted to major general, second-in-command under Stuart. Consequently, when Stuart was killed in the Wilderness Campaign in May 1864, Hampton took over as commander of the Confederate cavalry. One of his most famous accomplishments in this capacity occurred during the Petersburg Campaign. On September 16, 1864, while the Confederates were under siege in the city of Petersburg, Virginia, Hampton managed to raid Union encampments and take twenty-five hundred head of cattle, thereby providing the Confederacy with much-needed food. Four months later Hampton was promoted to lieutenant general.

In the closing days of the war, Hampton refused to surrender until Generals Robert E. Lee and Joseph E. Johnston had done so. By this time the conflict had become personal for him. One of his sons and his brother had been killed during the war, and another of his sons had been wounded. Moreover, the war had seriously drained his financial resources.

Long after the war ended, Hampton worked to restore and maintain white supremacy. In 1876 he ran for governor of South Carolina as a Democrat and won, largely thanks to his supporters' success in keeping blacks from voting. Hampton was reelected governor in 1878, but he left office in 1879 after being elected a U.S. senator; he served in the Senate until 1891. **See also** Petersburg Campaign; Reconstruction; Stuart, James Ewell Brown.

Hampton Roads

A Virginia waterway connecting the James and Elizabeth Rivers with Chesapeake Bay, Hampton Roads was the site of two important Civil War events, an 1862 naval battle and an 1865 peace conference. Neither of these events affected the course of the war; the battle ended in a draw, and the peace conference did not end the fighting.

The Battle of Hampton Roads was the Confederacy's attempt to break a Union blockade consisting of six wooden warships anchored in Hampton Roads, including the USS *Cumberland,* the USS *Congress,* and the USS *Minnesota.* To this end, the ironclad CSS *Virginia* (formerly the USS *Merrimack,* which had been captured and reconditioned) traveled from nearby Norfolk, Virginia, to Hampton Roads, and on the afternoon of March 8, 1862, the *Virginia*'s commander, Admiral Franklin Buchanan, launched an attack. His ship succeeded in ramming and sinking the

The Confederate navy sinks the USS Cumberland *during the Battle of Hampton Roads.*

Cumberland, after which Buchanan fired on the *Congress* until it caught fire and ran aground. Buchanan then turned his attention to the *Minnesota,* but decided to hold off his attack on this ship until the next morning. This proved to be a bad decision, because during the night the Union sent its own ironclad, the USS *Monitor,* into Hampton Roads, and shortly after dawn the two ironclads began to battle each other. Neither one was able to get into a position to ram the other, and each ironclad's shots failed to have any effect on the other because their hulls were so well protected. After about two hours of fighting, Buchanan noticed that the tide was starting to go out, so he ordered the *Virginia* back to Norfolk to avoid getting trapped in Hampton Roads, and the Confederacy abandoned its plan to break the blockade.

The Hampton Roads Conference took place roughly three years later, on February 3, 1865. Held aboard the U.S. steamship *River Queen,* this four-hour meeting between Federal and Confederate representatives included U.S. president Abraham Lincoln, U.S. secretary of state William H. Seward, Confederate vice president Alexander H. Stephens, Confederate senator Robert M.T. Hunter, and Confederate assistant secretary of war John A. Campbell. Both sides were there at the request of Missouri politician Francis P. Blair, who wanted America to unite against what he saw as a threat from the French, who had forces in Mexico. The conference quickly broke down over Lincoln's insistence that the South rejoin the Union and end slavery. The South was unwilling to accede to either demand, and in the end the two sides walked away without a treaty. **See also** Blair, Francis Preston; ironclads; *Merrimack,* USS/*Virginia,* CSS.

Hancock, Winfield Scott (1824–1886)

A veteran of the Mexican-American and Seminole Wars and a participant in U.S. military actions to protect Kansas settlers right before the Civil War, Union general Winfield S. Hancock was a highly successful and well-respected commander. In 1861 he was promoted to the rank of brigadier general in the volunteer army, and in this capacity he assisted General George McClellan in organizing the Army of the Potomac. The following year Hancock fought in the Peninsula Campaign, the Battle of Antietam, and the Battle of Fredericksburg, and in May 1863 he fought in the Battle of Chancellorsville and was made commander of the Second Corps, Army of the Potomac. While leading this corps in the Battle of Gettysburg (July 1863), Hancock was wounded in the thigh during the Southern attack known as Pickett's Charge. Nonetheless, Hancock subsequently commanded the Second Corps in the Wilderness Campaign and the Battle of Spotsylvania (May 1864) that immediately followed it. His men performed well in the campaign but suffered so many losses that some of them refused to participate in the August 1864 Battle of Ream's Station near Petersburg, Virginia, and the Second Corps was defeated there.

After the war, from 1866 to 1868, Hancock was given a series of administrative positions in the army as a major general, including control of the department overseeing Reconstruction in Louisiana and Texas. Although many Republican politicians of this period wanted the military to take a strong hand in managing such regions, Hancock insisted that civilians be allowed to resume their prewar level of authority. This position appealed to Democrats, who nominated Hancock for U.S. president in 1880. He lost by a narrow margin to James Garfield and afterward returned to his military duties. **See also** armies, Union; Garfield, James Abram; Pickett's Charge.

Hardee, William Joseph (1815–1873)

William J. Hardee was one of the Confederacy's most respected generals. In fact, his military knowledge was even respected in the North, because he had once trained cadets at the U.S. Military Academy and his 1855 book *Rifle and Light Infantry Tactics* was a training manual for the U.S. Army. Once the war began, this book was a guide for both Union and Confederate infantrymen.

A Georgia native, Hardee served in the U.S. Army until January 1861, when he resigned his commission to take command of Confederate troops in Arkansas. His Arkansas brigade, which became known as Hardee's Brigade, fought at the Battles of Shiloh (April 1862), Perryville (October 1862), Stones River (December 1862–January 1863), and Chattanooga (November 1863). During this time Hardee was promoted from major general to lieutenant general.

In May and September 1864, Hardee commanded his troops in several battles leading up to Union general William T. Sherman's capture of Atlanta, Georgia. Despite this failure, Hardee was subsequently given command of the military department of South Carolina, Georgia, and Florida, with his main focus being to stop Sherman's progression from Atlanta across Georgia to the sea. Unsuccessful in this venture, Hardee combined his troops with those of Confederate general Joseph E. Johnston. The war ended shortly thereafter, and Hardee settled on a plantation near Selma, Alabama. **See also** Johnston, Joseph Eggleston; Sherman, William Tecumseh.

Harpers Ferry

In 1859, a federal arsenal at Harpers Ferry, Virginia, became the site of an incident that inflamed passions on both sides of the slavery issue. On October 16 of that year, a group of twenty-two radical abolitionists, under the leadership of John Brown, seized the arsenal in order to arm themselves as part of a plan to start a slave rebellion in the area. In response, U.S. government troops attacked the arsenal in an attempt to capture Brown's gang. Ten of his men were killed in the process, but Brown was eventually taken prisoner. He was then tried for inciting insurrection, committing treason against the state of Virginia, and murder. Found guilty on all counts, Brown was executed by hanging on December 2, 1859. Thereafter, many Northerners viewed Brown as a martyr, while Southerners reviled him as a symbol of antislavery violence.

Brown's surviving followers were executed in January 1860. A year later, the federal arsenal at Harpers Ferry was abandoned to the Confederates shortly after the first shot of the Civil War was fired. The Confederates then dismantled the arsenal's weapons-producing machinery and sent it South to be put to work for the Confederate war effort. **See also** Brown, John; Virginia.

Harrison, Henry Thomas (ca. 1823–1913)

Tennessee native Henry T. Harrison was a Confederate spy and scout who successfully adopted a Northern accent and used disguises to gather information while among enemy troops. He began serving the Confederacy in 1861 as a scout in northern Virginia, then scouted in Mississippi in 1862. The following year he was assigned to work as a spy for General James Longstreet, who subsequently ordered him to spy for General D.H. Hill in North Carolina. While there he was captured as a suspected spy by a Union patrol, but was released after convincing the soldiers that he was a Northern sympathizer. Longstreet then sent Harrison to Washington, D.C., to learn about Union troop strength and movements in Maryland and Pennsylvania—information that later proved vital to the Confederates in preparation for the Battle of Gettysburg.

Harrison's subsequent contributions to the Confederate war effort are unknown, although he was spotted in New York City just before the war's end. According to some reports, by this time he had been relieved of his position because of drunkenness. However, this was most likely a story that had been invented to convince the enemy that Harrison was no longer a spy.

Harrison's activities after the war are equally mysterious. On April 7, 1866, he mailed a letter to his wife from Baltimore, Maryland, saying that he was going to be going on a long journey and might never come back. In 1867 she heard that he was in Montana Territory. No further word came of his whereabouts, and eventually she assumed that he had died out West. Thirty-four years later, in November 1900, he suddenly resurfaced, but by then his wife had remarried. Harrison left again, this time for Cincinnati, Ohio. The following year he let it be known that he was going to San Francisco, California, and was never seen again. **See also** Longstreet, James; spies.

Hayes, Rutherford Birchard (1822–1893)

Rutherford B. Hayes was president of the United States from 1877 to 1881, a time when Reconstruction was coming to an end. During this period he removed U.S. troops from occupied areas, allowed the South to wholly manage its own elections, permitted former Confederates to hold prominent positions in the U.S. government, and provided financial support to rebuild infrastructure that had been damaged in the war. Many of these actions were criticized, particularly by Hayes's fellow Republicans, for being too lenient on the South.

Prior to the Civil War, however, Hayes had often been at odds with Southerners as an Ohio lawyer who defended fugitive slaves and those who aided them. When the war broke out, Hayes volunteered to fight for the Union and served in combat. After the war he was elected to one term in Congress, then elected governor of Ohio.

In 1876 Governor Hayes ran for president as the Republican candidate against the Democrats' Samuel J. Tilden, the governor of New York. Tilden won the popular vote and might have won the electoral college as well had it not been for suspected ballot corruption in South Carolina, Florida, and Louisiana. As a result of voting irregularities, these Republican-led states decided to allow an election board to determine which candidate would win their electoral votes, and all three boards supported Hayes. Democrats immediately protested this Republican victory, and a supposedly national electoral committee consisting of fifteen members of Congress and the Supreme Court was called on to settle the dispute. In theory this committee was bipartisan, but Republicans held the majority, and they declared Hayes president.

This disputed election was significant to the South because, in the process of trying to reach a compromise prior to the national committee's decision, Hayes secretly promised some Southern politicians that if declared the winner he would end Reconstruction. When he followed through on this promise, so many of his Republican supporters complained that Hayes decided not to seek reelection when his term as president was up. After he returned to private life, he devoted himself to causes related to improving the lives of Southern blacks, particularly young people, and prisoners. **See also** Reconstruction.

Hill, Ambrose Powell (1825–1865)

Confederate general Ambrose P. Hill (most commonly known as A.P. or "Little Powell" Hill) is widely considered to be one of the best commanders of the Civil War, though also one of the most contrary. The division he led for much of the war, the Light Division, was among the most effective fighting units of the South.

The son of aristocratic Virginia landowners, Hill served in the U.S. Army as an artillery lieutenant and surveyor prior to the Civil War. He then entered the Confederate army as a colonel and was given command of a regiment in northern Virginia. In February 1862, though he had not yet fought in a battle, Hill was promoted to the rank of brigadier general, and less than three months later he participated in a Confederate attack at Williamsburg, Virginia, that was part of the Peninsula Campaign. Hill so distinguished himself there that he was promoted to major general and given command of the largest division of the Confederate armies, the six-brigade Light Division.

Hill commanded this division in the Seven Days' Battles (June–July 1862) at Mechanicsville, Gaines's Mill, and Frayser's Farm, each a defeat for the Confederacy. At Mechanicsville, Hill made the mistake of attacking the Union's right flank without waiting for the prearranged moment to do so, and a few days later he was arrested for not following orders. Because he had performed well on the battlefield, however, his superiors soon released him and placed him under the supervision of General "Stonewall" Jackson.

Hill had difficulty getting along with Jackson; the two often argued, particularly over the fact that Hill did not insist that his troops march as quickly or as formally as Jackson wanted. After one of these disputes, Jackson had Hill arrested for disobeying orders, but once again Hill was soon released. This time, however, the Confederate leadership kept the case open while they decided what to do about the charges against Hill. (The matter was finally dropped in 1863, when Jackson died of wounds received in a friendly fire incident at the Battle of Chancellorsville.) Yet Hill continued to reject formal military rules by wearing a red calico shirt rather than the shirt and jacket of a Confederate officer.

Meanwhile, even as he was quarreling with Jackson, Hill distinguished himself in battle after battle. At the Second Battle of Bull Run in August 1862, he was instrumental in fending off several Federal attacks, and he helped recapture Harpers Ferry in September 1862. He also participated in the Battles of Antietam (September 1862), Fredericksburg (December 1862), and Chancellorsville (May 1863), where he suffered minor wounds. Shortly thereafter, he was promoted to lieutenant general and given command of a new fighting unit, the Third Corps, under General Robert E. Lee. As the leader of this corps, Hill fought at the Battle of Gettysburg (July 1863), but he performed poorly due to an illness that continued to plague him in subsequent battles. Even so, he managed to hold off a Union siege at Petersburg, Virginia, for nearly a year, from June 1864 through March 1865. On April 2, 1865, Hill was shot and killed in a battle at the end of the Petersburg Campaign. **See also** Jackson, Thomas Jonathan; Lee, Robert Edward; Petersburg Campaign.

Hill, Daniel Harvey (1821–1889)

Confederate general Daniel H. Hill was known for his bravery—which bordered on recklessness—and his broad knowledge of military tactics. However, he was also notorious for being opinionated and having a tendency to insult people, which often made him difficult to deal with. Consequently, unlike his brother-in-law, "Stonewall" Jackson, he was not given the most prestigious commands.

A graduate of West Point (1847) and a veteran of the Mexican-American War (1846–1848), Hill taught college-level mathematics prior to the Civil War and wrote textbooks on the subject. In 1861 he joined the Confederacy in North Carolina and created the first training camp for its soldiers. Then a colonel, he was placed in charge of defending Yorktown, Virginia, but in September 1861 he was promoted to brigadier general and transferred to serve under Joseph E. Johnston. In this capacity, Hill led troops at the Battle of Seven Pines, the Second Battle of Bull Run, and the Battles of Antietam and Chickamauga. At Antietam he continued to fight even after his horse was shot out from under him, and at Chickamauga he made decisions that resulted in the capture of five thousand Union soldiers. After Chickamauga, however, Hill demanded that President Jefferson Davis remove Braxton Bragg, who had been in charge of all Confederate forces at the battle, from combat, saying that Bragg was not skilled enough to make command decisions. Instead, Davis relieved Hill from his battlefield duties and sent him to serve on the staff of General Pierre Beauregard. After other staff assignments, Hill returned to battle as the commander of the Army of Tennessee shortly before the end of the war, when this army was greatly reduced in size. **See also** Bragg, Braxton; Jackson, Thomas Jonathan.

Holmes, Oliver Wendell, Jr. (1841–1935)

Although best known for his later service as a Supreme Court justice, Oliver Wendell Holmes Jr. fought for the Union during the

Civil War. The diary he kept and the letters he wrote during this time in the army are notable for the vividness of their accounts of his war experiences. While serving as a captain with a unit fighting Confederate general Jubal Early's raiding forces just five miles from the U.S. White House, Holmes became famous after he noticed a civilian in a tall hat who kept peeking over the defensive fortifications and shouted, "Get down, you damn fool, before you get shot!" The man he had admonished, he later learned, was U.S. president Abraham Lincoln.

Holmes had enlisted as a private in the Fourth Battalion Infantry at the outset of the war, training at Boston's Fort Independence. However, he did not see battle until after he received a commission as first lieutenant in the Twentieth Massachusetts Volunteer Regiment in July 1861. He then fought in the Battles of Ball's Bluff, Antietam, and Chancellorsville, becoming a brevet (temporary) lieutenant colonel before leaving the army in 1864 with the rank of captain. During this period, he was wounded three times. After one of these injuries, his whereabouts were unknown for a time, and his father went looking for him. After Holmes Sr.'s account of this search, "My Hunt After 'The Captain,'" appeared in the November 1862 issue of *Atlantic Monthly* magazine, Holmes Jr.'s experiences in the war became popular knowledge. **See also** Early, Jubal A.; letters and diaries; Lincoln, Abraham.

Supreme Court justice Oliver Wendell Holmes Jr. earned the rank of captain while serving in the Union army.

Homer, Winslow (1836–1910)

Noted American artist Winslow Homer was employed in 1861 by the magazine *Harper's Weekly* to work as a war correspondent, submitting sketches that would be published as engravings in various editions. Homer primarily focused on scenes of camp life while following Union general George McClellan during the Peninsula Campaign and General Ulysses S. Grant during the Wilderness Campaign. However, he also sketched scenes from President Abraham Lincoln's 1861 inauguration. *Harper's* reproduced Homer's work in twenty-four engravings, and in 1866 his original sketches were displayed in an exhibition called "Prisoners from the Front" at the National Academy of Design. One of the most famous of these works is "The Surgeon at Work at the Rear During an Engagement," notable because it was rare for Civil War artists to depict physicians. **See also** artists and artwork.

homesteading

Homesteading was the practice by which settlers claimed ownership of government-controlled land by fulfilling various conditions, such as living on the selected parcel for a number of years and building a home on the land. Southerners opposed homesteading and worked to defeat legislation that would have encouraged the practice because they believed that most homesteading settlers would be abolitionists. This belief was strengthened when, in 1848, the abolitionist Free-Soil Party promoted a homesteading act that would have given a free plot of land to every man, white or black, who wanted one. After this, Southern slaveholders feared that homesteading would increase the number of antislavery votes in territories due to decide whether or not they would be admitted into the Union as free or slave states. As a result of such fears, pro-slavery guerrillas sometimes inflicted violence against homesteaders, and of the various homesteading bills introduced in Congress, none was able to pass into law until the South seceded from the Union.

As soon as the Homestead Act of 1862 went into effect on January 1, 1863, it began to benefit the Union war effort by putting more land into the hands of farmers, who then planted crops that ultimately helped boost the Union's food supply. Under the act, any U.S. citizen (or person whose citizenship was pending) who was the head of a household or over the age of twenty-one could apply to receive 160 acres of land, with title to the land to be given over once the applicant lived there for five years while making improvements to the property. A year after the act was put into effect, over 1 million acres of land west of the Mississippi River had been claimed by various individuals. **See also** guerrillas, partisan rangers, and irregulars; political parties.

Hood, John Bell (1831–1879)

Confederate general John Bell Hood held a variety of command positions during the Civil War, distinguishing himself as one of the fiercest fighters on the battlefield. One of these positions, in 1862, was as the commander of a military unit subsequently known as Hood's Texas Brigade, which was among the most active and courageous of the war, fighting in a total of thirty-eight battles despite many casualties. However, while Hood proved an able leader of brigades and divisions, as he moved up in responsibility to command larger forces he suffered many defeats due to poor decisions on the battlefield. This was perhaps understandable given that he had graduated from the U.S. Military Academy in 1843 near the bottom of his class.

Prior to the Civil War, Hood served as a brevet (temporary) second lieutenant in the Fourth U.S. Infantry, then a second lieutenant in the Second U.S. Cavalry in Texas, where he engaged in several battles with Indians. He resigned from the army and volunteered to fight for the Confederacy when Texas seceded from the Union. His initial rank in the Confederate army was captain, but shortly thereafter he was promoted to major and given command of the Fourth Texas Infantry (which was part of what later became known as Hood's Texas Brigade, along with thirty-one other volunteer infantry companies). Hood quickly rose to lead a division of General James Longstreet's First Corps of the Army of Northern Virginia. During 1862 Hood was promoted several more times, from major to brigadier general to major general, and within a year he was a lieutenant general. In July 1864 he became a full general.

As part of the Army of Northern Virginia, Hood fought in many major battles, including the Seven Days' Battles, the First and Second Battle of Bull Run, the

Battle of Antietam, and the Battle of Fredericksburg. He was seriously wounded in the left arm at the Battle of Gettysburg in July 1863, and at the Battle of Chickamauga in September 1863 he lost a leg. By the time his leg was injured, he had been transferred to the Army of Tennessee under General Braxton Bragg. Hood and Bragg did not get along, and largely because of Hood's complaints to his superiors, Bragg was eventually replaced by General Joseph E. Johnston. However, Hood continued to have problems with his commanding officer, because Johnston knew of Hood's role in Bragg's ouster and therefore disliked him. In response, Hood began to criticize Johnston to his superiors as well.

In July 1864 Confederate president Jefferson Davis removed Johnston as commander of the Army of Tennessee and put Hood in his place. This assignment, however, soon revealed Hood's inadequacies as a commander. For example, when charged with preventing Union general William T. Sherman from taking Atlanta, Georgia, Hood made a series of mistakes that weakened his army, attacking Sherman in several locations around the city without careful planning. As a result, he lost many of his men and, after five weeks of fighting, he lost Atlanta itself. Hood then suffered two more major defeats, the first in Franklin, Tennessee, in November 1864 and the second in Nashville, Tennessee, the following month. As he retreated from Nashville, Hood was pursued by Union general George H. Thomas, whose Army of the Cumberland obliterated most of Hood's Army of Tennessee. The next month Hood asked to be relieved of his command, and he never again commanded an army. However, he served the Confederacy in various other ways before surrendering in Natchez, Mississippi, in May 1865. After the war, Hood became a New Orleans businessman and wrote his memoirs under the title *Advance and Retreat*. They were published shortly after Hood died of yellow fever in 1879. **See also** armies, Confederate; Atlanta Campaign; Bragg, Braxton; Franklin and Nashville Campaign; Johnston, Joseph Eggleston.

Hooker, Joseph (1814–1879)

Also known as "Fighting Joe" for his courage under fire, Union general Joseph Hooker is notorious for leading the Army of the Potomac to a crushing defeat at the Battle of Chancellorsville in May 1863 despite the fact that he commanded more than twice as many soldiers (about 130,000) as his Confederate opposition. After this defeat, which resulted in the death of over 17,000 Union soldiers, Hooker asked to be relieved of his command. The U.S. Army immediately granted this request, although later Hooker did participate in other battles.

Prior to this incident, Hooker had a distinguished military career. Though a civilian in California when the Civil War broke out, he was given the rank of brigadier general in the volunteer Union army because of prior military experience in the Mexican-American War (1846–1848). Hooker participated in several eastern campaigns, and after being commended for his bravery during the Peninsula Campaign of 1862 he was made a brigadier general in the Regular Army and placed in charge of the First Corps of the Army of the Potomac. Hooker was then seriously wounded at the Battle of Antietam (September 1862), and after his recovery he was named the commander of the Army of the Potomac.

At the time Hooker took this command, in early 1863, the Army of the Potomac had recently experienced a serious defeat at the Battle of Fredericksburg (December 1862) under the command of General Ambrose Burnside. Hooker believed that this defeat had largely been due to organizational problems, so he immediately instituted a variety of reforms in how the army was managed. He also established his own network of spies under a new agency, the Bureau of Military Information, because he felt that the Union needed to receive more intelligence. Consequently, when he encountered the Confederacy at the Battle of Chancellorsville, Hooker was confident that his army would prevail. However, he made several mistakes during the battle, such as misperceiving the size and location of Confederate troops and leaving his left flank open to attack; the result was a surprising Union defeat that ended with Hooker's forces in retreat.

A month after the battle, Hooker pursued the enemy's forces, led by General Robert E. Lee, into Pennsylvania. During this pursuit he requested additional troops, but his superior officers refused to send them. Now certain that the leaders of the War Department had lost all confidence in his command abilities, he resigned as the leader of the Army of the Potomac the night before the Battle of Gettysburg in July 1863, whereupon General George Meade took over the post.

Three months later Hooker was assigned the task of commanding two corps of the Army of the Potomac while they were being sent by rail to relieve the forces of General William S. Rosecrans, who was under siege at Chattanooga, Tennessee. Once in Tennessee, Hooker remained a corps commander under the direction of General Ulysses S. Grant, and he was instrumental in capturing nearby Lookout Mountain from the Confederates in November 1863. Nonetheless, Hooker could not erase the stain that his loss at Chancellorsville had left on his reputation. In fact, when the commander of the Army of the Tennessee, General James McPherson, was killed during the Atlanta Campaign in July 1864, General William T. Sherman chose General Oliver Howard to replace McPherson, even though according to seniority and experience the position should have been Hooker's. Extremely disappointed at having been passed over, Hooker asked to be relieved from further battlefield duties, and he spent the remainder of the war serving in various insignificant positions away from the front lines. **See also** Chancellorsville, Battle of; Grant, Ulysses S.; Howard, Oliver Otis.

Howard, Oliver Otis (1830–1909)

In 1865 distinguished Union general Oliver O. Howard was placed in charge of the Bureau of Refugees, Freedmen, and Abandoned Lands (also known as the Freedmen's Bureau), a Reconstruction period government agency that helped former slaves.

Howard began his service in the Civil War as a colonel in a volunteer regiment in Maine, but after fighting in several battles, including the First Battle of Bull Run (July 1861), the Battle of Seven Pines (May 1862), and the Battle of Antietam (September 1862), he was promoted to major general. During the Battle of Seven Pines, Howard suffered a serious injury that required the amputation of his right arm. He then participated in the Battle of Chancellorsville (May 1863) and the Tennessee and Atlanta Campaigns (1863–1864). In July 1864, Howard was given command of the Army of the Tennessee. In this capacity, he participated in General William Tecumseh Sherman's march from Atlanta, Georgia, to the sea in late 1864 and the Carolinas Campaign of early 1865.

As soon as the war ended, Howard received a presidential appointment to head the Freedmen's Bureau, a position he held until 1872. Under his direction, this agency established a number of colleges for black students, among them the school that bears his name: Howard University, in Washington, D.C. From 1869 to 1874 Howard served as the president of this institution. He also served as the head of the U.S. Military Academy from 1880 to 1882, after a short stint fighting Indians in the American West as a general in the U.S. Army. Howard spent his later years writing about military history. In addition, in 1899 he published a novel, *Henry in the War, or the Model Volunteer,* that featured a main character he modeled after himself. **See also** Bureau of Refugees, Freedmen, and Abandoned Lands; West Point.

Hunley, CSS

The Confederate submarine *Hunley* was the first submarine to sink an enemy ship in war. The vessel was built in early 1863 in Mobile, Alabama, after the Confederacy offered a monetary reward to any private citizen whose ship sank a Union warship. Its builders were investors who hoped to reap the benefits of this offer, and they included Horace L. Hunley, for whom the submarine was named.

The *Hunley* was approximately thirty feet long and required a crew of nine men. One of these men steered the vessel, while the other eight turned a crank to run the sub's single propeller. To sink enemy ships, the *Hunley* towed a mine, then called a torpedo, with the idea that this device could be released below the enemy ship so that it would hit the ship's hull and explode. However, after the designers discovered that this system was unreliable, the torpedo was lashed to a long spar on the boat's bow, thereby allowing it to strike the enemy ship at what was theoretically a safe distance.

The *Hunley* was first launched at Charleston, South Carolina, after being transported there on a train car, but by some accounts the vessel immediately filled with water and sank. According to other accounts, it successfully made several short trial runs within the harbor. In either case, in August 1863 the Confederate government claimed the submarine for its navy. Commanded by Lieutenant John Payne, a new crew began learning to operate the vessel. At some point during their training, the submarine sank and five or six of the crew drowned.

The Confederacy then raised the vessel, repaired it, and sent it out in October 1863 with yet another crew, intending to sink the Union frigate USS *New Ironsides,* thc

The Hunley, *a Confederate submarine, was the first submarine to sink an enemy ship in war.*

Union warship USS *Housatonic,* or one of the other ships blockading Charleston's harbor. Again, the submarine sank, killing seven crew members. But by February 1864 it had been raised, repaired, and sent out once more. This time the *Hunley* sank the USS *Housatonic;* the warship went down just five minutes after being struck by the torpedo. However, the *Hunley* was damaged in the same explosion and subsequently sank as well, with all hands lost. **See also** blockades and blockade runners; navies, Confederate and Union; submarines.

Hunter, David (1802–1886)

On May 9, 1862, Union major general David Hunter acted without orders in issuing a proclamation abolishing slavery in Florida, Georgia, and South Carolina. He believed he had the authority to take this action because he had recently been placed in charge of these three states, but ten days later U.S. president Abraham Lincoln annulled the proclamation and rebuked Hunter for issuing it, fearing that without such a strong government response Hunter's action might cause the still-loyal slave states to secede.

A veteran of the Mexican-American War (1846–1848) Hunter served with distinction in several Civil War battles and led the first Union regiment consisting entirely of black soldiers (though its officers were all white). However, he suffered a serious defeat in June 1864 in Lynchburg, Virginia, and resigned his command less than two months later. Afterward Hunter remained with the military, and when Lincoln was assassinated he was one of the people responsible for bringing the conspirators to justice. **See also** assassination of President Abraham Lincoln.

Hunter, Robert Mercer Taliaferro (1809–1887)

Virginia politician Robert M.T. Hunter was the secretary of state of the Confederate States of America from July 1861 to February 1862 and afterward served as president of the Confederate Senate. He was also a participant in the 1865 Hampton Roads Conference, where various Northern and Southern officials met to negotiate (unsuccessfully) an end to the war.

Hunter first became involved in politics in 1834, after practicing law in Virginia for four years, serving first in the state legislature and then, beginning in 1837, in the U.S. House of Representatives. In January 1840 he was named Speaker of the House, earning the distinction at age thirty of being the youngest man yet to hold that position. At the time, he was a member of the Whig Party, but the positions that he subsequently took on various issues, including slavery, ran counter to his party's stances, and by 1843 his fellow Whigs had forced him out of office. Nonetheless, Hunter was once again elected to the House in 1845, this time as a Democrat, and in 1847 he became a U.S. senator. Within three years he became one of the three most powerful Southern Democrats in the Senate, the others being Jefferson Davis and Robert Toombs.

In 1860 Hunter worked with Senator John Crittenden and others to develop the Crittenden Compromise, a proposed packet of legislation designed to prevent the Southern states from seceding. When this legislation failed to pass, Hunter came up with his own series of proposed constitutional amendments designed to forestall secession. Among these were various protections related to slave commerce and transportation and a requirement that runaway slaves be returned to their owners or, if the slaves had reached a free state that refused to honor such property rights, that the government compensate slave owners for their losses. Hunter also suggested that two presidents be elected to run the country instead of one, with no action being taken unless both agreed on it, and that the Supreme Court be given greater authority to review state laws.

After his peers failed to embrace these proposals, Hunter resigned from the Senate. Shortly thereafter the Southern states seceded, and Robert Toombs was chosen as the Confederacy's secretary of state. When Toombs resigned this position in July 1861, Hunter took his place, and shortly thereafter the *Trent* Affair occurred, during which Union naval officers seized and boarded a British ship because it carried Confederate diplomats. Hunter tried to harness British anger over this incident to convince Great Britain to declare war on the United States or at least support the Confederacy's war effort.

In February 1862, Hunter resigned as secretary of state to join the Confederate Senate, where for the next three years he presented several bills related to taxes and other financial matters. By the time he attended the unsuccessful Hampton Roads Conference in 1865, he knew that the South did not have the money necessary to continue the war. Nonetheless, he objected to the North's terms for peace, which included a complete end to slavery. When the war ended, Hunter was trying to convince the Confederate Congress to support a new peace resolution that he himself had drafted.

After the Civil War the U.S. government imprisoned Hunter at Fort Pulaski in Georgia. He was released in January 1866, after which he settled in Virginia and returned to practicing law. He also wrote articles about the political decisions of the South during the Civil War. In addition, Hunter continued to be involved in state politics and served as the treasurer of Virginia from 1874 to 1880. **See also** Crittenden Compromise; Davis, Jefferson; Hampton Roads; Toombs, Robert A.; *Trent* Affair.

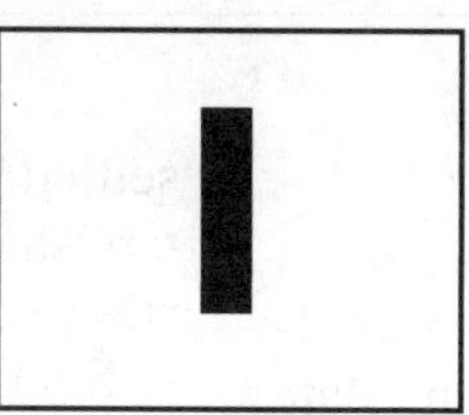

Idaho

Idaho saw no military action relating to the Civil War, although Union soldiers stationed there did sometimes have to fight Shoshone Indians. After the war, however, Idaho became a prime destination for Southerners wanting to start a new life. Consequently, the population of Idaho swelled from fewer than seventeen thousand in 1863 to more than ninety thousand in 1890. **See also** West, the.

Illinois

Some of the most prominent figures in the Union came from Illinois, including General Ulysses S. Grant and U.S. president Abraham Lincoln. Illinois also contributed about 250,000 men to the Union armies. Nonetheless, the state's citizens had mixed feelings about slavery. Prior to the 1830s, most whites in Illinois supported slavery, and many of them owned slaves. Then the abolitionist movement gradually took hold in northern Illinois, and by the late 1840s the state government was dominated by abolitionists. As a result, in 1848 Illinois officially banned slavery and the transportation of slaves into the state. However, it also forbade free blacks from entering the state.

Opposition to slavery was strong in northern Illinois, but many people in southern Illinois felt differently. Consequently, when the war broke out, a movement began in southern Illinois whose goal was to split the state so that southern Illinois would join the Confederacy while northern Illinois would remain with the Union. This movement failed, but the sentiments behind it did not disappear. As the war progressed, southern Illinois supported a growing peace movement advocating a truce between North and South. **See also** abolitionists; Grant, Ulysses S.; Lincoln, Abraham.

immigrants

In the two decades prior to the Civil War, the number of immigrants to the United States increased dramatically. Between 1851 and 1860, approximately 2.6 million immigrants arrived in the United States. This represented an approximate 50 percent increase over the 1.7 million who did so between 1841 and 1850.

During the war, immigrants were subject to the draft and many served in the Union army. There were approximately 200,000 German immigrants fighting for the Union and 150,000 Irish ones. This was enough for the Union to create all-German and all-Irish regiments. These regiments served as effectively as nonimmigrant ones, even though their members were not always convinced that the emancipation of slaves was worth fighting for. In particular, many Irish Americans resented being drafted into the Union army because they felt that an increase in the number of free blacks would result in a decrease in available jobs. This conviction was behind the worst draft riot of the war, which occurred in New York City from July 13 to 17, 1863, after striking Irish American dockworkers who had just been replaced by black workers learned that they were being drafted. **See also** conscription.

Indiana

Indiana was a free state from the time it first entered the Union in 1816, and although there were a few slaves in the state (just over 175) there was no significant proslavery sentiment there by the time the Civil War broke out. Since 1851 the state constitution had forbidden not only slaves but free blacks from entering Indiana under any circumstances. The restriction against free blacks would be declared unconstitutional by the U.S. Supreme Court in 1866.

During the Civil War, Indiana became an industrial center for the North. A site near its first state capital, Corydon, was also the location of a brief military battle on July 9, 1863. At that time, believing the war needed to be taken to the North, Confederate brigadier general John Hunt Morgan led approximately twenty-five hundred cavalrymen into Indiana, although he did so without permission from his superiors. During this raid he surprised the Union and captured approximately four hundred men from the Indiana Home Guard before heading on to Ohio (where he himself was captured). **See also** Morgan, John Hunt.

industry and technology

During the Civil War, the North had an extreme advantage over the South in terms of industry and technology. The North had long been home to most of the factories in the United States, whereas the South was largely agricultural. This meant that the Confederate states had difficulty manufacturing enough war matériel. So imbalanced was their manufacturing capacity that all of the Southern factories combined could not produce as many goods as those in New York City alone. Of particular significance was the fact that the South had only two gunpowder mills, while the North had sixty-seven just in Pennsylvania. This imbalance also left the South at a technological disadvantage, since many inventors—such as Samuel Colt, who developed and manufactured new types of firearms—had settled in the North, where they could establish or associate themselves with factories to build their inventions.

Southerners worked throughout the war to increase production at the few factories they did have and to strengthen fortifications around those cities where they were located. These included New Orleans, Louisiana; Richmond, Virginia; Nashville, Tennessee; Selma, Alabama; and Atlanta and Augusta, Georgia. Meanwhile, the Union military targeted these cities as part of its attempts to destroy Southern industry. The industrial imbalance forced the South to rely on imports, but the Union was able to greatly limit those through the use of blockades. **See also** Colt, Samuel; inventions.

infantry, Confederate and Union

When the Civil War began, there was no Confederate infantry, and the entire U.S. Army (which later also became known as the Regular Army) contained fewer than seventeen thousand officers and enlisted men. Consequently, both sides needed to increase their number of infantrymen. In the North, this was done not by enlarging the U.S. Army but by creating a second army, the volunteer army.

New recruits on both sides usually joined at the local level, then trained with their regiments at state capitals, the national capital (either Confederate or U.S.), or military training camps located in major cities. First, however, infantrymen had to pass a cursory medical examination and take two oaths, one to their state and one to their national government. Each soldier was then issued certain equipment, the type and amount of which varied during the war. In general, however, when supplies were plentiful, soldiers had to carry over ten pounds of guns and ammunition, along with several pounds of camping and personal gear and food. At the beginning of the war, infantrymen were also typically issued uniforms, which had to be replaced at the soldier's expense.

Both sides relied on experienced officers—most of whom, even those in the Confederacy, were graduates of the U.S. Military Academy at West Point—to train new recruits or to retrain those who had been taught incorrectly in their home states when their regiments were first formed. However, it took some time for Union and Confederate leaders to come up with the best methods for drilling volunteer soldiers, who were unaccustomed to taking orders. In fact, throughout the war both sides' infantries were plagued with problems related to the fact that volunteer soldiers had far less commitment to the military than professional soldiers did. **See also** armies, Confederate; armies, Union; camps and camp life; conscription; generals, Confederate and Union; military schools, bias against; uniforms and equipment.

inventions

During the Civil War, dozens of people on both sides developed new tactics and technologies to make the prosecution of the war easier. Among the most significant of these inventions in regard to combat conditions were machine guns; ironclads; land mines and bombs that could be exploded electronically; naval torpedoes; flamethrowers; repeating rifles; telescopic sights for rifles; revolving gun turrets; submarines that worked well enough to be sent on missions; aerial observation of troop movements (using balloons), along with blackouts and camouflage to combat it; the widespread use of field trenches; periscopes (for use in trenches); hospital ships; army ambulance corps; organized medical and nursing corps; the widespread use of anesthetics, where available, for patients in severe pain; military railroads and railroad artillery; and the military telegraph. **See also** ammunition; balloons; firearms; ironclads.

Iowa

Although Iowa supported the Union during the Civil War, none of the war's battles were fought in the state. Yet in terms of the number of people who went to war, Iowa contributed a larger percentage of its population than did any other state. Out of the approximately 675,000 people living in Iowa at the beginning of the war, more than 76,000, or more than 11 percent, became involved in the fighting, forming forty-five infantry regiments, two infantry battalions, nine cavalry regiments, and four light artillery batteries. By the war's end, approximately 14,000 of these men had died, either from disease or battle injuries. **See also** cavalry; infantry, Confederate and Union.

ironclads

Also called armorclads, ironclads were warships whose sides above the waterline were armored with metal plates. Such ships had been used in Europe prior to the Civil War, but they were not employed in America until the Confederacy converted the wooden warship USS *Merrimack,* which had been scuttled but recovered, into the ironclad CSS *Virginia.* Ironically, this decision was made more on the basis of ease and cost than on military strategy; it was simpler to repair the *Merrimack*'s damaged hull with metal plates than to replace broken planks. Nevertheless, even before the *Virginia* was put into action, both sides in the Civil War quickly saw the military advantages of having armored vessels, and the Union rushed to build one of its own. Named the *Monitor,* it was completed in less than four months and had a revolving gun turret. The *Monitor* and the *Virginia* met in combat shortly after both were launched. The battle at Hampton Roads, Virginia, on March 9, 1862, lasted four hours and ended in a draw. Both sides, however, subsequently built more ironclads, the Union sixty in all and the Confederacy twenty-one. The Confederates built all of these ironclads using the *Virginia* as a model, while the Union varied its designs. **See also** *Merrimack,* USS/*Virginia,* CSS; *Monitor,* USS; navies, Confederate and Union.

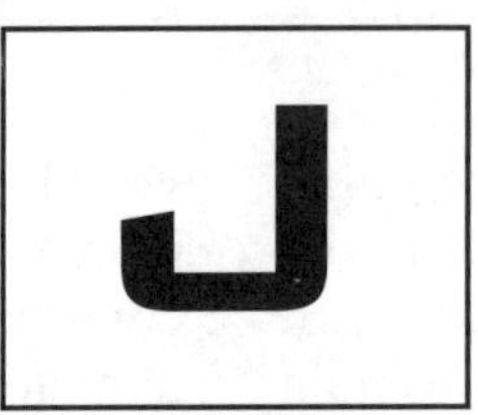

Jackson, Andrew (1767–1845)

Andrew Jackson, president of the United States from 1829 to 1837, died long before the Civil War began. However, he still played a role in Civil War politics because of the way he dealt with a secession crisis in 1832. At that time, South Carolina had threatened to leave the Union because it opposed federal tariff legislation. The state's position was that any state had the right to reject, or nullify, federal legislation through state legislation. Consequently, South Carolina's response to the tariff legislation has been called the Nullification Crisis.

In response to this crisis, President Jackson (himself a slave owner from Tennessee) demanded that South Carolina and all other states obey all federal laws, rejecting the legitimacy of nullification. In March 1833, after the U.S. Congress passed a bill that gave the president the right to make states comply with federal laws through the use of military force if necessary, Jackson made it clear that he would not hesitate to employ such force to prevent South Carolina's secession. At the same time, Congress passed a compromise measure that reduced the tariff. As a result, no other Southern states supported South Carolina in its cause, and the state's leaders soon backed down. The success of Jackson's strong response to South Carolina's threats encouraged President Abraham Lincoln to take an equally strong stance when the Southern states began seceding. **See also** South Carolina.

Jackson, Thomas Jonathan ("Stonewall") (1824–1863)

Confederate general Thomas J. "Stonewall" Jackson of Virginia was one of the most skillful commanders of the Civil War. After receiving formal military training at the U.S. Military Academy and serving as an artillery officer during the Mexican-American War (1846–1848), Jackson taught artillery tactics and philosophy at the Virginia Military Institute. When the Civil War began, Jackson took a group of his cadets to Richmond, Virginia, to train new recruits in the Confederate army. Within a few days he was made an infantry colonel in charge of volunteers and was sent to organize and train troops in the Shenandoah Valley. Highly effective at his job, he was promoted to brigadier general on June 17, 1861, and given command of a brigade.

This unit, consisting of five infantry regiments, fought under General Joseph E. Johnston at the First Battle of Bull Run on July 21, 1861. It was during this battle that Jackson received his nickname "Stonewall"; another Confederate commander, General Barnard E. Bee, pointed out to his men that Jackson—who had stationed his brigade in a line—was standing firm in his position "like a stone wall" despite heavy firing. As a result of his bravery, Jackson was made a major general and given command of all forces defending the Shenandoah Valley. In this capacity, he fought in several major battles and won every one of them, even when his men were seriously outnumbered, thanks to his superior command skills. He also prevented Union reinforcements from reaching General George McClellan, who was trying to take the Confederate capital of Richmond, Virginia.

During the subsequent Second Battle of Bull Run in August 1862, Jackson was largely responsible for the defeat of Union commander John Pope and his men. The following month Jackson captured Harpers Ferry, Virginia, and then joined General Robert E. Lee at the Battle of Antietam. Although this battle was inconclusive, many Southerners believed that had Jackson not been present the Confederacy would have lost. In any case, Jackson was promoted to lieutenant general and given command of one of Lee's two corps, with General James Longstreet leading the other. Shortly thereafter, in December 1862, Jackson's men were victorious at the Battle of Fredericksburg in Virginia.

General "Stonewall" Jackson led his Confederate troops to many victories.

Jackson's next major battle, Chancellorsville, was his last. In April 1863, he was ordered to slip around the forces of Union general Joseph Hooker so that his men would be positioned behind Hooker's when Lee made a frontal attack on them. Jackson was successful in positioning his troops before the fighting broke out on the evening of May 2. In the ensuing chaos, Jackson was accidentally shot in the left arm by one of his own men. Doctors amputated the arm to prevent gangrene, but Jackson subsequently developed pneumonia and died a week after the surgery. **See also** armies, Confederate; Jackson's Valley Campaign; Lee, Robert Edward.

Jackson's Valley Campaign

The series of military engagements that later became known as Jackson's Valley Campaign took place in Virginia's Shenandoah Valley from March 23 to June 9, 1862, between a Confederate army of approximately fifteen thousand led by Major General Thomas J. "Stonewall" Jackson and combined Union forces numbering about eighty thousand. Despite the fact that Jackson's troops were outnumbered, he managed to inflict heavy losses on the Union during his campaign and captured several wagonloads of supplies, which he then took with him when he left the valley to defend Richmond, Virginia.

The groundwork for Jackson's campaign was laid on October 28, 1861, when he was appointed to command the Valley District of Virginia. Two months later, with a force of about ten thousand men, he blew up a dam in order to destroy a Union camp in the valley. In January he took two towns, Bath and Romney, and established his own winter camp. By March he was ready to resume his operations against Union forces in the valley, and on March

23, 1862, his troops fought against about seven thousand Union soldiers at Kernstown, Virginia. After a day of fighting in which about 118 Union soldiers and 80 Confederate soldiers were killed, Jackson withdrew from the battlefield and shortly thereafter received reinforcements, so by May 1 his army numbered about fifteen thousand.

On May 8 Jackson again fought the Union, this time confronting a force of about three thousand at McDowell, and then retreated to some unknown hideout. (Patrols of Union cavalrymen failed to find him, despite blocking roads and questioning valley residents and travelers.) On May 23 he struck again at Front Royal, inflicting nine hundred casualties on a Union army numbering no more than one thousand. This time the Union responded by increasing the number of Union troops in the area and making it a priority for all of its valley forces to capture or kill Jackson; the Union commanders in charge of this action were John Frémont, Nathaniel Banks, and Irvin McDowell.

Banks confronted Jackson on May 24 at Newtown and ended up losing many men and supplies before retreating to Winchester. Jackson pursued him there, and on May 25 thc two sides fought the Battle of Winchester. The Confederates had few losses, but Banks's casualties for both the Battle of Newtown and the Battle of Winchester were about 62 dead, 243 wounded, and 1,700 captured or missing. Banks then fled across the Potomac River into Maryland, whereupon Jackson took some of his troops to Harpers Ferry to distract the Union while his other troops moved his prisoners and stolen supplies from Winchester to another town, Staunton. After this, Jackson fought in two more valley battles, at Cross Keys on June 8 and at Port Republic on June 9. In this last battle of his valley campaign, his forces outnumbered the Union forces about seventeen thousand to five thousand, and Jackson managed to prevent the Union from sending reinforcements by burning a bridge across the Shenandoah River. He then left the valley for Richmond. **See also** Banks, Nathaniel Prentiss; McDowell, Irvin.

jayhawkers

The term *jayhawkers* was used to refer to pro-Union guerrillas operating in Kansas and Missouri during the Civil War. The first bands of jayhawkers formed in Kansas in 1861 when Unionists there began to fear that neighboring Missouri, a slave state that had remained in the Union, would either secede or be taken over by Confederate forces. If this happened, the jayhawkers believed, Kansas would not only be cut off from the North but also be in danger of a Confederate takeover. To prevent this, the jayhawkers marched into Missouri and began wreaking havoc by burning crops, stealing livestock, kidnapping slaves, and destroying homes and barns of Confederate sympathizers, killing those who tried to fight back. Some of these jayhawkers, most notably Charles Jennison, also used such actions as an excuse to rape and torture innocent civilians; in fact, most jayhawker bands were made up of criminals rather than men dedicated to the Union cause.

After jayhawkers destroyed the town of Osceola, Missouri, in September 1861, burning it to the ground after carrying away anything of value, the federal government sent soldiers into the area to keep the peace. These troops, however, did virtually nothing to bring the jayhawkers to justice. This failure angered even those Missourians who had supported the Union, and as a result the number of Confederate sympathizers in the state rose. Moreover, some of these sympathizers formed their own guerrilla bands and began crossing the border to attack people in Kansas. These Confederate guerrillas became known as bushwackers, and the federal government soon became aggressive in tracking them down. **See also** bushwackers; guerrillas, partisan rangers, and irregulars.

Johnson, Andrew (1808–1875)

As vice president of the United States under Abraham Lincoln, Andrew Johnson became president after Lincoln's assassination. Therefore, he oversaw the implementation of Lincoln's Reconstruction policies after the Civil War. Johnson, who represented Tennessee in the U.S. Senate, also holds the distinction of being the only Southern member of that body who did not give up his seat after his state seceded.

Johnson first became involved in politics while working as a tailor in Greeneville, Tennessee, where he organized a workingman's party and eventually became mayor. In 1835 he was elected to the state legislature, and in 1843 he became a Democratic member of the U.S. House of Representatives. Johnson served in the House until 1853, when he became governor of Tennessee, and in 1856 he was elected to the U.S. Senate.

As a senator, Johnson consistently supported legislation to protect the South's right to keep its slaves. He opposed secession, however, and refused to support the Confederacy after the Southern states seceded. As a reward for his loyalty, Lincoln made Johnson the military governor of Tennessee once the federal government gained control of the state in May 1862. Then, when Lincoln ran for reelection in 1864, he chose Johnson as his running mate, a decision supported by the president's Republican Party, because the Republicans believed that having a Democrat on the ticket would strengthen their chances for victory.

After Johnson became president, he worked to implement Lincoln's plans. However, Johnson drew the ire of the Radical Republicans (a powerful faction within the Republican Party) for not dealing harshly with Southern states and former Confederate leaders during Reconstruction. Specifically, on May 29, 1865, Johnson pardoned all former Confederates (with a few exceptions) who agreed to take an oath of loyalty to the United States. He also admitted all former Confederate states to the Union without requiring them to implement broad civil rights for freedmen.

Andrew Johnson succeeded Lincoln as president, overseeing the implementation of Lincoln's Reconstruction policies after the war.

Radical Republicans grew even angrier with Johnson when the white planter aristocracy returned to power in the South and started enacting legislation that collectively became known as the Black Codes, which infringed on the blacks' newly won freedoms. These racist laws also resulted in an increase in the number of Northerners who supported Radical Republicanism. Consequently, in 1866 this faction became dominant in Congress, and the following year it passed several Reconstruction acts that went against Johnson's wishes, including one that gave blacks the right to vote.

The Radicals also pushed through a measure, the Tenure of Office Act, that made it impossible for the president to dismiss a member of his cabinet without congressional approval. In doing so, the Radicals sought to preserve the cabinet position of Secretary of War Edwin M. Stanton, a Lincoln appointee who was a major supporter of Radical Republicanism. When Johnson dismissed Stanton anyway, the president's enemies in the House impeached him. In the subsequent trial in the Senate, the Radical Republicans fell one vote short of the two-thirds majority needed to convict and remove the president. Although Johnson completed his term, continued opposition in the Congress made him an ineffective leader. After leaving the presidency he returned to Tennessee, where he was again elected senator in 1875. He died the same year. **See also** Radical Republicans; Reconstruction; Stanton, Edwin McMasters.

Johnston, Albert Sidney (1803–1862)

As soon as the war broke out, Albert S. Johnston became a full general in the Confederate army because of his previous experience as a military officer. A graduate of the U.S. Military Academy, he served in the Black Hawk War as a senior general and in many other positions as well, including the secretary of war for the Republic of Texas, a staff officer during the Mexican-American War (1846–1848), an army paymaster, a cavalry colonel, and the commander of a military operation against Mormon settlers in Utah Territory. Johnston left the U.S. Army, however, as soon as the state of Texas seceded from the Union. Johnston was blamed for the Confederacy's loss of two important Tennessee forts, Fort Henry and Fort Donelson, to the Union in February 1862, but he was also credited with showing great skill in positioning Confederate troops in preparation for the Battle of Shiloh in April 1862. Johnston was killed during heavy fighting on the first day of this battle. **See also** Fort Henry and Fort Donelson Campaign; Shiloh, Battle of.

Johnston, Joseph Eggleston (1807–1891)

Confederate general Joseph E. Johnston served in many major battles of the war and was close friends with the man who eventually commanded all Confederate armies, Robert E. Lee. A native of Virginia, Johnston studied engineering at the U.S. Military Academy and served in the U.S. Army in various assignments in the artillery and cavalry. By 1861 he held a dual rank, brigadier general (as a staff officer) and lieutenant colonel. Nonetheless, he resigned his commission to join an army being formed by the state of Virginia. His friend Lee did this as well, and at first both men held the same rank, major general. However, Lee was given command of the entire army, and eventually the Confederacy decided that Johnston should not have the same rank as Lee. Johnston was then demoted to brigadier general.

Johnston's first major battle was the First Battle of Bull Run, during which he so distinguished himself that he was promoted to full general, although within that grade he was ranked behind Samuel Cooper, Albert Sidney Johnston, and Robert E. Lee. This apparent slight angered Johnston and he quarreled with Confederate high officials, particularly President Jefferson Davis. For the rest of the war these two men were always at odds, with Johnston feeling that he never received his full due.

Johnston's career also suffered when he was seriously wounded during the Peninsula Campaign at the Battle of Seven Pines on May 31, 1862. When this occurred, Lee took over his command of the Army of Northern Virginia and performed far better than Johnston had, winning a series of important battles. Meanwhile, Johnston had to spend four months recuperating. After this, he was sent to command Confederate forces in Tennessee and Mississippi. In this capacity, he ignored Davis's wishes, which were for him to move these forces around in accordance with wherever the Union forces were located. Instead, Johnston concentrated his troops around Vicksburg. This decision not only caused many Confederate losses but failed to prevent the Union from taking the city. This defeat led to another quarrel between Johnston and Davis, after which Davis refused to give Johnston another command. Eventually, however, the president had no choice but to make Johnston the head of the Army of Tennessee, because there were no other generals available who could handle this important assignment.

After Johnston took over the Army of Tennessee, his problems with Davis intensified. The two argued over where the army should go, what it should do, and whether its supplies were adequate. Johnston subsequently had a series of serious losses with heavy casualties, and in July 1864 Davis removed him from his command. Johnston had many influential friends, and they sided with him against Davis. In addition, Lee asked Davis to give Johnston a new command, and as a result in February 1865 Davis sent Johnston to lead forces in the Carolinas. On April 26, Johnston surrendered those forces to the Union.

After the war, Johnston had a variety of jobs, including railroad president and railroad commissioner. He also wrote a memoir, *Narrative of Military Operations Directed During the Late War Between the States* (1874), in which he presented himself as a highly skilled commander hampered by his superiors. **See also** armies, Confederate; Lee, Robert Edward; Peninsula Campaign.

Kansas

Even before the Civil War, Kansas became a battleground for pro-slavery and antislavery forces. In large part this was because the U.S. Congress, as part of the Kansas-Nebraska Act of 1854, allowed the people of Kansas to decide by popular vote whether they would enter the Union as a slave state or a free state. In an attempt to influence this decision, proslavery and antislavery forces each sent people into the state, primarily along the eastern border, to establish residency prior to the vote so that they could participate in it and intimidate other voters—sometimes through physical violence—into siding with their respective positions. During this period, pro-slavery guerrillas from neighboring Missouri would frequently cross the border into Kansas to attack antislavery settlers.

In 1856 these guerrillas, who became known as border ruffians, sacked the antislavery town of Lawrence, Kansas. In response, abolitionist John Brown led an attack on a group of pro-slavery settlers who were innocent of any crime, massacring five men and boys. A retaliatory attack by pro-slavery forces soon followed. Hundreds of similar incidents subsequently took place in the region, and most were so violent that eventually Kansas became known as Bleeding Kansas. This guerrilla warfare continued even after Kansas entered the Union as a free state in 1861. **See also** border ruffians; Brown, John; guerrillas, partisan rangers, and irregulars.

Kansas-Nebraska Act

Passed by the U.S. Congress in 1854, the Kansas-Nebraska Act repealed part of the Missouri Compromise of 1820, which had established a dividing line within the territories acquired during the Louisiana Purchase (1803). According to this legislation, any territory located south of this line, which was at latitude 36°30', had to apply for admission to the United States as a slave state, and any territory north of the line had to prohibit slavery upon achieving statehood. However, according to a subsequent piece of legislation known as the Compromise of 1850, territories that were not part of the Louisiana Purchase could vote on whether they wanted to enter the Union as a slave state or free state. Soon citizens who lived in Louisiana Purchase territories demanded the same right, even though by the terms of the Missouri Compromise they would have been required to support slavery.

In response, Northern Democrat Stephen Douglas authored the Kansas-Nebraska Act, which decreed that the settlers within each state would vote on the slavery issue. This bill was initially extremely unpopular with other Democrats, particularly those in the South. Eventually, however, Senator David R. Atchison of Missouri, a slave state, convinced almost all of his fellow Southern Democrats to support the bill, on the theory that it would lead to the repeal of the Missouri Compromise's ban on slavery in the North.

But far from resolving the issue of slavery, the Kansas-Nebraska Act made the situation worse. Both pro- and antislavery forces sent their supporters into these territories to take up residence just long enough to cast their votes. The two groups then turned to violence as each one tried to gain dominance, and Kansas soon became known as Bleeding Kansas. In addition, the voting process was rife with corruption, voters were often threatened, and politicians tried to ignore results that displeased them. Specifically, pro-slavery Kansas politicians submitted a pro-slavery constitution as part of their statehood application, even though a majority of Kansas residents had voted against slavery. Their attempt to subvert the voters' wishes was stopped, however, primarily due to the efforts of Douglas, who was largely shunned by Southern Democrats after Kansas entered the Union as a free state. **See also** Compromise of 1850; Douglas, Stephen Arnold; Kansas; Missouri Compromise.

Kentucky

Although the U.S. government feared that Kentucky would be among the first states to secede, on May 20, 1861, the state's governor and legislature officially proclaimed Kentucky to be neutral. The state's citizens, however, opposed this position, wanting their government to support one side or the other in the war. In this regard they were fairly evenly divided until September 3, 1861, when the Confederate commander in charge of the Mississippi River Valley, Major General Leonidas Polk, decided that it was necessary to position Confederate troops in Kentucky to secure his hold on the valley. Many Kentuckians were angered by this invasion, and consequently support for the Union increased. In fact, during this period roughly seventy-five thousand Kentuckians volunteered to fight for the Union, compared to about twenty-five thousand for the Confederacy.

Meanwhile, the Union responded to this threat to its border state in kind, sending its own troops into the northern part of the state. From this point on, the state was technically no longer neutral. However, it never officially seceded, despite the fact that by the end of the year the Confederacy had taken over Kentucky's government and declared that the state was now a Confederate one.

Despite the tension caused by this situation, no battles were actually fought on Kentucky soil until August 1862, when Confederate general Braxton Bragg invaded the state from Chattanooga, Tennessee. He marched into Kentucky with roughly twenty-seven thousand men, capturing a garrison of four thousand Union soldiers in Munfordville, Kentucky, on September 17. By October, however, the Union had gained the upper hand in the area, and Bragg's army was driven back into Tennessee. No other Civil War battles were fought in the state, although guerrilla fighting was an ongoing problem.

Kentucky's land, therefore, was largely unaffected by the war. Its citizens, however, were not. A total of about ninety thousand Kentucky men ultimately decided to fight for the Union and about forty thousand for the Confederacy, with many Kentucky families contributing men to both sides of the battle. Thus a man fighting for the Union was likely to have a brother or son fighting for the Confederacy. **See also** Bragg, Braxton; guerrillas, partisan rangers, and irregulars.

Kershaw, Joseph B. (1822–1894)

Confederate officer Joseph B. Kershaw played a significant role in several important battles and is credited with preventing an incident of "friendly fire" in May 1864. During this incident, a group of Confederate soldiers, thinking they were shooting at the enemy, began firing on a group of their comrades in a wooded area in northern Virginia known as the Wilderness. Before the second group of soldiers could return fire, Kershaw realized what was happening and stopped them.

A veteran of the Mexican-American War (1846–1848) Kershaw was serving in the South Carolina legislature when the Civil War began. In early 1861, as his native state grappled with the question of whether to secede from the Union, he formed a regiment known as the Second South Carolina Infantry and became its colonel. After being involved in the siege on Fort Sumter and the First Battle of Bull Run, Kershaw was promoted to brigadier general. He subsequently fought in many major battles, including Chancellorsville, Gettysburg, Chickamauga, Spotsylvania, and those of the Wilderness Campaign. In May 1864 Kershaw was promoted to major general, after which he led an attack that was part of the Shenandoah Valley Campaign. He participated in several more battles before being captured by Union forces in the spring of 1865. After the war, Kershaw returned to practicing law, and in 1865 he was again elected to his state's legislature. Later he became a judge and then postmaster of Camden. **See also** South Carolina; Wilderness, Battle of the.

Ku Klux Klan

The Ku Klux Klan was a secret organization of white Southern racists whose goal was to restore white supremacy by keeping blacks—often through physical violence—from exercising the political and legal rights they had gained in the aftermath of the Civil War. The Ku Klux Klan originated as a sort of social club whose members were Confederate veterans in Pulaski, Tennessee. These men met regularly in 1866 merely to socialize and reminisce about the war. (The name Ku Klux Klan was based on the Greek word for "circle," *kyklos,* meaning "a group of people sharing an interest.")

Members of the Ku Klux Klan disguised themselves in white sheets with eyeholes.

Within a very short time, however, members' concerns about the rights being granted to blacks and the Radical Republicans' agenda in regard to these rights led the Klan to adopt an active form of resistance that involved violence against blacks. At the same time, word of the group spread not only in Tennessee but into other states as well. In the summer of 1867 the Ku Klux Klan held a convention in Nashville, Tennessee, attended by delegates from several Southern states, that established the group as a national organization with various leadership positions and rules. The membership list of the group was kept secret, and members disguised themselves in white sheets with eyeholes while conducting Klan business. However, historians suspect that the group's first leader, or grand wizard, was Nathan Bedford Forrest, a former Confederate cavalry general.

Between 1868 and 1870, the Ku Klux Klan—or KKK, as it was often called—attacked and killed dozens of blacks and their supporters in Tennessee, North Carolina, South Carolina, and Georgia, despite efforts by federal troops to stop such activities. In 1869, when it became clear that the federal government was going to take stronger measures against the organization, the KKK as a national organization officially disbanded. Local chapters, however, continued to operate, so in 1870 Congress passed the Force Act and in 1871 the Ku Klux Act, both of which made it possible for federal authorities to deal more harshly with the Klan by holding suspected members without charging them. The acts also allowed the government to use force to break up a gathering of Klan members and to deal with them severely when they were captured. (In 1881, the U.S. Supreme Court declared the Ku Klux Act unconstitutional, but by then the federal government had caught and imprisoned hundreds of Klan members.) Many KKK groups consequently disbanded, and by the end of the nineteenth century the Klan was considered dead.

In 1915 the Klan was resurrected by a Georgia preacher, Colonel William J. Simmons, who had learned about the group after taking an interest in fraternal organizations. Although this new Klan was modeled after the old one, historians do not generally consider it the same group because its aims were somewhat different, with the new Klan targeting not just blacks but members of a variety of minority groups and non-Christian religions. **See also** Forrest, Nathan Bedford.

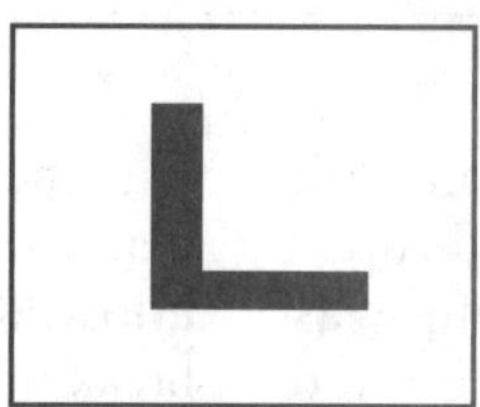

Langston, John Mercer (1829–1897)

When he became the clerk of Brownhelm, Ohio, in 1855, former slave John M. Langston became the first black American ever to achieve elective office in the United States. Much later, he was elected to represent Virginia in the U.S. House of Representatives, but he served for only three months in 1890–1891 due to challenges to his election that delayed his taking office until the term was nearly over. Langston also played an important role during the Civil War, recruiting black soldiers for the Union.

Born into slavery in Virginia, Langston was freed at the age of five by the white plantation owner who had fathered him. In 1849 Langston received a master's degree in theology from Oberlin College in Oberlin, Ohio, then attempted to enter law school. No such school in the United States would accept him, however, because he was black, so he studied on his own. A year after passing the bar exam in 1854, Langston won the first of many elections to local offices in Brownhelm and Oberlin. In 1864 he was also involved in creating the National Equal Rights League, dedicated to promoting civil rights.

After the Civil War, Langston practiced law in Washington, D.C., and taught law at Howard University. He also served as the dean of Howard's law department from 1869 to 1877 and as vice president of the university from 1872 to 1876. From 1877 to 1885 he was a U.S. diplomat in Haiti and Santo Domingo, after which he became president of the Virginia Normal and Collegiate Institute. **See also** black troops.

Lee, Robert Edward (1807–1870)

Virginia native Robert E. Lee commanded the most successful Confederate army during the war, the Army of Northern Virginia, and in 1865 became the general of all Confederate armies. Consequently, his surrender to the general of all Union armies, Ulysses S. Grant, at Appomattox Courthouse on April 9, 1865, is generally regarded as marking the end of the Civil War, even though the last Confederate army did not surrender until May 29, 1865.

Lee began his military career after graduating second in his class at the U.S. Military Academy in 1829, whereupon he joined the U.S. Army Corps of Engineers and went to work on a fort-building project in Georgia. Lee subsequently served with distinction under General Winfield Scott in the Mexican-American War (1846–1848), as a cavalry commander in Texas, and as the leader of troops that put down abolitionist John Brown's insurrection in 1859. By April 1861, Lee was such a respected military officer that the U.S. Army offered him the command of a new force whose purpose was to quash the secession movement before it involved too many states. Lee refused this position because, although he opposed secession, he did not support invading the South or using military force to keep the Union together.

When Virginia seceded shortly thereafter, Lee resigned from the U.S. Army and volunteered his services as the commander of all troops in Virginia, which eventually became part of the Confederate army. By September 1861 he was a full general in the Confederate army. Over the next several months, Lee held a variety of positions and contributed greatly to the Confederacy's military strategy. However, he did not command men in the field until the Battle of Seven Pines in May 1862, when he replaced an injured General Joseph E. Johnston as commander of a force that Lee would later name the Army of Northern Virginia.

Confederate troops celebrate General Robert E. Lee's victory at the Battle of Chancellorsville.

Lee led the Army of Northern Virginia in a series of military engagements in the Richmond, Virginia, area, experiencing many successes in the field. Above all, his goal was to keep Union soldiers away from the Confederate capital, and when he did engage the enemy, he did so with the goal of inflicting as much damage as possible in order to demoralize the Union and deplete its manpower and supplies. Despite his numerous victories, however, Lee was unsuccessful in his two attempts to pressure the Union by taking the war to Northern soil. Both efforts—the Battle of Antietam in Maryland and the Battle of Gettysburg in Pennsylvania—ended in defeat. By the Battle of Gettysburg in July 1863, Lee's army was plagued by shortages of food, supplies, and manpower, and the loss of some of his ablest commanders to battle wounds or illness. Nonetheless, he managed to slow (though not prevent) the taking of Richmond and nearby Petersburg by creating the most advanced field defenses and fortifications of the war.

After the war, Lee lost his Arlington, Virginia, home to the U.S. government, which then turned the grounds into Arlington National Cemetery and a housing project for freed slaves called Freedman's Village. Lee, who had no income, accepted a teaching position at Washington College in Lexington, Virginia, which later became Washington and Lee University. Lee and his family lived in a house on the college grounds until he died in 1870. **See also** Antietam, Battle of; Appomattox Campaign; field defenses; fortifications; Gettysburg, Battle of.

letters and diaries

In the nineteenth century, people routinely wrote letters to one another and kept diaries to share information about their daily activities and record their emotional responses to various events. In their letters to friends and family, soldiers typically told of the many hardships in camp and of the horrors they saw on the battlefield and in hospitals, and they spoke of the longing they had for home. They also offered their opinions about the war, not only through their words but often through pictures drawn on envelopes. For example, several Union soldiers decorated their envelopes with a sketch of Confederate president Jefferson Davis with a hangman's noose around his neck. Others sketched patriotic drawings, such as an eagle or a flag, accompanied by a patriotic slogan like "What God has joined let no man put asunder" (referring to the need to keep all states in the Union). In addition, most soldiers requested that their loved ones send them items such as baked goods, clothing, boots, medicines, writing supplies, sewing supplies, books, tools, and alcohol—although since alcoholic beverages were prohibited in military camps and on board naval vessels, requests for bottles of whiskey usually included instructions to hide them inside something else, such as a trussed turkey.

The responses that soldiers received in letters from home reveal the hardships endured by those they left behind. For example, women and children had to run farms and businesses by themselves and deal with losses in manpower and income, and in the South they also suffered from shortages of food and other necessities. Letters from home also expressed the grief that women and children experienced being separated from husbands, brothers, and fathers.

People also used diaries to express such emotions, as well as their observations and opinions about the war. One of the most notable Civil War diaries is that of Mary B. Chesnut, whose *A Diary from Dixie* provides the Southern perspective on the conflict. Other prominent female diarists include Phoebe Yates Pember, who wrote about nursing Confederate soldiers at a Richmond hospital; Kate Cumming, who wrote about her experiences as a nurse in Corinth, Mississippi; and Catherine Ann Devereux Edmondston, who told of her life as the mistress of a North Carolina plantation between 1860 and 1866.

Some diarists published their works in order to influence Civil War politics. Perhaps the most important diary in this regard was that of Frances Ann ("Fanny") Kemble, an English-born actress and prominent abolitionist. Kemble had kept a diary in 1838 and 1839 as the wife of a slave owner, Pierce Butler, and in 1863 she published it as *Journal of a Residence on a Georgian Plantation* to influence Civil War politics. Specifically, by presenting slavery in the worst possible light she hoped to contribute to efforts to prevent her native Great Britain from supporting the Confederate war effort. She succeeded in this regard after excerpts from her diary were read aloud in the British House of Commons.

Many Civil War soldiers also published their diaries, memoirs, and letters after the war, or their families published their works posthumously. In fact, there are hundreds of published first-person accounts of the war by people who served in it. One of the best examples is *A Soldier's Diary* by David Lane of the Seventeenth Michigan Volunteer Infantry, who decided to publish his diary in 1905 as a way of teaching his children and grandchildren about his life as a common soldier. A more politically oriented diary is *A Rebel War Clerk's Diary at the Confederate States Capital* by John Beauchamp Jones, published in 1866. Jones worked in the Confederate War Office in Richmond, Virginia, and his diary has provided historians with an idea of the Confederacy's concerns from 1861 to 1865. **See also** Chesnut, Mary Boykin; Strong, George Templeton.

Lincoln, Abraham (1809–1865)

As the sixteenth president of the United States, Abraham Lincoln led the country during the Civil War. Prior to going into

President Lincoln inspects the headquarters of the Army of the Potomac in October 1862.

politics, he held a variety of jobs, including flatboatman, postmaster, surveyor, and storekeeper, and in 1832 he served as a U.S. Army captain in the Black Hawk War. He eventually decided to become a lawyer, despite the fact that he had received no formal education as a boy. After studying law books on his own, he took and passed the bar exam in 1836, then joined a law practice in Springfield, Illinois (the state capital), and eventually settled into a partnership with William H. Herndon. Together, these two men made their practice one of the most successful in the state.

Lincoln first became involved in politics as a Whig in the 1830s, serving in the Illinois state legislature from 1834 to 1840 and the U.S. Congress from 1847 to 1849. By the time he entered Congress he had married Mary Todd, and over the years they had four children: Robert Todd; Edward Baker (who died of an illness at age four); William Wallace, or "Willie" (who died of malaria at age eleven); and Thomas (also known as Tad). Lincoln was devoted to his sons and to Mary, despite the fact that she suffered from regular bouts of depression and often flew into rages.

In 1856 Lincoln became a Republican, and two years later he challenged the Democratic incumbent Stephen A. Douglas for the U.S. Senate seat. Even though he lost the election, Lincoln's performance in a series of campaign debates brought him to national prominence. As a result, in 1860 the Republican Party nominated him as its presidential candidate, and Lincoln won the election—largely because the Democrats had split over the issue of slavery. Shortly thereafter, the Southern states began to secede, because Southerners considered Lincoln to be an abolitionist and an opponent of states' rights. By April 1861 the country was at war.

Lincoln at first struggled to identify an effective military strategy and to find the right generals to carry it out, and the Union armies suffered one loss after another. As time passed, however, he developed an efficient system of running the war effort, delegating responsibilities to different individuals. Specifically, by March 1864 Secretary of War Edwin Stanton was in charge of getting men and supplies to their proper locations; General Henry Halleck was the liaison between the president and all other military men as his personal adviser and chief of staff; and General Ulysses S. Grant was the general in chief who supervised all other generals and their armies.

As the war progressed, Lincoln negotiated various volatile political issues to prevent the Confederacy from gaining more support. For example, on January 1, 1863, he issued the Emancipation Proclamation, which officially freed most slaves—but only those who lived in Confederate states. In so doing, he increased support for the Northern cause among Europeans, who were staunchly antislavery, yet avoided giving slave states still loyal to the Union a reason to secede. Lincoln was equally adept at dealing with various political factions within Congress, both during the war and as the nation began to consider what would happen after the North won. He was also extremely popular among Union soldiers, and by 1864 his popularity was such that he easily won reelection against the Democratic candidate, General George McClellan.

At this point, Lincoln's goal was to heal the nation, and the Reconstruction policies he planned to implement would have dealt fairly leniently with the South. He never had a chance to implement these policies, though. In April 1865, just days after the Confederacy surrendered to the Union, Lincoln was assassinated by John Wilkes Booth while attending a play at Ford's Theater in Washington, D.C.

Shot in the head on the evening of April 14, Lincoln lingered until the next morning, dying at 7:22 A.M. His body was placed in a casket that was taken first to the East Room of the White House, then to the rotunda of the Capitol to lay in state, and then by train to Springfield, Illinois, for burial. Along the 1,662-mile train route, people lined up to pay their respects, and in certain cities the casket was removed from the train and placed in public buildings for viewing. In Cleveland, Ohio, there was no building big enough to hold the expected crowds, so the coffin was placed in a temporary outdoor pavilion; during one day of viewing, ten thousand people per hour passed through the pavilion.

On May 4, 1865, Lincoln's casket finally reached Springfield, where it was placed in the Illinois State House. Thousands of people viewed the body there, and thousands more lined the route from there to Oak Ridge Cemetery, where the coffin was taken for burial. Also carried to the cemetery was the coffin of Lincoln's son Willie; it had been removed from its Washington, D.C., grave so father and son could be buried side by side. **See also** assassination of President Abraham Lincoln; Lincoln, Mary Todd; Lincoln, Robert Todd.

Lincoln, Mary Todd (1818–1882)

As the wife of President Abraham Lincoln, Mary Todd Lincoln was the first lady during the Civil War. However, many Northerners questioned her loyalty to their cause, because she had been born in the South and many of her Kentucky relatives had joined the Confederate army. In fact, some Northern papers accused her of being a Confederate spy, though there was no evidence of this. Others were content merely to criticize various aspects of her behavior and personality, such as her violent temper and extravagant spending habits.

Mary Todd Lincoln not only flew into rages but suffered from bouts of depression, and she often retired to her bed complaining of what she called a sick headache.

Her behavior grew worse after Lincoln was elected president in 1860. In large part this was because she was unhappy having to move to the White House, but she was also suffering because she had lost one of their four sons, eleven-year-old William, in 1861. (The Lincolns had previously lost their four-year-old son Edward in 1850.) Three months after William's death, Mary Lincoln began inviting spiritual mediums to the White House, holding séances to try to contact not only his spirit but those of other relatives she had lost.

Mary Lincoln was with her husband when he was shot on April 14, 1865, and this experience destroyed her already fragile mental health. After he died the following day, she locked herself away in one room of the White House and refused to come out for five weeks, not even for the funeral. She then moved into a hotel suite in Chicago, Illinois, where she lived the rest of her life as a near recluse. She was officially declared insane in 1875 and died in 1882. **See also** assassination of President Abraham Lincoln; Lincoln, Abraham; Lincoln, Robert Todd.

Lincoln, Robert Todd (1843–1926)

The oldest son of President Abraham Lincoln, Robert Todd Lincoln left Harvard Law School in 1864 to support the war effort by becoming a U.S. Army captain. He was assigned to the staff of Ulysses S. Grant and accompanied the Union general on his campaigns during the last year of the war. After his father was assassinated, Lincoln moved to Chicago, Illinois, where he lived with his emotionally unstable mother so that he could help her raise his brother Tad. He also finished his law studies and established a legal practice.

Robert Lincoln remained in Chicago until 1881, when he went to Washington, D.C., to become secretary of war under President James A. Garfield. He continued in this position under President Chester A. Arthur until 1885, at which time he returned to his Chicago law practice. In 1889 he went to Great Britain as a diplomat under President Benjamin Harrison. Four years later, Lincoln was once again in Chicago, where he served on the board of directors of several major corporations. From 1897 to 1911 he also ran the Pullman Company, a manufacturer of sleeper cars for trains. **See also** assassination of President Abraham Lincoln; Lincoln, Abraham; Lincoln, Mary Todd.

literature, Civil War

Whether fiction or nonfiction, literature written shortly before or during the Civil War was primarily intended either to persuade readers to share the author's political views, usually regarding slavery, or to share a real-life, war-related experience, such as what it was like to be a soldier on the battlefield or a nurse working in a military hospital. One of the most important politically motivated works was Harriet Beecher Stowe's *Uncle Tom's Cabin* (1852), which focuses on the abuse of slaves on Southern plantations, but there were many others as well, including Southern novelist Augusta Jane Evans's *Macaria, or Altars of Sacrifice* (1864), which uses fictional characters to vilify the North and show why Southern secession was justified. Even popular Civil War fiction, which largely fell into the genres of romance and adventure, often had political undertones. For example, *The Aide-de-Camp* by James Dabney McCabe (1863) is a Southern adventure novel in which the hero is a Confederate spy and Abraham Lincoln an alcoholic. Many of the memoirs and diaries written during this period also included comments of a political nature, though the majority were not published until after the war, if at all. **See also** letters and diaries; poetry, Civil War; Stowe, Harriet (Elizabeth) Beecher; *Uncle Tom's Cabin.*

Livermore, Mary (1820–1905)

Along with Jane Hoge (1811–1890), Mary Livermore went on speaking tours in 1861 and 1862 to promote the activities of the U.S. Sanitary Commission, which worked to improve living conditions in military camps and hospitals, and to encourage the development of other relief agencies on the local level. They also delivered supplies to soldiers on the front lines. After the war both women wrote books about their experiences. Livermore's work, *My Story of the War: A Woman's Narrative* (1887), was the more widely read of the two, but Hoge's *The Boys in Blue* (1867) was also popular. **See also** Sanitary Commission, U.S.

Logan, John Alexander (1826–1886)

Union general John A. Logan is perhaps best known for his post–Civil War activities. In 1865 he helped create an organization of Union army veterans, the Grand Army of the Republic (GAR), and served as its commander in chief for several years. In this capacity, he established Memorial Day (then called Decoration Day) in 1868, asking all members of the GAR to honor those who had died in the Civil War by putting flowers on their graves every May 30.

Logan also had a distinguished career in politics both before and after the war. He represented Illinois in the U.S. Congress from 1859 to 1861, then gave up this position to organize the Thirty-first Illinois Infantry and serve as its colonel. Eventually he achieved the rank of major general of volunteers, and in 1864 he briefly commanded the Army of the Tennessee. In 1867 Logan returned to politics, representing Illinois in the U.S. House of Representatives until 1871, when he joined the U.S. Senate. Logan served as a senator from 1871 to 1877 and again from 1879 to 1886. **See also** veterans.

Longstreet, James (1821–1904)

Confederate lieutenant general James Longstreet fought in many major Civil War battles and was with General Robert E. Lee when Lee surrendered his Army of Northern Virginia to the Union at Appomattox. Longstreet was born in South Carolina but from the age of twelve he lived in Georgia. After Georgia seceded, Longstreet, by then a U.S. Army officer with two decades of military experience, joined the Confederate army as a brigadier general. His brigade won its first military engagement with the enemy, which took place at Blackburn's Ford, Virginia, just prior to the First Battle of Bull Run in July 1861. Two years later, as a lieutenant general, Longstreet was given command of a corps under Robert E. Lee. During this period Longstreet participated in such engagements as the Peninsula Campaign (spring of 1862), the Second Battle of Bull Run (August 1862), the Battle of Antietam (September 1862), the Battle of Fredericksburg (December 1862), and the Battle of Gettysburg (July 1863), during which he participated bravely in one of the most dangerous assaults of the war, Pickett's Charge.

Longstreet was then sent to the western theater to join the Army of Tennessee in fighting the Battle of Chickamauga (September 1863). This put him under General Braxton Bragg, with whom he had many disagreements. Finally Confederate president Jefferson Davis decided to end the difficulties between the two men by giving Longstreet a separate command and sending him to besiege the city of Knoxville, Tennessee, in November 1863. Longstreet argued constantly with his subordinates during this assignment, which ended in failure.

In April 1864 Longstreet was again placed under Robert E. Lee as part of the Army of Northern Virginia, and he remained with this army for the rest of the war. Longstreet's career was nearly ended, however, when his own men accidentally

James Longstreet led Confederate troops in many successful battles.

shot him in the throat and right arm during the Wilderness Campaign, and he had to take some time off to recover. He returned to the army in October 1864 with his arm paralyzed. In April 1865 Longstreet commanded troops during the Confederates' retreat from Petersburg to Appomattox, where he witnessed Lee's surrender to Union general Ulysses S. Grant.

After the war, several former Confederate generals, most notably Jubal Early, attacked Longstreet's reputation by suggesting in print that Longstreet was responsible for the Confederates' defeat at the Battle of Gettysburg because he had not arrived on the battlefield until the third day of fighting—a delay that Longstreet said was due to various unavoidable problems but that Early claimed Longstreet had arranged purposely. The Southern press also carried reports of Longstreet's many arguments with superiors and subordinates. In response, Longstreet wrote articles defending his actions at Gettysburg and criticizing those of Robert E. Lee.

Perhaps because of his problems with other Southerners, Longstreet became involved with the Republican Party during this period, thereby further angering his critics. This party affiliation allowed Longstreet to obtain not only a full U.S. pardon in June 1867 for his actions during the war but also a series of government appointments, including U.S. minister to Turkey (1880), U.S. marshal in Georgia (1881), and U.S. railroad commissioner (1898). **See also** Appomattox Campaign; armies, Confederate; Early, Jubal A.; Gettysburg, Battle of; Lee, Robert Edward; Pickett's Charge; Wilderness, Battle of the.

Louisiana

During the Civil War, Louisiana's economy was based largely on the harvesting of cotton and sugar cane, and slaveholding plantation owners dominated the state legislature. Therefore Louisiana voted to secede from the Union on January 26, 1861, even though the majority of its population opposed this decision. However, in April 1862 Louisiana's largest city (and indeed, with a population of about twenty-seven thousand the largest city in the Confederacy), New Orleans, fell into Union hands after a land-sea assault, largely due to the efforts of Union admiral David Farragut. This defeat was a major blow to the Confederacy, particularly since the city was located near the mouth of the Mississippi River and was strategically important in the Confederacy's defense of the Southern coast. **See also** Farragut, David Glasgow; population.

Magruder, John Bankhead (1807–1871)

Confederate general John B. Magruder was known for tricking the enemy into thinking he commanded a larger number of troops and had more weapons than he actually did. For example, at Yorktown, Virginia, in 1862 he had his soldiers create fake cannons out of logs and shout orders as though these weapons were manned, thereby convincing a Union army led by General George B. McClellan that it needed reinforcements before it could attack.

A brevet (temporary) lieutenant colonel of the First U.S. Artillery during the Mexican-American War (1846–1848), Magruder joined the Confederate army as a colonel when his native state of Virginia seceded in 1861. Shortly thereafter he was promoted to major general and given command of Confederate troops defending the Virginia peninsula. When Federal troops invaded this region in June 1861, Magruder defeated them at Big Bethel, Virginia. When he met the enemy again at Yorktown the following April, however, he was unable to achieve a victory. Therefore, after tricking McClellan into delaying a Union attack for a month, Magruder evacuated his men farther up the peninsula without McClellan's knowledge. Although this decision saved Confederate lives, some Southerners later criticized Magruder for sneaking away instead of fighting.

Magruder was also criticized for his actions during the Seven Days' Battles on the Virginia peninsula in June and July 1862. At times he would appear sleepy, but otherwise he was anxious and agitated. Although some people blamed his erratic behavior on drunkenness, it appears that it was the result of stress combined with an allergic reaction to some medicine he was taking. Nonetheless, when the Confederates lost over twenty thousand men in the conflict, Magruder took the brunt of the blame, even though he was not the only general on the battlefield. He was subsequently sent from the peninsula, first to Mississippi and then to Texas, where he continued to command troops until the war's end. **See also** Yorktown, Battle of.

Maine

As part of the Missouri Compromise of 1820, Maine entered the Union as a free state. In subsequent years, a majority of its citizens supported the abolitionist movement, and by the late 1850s the Republican Party dominated state politics there. Therefore Maine was firmly behind U.S. president Abraham Lincoln, a Republican, at the start of the Civil War. As a result of strong pro-Union sentiment, the state contributed thousands of soldiers to the North's war effort. **See also** Missouri Compromise.

Mallory, Stephen R. (1813?–1873)

Stephen R. Mallory was the Confederate secretary of the navy from February 28, 1861, to May 2, 1865. His first duty was to increase the size of the Confederate fleet, which at the beginning of the war had only twelve small ships and about three hundred officers who had come from the U.S. Navy. Mallory instituted a major recruitment and training effort to add hundreds of sailors to the navy and implemented plans to acquire ships through construction projects, purchases, and enemy captures. He also ordered Confederate workers to raise the sunken U.S. frigate *Merrimack* from the waters off Norfolk, Virginia, and recondition it as an ironclad ram named the *Virginia.* Moreover, Mallory supervised the placement of mines, then called torpedoes, in Southern waters in an attempt to sink enemy ships. Naval historians have judged Mallory to have been excellent at his job, though many of his peers thought he was not doing enough to advance the Confederate navy.

Mallory's experiences prior to the Civil War were varied; for example, while living in Florida he worked as a customs inspector, an attorney, a county judge, and a port collector. He also served in the Seminole Wars of 1836–1838 as the captain of a small boat in the Florida Everglades. During the 1850s Mallory served two terms as a U.S. senator and was appointed chairman of the Naval Affairs Committee. He left the Senate after Florida seceded in 1861.

After the war, Mallory was captured by Federal soldiers and spent nearly a year—from May 20, 1865, to March 10, 1866—imprisoned at Fort LaFayette in New York Harbor. Once released on parole, he returned to practicing law in Florida and wrote editorials for various publications, expressing his views on issues related to Reconstruction; in particular, he opposed giving blacks the right to vote. **See also** Florida; *Merrimack,* USS/*Virginia,* CSS; navies, Confederate and Union; Reconstruction.

Manassas, Virginia

Manassas, Virginia, was the site of what Northerners called the First Battle of Bull Run (July 1861) and the Second Battle of Bull Run (August 1862). This name is derived from that of a creek, Bull Run, that winds through the battlefield area. Southerners, however, called these two battles the First and Second Battles of Manassas. **See also** Bull Run, First Battle of; Bull Run, Second Battle of.

maps

For obvious reasons, maps were very important during the Civil War. However, in 1861 both the Union and the Confederate armies had difficulty obtaining accurate maps, because mapmakers did not routinely make maps of every part of the country. Therefore both governments supported mapmaking projects after the war began.

In the North, these projects were usually undertaken by government agencies already experienced in making maps, including the U.S. Army Corps of Topographical Engineers (which was eventually placed under the U.S. Army Corps of Engineers), the U.S. Coast Survey (under the Department of the Treasury), and the U.S. Navy's Hydrographic Office. In the South, there were no such mapmaking agencies when the war began, so General Robert E. Lee established one, the Topographical Department of the Army of Northern Virginia. Working out of offices in Richmond, Virginia, this department was charged with creating accurate maps of the area around the city. Once this assignment was finished, the department began making maps of other parts of Virginia, often at the request of various military commanders. These maps were drawn in black India ink on linen, and at first whenever someone requested a copy it was traced. By 1864, however, the Topographical Department had devised a way to make very crude photographic copies of these hand-drawn maps.

In addition to government mapmakers working out of Washington, D.C., and

Richmond, Virginia, military officers and soldiers in the field might also be assigned the duty of making maps during a military campaign. At first these men were amateur mapmakers, but eventually both governments assigned trained topographical engineers to certain armies, corps, and divisions. One such field mapmaker, Union colonel William E. Merrill of the Topographical Department of the Army of the Cumberland, traveled with his own mapmaking equipment, which included a printing press, two lithographic presses, and photographic devices, as well as a large staff. As a result, he was able to produce over two hundred maps for General William T. Sherman's Atlantic Campaign in 1864. **See also** engineers; Sherman, William Tecumseh.

marches

During the Civil War, armies traveled great distances on marches over all kinds of terrain in order to meet the enemy. In fact, many armies were forced to march twenty miles a day, and sometimes as much as thirty or forty, and the average marching speed of the infantry was two and a half miles per hour. To make travel easier, soldiers carried as little gear as possible, although their packs could still weigh several pounds. Generally, however, a soldier on a march took along just one blanket, if any; one pair of socks with no other change of clothing; one gun; two hundred rounds of ammunition; and a minimum amount of food. Whenever possible, supply wagons followed a marching army to carry grain for the army's horses and additional ammunition.

Soldiers cooked the food they would carry before they left camp so that they would not have to stop during their travels to prepare meals, and sometimes a man on a particularly tiring march would eat several days' rations at once just to avoid carrying such provisions. Consequently it was not unusual for a marching soldier to go a day or more without food. However, soldiers were also allowed to fish, hunt, and pick fruits, nuts, and berries along the way whenever time allowed in order to supplement their diet. They might also acquire food, as well as clothing, supplies, and personal items, from sutlers—traveling salesmen who followed regiments as they marched. However, sutlers charged high prices for their goods, and many soldiers did not have the money to patronize them.

The need for supplies was less of a problem for Confederate soldiers, at least in the war's early stages. Because they did most of their marching in the South, they often received gifts of food and supplies from civilians as they marched, particularly at the beginning of the war before food became scarce. Conversely, Northerners—who did most of their marching in enemy territory—were rarely offered anything.

Soldiers on both sides were allowed to forage for food and supplies, which meant that they could take provisions from citizens as needed. Union soldiers were supposed to give a receipt to each person from whom they took things, and the holder of the receipt theoretically could apply to the U.S. government for payment for the lost goods, but this procedure was rarely followed. As a result, marching armies often stripped families of their food, livestock, and possessions without leaving them with any way to buy replacements.

The longer the march, the greater the difficulty of dealing with one's possessions. On long marches, many of the men abandoned items as they went along in order to lighten their load. Sometimes they cast off blankets on a hot day only to wish they had them back again when the weather turned cold. Moreover, soldiers often found that even with careful planning they were inadequately supplied. For example, many soldiers wore out their shoes on long marches. When this happened, they might wrap rags around their bare feet or steal shoes from the dead. The need for a long march naturally placed an army at a disadvantage. Many men died while on marches, having suffered from heatstroke, frostbite, malnutrition, or illness. Moreover, those who survived might not have enough energy left to fight the enemy. **See also** food; shoes; sutlers; uniforms and equipment.

Maryland

Maryland had divided loyalties during the Civil War. When the war began, members of the working class and people living in western Maryland were largely pro-Union, while members of the upper class and people living along the eastern seaboard were largely pro-Confederate. The remainder of the population generally favored remaining neutral in the conflict between North and South. After some debate, this latter group prevailed, leading Maryland to declare its neutrality.

Nonetheless, the Union established a military presence in certain parts of the state, including the cities of Baltimore and Annapolis (where the U.S. Naval Academy was located). In Baltimore, where a majority of the population had been opposed to siding with the Union, citizens responded by attacking Union soldiers from a Massachusetts regiment that were marching through town on April 19, 1861. Their efforts were fruitless in removing Federal troops from their city, however, and soon the U.S. government had declared martial law throughout Maryland.

With Maryland in Union hands, the Confederate army invaded the state on three separate occasions, all resulting in battlefield defeats. The first resulted in the Battle of Antietam near Sharpsburg, Maryland, in September 1862. The second was part of the preliminaries to the Battle of Gettysburg in Pennsylvania in July 1863. The final Confederate invasion of Maryland was associated with a July 1864 failed attempt to attack Washington, D.C. **See also** Antietam, Battle of; Baltimore, Maryland; Gettysburg, Battle of; Washington, D.C.

Mason-Dixon Line

In the period just prior to the Civil War, a boundary dating back to colonial days known as the Mason-Dixon Line (or the Mason and Dixon Line), along with the Ohio River, had become the unofficial dividing line between the slave states of the South and the free states of the North. As such, it figured in the Missouri Compromise, a legislative package that established an official political boundary within the territories acquired in the Louisiana Purchase (1803), so all lands north of a geographic line at latitude 36°30' would prohibit slavery and those below would permit it.

The Mason-Dixon Line was originally established at 39°43' as a means of settling a border dispute between American colonies. In particular, the colonies of Pennsylvania and Maryland had competing claims to territory. To settle this and similar disputes, in the mid–eighteenth century the British government sent land surveyors and astronomers to America to draw the exact geographical boundaries of various regions. Two of these surveyors, Charles Mason and Jeremiah Dixon, worked on delineating the boundaries of Delaware and establishing the border between Pennsylvania and Maryland. The Maryland-Pennsylvania border, which was surveyed for 233 miles, involved cutting a swath through forests and placing small and large markers at one-mile and five-mile intervals, respectively. Completed in 1763 after four years of work, this boundary quickly became known as the Mason-Dixon Line. **See also** "Dixie"; Missouri Compromise.

Massachusetts

Massachusetts supported the Union during the Civil War with great enthusiasm. Home to many abolitionists, it was the first state to make an official commitment to the Union war effort, vowing on January 18, 1861, to send troops and funds to the federal government. (Minnesota, however, was the first state to actually send volunteers into the Civil War.) Some of the Massachusetts regiments sent to war, such as the Fifty-fourth Massachusetts, were peopled entirely by black soldiers. **See also** abolitionists; black troops; Minnesota.

McClellan, George Brinton (1826–1885)

Union general George B. McClellan was named the general in chief of the U.S. Army in November 1861 based on his having over a decade of military experience and his other contributions. A railroad president by the time the Civil War began, McClellan had previously distinguished himself by serving in the Mexican-American War (1846–1848), teaching military engineering at the U.S. Military Academy, and writing a military handbook on European armies after observing the battle tactics of Great Britain, France, Turkey, and Russia during the Crimean War (1855–1856). He had also designed a saddle to be used by the U.S. cavalry, a streamlined piece of riding equipment that soon became known as the McClellan.

At the outset of the Civil War, McClellan was involved in the first efforts to organize and supply Union troops. In May

George McClellan was a successful businessman at the time he was appointed commander of the Army of the Potomac.

1861 he was given command of the Department of the Ohio, which was charged with protecting western Virginia. In July 1861 he became the leader of what would soon become the Army of the Potomac, responsible for protecting Washington, D.C., and for destroying the Confederate troops in northern and eastern Virginia.

After he was named general in chief of the U.S. Army, McClellan proved to be skilled in matters related to organizing and supplying his troops, but he was reluctant to actually engage the enemy. Eventually, President Abraham Lincoln became frustrated with McClellan's reluctance to attack the Confederacy, and in January 1862 Lincoln issued an order, General War Order Number 1, that required all armies to move forward into enemy territory. Even then, McClellan waited two months before beginning his Peninsula Campaign, which took place in Virginia between March and July 1862. Although McClellan did win some battles during this campaign, he lacked aggressiveness and was quick to retreat, often convincing himself that the Confederate troops in any given battle were stronger and more skilled than his, even when this was not the case. As a result, he failed to take the Confederate capital of Richmond, Virginia, and eventually withdrew his army from the Virginia peninsula.

McClellan then returned to Washington, D.C., to command that city's defenses as the Confederates moved into Maryland. In September 1862 he succeeded in driving the Confederates from the battlefield during the Battle of Antietam, but he failed to pursue and destroy the retreating Confederate army. He also failed to take full advantage of a Confederate mistake prior to the battle. A Confederate courier had lost a document detailing the Confederacy's battle plans, which a Union agent later found on the ground and turned over to McClellan. This document indicated that McClellan's forces outnumbered those of the Confederates, but he did not believe this; as a result, he delayed attacking and when he did so he went into battle without conviction. Consequently, his success was not decisive. In November 1862 President Lincoln relieved McClellan of his command and never gave him another.

McClellan then publicly criticized Lincoln's handling of the war, even running against the president in the 1864 election. As the Democratic candidate, McClellan called the war effort a failure, an unpopular position that lost him the election. He then resigned his commission in the U.S. Army and moved to Europe. McClellan returned to the United States in 1868 and two years later took a job as chief engineer of the New York Department of Docks. In 1872 he left this position to become president of the Atlantic and Great Western Railroad. From 1877 to 1881 McClellan served as governor of New Jersey, after which he retired from public life. **See also** Antietam, Battle of; armies, Union.

McClernand, John Alexander (1812–1900)

Union general John A. McClernand was a politician prior to the war and had little skill as a commanding officer. He served in the U.S. House of Representatives from 1843 to 1851 and again from 1858 to 1861. Once the Civil War broke out, he fought in several major battles between 1861 and 1862 under General Ulysses S. Grant, whom he publicly criticized. In January 1863 McClernand formed a new version of the Army of the Mississippi with the intent of using it to take Vicksburg, Mississippi. However, Grant's army was already engaged in operations there, and McClernand's army was soon placed under his command. McClernand subsequently took part in the Red River Campaign, but in November 1864 he left the army because of poor health. From 1870 to 1873 he served as a circuit judge. **See**

also armies, Union; Grant, Ulysses S.; Vicksburg Campaign.

McDowell, Irvin (1818–1885)

Union brigadier general Irvin McDowell is best known for the defeat of his forces at the First Battle of Bull Run on July 21, 1861, despite the fact that his troops outnumbered the Confederates thirty-five thousand to thirty thousand. McDowell had been highly regarded before the war as a military strategist. A graduate of the U.S. Military Academy in 1838 and subsequently an instructor there, he fought in the Mexican-American War (1846–1848) and then served in a variety of staff positions until the Civil War broke out. At that time he began organizing Union troops and was chosen to defend the Washington, D.C., area. When Confederate troops took a position about twenty-five miles south of Washington, McDowell was sent to drive them away.

McDowell planned his attack carefully, and when he met the enemy at Bull Run Creek near Centreville, Virginia, he was confident that the complex strategy he had developed was sound. However, once the fighting began he had difficulty executing his plans, becoming indecisive on the field and proving unable to command large groups of men. (Instead, he would direct orders at individual regiments, sometimes losing sight of how they fit into the overall battle.) He also had problems with men disobeying his orders; some left the battlefield even as he was giving them commands. As the battle turned against the Union, the soldiers' retreat turned into a rout. Civilians who had come from Washington, D.C., to watch the battle got caught up in the panic, and in the resulting chaos several people were killed.

After the battle, McDowell was relieved of his command and George McClellan was put in his place. Meanwhile, McDowell was made corps commander under McClellan and John Pope. When McDowell again performed badly in the Second Battle of Bull Run in August 1862, he was relieved of command for the remainder of the war. Although he later led the Department of the Pacific from 1876 to 1882, he never regained the respect he had enjoyed prior to the Civil War. **See also** Bull Run, First Battle of; McClellan, George Brinton.

McPherson, James Birdseye (1828–1864)

James B. McPherson served the Union as both an engineer and a battlefield commander. A former engineering instructor at the U.S. Military Academy, he worked for the U.S. Army Corps of Engineers on a variety of projects in the West during the decade prior to the Civil War. After the war began he supervised the construction of fortifications near Boston, Massachusetts, and then spent several months serving as an aide-de-camp and engineer under General Henry Halleck in the Department of the Missouri. By the end of 1861 McPherson had become General Ulysses S. Grant's chief engineer.

McPherson contributed his engineering expertise to Grant's Tennessee Campaign and commanded troops in Grant's attacks on Fort Henry and Fort Donelson in February 1862. He was subsequently promoted to brigadier general of volunteers and participated in the Battle of Shiloh, as well as in Grant's attack on Corinth, Mississippi. After this McPherson was placed in charge of railways in the District of Western Tennessee, but by October 1862 he had been promoted to major general and given command of a division. By the time Grant made his second attack on Vicksburg, Mississippi, in 1863, McPherson was a corps commander. Once Vicksburg was taken, he was promoted to brigadier general in the Regular Army and placed in command of the District of Vicksburg.

In March 1864 McPherson became the commander of the Army of the Tennessee under General William T. Sherman and participated in Sherman's Atlanta Campaign. McPherson was killed during the Battle of Atlanta while facing Confederate troops under the command of John Bell Hood. When McPherson died, Grant reportedly said that he had lost his best friend. **See also** Atlanta Campaign; engineers; Grant, Ulysses S.; Hood, John Bell.

Meade, George Gordon (1815–1872)

As the commander of the Army of the Potomac, Union general George G. Meade defeated the Confederates at the Battle of Gettysburg in July 1863. A veteran of the Seminole and Mexican-American Wars, Meade began the Civil War as a brigadier general of the Second Brigade of the Pennsylvania Reserves, a volunteer army. He then fought and was wounded in the Seven Days' Battles (June–July 1862), but recovered in time to fight in the Second Battle of Bull Run in August 1862.

At the Battle of Antietam in September 1862 Meade took over command of the Union's I Corps when its general, Joseph Hooker, was wounded, and after the Battle of Fredericksburg in December 1862 Meade was given command of V Corps. He led these troops at the Battle of Chancellorsville in May 1863. In July he again replaced Hooker, this time as the commander of the Army of the Potomac, just days before the Battle of Gettysburg. Meade was subsequently praised for his tactical decisions during the battle but criticized for not pursuing the defeated Confederate army.

Meade remained the commander of the Army of the Potomac for the rest of the war, although in March 1864 this army (and all others in the Union) was placed under the ultimate command of General Ulysses S. Grant. In August 1864 Meade was promoted to major general in the Regular Army, and he continued to work for the U.S. military in various departments until his death from pneumonia in 1872. **See also** armies, Union; Grant, Ulysses S.; Hooker, Joseph.

medical facilities

During the Civil War, field hospitals served soldiers on the battlefield until they could be transferred to general hospitals located in cities and towns. Once at a general hospital, which did not limit its admissions and treated all types of injuries and diseases, a soldier might then be sent to a specialized hospital, which treated only certain types of problems. There were, however, very few of these specialized hospitals in either the North or the South, with most dealing with eye problems or sexually transmitted diseases.

The majority of general hospitals were established in the first years of the war in response to a severe shortage of such facilities. In 1861 there were only 2,000 hospital beds in all of Washington, D.C., but by the end of the Civil War there were nearly 137,000, divided among 204 Union general hospitals. Some of these new hospitals were built as part of a hospital construction program, but most were created by converting other structures into hospitals, either temporarily or for the duration of the war. For example, the Capitol Building in Washington, D.C., was used as a hospital until a new medical facility could be built nearby.

The Confederates had about 154 general hospitals by the end of the war, 20 of them in Richmond, Virginia, and most of the rest located near the southern Atlantic coast. Again, some had been built specifically as hospitals while others were converted structures. The South also had wayside hospitals, which were small, independent hospitals set up in private homes. A wayside hospital at High Point, North Carolina, served 5,795 Confederate soldiers between September 1863 and May 1865.

Among medical facilities built by both the North and the South after the war broke out, pavilion-style hospitals were the most common. Pavilion hospitals typically had several wooden buildings, known as pavilions, that were designed to house eighty to one hundred patients. Pavilions, which might be as long as 120 feet and were usually 14 or 15 feet wide, were designed so that their floors and ceilings could be opened in various places to provide ventilation. Pavilions were typically situated in an arrangement resembling a daisy, radiating from a center where additional structures such as treatment and operating rooms, the morgue, the pharmacy, the kitchen, and one or more icehouses were located. The South's Chimborazo Hospital in Richmond, which was the South's largest hospital, had five icehouses, as well as five soup houses, a brewery, a bakery, bathhouses, and eight thousand beds in thirty pavilions. In all, more than seventy-six thousand men were treated at this hospital during the four years of the war.

Field hospitals treated far more men over the course of the war than did general hospitals. At the beginning of the war, each regiment typically had its own field hospital, but by the end there was such a shortage of supplies and physicians, particularly in the South, that this was not always possible. When available, however, most regimental hospitals were set up in walled tents, although some were in the open air. When battlefields were near towns, doctors might take over a schoolhouse, barn, church, or other structure as a field hospital. Field hospitals of all types were typically located at least three to five miles away from the front lines, with the wounded being taken to these makeshift facilities by an ambulance corps.

Field hospitals offered only the crudest of comforts. While waiting to be treated by army surgeons, wounded soldiers typically lay on bare ground or on beds of hay, but even once they were treated there might or might not be a cot available for them to sleep on. Moreover, field hospitals could be extremely unsanitary. An inspection of Union field hospitals between November 1862 and March 1863 rated a third of them as very bad. Consequently, various individuals and relief organizations worked to better these conditions, most notably the U.S. Sanitary Commission. Nonetheless, thousands of soldiers died because their wounds became infected after treatment. **See also** casualties; diseases, dietary illnesses, and infections; drugs, medical; medical personnel and supplies; Sanitary Commission, U.S.; surgery.

medical personnel and supplies

Prior to the Civil War, all U.S. Army physicians were surgeons—that is, they knew how to remove bullets and amputate wounded limbs as well as treat a variety of injuries, illnesses, and diseases. However, in 1860 there were only 115 surgeons in the U.S. Army, and 24 of these left to join the Confederate military service. This number was completely inadequate, given the many men who would need to be treated, so as the war progressed, both the U.S. and the Confederate governments called on civilian physicians to volunteer their services with army medical corps. As a result, eventually more than 10,000 doctors of various types treated soldiers during the Civil War, usually after subjecting themselves to an examination by either a Union or Confederate board of medical examiners. They were then assigned to be a surgeon or assistant surgeon, depending on their experience, with a military unit, for which they would not only provide medical services but also keep medical records, determine which men were fit for service, requisition medical supplies as needed, and establish field hospitals.

In performing their duties, surgeons relied on the help of nurses, who were also in short supply at the outset of the war. At that time all army nurses were male, because it was generally considered improper for women to bathe grown men or dress their wounds. Because of this shortage, most men assigned to nursing duties had no formal training. Sometimes, a soldier recovering from an illness or injury that made him unfit for battle would be assigned such duties. In July 1862, however, the Union decided to recruit the first female military nurses, and to this end the U.S. surgeon general decreed that one-third of the Union's hospital nurses should be women. Two months later the Confederacy adopted a similar policy. By the end of the war, approximately three thousand women had officially become nurses, with many more acting as nurses on an informal basis whenever wounded men showed up in their towns after a nearby battle. There were also a few female doctors, even though medical schools of the period generally refused to admit women. One of the most prominent female physicians was Mary Walker, who was commissioned as a Union army surgeon in 1864.

By the time women had begun to provide medical services on the battlefield, both the North and the South had decided to consider doctors and nurses as neutral in the conflict. This meant that all medical personnel captured during a battle were supposed to be immediately returned to

A nurse cares for two wounded Union soldiers. Despite a severe shortage of qualified medical personnel, women were not allowed to work in military hospitals until 1862.

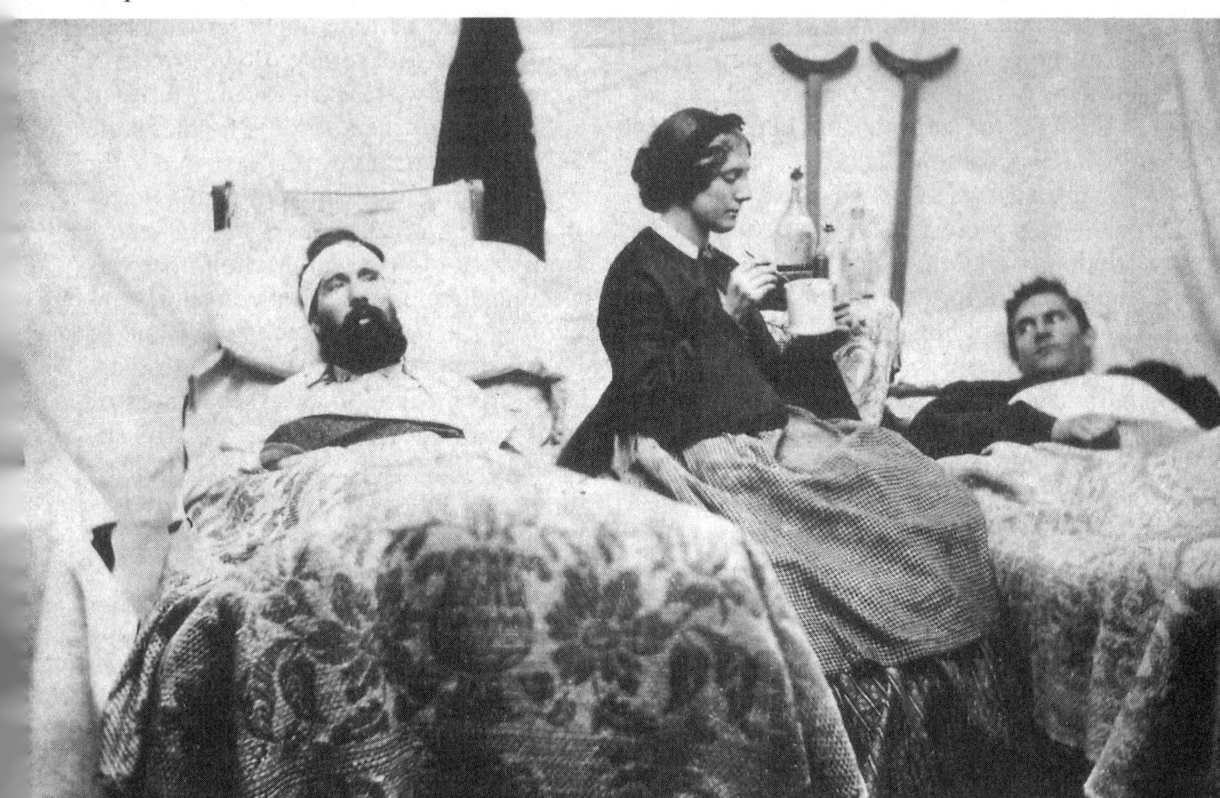

their own military forces (although Union records show that at least 4 Union medical officers died in Confederate prisons). In addition, both the Union and the Confederate armies tried to avoid injuring medical officers on the battlefield, identifying them by certain marks and insignia on their uniforms. For this reason, Union army records indicate that only 42 medical officers were killed as a result of battlefield or guerrilla-warfare injuries, with another 73 receiving nonfatal battlefield wounds. However, at least another 281 died of diseases they contracted while treating patients.

Each medical officer used surgical instruments that had been furnished by the government, which he (or, very rarely she) was then responsible for maintaining. These instruments were typically divided among two to four medical bags. One of these, known as the "surgeon's field companion," was a case that the physician personally carried onto the battlefield in order to treat wounded men where they fell. Another was the "hospital knapsack," which was carried by the physician's assistant for the surgeon's use in performing hospital operations. This bag might weigh as much as twenty pounds. Two other possible bags were a pocket case, which carried a small amount of supplies for the treatment of minor ailments and injuries, and a bag holding only those instruments needed for minor operations. Physicians also had access to a medicine chest, which was transported in a wagon whenever a regiment was on the move. Other bulky medical, surgical, and hospital supplies were also transported by wagons, at first along with other types of supplies but eventually in special wagons designated as being only for medical use.

Special wagons were also used to transport wounded men from the battlefield to hospitals. Known as ambulances, these vehicles were initially driven by enlisted men assigned to the duty by the Quartermaster Corps, usually because they had displayed cowardice in battle. However, such individuals tended to repeat their cowardice and often pretended to be busy elsewhere when wounded soldiers needed to be evacuated in the midst of battle. Therefore in 1862 Union general George McClellan created the first Ambulance Corps for his Army of the Potomac, which was an organized, trained group of ambulance drivers under the control of the army's medical director. Although the Quartermaster Corps protested this action, the Ambulance Corps proved to be so effective that many other armies established similar units, and in 1864 the U.S. government officially decreed that every Union army had to have its own Ambulance Corps. **See also** diseases, dietary illnesses, and infections; drugs, medical; surgery.

Memminger, Christopher Gustavus (1803–1888)

Christopher G. Memminger served as the Confederate secretary of the treasury from February 21, 1861, to July 18, 1864. A South Carolina attorney, former state assemblyman, and plantation owner whose family had many political connections, Memminger was a strong secessionist prior to the war. Memminger was also the director of several companies, including the Farmers Exchange Bank of Charleston. At the 1861 convention establishing the Confederate States of America (CSA), Memminger was selected to help draft a provisional constitution and shortly thereafter became Jefferson Davis's first choice for CSA secretary of the treasury.

Despite his banking experience and an honest desire to succeed, Memminger was unable to solve the Confederacy's many financial problems. For example, he was unsuccessful in fighting inflation and had difficulty getting enough currency printed to pay the Confederacy's bills. Initially he tried to pay for the war by borrowing money, but later he decided to pay for it through taxes. Even when these taxes were enacted, however, he still could not raise enough money to keep the Confederacy from going bankrupt. When this finally occurred, Memminger resigned as secretary of the treasury, having received a vote of no confidence from the Confederate House of Representatives in May 1864. His main adviser and friend, George A. Trenholm, then took his place, but did no better than Memminger had.

Meanwhile, Memminger returned to his law practice. After the war, unlike many other Confederate high officials, he was neither pursued nor arrested by the U.S. government. In 1876 he was elected to the South Carolina Assembly, and he continued to be active in his state government until his retirement in 1879. **See also** cabinet, Confederate; Trenholm, George Alfred.

Merrimack, USS/*Virginia,* CSS

In an attempt to prevent the enemy from acquiring a valuable ship when the Confederates closed in on the Gosport Navy Yard in Norfolk, Virginia, Union soldiers burned and sank their steam frigate USS *Merrimack* in April 1861. Two months later, however, the Confederacy raised and repaired the ship. To speed the repairs, the Confederate decided to convert it into an ironclad warship. At the time, the Confederates knew that the Union was also working on an ironclad warship, the *Monitor,* in New York, so they worked quickly on the *Merrimack,* which they renamed the CSS *Virginia.* The ship left port on March 8, 1862, under the command of Commodore Franklin Buchanan and headed north to Hampton Roads, a waterway connecting the James and Elizabeth Rivers with Chesapeake Bay. There it fought in the Battle of Hampton Roads against several Union warships, including the *Monitor* (against which it battled for four hours, with neither side gaining the advantage), but it had to break off the engagement before the outgoing tide lowered the water in the bay. This was because, like other ironclads, the ship was heavy in the water and could therefore easily run aground.

After this battle the *Virginia* was placed under the command of Captain Josiah Tattnall and sent to attack other Union ships. However, its home port remained Norfolk, Virginia, and it was there when the Confederates were forced to evacuate the city. Unfortunately for the *Virginia,* at that time the water level of the James River was too low for the ship to make it out to sea, so on May 11, 1862, the Confederacy scuttled it, and the ship never returned to service. **See also** Hampton Roads; Norfolk, Virginia.

Michigan

Michigan, a free state, supported the Union during the Civil War. It contributed approximately ninety thousand soldiers to the war effort, of whom nearly fifteen thousand died. In addition, the state provided a regiment made up of black men not only from Michigan but from other states and from Ontario, Canada, as well. **See also** black troops.

military schools, bias against

During the Civil War, officers who had previously been trained at military schools believed that officers who had had no military training lacked the knowledge of military tactics necessary to successfully prosecute the war. (This bias was particularly prevalent in the South, which had ninety-six military schools prior to the war in comparison to the North's fifteen.) Meanwhile, officers without military training, as well as some civilian politicians, believed that men trained in military schools were so steeped in military theories that they often ignored commonsense approaches to the war.

Clashes between the two types of officers typically occurred within the Union and Confederate volunteer armies, because both the North and the South usually assigned experienced Regular Army officers the duty of leading volunteer regiments and brigades and teaching their inexperienced soldiers and officers about weaponry and military tactics. These Regular Army officers often complained that by the time they took charge, volunteer regiments had already been badly trained by leaders the men had elected from among their ranks—typically the most popular men or those who had been wealthy enough to finance the regiment.

Because of such complaints, as well as the poor performance of inexperienced officers on the battlefield, beginning in 1862 Union and Confederate volunteer commanders had to take an examination to show that they possessed a rudimentary knowledge of battlefield skills, though politically powerful men were often able to get around this rule. In addition, upon taking command, volunteer officers were required to study military texts, drill their men, and stage mock battles on a regular basis.

Complaints regarding the supposed weaknesses of officers trained in military schools gradually diminished as many of these men continued to perform brilliantly on the battlefield. One particularly notable example of the value of military training occurred at the Battle of New Market, which was fought in the Shenandoah Valley on May 15, 1864. Confederate forces in this battle included 247 cadets from the Virginia Military Institute who made a heroic charge at the Union forces of Major General Franz Sigel, thereby helping the Confederacy achieve a victory and becoming heroes in the South. **See also** Virginia Military Institute; West Point.

military strategies, Northern vs. Southern

When the Civil War began, leaders in both the North and the South thought that it would be a short war, but the two sides had very different military strategies regarding how to bring about a quick end to the conflict. In the North, the first proposed military strategy was General Winfield Scott's Anaconda Plan, so named because the idea was to destroy the South by shutting off its supplies via a blockade, much as an anaconda snake squeezes the life out of its prey. Once this occurred, Scott suggested, the Union could take an army down the Mississippi River to split the weakened Confederacy in two. President Abraham Lincoln rejected this plan at first, because he knew that the Northern public wanted to see aggressive, immediate military action against the South in general and the Confederate capital of Richmond, Virginia, in particular. Later, however, he decided to blockade Southern ports, although he stuck to the plan of invading the South. With this strategy in mind, Lincoln ordered General George McClellan to advance on Richmond.

McClellan, however, was slow to move into enemy territory, even after Lincoln ordered him to speed up his military campaign, and he hesitated to attack the Confederates even when it was the right time to do so. As a result, Lincoln replaced McClellan with another general, Henry Halleck, who led the Union forces from 1862 to 1864. During this period, the blockade began to take effect, and the Union gained control of the Mississippi River in order to split the Confederacy, just as Winfield Scott had originally suggested. Then in November 1863 a Union force led by General Ulysses S. Grant took control of Chattanooga, Tennessee, which was the gateway to the interior of

Confederate territory. Lincoln realized that in Grant he had found a commander who was willing to prosecute the war on Southern soil with the right amount of forcefulness, and he replaced Halleck with Grant as his general in chief. Grant then took over the development of the Union's military strategy and ordered his armies to cut a swath of destruction from Tennessee down through Atlanta, Georgia, to Savannah, Georgia, on the sea, then drive upward through the Carolinas to meet Union forces already at Richmond, Virginia. Only by using this aggressive, bloody strategy, Grant believed, could the Union bring the war to an end.

In contrast, the Southern strategy was largely defensive rather than offensive. Going into the war, the Confederates believed that European dependence on cotton would be the key to their victory. Under this theory, sometimes referred to as the King Cotton strategy, England and France would get involved in the war in order to keep up their supplies of cotton, and their military strength would make it impossible for the Union to prevail. However, the Confederacy realized that these countries would not jump into the conflict right away, so in the meantime President Jefferson Davis adopted what he called an "offensive-defensive" military strategy. His idea was that the South build up its forces in key defensive positions to block Union attacks, but when attacked the Confederate armies would always fight aggressively enough to put the Union on the defensive.

A few Confederate generals argued that this was the wrong strategy. Instead they wanted the war taken into the North, and indeed Generals Robert E. Lee and Jubal Early did attempt to do this on a few occasions. However, these attempts failed because the Confederacy's leaders were unwilling to commit enough forces to an attack on the North, fearing that this would weaken their defenses of key positions. Indeed, shortly after troops were sent from New Orleans, Louisiana, in 1862 to participate in battles in Tennessee, that city fell into Union hands due to a lack of defensive manpower.

Since state and city leaders did not want to part with their defensive troops, the Confederacy maintained its offensive-defensive strategy even after it became apparent that European countries were not going to become involved. By this point, the South was hoping that it could hold on to its lands until the North either decided that it could never achieve a total victory over the South or simply grew tired of war. With this in mind, Confederate agents in the North secretly worked to support the peace movement there, but before they could make much headway the South experienced a series of crushing defeats from which it could not recover. **See also** Anaconda Plan; cotton; foreign countries, involvement of.

militias, state

A militia is a military force that is not part of the regular armed forces but is ready to be called on for help in an emergency. At the beginning of the Civil War, the federal government called on seventy-five thousand men from state militias, and other groups of militiamen in both the North and the South were eager to volunteer for battle. However, there was some friction between these soldiers and the professional soldiers of the Regular Army, who felt that the training of state militiamen was generally inadequate. The effectiveness of some militiamen was also limited when they made easy targets of themselves by wearing brightly colored state militia uniforms into battle during the first weeks of the war. Soon, however, many realized that it was wiser to adopt the muted gray or blue of the Confederate and Union armies, respectively, which enabled men to blend into shadows. **See also** conscription; uniforms and equipment.

Minnesota

Although it was far from the fighting, Minnesota was the first state to send volunteer soldiers into the Civil War. However, other than sending troops in the numbers and at the times requested by the government, Minnesota had little involvement in the war. Instead, its main focus during the war years was on dealing with its Sioux Indians, who often left their government reservations to attack nearby towns and farms. Consequently, many men who might have left Minnesota to fight for the Union stayed home to protect their families from such attacks. **See also** Native American soldiers.

Mississippi

After seceding from the Union on January 9, 1861, Mississippi became a vital part of the Confederacy, largely because it controlled a long stretch of the Mississippi River. In order to keep from losing this waterway, which was used to transport troops and supplies, the Confederacy established forts along its banks and patrolled its waters with gunboats. Meanwhile, the Union made taking control of the Mississippi River a priority. In April 1862, Union naval forces captured New Orleans, Louisiana, which was situated near the point where the Mississippi River reached the sea. Union gunboats then worked their way up the river to Mississippi, easily taking the city of Natchez before heading north to Vicksburg, a fortified city on a bluff overlooking the river. From November 1862 to July 1863, the Union launched both naval assaults and land attacks against Vicksburg until it surrendered on July 4, 1863. Several other Mississippi towns also saw heavy fighting, including Corinth, which was the terminus of two important railroad lines. Because of the extensive fighting, Mississippi's lands were devastated, which added to the state's economic problems after the war. **See also** Corinth, Mississippi; Vicksburg Campaign.

Missouri

Missouri was admitted to the Union in 1820 as a slave state under the terms of the Missouri Compromise; a free state (Maine) was also admitted at the time in order to maintain the balance between pro- and antislavery forces in Congress. After Missouri achieved statehood, an influx of new settlers who opposed slavery threatened the slave owners who had already achieved dominance in Missouri. This resulted in violent clashes between the two sides long before the Civil War began.

As the number of abolitionists increased in Missouri, the state legislature passed laws designed to ensure that blacks would remain oppressed. Specifically, it prohibited blacks from learning to read or write and it closed its borders to all free blacks. Later, as the threat of secession loomed, the U.S. Army established a strong presence to keep Missouri in the Union. The state government disagreed on whether Missouri should remain with the Union, although the governor, Claiborne F. Jackson, favored secession. The decision was ultimately made that the state should officially side with the Union, largely for economic reasons. On June 11, 1861, however, Jackson and other officials met with Union brigadier general Nathaniel Lyon to discuss the possibility of Missouri seceding, and Lyon announced that he would declare war on the state rather than see it leave the Union. Lyon then launched a military campaign that ultimately led to the Battle of Wilson's Creek (also called the Battle of Oak Hills) on August 10, 1861, between Lyon's forces and those of Confederate general Ben McCulloch. This battle resulted in a Confederate victory and Lyon's death, as well as the belief among Confederate sympathizers that Missouri might be able to secede.

In October, Jackson established a second Missouri government in the southwestern part of the state, in opposition to the pro-Union one, and this government joined the Confederacy. The Union, though, refused to recognize this political body and declared that Missouri was still officially a Union state. Nonetheless, for every four Missourians who became Union soldiers, one became a Confederate. Others became Confederate guerrillas, also known as bushwackers—violent individuals who attacked Union soldiers and abolitionists, particularly along the Kansas-Missouri border.

Despite the divisions within the state, the Union retained control of most of Missouri. The closest the Confederacy came to threatening this control was the Battle of Pea Ridge in neighboring Arkansas on March 7–8, 1862. The battle involved about 16,000 Confederate soldiers, including members of the Missouri State Guard under Major General Earl Van Dorn, who planned to solidify his presence in Arkansas so that he could launch attacks in Missouri. However, after he was defeated by about 10,250 Union men from Brigadier General Ryan Curtis's Army of the Southwest, Van Dorn withdrew from the area, having lost about 800 soldiers. **See also** abolitionists; bushwackers; guerrillas, partisan rangers, and irregulars; Missouri Compromise.

Missouri Compromise

A legislative package passed by Congress in 1820, the Missouri Compromise was designed to maintain a balance in the United States between free states and slave states. Its passage was prompted by the Missouri Territory's request to be admitted into the Union as its twenty-third state. At that time, there was an equal number of free and slave states, so Missouri's entrance into the Union as one or the other would affect the balance of power in Congress. Moreover, Missouri's bid for statehood was the first to come from the western territories acquired by the United States as part of the Louisiana Purchase (1803), and any decision by Congress on this issue would affect all other states that might develop within this region. Therefore, many senators argued passionately over whether Missouri should support slavery.

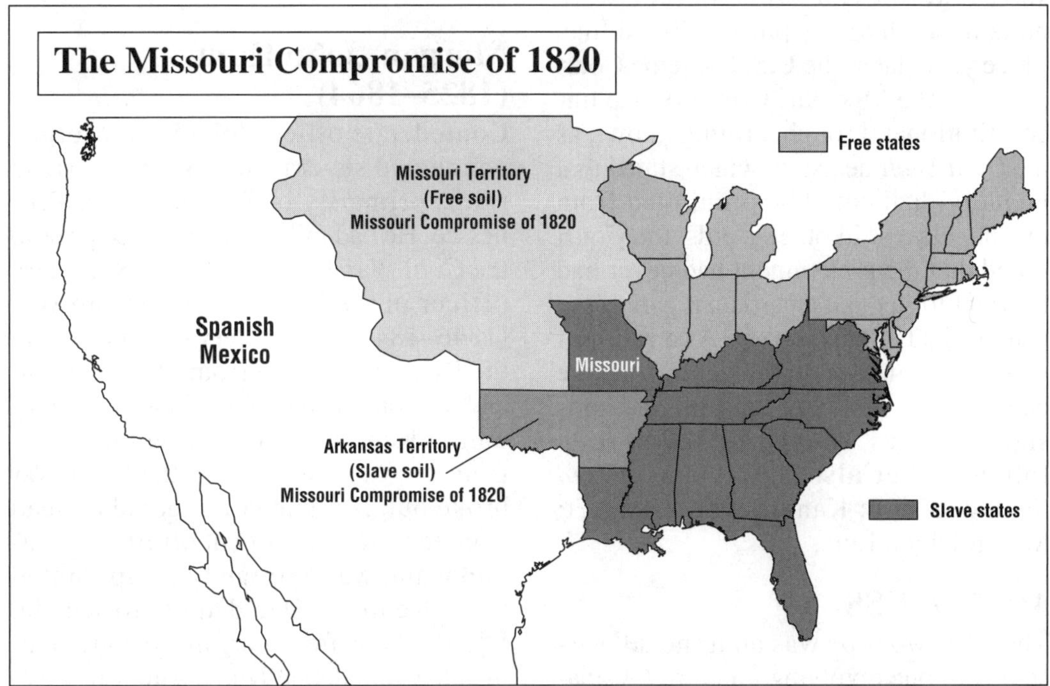

As part of these arguments, Congress considered the fact that a colonial era boundary known as the Mason-Dixon Line, located at latitude 39°43', was already the unofficial dividing line between the slave states of the South and the free states of the North. Eventually Kentucky congressman Henry Clay suggested that a similar line be drawn within the territories of the Louisiana Purchase so that all lands north of a geographic line at latitude 36°30' would prohibit slavery and those below would permit it. Under this system, Missouri—which was in the South—would enter the Union as a slave state. To maintain the balance between free and slave states, Clay further proposed that another new state, Maine, be carved out of Massachusetts and admitted to the Union as a free state. Once the balance between pro- and antislavery forces in Congress was ensured, the legislation passed.

In 1854, much of the Missouri Compromise was invalidated by the passage of the Kansas-Nebraska Act, which decreed that all territories could vote on whether they would enter the Union as free or slave regardless of whether they were north or south of any preestablished line. Three years later, the U.S. Supreme Court declared the Missouri Compromise unconstitutional through a ruling known as the *Dred Scott* decision, which stated that no individual could be prohibited from owning slaves. In other words, the Court found that the government had never had the right to say that a particular part of the country had to ban slavery. As a result of this decision, no further compromise could be reached between pro- and antislavery forces, and the Civil War soon followed. **See also** Clay, Henry; *Dred Scott* decision; Kansas-Nebraska Act; Mason-Dixon Line.

Monitor, USS

The USS *Monitor* was an ironclad warship with one revolving gun turret. Capable of holding a crew of fifty-eight men, the *Monitor* went into service in February 1862, and the following month it fought the Confederate ironclad *Virginia* at Hampton Roads, Virginia. This was the first battle between two ironclads, and it ended with neither side gaining the advantage. (The *Virginia,* which initiated the attack, was forced to withdraw from the area because of a shifting tide.) However, the *Monitor* was able to participate in only two more actions, both naval assaults on Virginia land fortifications (one on Sewall's Point in May 1862 and the other on Drewry's Bluff in December 1862), because it sank in a storm off the North Carolina coast in December 1862.

Monitor became the term most commonly used for Union ironclads (armored warships with metal hulls) that had a flat deck and at least one gun turret (except for monitors of the Casco class, which were created by replacing twin gun turrets with a torpedo mount, or spar). By the end of the war, the Union had employed twenty-eight monitors of various classes. **See also** ironclads; *Merrimack,* USS/*Virginia,* CSS.

Morgan, John Hunt (1825–1864)

Confederate officer John Hunt Morgan conducted several successful guerrilla raids, primarily in Kentucky and Tennessee. He had military experience prior to the Civil War, having been a U.S. cavalry officer in the Mexican-American War (1846–1848), an artillery commander in the Kentucky militia from 1852 to 1854, and the commander of a volunteer infantry unit in Kentucky, the Lexington Rifles, from 1857 to 1860. When the Civil War broke out, Morgan volunteered to head Confederate recruitment efforts in Kentucky and was extremely disappointed when Kentucky decided not to secede. Shortly thereafter, Morgan led a group of men to Confederate-held territory in western Kentucky and joined the Confederate army as the captain of a cavalry company. In April 1862 he commanded a squadron at the Battle of Shiloh as its colonel, and in December 1862 he was promoted to brigadier general and given command of a division of nearly four thousand men.

His first significant raids took place in Kentucky and Tennessee in the summer of 1862. On one of these raids, Morgan destroyed two railroad tunnels, which led to the crippling of the Louisville and Nashville Railroad, which had been transporting supplies to the troops of Union general Don Carlos Buell. As a result, Buell had to delay a planned attack on Chattanooga, Tennessee. Morgan attacked this railroad again at the end of December 1862, when his division destroyed two railroad trestles north of Elizabethtown, Kentucky. As a result, the railroad could not operate for five weeks. Moreover, as part of the operation Morgan's troops captured approximately seventeen hundred Union soldiers from a brigade of slightly over two thousand men stationed at nearby Hartsville, Tennessee.

In July 1863, Morgan took twenty-five hundred of his four thousand men on a raid through Indiana and Ohio. Known as the "Great Raid," this operation—which took place without authorization from Confederate leaders—proved to be his undoing. Union troops captured seven hundred of his men on July 19, and seven days later Morgan himself was captured. But once again one of Morgan's raids had delayed a Union action; by sending troops after Morgan, the Union had to postpone a planned invasion of east Tennessee. Moreover, Morgan managed to escape from the Ohio State Penitentiary, where he had been imprisoned, in November 1863. The following year he was given command of the Department of Western Virginia and East Tennessee, and in May and June 1864 he led over two thousand men on raids in Kentucky and Tennessee, doing a great deal of damage before being stopped by a Union cavalry brigade. Surrounded by Federal cavalry in Greeneville, Tennessee, Morgan tried to escape but was killed. **See also** guerrillas, partisan rangers, and irregulars.

Mosby, John Singleton (1833–1916)

Also called the "Gray Ghost," John S. Mosby conducted guerrilla operations for the Confederacy as the leader of the Forty-third Battalion of Virginia Cavalry, also known as Mosby's Raiders. He enlisted as a private in the First Virginia Cavalry at the outset of the war and fought in the First Battle of Bull Run. Shortly thereafter Mosby was transferred to the cavalry of General J.E.B. Stuart, participating in the Second Battle of Bull Run and the Battle of Antietam, and became one of Stuart's scouts.

Stuart sent Mosby on his first guerrilla operation in January 1863, in keeping with the Confederate Partisan Ranger Act of April 1862, which authorized the commission of military units to conduct guerrilla warfare. For the next two years Mosby, soon promoted to colonel, continued to attack Union troops, wagon trains, bridges, and railroad lines in northern Virginia near Washington, D.C., capturing enemy soldiers, horses, and supplies; destroying transport systems; and providing the Confederacy with information about the size and movements of Union forces. The number of Confederates involved in his guerrilla operations grew steadily, although only a few dozen men went on any given raid (each of which usually lasted no more than three days). At the time Mosby dissolved his unit—by then considered part of the Army of Northern Virginia—it contained two battalions of eight companies, in which about two thousand men had served (although about a third of them were killed and around five hundred captured). After the war, Mosby returned to a law practice that he had established in

Virginia prior to the war. In his later years he served the federal government in a variety of positions, including acting as an attorney for the Department of Justice. **See also** cavalry; guerrillas, partisan rangers, and irregulars; Stuart, James Ewell Brown.

musicians

During the Civil War, musicians were considered a vital part of the army for both the North and the South. Buglers, drummers, and fife players played as a means of communicating commands on the battlefield or to mark certain moments in camp life. For example, in cavalry and artillery units, bugle sounds directed soldiers to charge or fire their weapons; in infantry units, the soldiers relied on drumbeats to help them keep time while marching or to inspire them on the battlefield. In camp, drums and fifes signaled when to wake up or perform certain tasks and announced meetings and other activities. In addition, soldiers facing dismissal as punishment were literally "drummed out of the corps" (i.e., kicked out of camp to the beat of drums). Each company typically had at least one musician, while regiments and brigades often had bands. Many of the men who became army musicians at the company level learned to play their instruments after they enlisted. This was particularly true of individuals who played the drums, who were often chosen for this duty because they were the youngest men in a company. Confederate drummer Charles C. Hayes, for example, was only eleven years old, and Union drummer Edward Black was only nine. The reason youth was a factor in choosing a musician

Regiment bands were an important component of the armies of both sides. Bands were used to communicate commands on the battlefield and to mark significant moments of camp life.

was that soldiers assigned to play the drums, fife, or bugle were exempted from fighting. Once a young drummerboy became old enough to fight, he was often transferred to combat duty.

Regiment and brigade bands were often made up of professional musicians, and in some cases, these musicians had played together prior to the war and enlisted as a group. There were approximately 400 such army bands in the Union and 125 in the Confederacy. In addition to performing their duties in camps and on battlefields, these units might also play at special events, such as official ceremonies attended by dignitaries. All military musicians were also sometimes called on to perform other duties. Trained as infantrymen in both the North and the South, they might have to fight in a battle, but more often these musicians acted as messengers or assisted physicians in transporting and treating patients. **See also** children in the Civil War.

names

Northerners used different names than Southerners did for various battles in the Civil War, as well as for the war itself. For example, the Union's Battle of Bull Run, named after nearby Bull Run Creek, was the Confederacy's Battle of Manassas, named after the nearby Manassas railroad station. Similarly, a battle that Union soldiers called Antietam, after a stream, the Confederates called Sharpsburg, after a town, and the Union's Battle of Chickahominy, a river, was the Confederacy's Battle of Cold Harbor, named for a local tavern. As with these examples, most Union names for battles were taken from geographical features such as rivers, streams, and mountains, whereas most Confederate names were taken from man-made structures such as taverns, inns, and churches. (Confederate general D.H. Hill once remarked that he thought this difference was due to the fact that Union soldiers, who typically lived in the city, were most fascinated with the countryside, whereas Confederate soldiers, who usually grew up in rural areas with vast farmlands, were impressed by buildings.)

Such discrepancies in names have caused difficulties for historians. However, in writing about the Civil War, most have chosen to use the Union names unless a particular Confederate name is better known. For example, even historians who habitually use Union names typically refer to a battle on April 6–7, 1862, as the Battle of Shiloh, which the Confederates named for a nearby church, rather than the Union name, the Battle of Pittsburg Landing.

All historians use the name "Civil War" in referring to the war between North and South, and this was by far the most popular name during the war itself. However, other terms were used as well. In the North, "War of the Rebellion" was a common name, while "War for Southern Independence" and "War of Secession" were common in the South; the "Confederate War" was common abroad. After the war, Southerners often referred to the Civil War as the "War Between the States," which they drew from the title of an 1868 book, *A Constitutional View of the Late War Between the States* by Alexander H. Stephens. In fact, at one point Stephens, who was a U.S. congressman and had served as the Confederate vice president, tried unsuccessfully to get the U.S. government to make the "War Between the States" the official title of the conflict. Other Southern names for the war included "Mr. Lincoln's War" and the "War of Northern Aggression." **See also** Stephens, Alexander Hamilton.

Nast, Thomas (1840–1902)

During the Civil War, artist Thomas Nast produced numerous battlefield and camp-life sketches for Northern newspapers, but he was primarily known for his editorial cartoons and patriotic drawings supporting the Northern cause. He also holds the distinction of being the only Civil War artist-correspondent to have prior battlefield experience, having covered the Italian military campaign of Giuseppe Garibaldi in 1860 for the *Illustrated London News*. Prior to this he worked as a draftsman for *Frank Leslie's Illustrated Newspaper* and *Harper's Weekly*. When the Civil War began, Nast was again working for *Harper's Weekly*, this time as a cartoonist. Many of his cartoons were in support of Abraham Lincoln and his policies. However, one of his best-known wartime editorial cartoons is "Emancipation," an 1863 depiction of the horrors of slavery. During the Reconstruction era, many of Nast's cartoons portrayed Southerners as continuing to treat blacks cruelly. **See also** artists and artwork.

National Currency Act

The National Currency Act was U.S. legislation passed in February 1863 to encourage investment in government bonds, which were a major source of financing for the war. Prior to this act, most state banks issued their own currency, and although all of this currency was supposed to be backed by gold, this was not always the case. Therefore the currency given out by some banks was not worth the amount printed on it (the face value) or possibly had no value at all, making investors less likely to trust banks.

To solve this problem, the National Currency Act—which was expanded and renamed the National Banking Act in 1864—created a system of national banks that used a uniform currency secured by federal bonds that each bank had to deposit with the administrator of the system. Moreover, all banks in the system had to have a certain amount of money on hand based on their loans and deposits, and there were restrictions regarding what kind of loans could be made. This system, which ended what is commonly called the Free Banking Era (1837–1863), inspired more confidence in banks, but it also brought protests from Democrats, who did not share the Republican view that the central government should hold more power than the states. **See also** economy, Southern vs. Northern.

Native American soldiers

Approximately twenty thousand Native Americans served in uniform during the Civil War, fighting for either the Union or the Confederacy; a few even became noncommissioned or commissioned officers. The majority of Native Americans fought in the Trans-Mississippi Theater of war, although some participated in major battles in other theaters as well. In addition, five tribes of Native Americans had nonvoting representatives in the Confederate Congress: the Cherokee, Creek, Choctaw, Chickasaw, and Seminole.

The Cherokee bands who lived east of the Mississippi River provided the largest number of Native American soldiers in the Confederacy. Those who lived in Indian Territory (primarily Oklahoma), however, were more divided in their support, with the majority fighting for the Confederacy but some siding with the Union. The Catawba Indians of South Carolina were also strong allies of the Confederacy, even going so far as to hunt down runaway slaves for Southern plantation owners. In fact, the Catawba were the first Native Americans to create an Indian regiment for the Confederacy, serving as volunteer infantrymen in the Army of Northern Virginia.

Native Americans who supported the Union included the Delaware, the Ottawa, the Ojibwa, the Pequot, the Mohegan of Connecticut, the Tonawanda band of the Seneca, the Pamunkey of Virginia, and the Lumbee of North Carolina. The Delaware typically served as scouts (as they often had for the U.S. Army prior to the war) or as guards, while the Ottawa and Ojibwa primarily served as sharpshooters. The Lumbee engaged in guerrilla warfare during Union general William T. Sherman's Carolinas Campaign in 1865. The Pamunkey served the Army of the Potomac as river pilots in North Carolina.

Some Native Americans chose to serve as either Union or Confederate soldiers because they were extremely poor and needed the money, food, and clothing that the military offered. Sometimes, however, entire tribes decided to serve if they felt that after the war they would be rewarded for their loyalty with certain benefits, which might include being allowed to remain on their native lands. Even for those who fought for the Union, such hopes did not bear fruit. In fact, although blacks were emancipated as a result of the war, Native Americans received no new legal rights in exchange for their service. Indeed, many legal decisions made in the years after the war reduced their rights rather than expanding them. For example, one 1884 U.S. Supreme Court decision, *Elk v. Wilkins,* declared Indian tribes to be "alien nations," which meant that a Native American was not a U.S. citizen. Even though Native Americans did not receive any benefits from the war, they still had to endure its hardships, and those who served often came home maimed—if they came home at all. **See also** Oklahoma.

navies, Confederate and Union

When the Civil War broke out in 1861, the U.S. Navy had about ninety vessels, while the Confederate navy had to be built from scratch. However, having existing vessels did not give the Union much of an advantage. Of the U.S. Navy's ninety ships, only fourteen were immediately able to participate in the Northern blockade of Southern ports that was instituted at the start of the war. Of the remaining seventy-six, twenty-eight were either in foreign ports or far out into the Atlantic, twenty-seven were being repaired in various American ports, and twenty-one were seriously damaged but not yet being repaired (if repair was at all possible). Moreover, at least fifty of the U.S. Navy's ships were sailing ships of various types (e.g., frigates, sloops, and brigs) and therefore obsolete given new technologies and ship designs that had been developed over the previous twenty years. Specifically, beginning in 1840, when the steam engine was introduced, the sailing ship was gradually replaced by various kinds of steamers, which might still have sails but only as auxiliary propulsion. These new kinds of ships could move in any direction regardless of wind conditions, giving them a definite advantage in battle over sailing ships.

Unfortunately for the Union, of the approximately forty steamers in service to the U.S. Navy in 1861, five were in such disrepair that they were useless, seventeen were abroad, one was stationed in Lake Michigan, and nine were awaiting repairs. Of the remaining eight, one was on its way back to Florida from Veracruz, Mexico, while the others were stationed at various East Coast ports, from Washington, D.C., to Florida. Therefore at first this fleet was too scattered to be of much use, and even after some of the ships abroad were brought back to the United States and some of the ships under repair were made fit for duty, the Union still had only thirty steamers at its disposal.

Desperate for more ships, the U.S. government either bought or borrowed vessels belonging to private citizens and ordered new ships to be constructed. One year later, it had increased the number of its vessels to 390, and by the end of the war this number was 716. Of the 626 ships it had added to its fleet since the start of the blockade, 418 were purchased and 208 built. The purchased vessels were widely varied, since the Union used whatever ships it could find, including ferryboats, fishing boats, harbor tugboats, barges, and ocean liners. The new warships were also of various types, with 60 being ironclads, the most advanced steamers of the time. Ironclads were wooden ships with metal plating nailed to their sides above the waterline, making them nearly impervious to gunfire, and those built by the Union were equipped with revolving gun turrets that could fire in any direction.

The Confederate navy built ironclads as well (in fact it built the first such ship), although it only had two dozen by the end of the war. Like the Union, the Confederacy acquired its fleet of warships both by building new ships and by purchasing and converting existing ones. In addition, the Confederacy seized certain ships along the Mississippi River to better defend this important waterway. (However, the ships of this flotilla, known as the River Defense Fleet, were all soon captured or destroyed by the Union.)

The Confederacy also seized any U.S. vessels that were in Southern ports and navy yards at the start of the war. These included the *William Aiken* at Charleston, South Carolina; the *Lewis Cass* at Mobile, Alabama; the *Fulton* at Pensacola, Florida; the *Robert McClellan* and the *Washington* at New Orleans, Louisiana; the *Henry Dodge* at Galveston, Texas; the *Jamestown* and the *Yorktown* at Richmond, Virginia; and the *Duane* at Norfolk, Virginia. However, the Confederacy also lost some U.S. vessels at Norfolk after Federal employees at the Gosport Navy Yard set fire to seven warships rather than let the Confederacy have them. (One of these ships, the frigate steamer *Merrimack,* was later salvaged by the Confederates and turned into the first ironclad, the *Virginia.*)

Steamships like this one were typically converted to gunboats for wartime use.

Of the U.S. ships that the Confederacy seized, only the *Fulton* was a true naval vessel, a side-wheeled steamer built in 1837. Most of the rest were small sailing ships, river steamers, and tugboats. Therefore the Confederate Congress authorized the construction of new ships, both in the South and abroad in England and France. However, in ordering the construction of ships in Great Britain, Confederate agents had to promise the British government that the vessels were not intended for war, and they could not add guns to the vessels until they were out to sea. This subterfuge was necessary because the British government, having declared its neutrality in the American conflict, would not allow its shipbuilders to supply warships to either the Union or the Confederacy.

Due to such efforts, the Confederate navy raised its number of vessels from twelve small ships at the start of the war to thirty-five by the end of the first year. Of these thirty-five, twenty-one were steam vessels, the majority of them small and fast. In addition, there were many state-owned vessels aiding the Confederacy as well as private vessels acting as blockade runners, ships that got past the Northern blockade in order to bring goods to the South. By 1862, blockade runners were traveling from Great Britain to the South with as much frequency as transatlantic steamships, and pursuing them was stretching the limited resources of the U.S. Navy. Also by this time, the Confederacy had established the James River Squadron, consisting of several civilian steamers converted into gunboats to defend the James River below Richmond, Virginia. Eventually three ironclads were added to this fleet as well.

Meanwhile, both the Union and the Confederacy were struggling to recruit enough sailors to man their growing fleets. The U.S. Navy had approximately seventy-five hundred sailors and one thousand officers in 1861. The Union needed thousands more, but recruiting was no easy task. At the time the war broke out, the navy had a poor reputation. For years the service had moved men up in rank solely on the basis of seniority, which meant that there were many officers of inferior skills, the majority of them far older and less open to change than the sailors under their command. (In fact, some of these officers were extremely old, the navy having no mandatory retirement.) At the same time, lower-ranking officers often grew frustrated over having to wait so long for advancement, and some of them had quit the navy altogether. Therefore by 1861 the U.S. Navy was experiencing a serious shortage of junior officers.

One way that the U.S. government tried to solve this problem was by immediately ordering all of the upperclassmen at the U.S. Naval Academy into active service. Located in Annapolis, Maryland (although it was temporarily moved to Newport, Rhode Island, during the Civil War), this institution had been established in 1842 as the main training ground for naval officers. Originally the course of study at the academy was five years (the middle three years of which were spent at sea), but in 1850 this was shortened to four years to put more officers into service more quickly. During the Civil War the course of study was shortened even more so that officers graduated just as soon as they were deemed minimally competent to serve.

When this still did not provide enough officers, the U.S. Navy began calling for volunteer officers. These men might have no naval training but they did have nautical experience, usually as sea captains on civilian vessels. A similar call for volunteers took place for sailors, but many of these men had never before been to sea. As a result of these recruitment efforts, by the end of the war the U.S. Navy had increased its number of officers to over seven thousand and its number of sailors to approximately fifty-one thousand.

Meanwhile, the Confederate navy was formed with approximately three hundred officers who had left the U.S. Navy to join the Confederacy in 1861. Upon taking office, the Confederate secretary of the navy, Stephen Mallory, immediately instituted a major recruitment and training program to add manpower to this navy. To convince sailors and officers to leave the U.S. Navy and join the Confederacy, Mallory made sure that the Confederate navy's pay scale was slightly higher than the U.S. Navy's. (In both navies, pay was based on rank and experience, with admirals making around $6,000 a year and captains commanding squadrons about $5,000.) In addition, in 1863 the Confederacy increased its number of officers still further by establishing its own naval academy, on board the steamship *Patrick Henry* in the James River, to train junior officers. Records have been lost regarding exactly how many men served in the Confederate navy, but there were more than enough for the number of vessels in the fleet. Sailors who were not needed at sea were typically assigned to garrison coastal and river forts, although they might be assigned to the army instead.

While he was increasing the Confederate fleet, Mallory also supervised the placement of underwater mines (then called torpedoes) in Southern waters to defend against enemy ships. Since ironclads were plated only to the waterline, these mines worked against them as well as against older models of warships. The Confederates also built a torpedo-armed submarine, the *Hunley,* that became the first such vessel to sink a ship during war. In addition the Confederacy began adding rams to its steamships, realizing that unlike sailing ships these vessels were capable of heading straight toward an enemy ship at will. But despite these innovations, as the war progressed the U.S. Navy was able to tighten its blockade on Southern ports and take control of important Southern waterways. Ultimately, as with the Confederate army, the Confederate navy could not overcome the fact that the North had far more military resources than the South. **See also** blockades and blockade runners; *Hunley,* CSS; Mallory, Stephen R.; sailors.

New Hampshire

Home to many abolitionists, New Hampshire supported the Union throughout the Civil War, contributing roughly thirty thousand men to various branches of the U.S. military. However, it was far from the actual fighting, so no battles took place on its soil. **See also** abolitionists.

New Jersey

New Jersey supported the Union during the Civil War. Its major contribution to the war effort was industrial. In particular, the state provided iron for making cannons and ammunition. **See also** ammunition; artillery.

New Mexico

Part of lands ceded to the United States following the Mexican-American War (1846–1848), New Mexico achieved territorial status in 1850. Under the terms of the Compromise of 1850, New Mexico (along with Utah) would be considered neutral until it applied for statehood, whereupon its citizens would decide whether the state would be slave or free. (As it happened, New Mexico did not achieve statehood until 1912, by which time slavery had been outlawed nationwide, making the question moot.) When the Civil War broke out, the U.S. Army was already a strong presence in the territory. Consequently, when the Confederates tried to invade the territory they were repelled by a Union regiment known as the Colorado Volunteers. **See also** Compromise of 1850.

newspapers

Newspapers covered the Civil War extensively, although that coverage did not include photographs. However, illustrations reproduced from artists' sketches became popular in American newspapers during the 1850s, and this demand increased during the Civil War. People wanted to see depictions of major battles, military leaders, and military life, and they expected newspapers to provide them. Eventually, the demand for illustrated periodicals became so great that there were not enough to go around, particularly in military camps. For this reason, Union general William T. Sherman once ordered that men who had been in battle were to be given their copies of a periodical first, just in case they ran out.

The most popular illustrated periodicals during the war were *Harper's Weekly, Frank Leslie's Illustrated News,* and the *New York Illustrated News* in the North and the *Southern Illustrated News* in the South. The *Southern Illustrated News* was established in Richmond, Virginia, in 1862 and ended publication in 1864. During this time, it often skipped issues due to shortages of materials, and by the last year of publication it had no engravers and therefore could provide no illustrations. In contrast, *Harper's Weekly* featured nu-

This illustration of Civil War refugees appeared in Frank Leslie's Illustrated News. *Newspapers printed illustrations of battles and other scenes of life during the war.*

merous pictures, some taking up a full page, as well as cartoons. Established in 1857 by Fletcher Harper of Harper and Brothers Publishers, this weekly periodical had a circulation of 100,000 in 1860 and 120,000 by 1863. The circulation of *Frank Leslie's Illustrated News,* founded in 1855 by publisher, artist, and engraver Frank Leslie, averaged 100,000 readers throughout the war, although during a short period from 1861–1862 this figure ran as high as 200,000. A sixteen-page periodical, it employed a large staff of artists, as did *Harper's.* In contrast, the *New York Illustrated News,* established by publisher John King in 1859, employed only one artist. Eventually that man resigned, leaving the paper unable to offer illustrations. Thus, although it approached the circulation of Frank Leslie's periodical in 1861, the *New York Illustrated News* gradually lost readers, fell into financial troubles, and was out of business by the end of 1864.

In the North, in addition to illustrated periodicals, black-owned newspapers and abolitionist papers gained in popularity in the years leading up to the war. The first black-owned newspaper, *Freedom's Journal,* appeared long before the war, in 1827, but many more appeared during the late 1850s. These included the *Christian Recorder,* established in 1856 by the African Methodist Episcopal Church, and *Douglass' Monthly,* published by abolitionist Frederick Douglass. The leading abolinionist paper, the *Liberator,* was established in 1831 by William Lloyd Garrison and continued to be published until the Thirteenth Amendment to the Constitution outlawed slavery nationwide. **See also** artists and artwork; Douglass, Frederick; Garrison, William Lloyd.

New York

New York supported the Union during the Civil War. However, New York's leaders did not support all of the Union's policies. In particular, they questioned the system by which men were enlisted in the army, arguing that Union physicians were sloppy in examining potential soldiers to determine whether they were fit to serve. A state investigation discovered that out of fifty thousand New Yorkers certified by the Union as being healthy enough to face the rigors of war, fewer than forty-five thousand were actually in good physical condition. **See also** conscription.

Norfolk, Virginia

Norfolk, Virginia, was the site of the Gosport Navy Yard, a U.S. Navy shipbuilding and maintenance facility before the Civil War. On April 18, 1861, Virginia troops captured the city for the Confederacy, but before the soldiers could enter the navy yard its commander, Commodore Charles McCauley, set many of its ships and supplies on fire. The Confederates later salvaged one of these ships, the USS *Merrimack,* and turned it into an ironclad named CSS *Virginia,* and also managed to salvage other equipment and supplies in the yard. Norfolk remained in Confederate hands until May 1862, when the approach of Union troops forced its evacuation. As before, however, the men defending the navy yard destroyed its vessels, equipment, and supplies in an attempt to keep them out of enemy hands. **See also** ironclads; *Merrimack,* USS/*Virginia,* CSS; navies, Confederate and Union.

North Carolina

North Carolina contributed thousands of soldiers to the Confederacy, and a majority of them died in combat. The state, however, had difficulty deciding which side it would support in the Civil War. On February 28, 1861, the state legislature voted to remain with the Union, but it objected to providing any soldiers to the cause. When the federal government insisted that North Carolina contribute to the war effort, the state decided to secede from the Union. On May 20, 1861, it became the last state to join the Confederacy, although many of its citizens remained Northern sympathizers.

Another significant contribution that North Carolina made to the Confederate war effort was related to blockade running. The North Carolina city of Wilmington was the most important blockade-running port in the South, as well as the site of important shipyards and railroads. In fact, after the Battle of Mobile Bay on August 5, 1864—which resulted in U.S. admiral David Farragut taking Mobile, Alabama, for the Union—Wilmington was the only Confederate port with the capability of sending ships abroad. This changed after the Union captured nearby Fort Fisher, which offered Wilmington's main defense against attack, in February 1865. Shortly after the fort was taken, the Confederates evacuated the city; Union forces occupied Wilmington on February 22, 1865. The largest battle fought in North Carolina occurred in March 1865 at Bentonville. A total of 81,000 soldiers participated in this three-day battle, which was part of Sherman's Carolinas Campaign; 2,606 Confederate soldiers and 1,527 Union soldiers died. **See also** Carolinas Campaign; Farragut, David Glasgow; Fort Fisher.

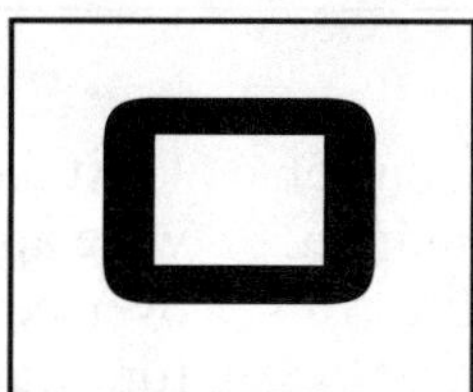

Ohio

A major industrial state, Ohio supported the Union during the Civil War, even though many of its citizens were involved in peace movements. In the summer of 1863, the Confederacy carried the war to Ohio through a campaign known as the Great Raid, in which Colonel John Hunt Morgan led twenty-five hundred men on an invasion of Indiana and Ohio. When they reached Buffington Island, Ohio, approximately seven hundred of them were captured by the Union, and Morgan himself was taken prisoner near West Point, Ohio, on July 26, 1863. He was then held in the Ohio State Penitentiary until November 27, 1863, when he escaped and returned to duty for the Confederacy. **See also** Morgan, John Hunt.

Oklahoma

At the time of the Civil War, what would one day be Oklahoma was part of Indian Territory. Some of the tribes there coalesced into a political body that became known as the Five Civilized Tribes of the Indian Territory: the Cherokee, the Choctaw, the Creek, the Chickasaw, and the Seminole. In early 1862, this entity joined the Confederate States of America, and representatives from each tribe were allowed to attend sessions of the Confederate Congress as nonvoting members. Prior to this, however, Oklahoma was the site of several skirmishes between Native Americans who supported the Confederacy and those who favored the Union, and similar fights continued on a small scale throughout the war.

After the Civil War, the Five Civilized Tribes' support of the Confederacy resulted in the U.S. government putting them under military rule during Reconstruction. Moreover, the government moved additional Native American tribes into Oklahoma and took over parts of the region for new railroad lines. The federal government also began encouraging blacks to settle in Indian Territory. As a result of the government's policies, by 1886, over sixty Native American tribes and approximately forty thousand blacks were living in Oklahoma. **See also** Congress, Confederate; Native American soldiers.

ordnance accidents

Technically, the word *ordnance* means any kind of military supplies, but in the Civil War it was primarily used to refer first to ammunition and then to weapons. Therefore an ordnance laboratory or factory was one that manufactured ammunition. Most of these facilities, North and South, were largely staffed by women, so when accidents occurred, most of the victims were women. The worst accident took place in March 1863 when an explosive primer at the Confederate States Laboratory, an ordnance laboratory in Richmond, Virginia, accidentally ignited, resulting in a blast that killed sixty-two female and seven male workers. The same kind of accident happened at a Washington, D.C., arsenal in June 1864, at which time more than twenty-five people, at least twenty-one of them women, died. **See also** ammunition; weapons; women, contributions of.

overseers

An overseer was a white man—or on rare occasions a black man—who supervised the work of slaves on farms and plantations with large work forces, reporting directly to the plantation owner. The overseer's main responsibility was determining slaves' work assignments in accordance with the needs of the plantation and the desires of the plantation owner. On small plantations, the overseer gave these assignments directly to the slaves, disciplined any who disobeyed, handled any problems related to the health and living conditions of slaves, and made decisions regarding the buying and selling of slaves. On large plantations, these duties were handled by one or more slave drivers—more often black than white, particularly in the lower South (i.e., the states south of Virginia and Maryland)—who worked for the overseer.

Some slave drivers and overseers performed their jobs with more compassion than others. Those who were particularly callous in their treatment of their charges were often the subject of abolitionist literature, fueling anti-South sentiment in the North prior to the Civil War. Those overseers who treated slaves well were typically not spoken of in the North, either before or during the war.

At the outbreak of the Civil War, there were approximately thirty-eight thousand overseers working on rice, sugar, and cotton plantations and tobacco and grain farms throughout the South, with the majority located in Louisiana, North and South Carolina, Alabama, Georgia, and Virginia. Prior to the war, on rice plantations in Georgia and South Carolina, there was typically one overseer for every three hundred slaves; on other plantations and farms the ratio was more typically one overseer to every seventy-five or one hundred slaves. After war broke out, however, these numbers changed as a shortage of overseers developed.

In 1862 the Confederacy exempted overseers on large plantations from military service after slave owners insisted that these men were indispensable in preventing slave uprisings. By the end of 1863, however, this exemption was rescinded due to the increased need for soldiers. Consequently, women began to serve as overseers on some plantations, while on others the plantation owner himself took on the duties of an overseer. However, given the large number of slaves working on some of these plantations, it was difficult for one man to supervise an entire agricultural concern, and as a result work failed to get done and farm productivity fell. **See also** conscription; plantations; slavery and slave life.

pay, soldiers' and sailors'

In both the North and the South, soldiers and sailors were paid for their wartime service. In the North, white Union army privates received $13 per month and blacks $10 per month, until June 1864 when their pay was raised to equal that of their white counterparts. Union army officers were paid substantially more, with the salary depending on rank: A first or second lieutenant received $105.50 a month, a captain $115.50 a month, a major $169, a lieutenant colonel $181, a colonel $212, a brigadier general $315, a major general $457, and a lieutenant general $758. Noncommissioned army officers (enlisted men appointed to subordinate ranks like sergeant or corporal) made anywhere from $2 to $13 more than a private, depending on rank. This was true in the South as well, where army privates made $11 a month. (In June 1864, this was raised to $18.) Southern army officers made slightly less than their Northern counterparts; a brigadier general, for example, made $301 a month.

In both the Union and the Confederate navies, pay was based on experience. In the North, a beginning sailor made $12 a month, a sailor with somewhat more experience $14, and an experienced seaman $18. The Confederate navy's pay scale was slightly higher, but in both North and South boys who went to sea (in the Union, they had to be over age thirteen, and in the Confederacy, over age fourteen) were paid less, and again the amount was based on experience. An inexperienced boy—also known as a third-class boy—was paid $7 a month, with second- and first-class boys paid $8 and $9, respectively. In addition, sailors received bonuses based on the value of prizes of war (captured enemy vessels and cargo), as did officers. Officers' pay was significantly higher, with top-ranking officers making more than low-ranking officers. Under this system, an admiral could earn as much as $6,000 a year, captains $5,000. **See also** navies, Confederate and Union.

peace movements and societies

As it became obvious that the Civil War would be long and bloody, various peace movements and societies sprang up in both the North and the South. The first peace societies, however, appeared in the South either right before or immediately after the war began, established by people opposed to secession. These groups included the Heroes of America, located in North Carolina and Tennessee; the Peace Society, located in Alabama; and the Peace and Constitutional Society, located in Arkansas.

By 1862, the peace movement in North Carolina had become so strong that in March of that year fifty members of a state militia held a peace protest; it took three hundred Confederate troops to quell the demonstration. The following year, North Carolina plantation owner James T. Leach wrote a letter to his local newspaper arguing that the South should return to the Union. Leach's position was popular enough that shortly thereafter he was elected to the Confederate House of Representatives and became one of the South's most passionate advocates for reunification with the North. Moreover, his letter led to an increase in participants in North Carolina's peace movement, as did an 1862 book by peace advocate Bryan Tyson titled *A Ray of Light.* Tyson insisted that the Confederacy would lose the war, and he proposed that the South rejoin the Union in exchange for a constitutional guarantee that existing slave states would not have to give up slavery.

In January 1863, Northern Democrats in the U.S. Congress made the same proposal, inspiring a Northern peace movement that in turn fueled the growth of the Southern peace movement. Within six months, hundreds of peace rallies had taken place throughout North Carolina. Confederate troops eventually ended all political protests in the state, even going so far as to destroy the offices of a pacifist newspaper, the *North Carolina Standard.* But in the meantime, the peace movement spread to other Southern states, and as it did other peace candidates were elected to the Confederate Congress. Throughout 1864, they attempted to persuade President Jefferson Davis to support the Northern Democrats' proposal but he refused, arguing that any peace proposal should include a guarantee of Southern independence rather than reunion with the North. Meanwhile, the Southern press condemned the peace movement as being bad for Confederate morale—an understandable criticism given that the number of military desertions increased as the calls for peace and reunion increased (although most desertions were undoubtedly based on personal reasons rather than on the desire to support a political movement).

In December 1864, a member of the Northern peace movement, Missouri politician Francis Blair, traveled to Richmond, Virginia, to speak with the Confederate congressmen who favored peace. Together they arranged for official peace talks between representatives of the Union and the Confederacy at Hampton Roads, Virginia, on February 3, 1865. Held aboard the U.S. steamship *River Queen,* this four-hour meeting, which included U.S. president Abraham Lincoln and Secretary of State William H. Seward and from the Confederacy Vice President Alexander H. Stephens, Senator Robert M.T. Hunter, and Assistant Secretary of War John A. Campbell, was a failure. Lincoln demanded that the South rejoin the Union, while Davis's representatives were bound by their president's insistence on Southern independence. Moreover, Lincoln insisted that slavery in the South would have to end, although he offered to compensate slave owners monetarily for the loss of their human property. The Confederates, however, refused to emancipate their slaves.

With the failure of the Hampton Roads Peace Conference, all talks of peace between the Union and Confederacy came to an end. Nonetheless, various peace movements and societies continued to push for new diplomatic efforts. In addition, membership in Southern peace societies continued to increase. By the end of the war, these groups collectively had well over 100,000 official members and countless other unofficial ones. **See also** Blair, Francis Preston; Hampton Roads.

Pemberton, John Clifford (1814–1881)

Confederate lieutenant general John C. Pemberton was charged with defending the city of Vicksburg, Mississippi, against the forces of Union general Ulysses S. Grant in late 1862 and early 1863. After a forty-seven-day siege, however, he surrendered the city on July 4, 1863. Afterward Pemberton was criticized in the South for the way he handled Vicksburg's defense.

Lieutenant General John Pemberton surrendered the city of Vicksburg, Mississippi, on July 4, 1863.

A native of Pennsylvania, Pemberton decided to fight for the Confederacy based on both his political beliefs and the fact that his wife was from the South. However, during the Civil War some Southerners questioned his loyalty and bravery (even though he had been previously honored by the U.S. Army for bravery during the Second Seminole War and the Mexican-American War) because, as head of the Department of South Carolina and Georgia, he said that he valued his men's lives more than a piece of land and would sacrifice the latter in order to save the former. Because of such comments, Pemberton was rebuked by Confederate officials, and South Carolina and Georgia state officials asked the Confederacy to transfer Pemberton elsewhere. In doing so, they questioned whether any Northerner was capable of fighting vigorously for the South—a lack of trust that would continue to plague him throughout the war.

Eventually Confederate president Jefferson Davis did reassign Pemberton, making him the head of the Department of Mississippi and East Louisiana in October 1862. In this capacity Pemberton was charged with defending Vicksburg, a key to the Confederacy's preventing Union forces from crossing the Mississippi River. In his first months on the job, he concentrated on administrative activities, and by all accounts he was a far better administrator than a commander, making many improvements related to supply distribution and the comfort of soldiers. Pemberton was also effective at first in protecting Vicksburg from Grant's attack. By the spring of 1863, however, Grant had crossed the river, because Pemberton decided to concentrate on holding Vicksburg instead of preventing Grant's river crossing.

After Grant crossed the river, Pemberton received an order from General Joseph E. Johnston to attack Grant. However, this could be done only by pulling soldiers out of Vicksburg, and Pemberton decided that the defense of the city was paramount. Consequently, he ignored Johnston's order, and Grant scored a series of victories on nearby battlefields. Once again Pemberton received an order from Johnston, this time demanding that he send soldiers to help Johnston defeat Grant. Pemberton followed this order, but before his men could reach Johnston they encountered some of Grant's troops. During the ensuing battle at Champion Hill, Pemberton's men were forced to retreat to Vicksburg.

In the aftermath of the loss of Vicksburg, Pemberton was chastised by Johnston for disobeying his orders. In response, Pemberton requested that his punishment be in the form of reduction in rank from lieutenant general to lieutenant colonel. The Confederacy granted this request, then reassigned Pemberton to serve with an artillery unit in Virginia and South Carolina. He was still with this unit when the war ended. **See also** Johnston, Joseph Eggleston; Vicksburg Campaign.

Peninsula Campaign

An unsuccessful Union attempt to take the Confederate capital of Richmond, Virginia, the Peninsula Campaign took place from March to July 1862. Under the command of General George B. McClellan (who had recently been removed as general in chief of all Union armies), approximately 105,000 men of the Army of the Potomac went by ship to Fort Monroe, Virginia, and headed up the James River peninsula toward Richmond, fighting various battles en route. Their first conflict occurred from April 5 to May 3 at Yorktown, Virginia, where they laid siege to the city and then drove its defenders—approximately 17,000 men under General John B. Magruder—from the area. On May 5 they took the city of Williamsburg and on May 9 Norfolk, Virginia. On May 15, Union naval forces joined the campaign in the first Battle of Drewry's Bluff when they attempted but failed under heavy fire to reach Richmond via the James River. From May 31 to June 1 the Union and Confederates clashed again in the Battle of Seven Pines, during which Confederate general Robert E. Lee took command of the Army of Northern Virginia after its commander, Joseph Johnston, was wounded. On June 12, on Lee's orders, Brigadier General Jeb Stuart successfully led a cavalry troop around and behind the Union forces to gather information, capture enemy soldiers, and destroy Union supplies. Lee then took the offensive, instigating a series of battles known as the Seven Days' Battles (June 25 to July 1) that eventually resulted in McClellan withdrawing from the area. **See also** Johnston, Joseph Eggleston; Lee, Robert Edward; McClellan, George Brinton; Seven Days' Battles; Stuart, James Ewell Brown.

Petersburg Campaign

The Petersburg Campaign, which took place from June 15, 1864, to April 3, 1865, was Union general Ulysses S. Grant's successful attempt to take the Confederate city of Petersburg, Virginia, in preparation for an attack on the nearby Confederate capital of Richmond, Virginia. On the first day of the campaign, the Union, with approximately forty-eight thousand troops, attacked fifty-four hundred Confederates defending Petersburg's rail lines. After this attack failed, the Confederates, led by General P.G.T. Beauregard, established a strong line of field defenses, including numerous trenches, and a Union siege on Petersburg began. This siege lasted ten months, making it the longest campaign of the war. It also included the Battle of the Crater, one of the biggest Union disasters of the war. In the end, however, the Union took Petersburg and Richmond as well. **See also** Crater, Battle of the.

pets and mascots

Civil War soldiers often kept animals as pets or as mascots for an entire army. The most common pets were small animals that a soldier could carry in his pocket, such as a mouse, snake, or lizard. Some men also kept cats, but dogs were far more common as both mascots and pets. Another popular mascot was the rooster. Most regiments had at least one of these animals. Some were treated with great care and allowed to ride on cannons or on the arm of a mounted soldier during a march. However, camp roosters might also be made to fight with another rooster—perhaps from another regiment—to demonstrate their strength and courage as a symbol of the regiment to which they were attached. Chickens might also be kept as personal pets, with the most famous being one that belonged to Confederate general Robert E. Lee. Lee traveled with this chicken for much of the war and kept it in his tent with him each night, where it was said that the bird laid an egg on his cot every morning. A few Union regiments kept eagles as a symbol of the Union and carried them into battle on special perches. There are also reports of soldiers keeping pigs as pets, but their attachment could not have been great because pigs were usually slaughtered and eaten as soon as they reached maturity. Horses, although not considered pets, were highly prized. Cavalry men often developed very close attachments to their horses and grieved when they were killed in battle. **See also** cavalry.

photography

Photography was a relatively new development when the Civil War broke out, but it had already been established as a way to record military engagements. However, the technology was so crude that any movement by the subject would result in the picture being blurry. Therefore Civil War photographers did not take pictures during battles themselves; instead, they produced portraits of soldiers, scenes of stationary people and objects, and landscapes that might include battlefield dead.

At the outset of the war, there were approximately three thousand men involved professionally with some form of the photographic process. Most, however, were in the North, which was then the center of the country's industry and technology, and those few photographers working in the South had trouble getting paper and chemicals for their work as the war progressed. Consequently, of the roughly 1 million photographs depicting Civil War subjects, most were taken by Northern photographers working in the Eastern Theater of the war. Moreover, most of the Civil War battlefield photographs depict Union victories.

Nonetheless, the first photographs made of Civil War subjects were produced in the South, by New Hampshire photographer J.D. Edwards. He was working in New Orleans, Louisiana, when the first states began to secede from the Union, and he took pictures of the city's volunteer soldiers. After the war broke out, he went to Florida to take dozens of pictures of military subjects there.

The most famous Civil War photographer, however, was Mathew Brady of New York, who along with a staff of assistants took pictures of Northern troops. Brady set out to make a photographic record of many of the most significant events and people of the war, and when President Abraham Lincoln refused to authorize government funds for this project, Brady financed it himself, expecting to be able to sell his work after the war was over. Instead, he found no market for his photographs and died in poverty.

A protégé of Brady's, George Smith Cook, became the most prominent photographer in the South. Nicknamed the "Photographer of the Confederacy," Cook was a native of South Carolina who left Brady's New York studio and headed to the South as soon as his home state seceded from the Union. His best-known work was the first picture showing ironclads in battle, taken of the Union monitors *Weehawken, Montauk,* and *Passaic* attacking a Confederate coastal fort in September 1863. **See also** artists and artwork; Brady, Mathew.

Pickett, George Edward (1825–1875)

Confederate major general George E. Pickett participated in several campaigns but is best known for his association with a July 3, 1863, Battle of Gettysburg assault on Union positions known as Pickett's Charge. Pickett's name was connected to this event because three brigades from his division suffered the most serious losses in the charge: Approximately two-thirds of the forty-three hundred men were killed, and all of his thirteen colonels were either killed or seriously injured. However, Pickett's brigades made up less than one-half of the forces taking part in the charge, and other generals actually figured more prominently in the attack than Pickett did.

Pickett suffered substantial losses in other battles as well, including the Seven Days' Battles and the Appomattox Campaign, but he was rarely wounded himself. On at least two occasions this was because he disappeared from the battlefield either right before or during the conflict. Such was the case, for example, at the Battle of Five Forks on April 1, 1865. While his men were undergoing a Union attack that resulted in a loss of approximately five thousand of their number, Pickett was enjoying a cookout with two other generals two miles away from the front lines.

Pickett was severely criticized for such behavior, as well as for hanging twenty-one Union soldiers captured in North Carolina in February 1864. Pickett later insisted that he thought the men were not Union soldiers but Confederate deserters. (Deserters were often hanged, whereas prisoners of war were customarily imprisoned.) Nonetheless, after the war the U.S. secretary of war recommended that Pickett be prosecuted for murder, although no such action was taken.

A Virginia aristocrat, Pickett had been ranked last in his class at West Point, from which he graduated in 1846, but he did receive a commendation for bravery during the Mexican-American War (1846–1848) as part of the Eighth Infantry Regiment; specifically, during the storming of Chapultepec under heavy fire in September 1847, he was the first person to climb over a wall erected by the defenders. After this conflict Pickett served in Texas and in Washington Territory, but he left the U.S. Army in 1861 to fight for the Confederacy, first as an infantry captain and then as a colonel.

In 1862 Pickett was promoted to the rank of brigadier general. Shortly thereafter he was assigned to lead a brigade under Lieutenant General James Longstreet. In this capacity, Pickett fought in the Seven Days' Battles in June and July 1862, during which he suffered a shoulder injury that prevented him from performing his duties for the next three months. He was then promoted to major general and assigned to command a division under Longstreet known as the First Corps. As its commander he fought at the Battle of Fredericksburg (December 1862) and at the Battle of Gettysburg (July 1863). However, he reached the three-day Battle of Gettysburg late—that is, toward the end of its second day—and subsequently faced accusations that he had purposely delayed his arrival to avoid combat.

After Gettysburg, Pickett was sent to a garrison near Richmond, Virginia. From there he launched an attack on New Bern, North Carolina, in February 1864 that was unsuccessful. It was following this engagement that he ordered his notorious execution of twenty-one Union soldiers. Three months later, in May 1864, Pickett fell into a deep depression, refused to perform his duties, and was removed from command. He was reinstated a month later, apparently fully recovered, but did nothing to distinguish himself until a year later, and then it was his absence at Five Forks for which he was known. Shortly thereafter he was permanently relieved of command. Pickett spent several years in Canada before settling in Norfolk, Virginia, working as an insurance salesman.

See also Gettysburg, Battle of; Longstreet, James; Pickett's Charge.

Pickett's Charge

Named after Confederate major general George E. Pickett, Pickett's Charge was a rushing attack undertaken by the Confederates during the Battle of Gettysburg in Pennsylvania on July 3, 1863. This attack involved not only three brigades from Pickett's division but other Confederate forces as well. In fact, Pickett's brigades made up less than one-half of the force of the charge, and General Robert E. Lee, not Pickett, ordered the attack. Nonetheless, Pickett's name was associated with the charge because it was his brigades that suffered the most serious losses: Approximately two-thirds of his forty-three hundred men were killed, and all of his thirteen colonels were either killed or seriously injured. However, other brigades participating in the charge also suffered heavy casualties, with most soldiers dying before ever reaching the Union line.

At the time the charge was initiated, the Union front line stretched for several miles, from a site called Little Round Top north along a stretch of high ground known as Cemetery Ridge, then northeast to Culp's Hill. General James Longstreet believed it was best to concentrate the Confederate attack on the Union troops around Little Round Top. General Lee, however, decided to launch a full frontal charge straight through the Union line along Cemetery Ridge. To do this, Confederate soldiers would have to cross fourteen hundred yards of open ground in order to reach the Union soldiers.

On Lee's orders, at approximately 3 P.M. Pickett's brigades and others formed into a line over a mile wide and began marching in formation toward the Union soldiers. In response, Union infantrymen and artillery began firing on them; their barrage was so intense that firing was heard over one hundred miles away in Pittsburgh, Pennsylvania. Under such a heavy assault, only a few Confederates managed to reach the Union line. One of them,

Confederate troops storm Cemetery Ridge during the Battle of Gettysburg in the rushing attack known as Pickett's Charge.

General Lewis A. Armistead, led approximately 150 men over a Union-built wall on Cemetery Ridge and reached the enemy's cannon, whereupon he was shot and killed by a Union soldier.

Finally the remaining Confederates fell back, and the next day General Lee withdrew all of his forces and retreated into Virginia. Afterward Lee blamed himself for the heavy Confederate losses at Gettysburg, particularly during Pickett's Charge. He offered to resign, but Confederate president Jefferson Davis refused to accept his offer. **See also** Armistead, Lewis Addison; Gettysburg, Battle of; Pickett, George Edward.

Pierce, Franklin (1804–1869)

As the president of the United States from 1853 to 1857, Franklin Pierce was ineffective in settling disputes related to the slavery issue. In particular, he was highly criticized by the Northern press and in certain political circles for his support of the Kansas-Nebraska Act. Prior to becoming president, Pierce, a Democrat, served in the New Hampshire state legislature (1829–1833), the U.S. House of Representatives (1833–1837), and the U.S. Senate (1837–1842). He then practiced law and was a federal district attorney until the outbreak of the Mexican-American War in 1846, during which he served as an officer.

During his presidential campaign, Pierce benefited greatly from the public's perception of the Democrats' being better able than the Whigs to reach a permanent compromise over the slavery issue. Therefore Pierce was elected by a landslide. Once in office, he favored a continuation of slavery on economic grounds, believing that if the South were forced to give up its slaves the country's prosperity would suffer. Consequently, he did not support antislavery legislation, much to the dismay of many of his fellow Northerners. As a result, the Northern-dominated Democratic Party refused to renominate him when his term in office ended. **See also** Kansas-Nebraska Act; political parties.

Pinchback, Pinckney Benton Stewart (1837–1921)

During the Civil War, former slave Pinckney B.S. Pinchback served as a Union officer, and afterward he was involved in Reconstruction politics. He also holds the distinction of being the first black to serve as a state governor, a position he held for thirty-six days while the Louisiana governor, Henry Warmouth, was undergoing impeachment proceedings.

Pinchback was born into slavery but freed by the Georgia plantation owner who had fathered him. When this man died in 1848, Pinchback, his mother, and his nine siblings moved to Ohio to escape being returned to slavery. Pinchback then began working as a servant on various boats, eventually becoming a steward aboard a steamboat that traveled along the Mississippi, Red, and Missouri Rivers. This job placed him in the South when the Civil War started.

Wanting to join the Union army, Pinchback managed to elude a Confederate blockade on the Mississippi River to reach New Orleans, Louisiana, then held by the North. Once there, Pinchback formed the Corps d'Afrique, a volunteer group of black soldiers, and became its captain. In 1863, however, disaffected over the fact that even in the North black soldiers were treated poorly in comparison to their white counterparts, Pinchback quit the military.

After the war, Pinchback went into politics in Louisiana, organizing the Fourth Ward Republican Club in New Orleans. In 1868 he was elected to the Louisiana Senate, which in 1871 led to his becoming the state's lieutenant governor and then, briefly, the acting governor. The following year he was elected to the U.S. Congress, but his opponent claimed the election had been fraudulent and got the results overturned. The next year Pinchback was elected to the U.S. Senate, but once again the results were overturned due to charges of fraud. Scholars believe that, in both cases, Pinchback was unfairly denied his victory and that the vote-tampering charges were concocted by white racists. Consequently, Pinchback decided not to make another bid for office. Instead he worked as a surveyor of customs in New Orleans until 1887, then entered law school and became a lawyer in Washington, D.C. **See also** Reconstruction.

Pinkerton, Allan (aka E.J. Allan) (1819–1884)

At the beginning of the Civil War, private detective Allan Pinkerton worked as the head of a network of Union spies under the name E.J. Allan. His agents operated throughout the Southern states, gathering massive amounts of information about Confederate activities, supplies, and equipment. However, Pinkerton made many mistakes in his interpretation of this information. For example, in October 1861 he provided General George McClellan with an intelligence report stating that Confederate general Joseph Johnston had over 150,000 men, when in fact Johnston had fewer than 50,000 under his command. Similarly, in April 1862 he provided an estimate of 120,000 Confederate troops in a Virginia location where there were actually fewer than 17,000. Consequently, although he had some successes—including the capture of Confederate spy Rose O'Neal Greenhow—he was forced out of his job in late 1862.

An immigrant from Glasgow, Scotland, Pinkerton originally came to the United States in 1842 as a cooper (a person who constructs barrels). Shortly thereafter, while living in Dundee, Illinois, he became an amateur detective and solved a few local crimes. As a result, he was made deputy sheriff of his county, Kane County, in 1846, and after a few months he became deputy sheriff of Cook County, which encompassed the city of Chicago, Illinois.

In 1850 Pinkerton opened his own private detective agency, the Pinkerton Detective Agency, which specialized in protecting railroads from train robbers. In early 1861, one of his railroad clients, President Samuel E. Felton of the Philadelphia, Wilmington, and Baltimore Railroad (PW&B), asked him to protect the PW&B railway lines from sabotage by secessionists who wanted to prevent supplies from reaching Washington, D.C. As part of this assignment, two of Pinkerton's agents, Harry Davies and Timothy Webster, learned that a group of at least thirty men in Baltimore, Maryland, were conspiring to assassinate president-elect Abraham Lincoln before he could take office. The conspirators were led by a barber known only as Captain Ferrandini, who was also the head of a local military society known as the Constitutional Guards.

Posing as E.J. Allan, Pinkerton met with Ferrandini at a Baltimore restaurant and pretended to be interested in helping him with his plan. Ferrandini then provided him with details about the plan. When Lincoln took the train from Springfield, Illinois, to Washington, D.C., for his inauguration, it would make a brief stop in Baltimore so that the train car could be switched from one track to another. Since most people got off of the train while this transfer was taking place, Lincoln was expected to do so as well, and when this happened one of eight would-be assassins planted in the waiting crowd would shoot him. To distract the crowd prior to the shooting, some of Ferrandini's men would start a fistfight; Baltimore police were certain to concentrate on breaking up this fight rather than protecting Lincoln because, according to Ferrandini, the Baltimore superintendent of police, George P. Kane, was in on the assassination plot.

Armed with this information, Pinkerton met with Lincoln, who did not believe

Allan Pinkerton was a private detective who worked as a Union spy during the Civil War.

him. A few hours later, however, Pinkerton's story was corroborated by New York City police superintendent John A. Kennedy, who had been asked by a Congressional committee to investigate the safety of Lincoln's inaugural trip and who had heard that a plot against Lincoln was afoot. Lincoln then asked Pinkerton to protect him as he passed through Baltimore. Pinkerton stationed several of his agents at various points along the track, and the railroad hired an additional two hundred men to assist him. In addition, the train was timed to reach Baltimore at 3 A.M., when no crowd would be waiting, and Lincoln stayed on the train. Afterward, Pinkerton provided information that led to Kane's arrest, although Ferrandini had disappeared.

Once Lincoln took office, Pinkerton met with him to encourage the creation of a federal secret service, which was conceived as a national network of spies. The president was not interested in Pinkerton's proposal, but General George B. McClellan was. He hired Pinkerton to work for him out of Washington, D.C., as both a spy and a spymaster—the head of a network of spies that Pinkerton would later claim was indeed the beginning of the U.S. Secret Service even though it was not a national agency. Pinkerton worked for McClellan until the general was removed from his command of the Army of the Potomac in 1862, whereupon Pinkerton lost his position as well.

Pinkerton then returned to running his detective agency. After the war he also wrote books about his experiences. They included *The Spy of the Rebellion* (1883) and *Thirty Years a Detective* (1884), both of which have numerous errors and exaggerations. **See also** Lincoln, Abraham; McClellan, George Brinton; spies; Webster, Timothy.

plantations

The vast majority of plantations at the beginning of the Civil War were small, and only about 5 percent of plantation owners had more than one hundred slaves. The large plantations, however, could be extensive and elaborate. They might include buildings that served as child-care centers, hospitals, and churches for slaves, as well as numerous other structures for housing slaves and livestock and storing farm tools and supplies. Plantations also typically had at least one smokehouse for curing meat; a "kitchen garden" that provided fruits, vegetables, and herbs for consumption by the people living on the plantation; and workshops where slaves might make goods as varied as furniture, cloth, barrels, and horseshoes. Some plantations also had a schoolhouse for any white children who lived on or near the plantation. (In the South, black children were not allowed to go to school.) In addition, all plantations had what was known as the "big house," the place where the slave owner lived. This home was typically three stories tall, with a grand entrance and many rooms lavishly appointed with fine furniture and artwork. Many of them were destroyed during the war, however, by Union soldiers who set them on fire after looting their treasures, particularly during William T. Sherman's March to the Sea. **See also** Sherman's March to the Sea; slavery and slave life.

poetry, Civil War

Hundreds of poems were written during the Civil War, some signed and some anonymous. Many of these were published in newspapers and journals and/or as single sheets known as broadsides, which were intended for display as posters. Some poems also became song lyrics, such as Julia Ward Howe's "Battle Hymn of the Republic." At the outset of the war the majority of poems were patriotic and intended as calls to arms. Later poems commemorated certain battles or heroes, although as the war dragged on some poets chose to focus instead on more melancholy subjects, such as the homesickness of soldiers or the death and destruction they saw on the battlefield.

One of the most popular poems in the North was "Sheridan's Ride" by Thomas Buchanan Read, who created many other poems during the war. "Sheridan's Ride," which was recited to Northern audiences and memorized by Northern schoolchildren, commemorates Union general Philip Sheridan's rallying of his troops during the October 19, 1864, Battle of Cedar Creek, Virginia. One of the most popular Southern poems was "The Burial of Latane," written by John Reuben Thompson in 1862 to commemorate the death of William D. Latane, a soldier in Jeb Stuart's cavalry who was killed in Virginia.

Neither Read's nor Thompson's poems, however, achieved lasting popularity. On the other hand, the Civil War poetry of Walt Whitman—two volumes, *Drum-Taps* (1865) and *Sequel to Drum-Taps* (1866), and an elegy to Abraham Lincoln, "O Captain! My Captain!"—continue to be widely read into the twenty-first century. **See also** "Battle Hymn of the Republic"; literature, Civil War; Whitman, Walt.

political parties

There were several political parties prior to the Civil War, many whose stated principles referred directly to slavery or related issues. These include the American Anti-Slavery Society; the American Colonization Society, which argued that blacks should be sent from the United States to colonize Africa; the American Party (also called the Know-Nothings), which opposed allowing any more European immigrants into the country; the Constitutional Union Party; the Free-Soil Party, which opposed allowing slavery in U.S. territories; the Liberty Party, which was founded by abolitionists; the Democratic Party, formed in 1800 on the principle of limited government; the Whig Party, which was created in 1834 to oppose certain Democratic positions, particularly those related to the economy, but dissolved in 1852; and the Republican Party, which was formed two years later as an antislavery coalition that included many former Whigs, Free-Soilers, and Democrats who favored emancipation. During the war, most parties dissolved and only two, the Republican party and the Democratic Party, remained, with the Democratic Party divided into several factions.

Once the war broke out the Democratic Party lost all of its Southern members, but the Democrats who remained in the Union were still divided. Some, known as War Democrats, supported President Abraham Lincoln's decision to go to war in order to keep the South in the Union, although many of them did not support emancipation or the enlistment of black soldiers. Others, known as Peace Democrats, opposed the war and all war-related legislation, including the increase of taxes to pay for the war effort.

Among these Peace Democrats were men who openly supported the Confederacy in its bid for independence. The Republicans called these antiwar Northern Democrats "Copperheads," referring to a poisonous snake common in the South. The largest contingent of Copperheads was in southern Illinois, although there were many Copperheads in southern Ohio and Indiana as well. In general, the people of these regions not only opposed emancipation but also intensely disliked New Englanders, particularly abolitionists.

Meanwhile, the Democratic Party of the South divided into so many factions that it essentially ceased to exist. Some of these factions opposed and some supported various aspects of President Jefferson Davis's political policies, including decisions related to the prosecution of the war, the Confederate economy, and the organization of the new Confederate government. One of the main points of disagreement was over whether the Confederate government should be centralized. Some politicians argued that it was hypocritical for the South to support states' rights prior to the war while allowing Davis to create a strong central government once the war began.

There was also no Republican Party in the South, since the party was founded with emancipation as one of its core issues. In fact, it was the election of the Republican candidate for U.S. president, Abraham Lincoln, in 1860 that brought about the secession of the Southern states. During the 1864 election, the Republicans began calling their party the National Union Party in order to attract War Democrats into their fold, but after the election they went back to their original name and took positions related to emancipation and black civil rights that quickly alienated whatever War Democrats they had attracted. **See also** Radical Republicans; Reconstruction.

Polk, Leonidas (1806–1864)

Lieutenant General Leonidas Polk served with distinction in the Confederate army, but he was something of a contradiction in that he was also a bishop of the Protestant Episcopal Church. In addition, in 1860 he established the University of the South in Sewanee, Tennessee, which was designed as a training center for slave owners who would have to learn how to work with free blacks should the North succeed in emancipating the slaves. Polk had decided to become a bishop while a cadet at the U.S. Military Academy at West Point, from which he graduated in 1827. He then entered the Virginia Theological Seminary, and in 1830 he was ordained as a deacon. A year later he was a priest, and within ten years he had served as a bishop of the Southwest and a bishop of Louisiana. When the Civil War began, Polk joined the Confederacy as a major general, leading troops in the defense of the Mississippi River. He participated in the Battle of Shiloh in April 1862 and six months later was promoted to lieutenant general. In June 1864 he was mortally wounded in the Battle of Pine Mountain in Georgia. **See also** Shiloh, Battle of.

Pope, John (1822–1892)

A professional soldier and military engineer who had served in the Mexican-American War, Union general John Pope commanded the Army of Virginia, but after a serious defeat at the Second Battle of Bull Run (August 1862) he was relieved of command. At the outset of the Civil War Pope was made a brigadier general in the volunteer army. A year later he was promoted to major general, having achieved recognition for gaining Union control of a large section of the Mississippi River. Pope was then made a brigadier general in the Regular Army and placed in charge of the Army of Virginia. This command, however, proved beyond his ability. Just prior to the Second Battle of Bull Run, Pope misjudged the strength and location of the enemy's forces, and during the battle he became confused and gave contradictory orders. As a result, 1750 of his men were killed. After being relieved of his command, Pope was sent to Minnesota to fight Indians. After the Civil War ended he continued to be concerned with Indian attacks in the West as a commander of the Department of the Missouri (1870–1883). **See also** armies, Union; Bull Run, Second Battle of.

popular sovereignty

Also called squatter sovereignty, popular sovereignty was a doctrine that held that settlers in a U.S. territory could decide for themselves whether to allow slavery. Southerners generally opposed this concept, because they believed it was unconstitutional for any entity to prevent an individual from owning a particular piece of property (i.e., a slave). Nonetheless, in 1854 the doctrine formed the basis of the Kansas-Nebraska Act. **See also** Kansas-Nebraska Act.

population

According to the U.S. census of 1860, the population of the District of Columbia, the seven U.S. territories, and the twenty-three states that would later remain with the Union was 22,339,989, while the eleven Southern states that would eventually form the Confederacy had 9,101,090. Therefore at the outset of the Civil War the North had two and a half times more people than the South. Of these Northerners, about one-third were recent immigrants, as compared to only 9 percent of the Southern population.

Of the more than 22 million people in the North, over 355,000 were free blacks and over 432,000 were black slaves in U.S. territories and slaveholding states that remained loyal to the Union. Of the more than 9 million people in the South, over 3.5 million were black slaves. However, only about 1.7 million whites were slave owners or family members of slave owners, which means that most Southerners were either black slaves or whites who did not own slaves. The number of farmers in the North and South combined was 4.9 million, out of a total of 7.7 million people with jobs.

The largest states in the upper South were Virginia with over 1 million free men and about 490,000 slaves, Tennessee with over 830,000 free men and 275,000 slaves, and North Carolina with more than 661,000 free men and 331,000 slaves. The largest states in the lower South were Alabama with about 520,000 free men and 435,000 slaves, Georgia with about 505,000 free men and 460,000 slaves, Mississippi with about 350,000 free men and 436,000 slaves, and South Carolina with about 300,000 free men and 400,000 slaves. The largest states in the North were New York, with a population of about 3.8 million, Pennsylvania with about 2.9 million, Ohio with about 2.3 million, Illinois with about 1.7 million, Indiana with about 1.35 million, and Massachusetts with about 1.23 million.

The largest city in the United States in 1860 was New York City, with about 124,000 people. In comparison, the largest city in the South at that time was the fifth largest city in the United States: New Orleans, Louisiana, with about 27,000 people. **See also** plantations; slavery and slave life.

Porter, David Dixon (1813–1891)

At the time the Civil War began, David D. Porter was an experienced army officer, having served in the Mexican-American War (1846–1848), but he was given command of a Union gunboat, the *Powhatan,* in the Gulf of Mexico. In April 1862, as part of the West Gulf Blockading Squadron, Porter participated in an attack on New Orleans, Louisiana, via the Mississippi River as the commander of the mortar flotilla. This operation was led by Porter's adoptive brother David Glasgow Farragut, and by some accounts it was Porter who suggested both the attack and placing Farragut in charge of the attack.

By the end of 1862, Porter had been given command of his own squadron, the Mississippi Squadron, and ordered to maintain the Union's hold on the Mississippi River above the city of Vicksburg. By the end of 1863, Porter had been promoted to rear admiral and was now defending an even larger stretch of the Mississippi River. Once the Union was certain that it had control of this river system, Porter was transferred to the Atlantic Ocean as commander of the North Atlantic Blockading Squadron. In January 1865 he led a successful attack on Fort Fisher, on the North Carolina coast.

After the war, Porter was appointed the superintendent of the U.S. Naval Academy at Annapolis, Maryland, and was promoted to vice admiral. In 1870 he was promoted to full admiral. **See also** blockades and blockade runners; Farragut, David Glasgow; navies, Confederate and Union.

Port Hudson, Louisiana

Port Hudson, Louisiana, was located on the Mississippi River about 25 miles from Baton Rouge, Louisiana, and about 240 miles from Vicksburg, Mississippi. Because of this strategically significant position, the Confederates established a garrison on the site, and on May 25, 1863, the Union attacked it with five divisions of soldiers under the command of General Nathaniel Banks. The Confederates fought back, and the Union soon realized that it would not be easy to take the garrison. Consequently, Banks decided to put the garrison under siege. On June 14, after it had become obvious that this tactic was ineffective, Banks attacked the garrison again. Once more the Confederates withstood the attack, but when they learned that Vicksburg had fallen to the Union they knew that they would never receive reinforcements and decided to surrender. The garrison passed into Union hands on July 9, 1863. **See also** Banks, Nathaniel Prentiss; Vicksburg Campaign.

Price, Sterling ("Old Pap") (1809–1867)

Affectionately nicknamed "Old Pap" by his men, Sterling Price was a Confederate general who led a September 1864 cavalry raid from Arkansas into Missouri, then held by the Union. His idea was not only to capture the state for the Confederacy but also to strike a blow at the North just before it would vote on U.S. president Abraham Lincoln's reelection. Although he was not successful in either capturing Missouri or discrediting Lincoln, he did manage to destroy several miles of railroad tracks and distract Union soldiers who were intended to reinforce General William Tecumseh Sherman's attacks in Georgia.

Price had military experience prior to the Civil War, having served in the Mexican-American War (1846–1848) as a colonel and then a brigadier general with the Second Missouri Infantry. He also had experience in politics, having served in the U.S. House of Representatives and as governor of Missouri. When Missouri decided not to secede from the Union but instead to remain neutral in the conflict, Price and much of the state guard went to Arkansas to ask Confederates there to help him attack Union troops in Missouri. After a few successful Missouri raids, Price officially joined the Confederacy and served under Earl Van Dorn in the Army of the West. He fought in several battles before launching his September 1864 raid into Missouri.

For this mission, the Confederacy gave Price all cavalry west of the Mississippi, a force of over twelve thousand men and fourteen guns. However, just south of St. Louis, Missouri, he lost one thousand of his most experienced men within the first twenty minutes after attacking a Union fort. Though he later increased his troops to fifteen thousand as he traveled west toward Jefferson City, Missouri, he was unable to prevail against the Union, which increased its forces in Missouri to counter Price's plans. Eventually Price was forced to retreat across the Arkansas River and travel into Indian Territory before heading back east to Arkansas. By the time he reached Laynesport, Arkansas, on December 2, 1864, he had lost over four thousand men. In all, his cavalry had traveled nearly fifteen hundred miles.

When the Civil War ended, Price fled to Mexico, where he established a colony called Carlota for former Confederates. Due to political unrest in Mexico, however, in 1869 he decided to return to Missouri, where he died a few months later. **See also** armies, Confederate; cavalry; Missouri.

prisons and prisoners of war

During the Civil War the Union captured about 462,000 Confederate soldiers and sailors, while the Confederates captured about 211,000 Union soldiers. Of these men, approximately 425,000 were housed in 150 Union and Confederate prisons, overseen by Colonel William Hoffman of the Union and Brigadier General John H. Winder of the Confederacy, respectively. Due to limited space in these facilities, however, many more prisoners of war (POWs) were released before they even left the battlefield, particularly during the first year of the war. As part of their release, these POWs were recorded as being "paroled" and had to vow not to take up arms again until they had been exchanged on paper with a POW in the opposing army.

By 1862, a formal system of exchange was established between the two armies. A private could be exchanged for a private, a sergeant for two privates, a lieutenant for four privates, and so on, with a general being worth sixty privates. Under this system, the Union paroled at least 247,000 men, the Confederacy about 16,000. The exchange system collapsed in December 1862, however, because the Confederacy refused to exchange captured black soldiers. Instead, these men were sold into slavery, and any whites who had led them into battle were executed. As a result of this policy, on July 30, 1863, U.S. president Abraham Lincoln declared that for every POW execution in the South there would be a corresponding execution in the North, and for every enslavement of a black soldier a Confederate POW would be forced to perform hard labor.

Once the prisoner exchanges ended, all prisons became horribly overcrowded, and this led to disease and death among prisoners. Approximately 56,000 men died in Union and Confederate prisons, although some POW facilities were worse than others in this regard. For example, one-fourth of all Confederate prisoners died in a prison camp at Elmira, New York; 29 percent of Union prisoners died at Camp Sumter at Andersonville, Georgia (also known as the Andersonville Prison Camp); and 30 percent of Union soldiers died at the Salisbury Prison Camp in North Carolina.

There were six types of prisons during the war. The first prisons used during the war were facilities that had existed as jails or prisons prior to the war. Next were forts, such as Fort Warren in Massachusetts's Boston Harbor, that had been converted into prisons. Vacant buildings and warehouses were used as prisons once all existing facilities had become full. Another type of prison was the converted military training camp. The last two types of prisons were built to house large numbers of prisoners: stockades without shelters and stockades with tent cities.

One of the most notorious prisons created from a vacant building was Libby Prison in Richmond, Virginia. Libby Prison was originally a four-story factory that supplied materials for shipbuilding. The Confederacy primarily housed Union officers there beginning in March 1862. Due to the overcrowding caused by the cessation of prisoner exchanges, by the beginning of 1864 there were at least twelve hundred prisoners on each floor of the building, a third of whom were seriously ill by March of that year. Overcrowding was so bad at Libby Prison that not everyone could lie down to sleep at the same time, and those whose turn it was to sleep had to lie on their sides. Moreover, prisoners were forbidden to look out of the windows; if they did so, they would be shot. And during the night they were not allowed to use the latrines, so they often soiled themselves.

Given such conditions, a group of more than two dozen prisoners at Libby Prison devised an escape plan. They punched a hole in a second-floor wall behind a stove, made a passageway within the wall down to the building's basement, and worked in shifts to secretly dig a tunnel through the basement floor and underground to a shed across the street from the prison. They hid the dirt they had removed by scattering it under a pile of straw that was already in the basement. After forty-seven days of effort, the escape route was complete, and on February 9, 1864, 109 Union officers gained freedom by crawling through the tunnel and emerging inside the shed. Once outside the shed, they walked individually or in very small groups out of the city and headed north. However, only fifty-nine of them made it to safety. Of the remainder, two drowned while trying to swim across the James River and the rest were recaptured by the Confederates.

Another camp plagued by escape attempts, though none were successful, was Camp Douglas in Chicago, Illinois. It was also one of the worst of the prisons established in former military camps. This twenty-acre prison was located on land that had once belonged to Senator Stephen A. Douglas, and was named for him. Camp Douglas acted as a military camp in 1861 and part of 1862, then was converted into a prison with sixty-four barracks and began accepting Confederate prisoners in February 1863. Each barracks was intended to house ninety-five men, but eventually every one of them held about 190, so by December 1864 there were over twelve thousand prisoners in the camp. Diseases such as smallpox, pneumonia, and typhoid fever spread quickly under such conditions, particularly during the winter because the weather was too bad for the men to go outside for fresh air. As a result, the death rate during the winter of 1863 was eighteen men per day.

Rules at Camp Douglas were highly restrictive. For example, no prisoner was allowed to light a candle or talk at night.

When a prisoner caused trouble for his guards, they might lock him for several days in a room that was only eight feet square and seven feet high and had only two airholes. Given such conditions, so many men tried to escape that in May 1864 the Union not only added an elevated walkway for guards to the perimeter of the camp but also raised all of the barracks up on platforms so that the men could not tunnel beneath them.

Another military-camp-turned-prison was a facility at Elmira, New York. It began as a forty-acre Union training camp for twenty-one thousand soldiers, but became a prison for more than ten thousand Confederate captives in July 1864. The Elmira prison had thirty-five buildings surrounded by a twelve-foot-high wall with an observation tower, which officials allowed citizens to climb to view the prisoners for a fee of 10 cents. Prisoners at Elmira were forced to eat extremely poor food, and punishments included being locked in a "sweat box" (a box only seven feet tall, twenty inches wide, and twelve inches deep) for long periods of time. One-quarter of the men housed at the Elmira prison died of disease, although the prison was used for only one year. In October 1864 alone, the death rate just from disease was five men per day. In the previous month, nearly two thousand men died of scurvy, a nutritional deficiency.

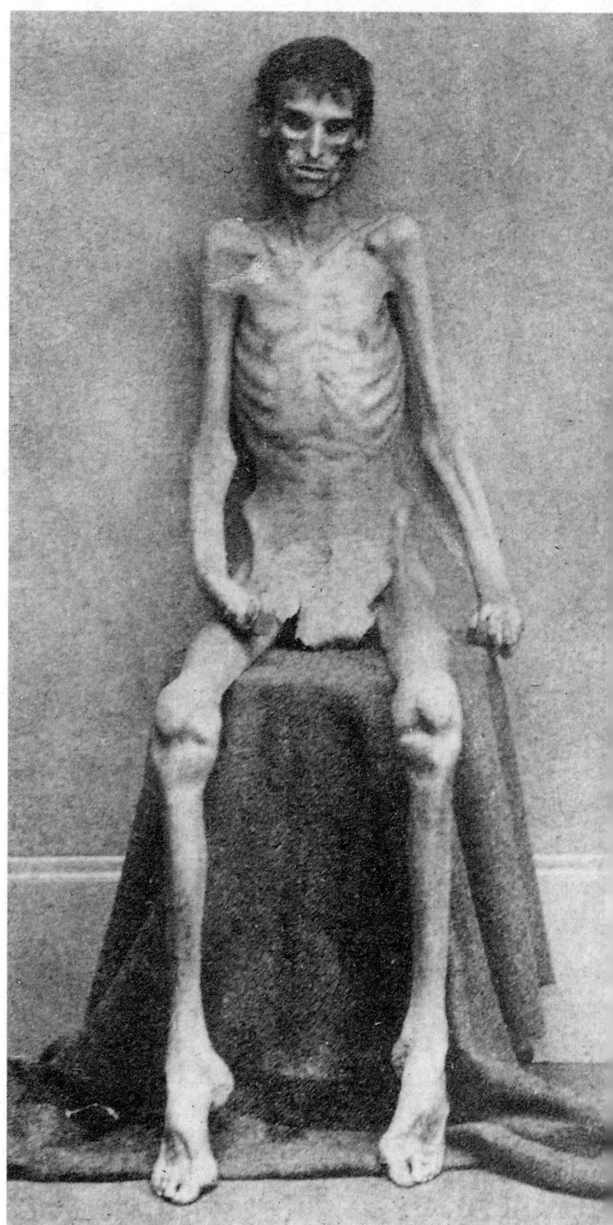

An emaciated prisoner of war from the Andersonville Prison Camp in Georgia.

The prisons with the worst conditions, however, were stockades, either with or without shelters. Of these, the three most notorious were Confederate prisons: Camp Salisbury in North Carolina, Belle Isle on the James River near Richmond, Virginia, and Camp Sumter at Andersonville, Georgia. Camp Salisbury comprised sixteen acres surrounded by a wooden stockade. It had a few small buildings and a four-story cotton factory that was used as housing, although prisoners also slept outside. The prison was intended to hold two thousand men, but by October 1864 there were over ten thousand housed there, and by April of the following year at least thirty-four hundred had died. The Belle Isle prison had a maximum capacity of about three thousand men but actually held at least double that number. Some prisoners slept in groups of ten or twelve in small, tattered tents, but most slept on the ground in open air. In either case, the men were packed closely side by side. Even in the camp's five hospital tents, which were located near a large graveyard, patients slept on straw with logs as pillows. As in other camps, disease spread rapidly, more than 90 percent of the men were malnourished, and many prisoners froze to death in the winter.

Finally in the winter of 1863–1864 the conditions at Belle Isle became so bad that the Confederacy decided to relocate the prisoners to another facility: Camp Sumter, also known as Andersonville Prison. Unfortunately for the prisoners, this soon became a far worse place to live than Belle Isle. Intended to hold 10,000 Union soldiers, within a few months of operation it had approximately 32,000. Of the 49,485 prisoners who lived at the camp between February 1864 and May 1865, over 13,000 died, and most of the remainder developed serious illnesses that continued to plague them after the war was over.

By the end of the war, Confederate prisons were responsible for the deaths of over 30,000 Union soldiers, out of approximately 197,000 men held in such facilities. Meanwhile, Union prisons were responsible for the deaths of at least 26,000 Confederate soldiers, out of approximately 225,000 men held. Still more men died of either disease or accidental injuries while being transported to prison. For example, on July 16, 1864, forty-eight Confederate prisoners were killed when a train carrying them to the Elmira prison crashed. And more than 1,700 Union soldiers died right after being released from Confederate prisons at the end of the war after the boiler on their overloaded ship, the *Sultana,* exploded on its way to Illinois. **See also** Andersonville; *Sultana.*

propaganda

Many private groups, particularly abolitionist ones, used propaganda to convince Americans that their side was the right one. Such groups typically printed pamphlets and books expressing their views, distributing them to hundreds or perhaps thousands of people. For example, the Loyal Publication Society of New York published ninety pamphlets and distributed 900,000 copies of them, all supporting the Northern cause. In addition, private citizens who wanted to form regiments used propaganda to encourage men to volunteer, playing on their emotions in regard to their beliefs about their country and about the slavery issue. Patriotism was further fueled by soldiers at the front, who wrote letters to newspapers asking people at home to remain steadfast in their support for the war.

The leaders of the North and the South also gave speeches intended to boost morale and explain the rationale behind certain aspects of the war. However, these speeches were not made as part of a deliberate government propaganda effort. Both the U.S. and Confederate governments did pursue propaganda efforts abroad, though. In 1861, they sent representatives to England and France to influence foreign politicians and citizens, through personal appearances and the press, in an attempt to gain European allies. Both governments were unsuccessful in this regard (European countries maintained a position of neutrality during the Civil War), but they did manage to raise funds from various private sources for their war efforts. **See also** abolitionists; foreign countries, involvement of.

prostitutes

Prostitutes plied their trade near army encampments and in cities where they knew that soldiers would be passing through on their way to other cities or to battlefields. Consequently, Richmond, Virginia, and Washington, D.C., both had large numbers of prostitutes. Wherever they were, prostitutes spread disease. By some estimates, there were at least a half-million cases of sexually transmitted diseases contracted during the war, and by the end of the war special hospitals had been established that were dedicated to treating these diseases. **See also** medical facilities.

punishments

There were many problems with discipline during the Civil War, and traditional military punishments were not always effective in dealing with them. The reason for this had to do with certain differences between pre–Civil War and Civil War enlisted men. Before the Civil War, most soldiers and sailors came from lower social classes than the officers they served, and obedience to one's social superior was the norm. During the Civil War, however, many volunteer soldiers, particularly in the South, were of a higher social class and also were usually wealthier than the professional officers under whom they served. Thus, these soldiers felt comfortable arguing with officers or even refusing their orders. Moreover, volunteer regiments were typically formed in local communities where everyone knew one another, and this familiarity often made it more difficult for one man to tell another what to do. Adding to discipline problems was the fact that the government, whether Union or Confederate, was desperate to get and keep a large number of troops. As a result, commanding officers were reluctant to take a firm hand with soldiers or sailors out of fear that they might desert.

Still another factor was that many volunteers had joined the military thinking their service would be easy. When conditions grew difficult, or even merely boring, these men often deserted the military and returned home. Thousands of men deserted from both armies during the war, with the largest number leaving right before a major battle. For example, more than 8,000 soldiers and 250 officers deserted from Union armies just prior to the Battle of Antietam. Sailors at sea, who were unable to desert, sometimes mutinied to avoid service. In addition, many sailors and soldiers also threatened to kill officers with whom they disagreed. Confederate brigadier general Charles S. Winder received several such threats from the men in his five volunteer regiments after the Second Bull Run Campaign as a result of his using corporal punishment on soldiers who did not keep pace with their peers on the march to the battlefield. (Most of those soldiers who did not threaten to kill him deserted.)

In punishing his men, Winder employed a method known as bucking and gagging. The soldier being punished was gagged and a log placed behind his elbows and behind his knees. Then his hands were tied to his ankles and he was left to endure the situation for several hours. Alternatives to bucking and gagging included making a man carry a heavy saddle, a heavy log, or a bag of rocks instead of a rifle while marching or performing guard duty; making him perform such actions with a cannonball chained to his leg; or forcing the man to sit astride a "wooden mule," a thin rail as high off the ground as a horse, for hours. Other punishments included reducing a soldier's time for relaxation and/or assigning him to difficult or offensive tasks, such as digging or maintaining latrines or burying bodies. On board ship, a common punishment was withholding meals or providing only bread and water. (Prior to the Civil War, flogging was also a common punishment for disobedient sailors, but it was outlawed shortly before the war began.) Meanwhile, disobedient cavalrymen and artillerymen might be hung by their thumbs, tied spread-eagled to wheels, or otherwise restrained in ways that were painful but not lethal.

All of these punishments were administered by officers in the field or at sea for minor offenses as soon as they occurred. More serious offenses were met with punishment determined by court-martial.

There were two types of court-martials, the special and the general. A special court-martial, which was for a medium-level offense, was presided over by three officers who served as judges and jurors. They heard any accusations against the offender, spoke to witnesses, and decided the offender's punishment, which might include the loss of a month's pay, thirty days in prison, or performing hard labor, or—for noncommissioned officers—demotion to a lower rank. Commissioned officers were usually just fined or given an inferior command assignment, although in some cases they were encouraged to resign or, more rarely, dismissed from the military.

A general court-martial, which was for very serious offenses (such as desertion, murder, sleeping on duty, supporting a mutiny, or being a coward, thief, or spy), required five to thirteen officer judges and a judge advocate who questioned witnesses. The mildest punishment for someone found guilty in a general court-martial was branding, which was reserved for deserters, thieves, and cowards. These men would be branded on the hip, face, hand, or some other part of the body with a letter in accordance with the crime: Deserters would be branded with a D, cowards with a C, and thieves with a T. A person who was branded might also be "drummed out of the corps," which meant that he would be sent away from his unit of service to the beat of drums after first having his insignias of rank stripped away and his head shaved. (Sometimes, instead of a simple drumbeat, the offender was kicked out to the tune of "Yankee Doodle" in the North or "The Rogues' March" in the South.) The most serious crimes were punished by death, either by hanging or firing squad. Once the judges of a general court-martial voted for this punishment (with at least a 2-to-1 majority required), only the U.S. or Confederate president or the general who had brought the offender to court could issue a pardon to stop the execution. **See also** desertion; execution; spies.

Quakers (aka Friends)

Members of a Protestant sect called the Society of Friends, Quakers were among the first and most active abolitionists in America. The most prominent Quaker abolitionists prior to the Civil War include Sarah Grimké and Angelina Grimké Weld, two sisters who wrote, respectively, the pamphlets *Appeal to the Christian Women of the South* and *Epistle to the Clergy of the Southern States* in the 1830s to call for an end to slavery; poet and journalist John Greenleaf Whittier, who became a lobbyist for antislavery legislation; and Isaac Hopper, Thomas Garrett, and Levi Coffin, who were responsible for helping thousands of slaves escape to freedom as part of the Underground Railroad.

Quakerism began in the seventeenth century, when it was created by English Puritan George Fox (1624–1691), and quickly spread from England to the American colonies. By the Civil War, Quakers were particularly prevalent in New England, New York, Maryland, and Virginia. Together with a religious group with similar beliefs, the Mennonites, they numbered about 200,000.

Quakers believed that all human beings deserved respect regardless of race, and therefore from America's colonial years onward they were involved in abolitionist activities. In fact, during the 1820s—long before most Americans questioned whether slavery was morally right—they were working to establish abolitionism in the upper South. However, Quakers were also pacifists, which meant that they avoided actively participating in battles to free the slaves. For this reason, when the Union discovered that the Confederates had painted logs to look like cannons so that their forces would appear stronger during the 1862 Battle of Yorktown, Northern reporters dubbed these harmless cannons "Quaker guns."

Because of their pacifism, Quakers tried to get the Confederate and Union armies to exempt their members from conscription on the grounds of conscientious objection. They succeeded with the Confederacy—although sometimes a soldier's request for exemption was ignored—but failed to convince the Union of the need to give pacifists the right not to fight. Quakers also expressed their pacifist views by refusing to pay war-related taxes, an action that often resulted in the seizure of their property. **See also** abolitionists; conscientious objectors; Underground Railroad; Whittier, John Greenleaf.

Quantrill, William Clarke (aka Charley Hart) (1837–1865)

During the Civil War, William C. Quantrill was a bushwacker, or Confederate guerrilla, who led a band of men in attacking antislavery settlers and Union soldiers in Kansas towns near the Kansas-Missouri border. The most famous such attack took place on August 21, 1863, when Quantrill led over 450 guerrillas in an assault on the citizens of Lawrence, Kansas. Quantrill's men slaughtered about 150 defenseless men and boys during this attack.

A former schoolteacher from Ohio who had once been accused of petty thievery, Quantrill was living near the Missouri-Kansas border when the Civil War broke out. This area had long been the site of conflict between antislavery and proslavery forces, and Quantrill soon allied himself with violent guerrillas who routinely raided antislavery towns. Some of the men with whom he associated included Frank and Jesse James and the Younger brothers (Thomas Coleman, or "Cole," John, James, and Robert), who later became notorious Wild West outlaws, and "Bloody Bill" Anderson, who was even more brutal than Quantrill.

In the aftermath of the attack on Lawrence, Kansas, Federal troops tried to capture Quantrill and his most notorious followers, but they escaped into Texas and operated there for a time. Eventually, however, their band splintered into several guerrilla groups that operated in various parts of the country. On May 10, 1865, Quantrill was leading one of these groups, with approximately thirty guerrillas, in Kentucky. While they were spending the night in a barn, Union soldiers who had been tipped off as to Quantrill's whereabouts began firing on the structure. Quantrill tried to escape on horseback but was mortally wounded. He died several days later, on June 6, 1865.

See also Anderson, William; bushwackers; Kansas.

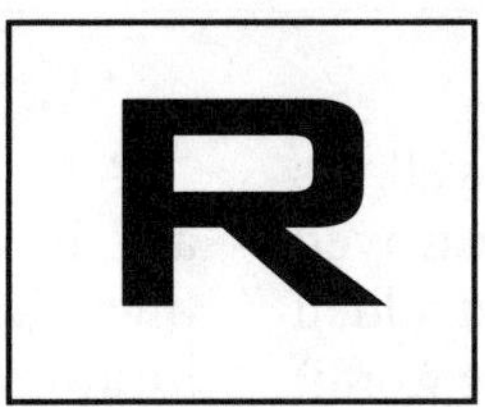

Radical Republicans

The Republican Party was formed in 1854 as an antislavery coalition composed of former Whigs, Free-Soilers, antislavery Democrats, and others who supported emancipation. In the years just prior to the Civil War, a faction developed within this party known as the Radical Republicans; members of this faction held relatively extreme views in regard to black civil rights. For example, Radical Republicans called for immediate and total emancipation, the creation of laws that would establish black equality, and the repeal of fugitive slave laws. Once the Civil War broke out, Radical Republicans became even more vociferous in expressing these views and were therefore often at odds with many fellow Republicans, including President Abraham Lincoln, who favored a more moderate approach to the slavery issue during that period. One of the most aggressive and extreme Radical Republicans in Congress was Pennsylvania representative Thaddeus Stevens, who was instrumental in convincing the government to use black troops. During Reconstruction, Stevens led the Radical Republicans in Congress in promoting black civil rights and calling for the U.S. government to deal harshly with all former Confederate states. When President Andrew Johnson instead adopted a policy of leniency toward the South and allowed the Southern states to enact laws that denied blacks equal rights despite emancipation, the Radical Republicans gained support among the general public, and in 1866 this faction became dominant in Congress. Consequently in March 1867 Congress began passing Reconstruction acts that went against Johnson's wishes, including one that gave blacks the right to vote. **See also** Johnson, Andrew; political parties; Stevens, Thaddeus.

railroads

Railroads figured prominently during the Civil War because they could move troops and supplies great distances within a relatively short time. For example, when Union forces were under siege at Chattanooga, Tennessee, in the fall of 1863, the Union sent twenty thousand reinforcements from the Army of the Potomac—along with equipment, weapons, and horses—by rail over a distance of twelve hundred miles in just eleven days. Similarly, in July 1862 Confederate general Braxton Bragg sent thirty thousand men on a roughly two-week rail trip from Mississippi to Chattanooga, Tennessee, over a 776-mile route that skirted Union positions.

There were approximately nine thousand miles of rail line in the eleven Confederate states when the war started (roughly one-third of the country's rail mileage), managed by more than one hundred railroad companies. However, only nine rail lines were longer than two hundred miles; most were about eighty-five miles in length. The main railroad centers in the South were Richmond, Virginia; Atlanta, Georgia; and Chattanooga, Tennessee, although many other major cities were served as well. As the war progressed, the Union destroyed many of the South's rail lines, but added new ones (about four thousand miles worth) to move military personnel, equipment, and supplies to various areas of combat.

During the war, roughly one-third of the passengers carried on Southern railroads were associated with the military. Passenger cars, which were about fifty feet long, could hold roughly fifty people and usually had a toilet and a stove. Freight cars were about twenty-four to thirty-four feet long and could hold eight to twelve tons. By the end of 1863, many Southern railroad cars of both types were in disrepair, as were many locomotives, but the South lacked the resources to fix them. The Confederacy also had difficulty maintaining rail lines as iron became scarce and there were few men available to cut new railroad ties (even when wood was available).

A far greater problem for the Confederacy, however, was Union attacks on rail lines. Union soldiers not only destroyed hundreds of miles of track but also wrecked locomotives, railroad cars, trestles, and depots, and whatever they did not destroy they took for their own use. As a result, Confederate armies often did not receive necessary supplies on time, if at all. This was particularly true in 1864 and 1865, when the armies of Robert E. Lee went without new supplies of food for days while attempting to defend the Confederate capital. **See also** transportation.

Randolph, George Wythe (1818–1867)

The grandson of U.S. president Thomas Jefferson, George W. Randolph served as the Confederate secretary of war from March 23, 1862, to November 17, 1862. Randolph had practiced law and served in both the U.S. Army and U.S. Navy prior to

Railroad cars lie exposed in Atlanta, Georgia, after the depot was destroyed in a Union attack.

the war but joined the Confederacy as soon as his native state of Virginia seceded. As secretary of war, he oversaw the creation and enactment of the first Confederate conscription law. However, he disagreed with President Jefferson Davis on many issues related to how the war should proceed and how the army and War Department should be organized, and soon he decided to resign his position. He then went to Europe to further Confederate concerns there. **See also** cabinet, Confederate.

Reagan, John H. (1818–1905)

A lawyer and former U.S. congressman from Texas, John H. Reagan was the Confederate postmaster general for the duration of the war. In creating the Confederate postal service he used the federal one as a model, and even hired away federal postal workers to work in his own postal service. Reagan also met a Confederate Constitution requirement to make the postal service self-supporting by March 1, 1863, by streamlining the organization to make it more efficient and charging higher amounts for mail. Reagan was with President Jefferson Davis when he was captured by Union soldiers at the war's end. **See also** Davis, Jefferson.

Reconstruction

Reconstruction was a period of American history lasting from roughly 1865 to 1877 during which the federal government instituted policies to bring the South back into the Union and to define the rights of newly emancipated blacks. Historians disagree on whether the primary purpose of these policies was to punish the South or whether they were sincere attempts to establish and protect civil rights.

The first Reconstruction policy was proposed by U.S. president Abraham Lincoln in December 1863. Known as the Ten Percent Plan, this policy allowed a Southern state to apply for readmission to the Union once one-tenth of its prewar voters had taken an oath of loyalty to the United States. The state's citizens also had to elect a new state government and alter their state constitution so that it officially abolished slavery. However, states were not required to allow blacks to vote or hold political office. Therefore toward the end of 1864, the U.S. Congress—which was controlled by Radical Republicans who wanted to deal harshly with the South—rejected the plan in favor of the Wade-Davis Bill, which stated that in order to be readmitted to the Union the Southern states had to give blacks equal rights under the law. The bill also increased the percentage of Southern voters in a state who had to take an oath of loyalty from 10 to 50 percent. Lincoln did not sign this bill, however, before Congress went into recess in March 1865 (by which time it had passed the Thirteenth Amendment abolishing slavery throughout the United States), and at the time he was assassinated the following month, he apparently still intended to push the adoption of his Ten Percent Plan.

Lincoln's successor, Andrew Johnson, did not adopt either the Ten Percent Plan or the Wade-Davis Bill. Instead, he enacted Reconstruction policies that did not demand much from Southerners. Specifically, Johnson did not demand that a certain percentage of Southerners take an oath of loyalty to the Union, although he did require former Confederate leaders and wealthy Southerners to apply for a presidential pardon of their Confederate war activities. Moreover, a Southern state could rejoin the Union simply by abolishing slavery and officially stating that it was wrong to secede, without having to elect a new state government. Johnson also ordered that all Southern plantations taken by the Union be returned to their owners.

Because of Johnson's concessions to the South, when the U.S. Congress convened in December 1865 with its first Southern representatives since before the

The first black senators and members of Congress, some of whom are pictured here, were elected to Congress in 1870 when blacks were given the right to vote.

war, it contained many former leaders of the Confederacy. This angered Northern congressmen, who began passing new civil rights and Reconstruction bills and constitutional amendments despite Johnson's opposition to them. By March 1868, these included the Reconstruction Acts, which placed certain Southern states under military control and forced them to write new constitutions that gave blacks more rights. Congress also banned certain former Confederates from holding political office, and it tried to impeach Johnson and nearly succeeded. The following year, Congress passed a constitutional amendment (ratified in 1870) giving blacks the right to vote.

Meanwhile, blacks were trying to adjust to their new lives as freedmen. Some continued to work on plantations, just as they had when they were slaves, although now they could come and go as they pleased. Others started new lives in new locations, perhaps buying or renting land through a government agency called the Bureau of Refugees, Freedmen, and Abandoned Lands so that they could become self-supporting farmers. The Bureau of Refugees, Freedmen, and Abandoned Lands also established black churches and schools, and by 1877 approximately 600,000 blacks had enrolled in classes to learn to read and write.

A few blacks also became involved in politics, supporting Republicans in large numbers at the polls. In addition, over 260 blacks served as delegates to state political conventions during the 1866 congressional elections. A few blacks even held local or state office. Of these, the most notable is the first black governor, P.B.S. Pinchback of Louisiana. He and fifteen other blacks also served in the Congress at some point or another during the Reconstruction period.

But despite such signs of progress, life in the South was still very difficult for blacks after the war. Some whites took advantage of the freedmen's naïveté in order to cheat them in various ways, and many white Southerners continued to prevent blacks from exercising their rights. For example, some employers told their black workers that if they voted they would be fired, and secret societies such as the Ku Klux Klan were formed to perpetrate violent attacks on blacks who tried to better themselves. Meanwhile, in Tennessee, Georgia, North Carolina, and Virginia, white voters managed to force Republicans out of office, so by 1871 the Democrats controlled those state governments. After the 1876 elections, Democrats also gained control of South Carolina, Florida, and Louisiana as part of a political deal brokered by Republicans to get their presidential candidate, Rutherford B. Hayes, into office.

Once the Democrats regained control of the South, they began enacting laws (known as Black Codes) that placed restrictions on black rights as part of a campaign to restore white supremacy that became known as Redemption. For example, blacks were now segregated from whites in schools, hospitals, restaurants, train cars, and many other places, and blacks were banned from marrying whites. As a result, Reconstruction ended. **See also** Black Codes; Bureau of Refugees, Freedmen, and Abandoned Lands; Ku Klux Klan.

Red River Campaigns

As part of a plan to invade Texas, the Union launched two land-sea campaigns along Louisiana's Red River, both of them failures. The first took place in 1863 after the Union took Port Hudson, Louisiana, on the Mississippi River. Although the commander of that operation, Major General Nathaniel P. Banks, wanted to go on to attack Mobile, Alabama, President Abraham Lincoln instead ordered him to advance into Texas. Banks was unable to get his troops very far along the Red River, nor was he able to move them along an inland route, but Union naval forces under the command of Rear Admiral David Porter did take several port cities along the Gulf Coast.

The second Red River Campaign took place in March and April 1864, with the intent that several Union forces would meet along the Red River at Alexandria, Louisiana, and then proceed to the Confederate city of Shreveport, Louisiana. Due to delays and other problems, very little went right for the Union during this campaign. For example, Banks's force of seventeen thousand was supposed to be reinforced by fifteen thousand men under Brigadier General Frederick Steele, but they were unable to reach him. Meanwhile, the Confederates sent about twenty-five thousand men into the area under the command of General Edmund Kirby Smith. After a few skirmishes with just part of this force, Banks retreated, as did Porter after his ships met heavy fire from troops stationed on the banks of the river.

In all, the two Red River Campaigns cost the Union about fifty-two hundred soldiers and the Confederacy about forty-two hundred. The second campaign also cost Banks his command. **See also** Banks, Nathaniel Prentiss; Porter, David Dixon.

refugees

As Southern towns and farms were devastated by war, disease, and/or food shortages, their residents fled to other areas of the South as refugees. There were approximately 200,000 Southern refugees, many of them women and children. Of these, most relocated to major cities in Virginia, particularly Richmond. In the West, the primary state destination for refugees was Texas. Other Confederate cities that received large influxes of refugees were Raleigh, North Carolina; Columbia, South Carolina; and Atlanta, Georgia. As the populations of such cities increased, housing and jobs became scarce and prices for various goods and services rose. Therefore refugees often found themselves living on the streets in poverty, perhaps in worse circumstances than before they had left their homes. **See also** economy, Southern vs. Northern.

relief societies

As soon as the war began, both Northerners and Southerners began forming soldiers' relief societies, and eventually there were over twenty thousand such agencies. Most were run by women who concentrated on helping soldiers who had come from their own communities or states. Their aid typically came in the form of preparing food and sewing and knitting clothes, blankets, and flags for the troops. However, a few relief societies were broader in scope. For example, in the North the Women's Central Association for Relief coordinated the activities of local and state relief societies, and eventually its actions led to the establishment of the U.S. Sanitary Commission, which worked to better Union soldiers' living conditions.

All types of relief societies also devoted a great deal of time to raising funds for the war effort, either in general or for a specific purpose (such as buying gunboats). In addition, as the war progressed, new relief societies were established specifically to help blacks. One of the most significant of these was the Contraband Relief Association, which later became the Ladies' Freedmen and Soldiers Relief Association. One of the leaders of this group, which was founded in 1862, was Elizabeth Keckley, a former slave who was Mary Todd Lincoln's seamstress. **See also** Sanitary Commission, U.S.; women, contributions of.

Richmond, Virginia

Richmond, Virginia, was the Confederate capital for much of the war. As such, the Union launched many attempts to take the city, which resulted in a great deal of fighting in the surrounding area. On April 2, 1865, the Confederates abandoned the city, setting it ablaze to prevent the Union soldiers who then occupied Richmond from gaining any important supplies. The Confederate capital was then moved to Danville, Virginia, but a week later Robert E. Lee surrendered the Confederacy's Army of Northern Virginia and the war was essentially over. **See also** Lee, Robert Edward; Virginia.

riots

Both the North and the South had to deal with civilian riots during the war. In the South, these riots were responses to starvation and economic problems. The most famous such riot occurred in Richmond, Virginia, in 1863, when hundreds of people, most of them women, looted stores while protesting food shortages. Similar events took place in other cities throughout the Confederate states, including New Orleans, Louisiana; Salisbury, North Carolina; Petersburg, Virginia; and Savannah, Georgia.

In the North, riots occurred as responses to the draft and other government policies related to the war. Fueling opposition to these policies was the resentment toward blacks on the part of many industrial workers who did not want to fight to free people they feared might eventually compete with them for jobs. In fact, many riots were prompted by incidents in which blacks took whites' jobs. For example, Irish American dockworkers in Cincinnati, Ohio, in 1862 and in New York City in 1863, who had gone on strike rioted after blacks replaced them on the docks. The New York riots, which lasted four days, started when some of these striking workers heard that they were being drafted into the military. **See also** conscription.

rivers, significant

Rivers that formed natural boundaries or provided a good means of transportation to areas of combat were particularly significant during the Civil War. Among these were the Mississippi River, the Rapidan River, the Rappahannock River, the Chickahominy River, the Potomac River, the Tennessee River, and the James River. The Mississippi River was used to launch numerous Union attacks on the South after all Confederate forts on the river were taken by Union general Ulysses S. Grant in 1862. The Rapidan River and the Rappahannock River were front lines between the forces of the North and those of the South for much of the war, and a great deal of fighting took place along the Chickahominy as well. The Potomac was the natural boundary between the North and the South, which meant that fighting rarely took place north of the Potomac. Many of the most important battles of the western theater of the war were fought along the Tennessee River, which runs through Kentucky, Tennessee, and Alabama. The James River, which runs through the center of Virginia, was the means by which Union general George McClellan attempted to take the Confederate capital of Richmond, Virginia, during his Peninsula Campaign in 1862. In addition, the place where it empties into Chesapeake Bay is the site of Norfolk, Virginia, where the South's largest navy yard was located. **See also** Alabama; Kentucky; Mississippi; Tennessee; Virginia.

Root, George Frederick (1820–1895)

George F. Root was the most prolific of all Civil War song composers. Born in Massachusetts, he could play thirteen different musical instruments by the age of thirteen. At the age of twenty-five he took a job playing the organ at a New York City church and teaching music and voice at a girls' school there. Five years later he became an instructor at the Boston Academy of Music. Shortly thereafter he began composing music, and in 1859 he became a partner in a Chicago, Illinois, music publishing company, Root and Cady. He also published a periodical, the *Song Messenger of the Northwest,* dedicated to music.

Root's early compositions were classical pieces, but by the time the Civil War broke out he was writing popular pieces as well, sometimes under the pseudonym Wurzel ("root" in German). His Civil War works include "Battle Cry of Freedom," "Just Before the Battle, Mother," "Starved in Prison," "The Vacant Chair," and "Tramp! Tramp! Tramp!" **See also** songs.

Ruffin, Edmund (1794–1865)

Edmund Ruffin is believed to be the person who fired the first shot on Fort Sumter, thereby officially starting the Civil War. Before the war, he was a fire-eater (an ardent Southern secessionist) and an agricultural expert, writing books and articles on such topics as fertilizer and crop rotation. Two months after Robert E. Lee surrendered the Confederacy's Army of Northern Virginia, Ruffin became so despondent over the loss that he killed himself. **See also** fire-eater; Fort Sumter.

sailors

Both the Confederacy and the Union suffered from a shortage of sailors during the Civil War. In 1863 the Confederacy solved this problem fairly easily by enacting a law in which any soldier who wanted to do so could transfer to naval duty. The North, however, had more difficulty with its shortage of sailors, because it had far more ships than the South and far fewer men willing to serve on them. The Union had to offer monetary bonuses and promises of easier duties to convince soldiers to become sailors. When these incentives proved insufficient, some draftees were sent to the navy. In addition, on certain navy vessels, members of the U.S. Marine Corps were brought on board to serve as guards, even though their normal service was in coastal barracks.

Despite their need for sailors, both navies had certain minimum requirements for crew members. No one under the age of fourteen in the Confederacy or thirteen in the Union could serve on board a ship (although this rule might be ignored when cabin boys were needed), and boys under age twenty-one in the Confederacy and eighteen in the Union needed parental consent to enlist. There was a maximum age for enlistees as well, unless a man was an experienced seaman or had a trade that would be of value at sea. In the South the maximum age was thirty-five; in the North it was thirty-eight for skilled tradesmen but thirty-three otherwise. There were also minimum height requirements in both navies: four feet eight inches or taller for Confederate sailors and five feet eight inches or taller for Union sailors.

When the war began the North had yet another restriction: Only one out of every twenty men on any naval vessel could be black. During the war this restriction was eliminated, but blacks were often assigned to the most backbreaking duties on ship, such as shoveling coal or raising anchors. Alternatively, blacks might be assigned to work as officers' servants.

Once a man was accepted into either navy, he was usually trained on a receiving ship, an old vessel designated for use by only new recruits and their instructors. Prior to the war, the training period for a sailor might last months, but during the war a recruit might spend as little as a week in training. He would then be sent to his permanent assignment and given specific duties to perform, usually depending on the ship's needs rather than his own preferences or abilities. Once at sea he would continue his naval education, because any recruit who wanted to be promoted had to master knot tying, sail and rope repairing, and dozens of other skills.

Whatever a sailor's assignment, the majority of his time was spent out of harm's way. There was very little ship-to-ship fighting—by some estimates, less than one week's worth during the entire war—but a ship's guns were often used to bombard a coastal fort. Some sailors were accidentally killed while using these guns, whether during a military action or a training session. Other sailors were killed when their ship hit an enemy mine, when a sniper shot at them, or when they slipped and fell from their ship's rigging.

Most days on board ship were very routine. Depending on their captain's wishes, sailors generally rose at 4 or 5 A.M. to the sound of a bugle, stowed the hammocks they slept in each night, and then began washing down the decks and cleaning other parts of the ship and its weaponry. Once the ship was clean, the men usually washed themselves in preparation for an inspection at 7:30 A.M. A half-hour later, men who had stood watch in a four-hour shift were relieved of their duty and the crew ate breakfast, which was typically coffee, salted beef, and a hard cracker known as hardtack. When eating meals, sailors sat with their "mess," which was a group of eight to fourteen men.

Usually at 9:30 A.M., there was another inspection, this time of weaponry. After this, sailors on some ships had time to themselves, which they usually spent reading, playing cards or other games (often gambling on the outcome, even though this was forbidden by both the Union and the Confederate navies), playing musical instruments, mending their clothes, or practicing various skills. On other ships, however, the time between breakfast and lunch was spent in training and/or in repairing sails and other equipment on board ship.

At noon there was another change of watch and the crew ate lunch, which was typically the same as breakfast with the

Sailors on a navy vessel pass the time with checkers and card games. Civil War sailors fought in few battles, but their service was still important to the war effort.

addition of rice and/or beans. In the Confederacy this meal might be supplemented by stores captured from merchant vessels, with cheese being a particular favorite. In the Union, ships had occasional opportunities to go ashore to acquire fresh fruit, vegetables, and other provisions. In both navies, men were allowed to fish to supplement their diets, and they were given a daily allotment of rum or whiskey (if they refused it, the value of the alcohol was added to their pay).

Afternoons were spent drilling and training until 4 P.M., when the watch was relieved and dinner served. By 5:30 or 6 P.M. the men were expected to be in their hammocks, where they could read or otherwise entertain themselves until lights out. Depending on the time of year and the wishes of the captain, this might occur at 8 or 9 P.M. or perhaps later. For ships on blockade duty, watches were kept up throughout the night, perhaps in the same four-hour shifts as during the day but usually in shorter shifts in order to ensure that the men on duty were at their best. Keeping a sharp lookout was particularly important at night because this was when most blockade runners tried to sneak in and out of Southern ports.

Given the sameness of each day in the navy, as well as the fact that there were many hours in a day when nothing much occurred, many sailors were plagued by boredom. In addition, due to the close quarters on board ship, sailors were at high risk of contracting diseases, as well as of becoming malnourished due to a frequent lack of fresh fruit and vegetables (although most ships tried to keep a supply of limes on board to prevent scurvy, a nutritional disease caused by a lack of vitamin C). Therefore, many sailors grew unhappy with their lives, and out of this unhappiness some started disobeying orders and/or deserting their ship when it docked in a port. **See also** food; navies, Confederate and Union; pay, soldiers' and sailors'; punishments.

Sanitary Commission, U.S.

The U.S. Sanitary Commission was established in the North in 1861 to improve living conditions and medical treatment for Union soldiers. The idea for the organization came out of a public meeting called by two women physicians, Elizabeth and Emily Blackwell, on April 15, 1861, at their New York women's infirmary to discuss medical issues related to the war. There was so much interest that they held a second meeting four days later, at which more than ninety women signed a petition asking President Abraham Lincoln to create a government agency responsible for the well-being of soldiers. When he did not do this, the women formed the Women's Central Association for Relief and sent a delegation to Washington, D.C., to speak with Lincoln in person.

As a result of this meeting, on June 9, 1861, the U.S. government established the U.S. Sanitary Commission and assigned it the duty of inspecting army camps and hospitals to make sure they were sanitary and improving ones that were not. The agency also provided nurses, medical supplies, clothing, and personal items for the comfort and care of soldiers, and when necessary it helped evacuate wounded soldiers from areas under heavy attack.

Most of the workers in the agency were women, although it was headed by a number of men. The Sanitary Commission was headquartered in Washington, D.C., but there were regional offices in ten Northern cities as well. These offices not only carried out the duties of the national organization but also oversaw the activities of local soldiers' relief societies. These societies in turn joined the Sanitary Commission in fund-raising activities that supported the commission's efforts. By some estimates, the Sanitary Commission raised over $20 million worth of money and supplies for the betterment of Union soldiers. **See also** Blackwell, Elizabeth; medical personnel and supplies; relief societies.

Scott, Winfield (1786–1866)

General Winfield Scott was the commander of the U.S. Army at the beginning of the Civil War. As such, he proposed the Anaconda Plan, a strategy for winning the war in which the South would be "squeezed to death" (like the prey of an anaconda snake) via a blockade on its ports and a gradual lessening of its territory. This plan was rejected and ridiculed at the outset, but eventually its principles were adopted with great success. By this time, however, Scott had been forced to retire from the army, largely because of his advanced age.

Scott began his military career as an artillery captain in 1808, and within a short time he had become a major general. Scott held the rank of general in three American wars: the War of 1812, the Mexican-American War (1846–1848), and the Civil War. He also fought in various battles against Native Americans. He was named the commanding general of the U.S. Army in 1841 and remained in charge of all U.S. military forces until November 1861. During this period he was such a stickler for following military rules that his men nicknamed him "Old Fuss and Feathers," but he was still an extremely popular commander. Nonetheless, when in 1852 Scott ran for president as the Whig nominee against Democrat Franklin Pierce he lost. **See also** Anaconda Plan.

Seddon, James A. (1815–1880)

Virginia slave owner and politician James A. Seddon served as the Confederate secretary of war from November 21, 1862, to February 6, 1865. After practicing law in Richmond, Virginia, during the 1830s and 1840s, Seddon served in the U.S. House of Representatives for two terms, where he supported slavery and states' rights. He also favored secession but kept this view to himself while in Congress. However, once the first shots of the Civil War were fired at Fort Sumter, Seddon argued successfully at a state convention that Virginia should leave the Union. Shortly thereafter Seddon was chosen to be a member of the Provisional Confederate Congress, and he influenced many of the first decisions of the Confederacy regarding its government, economy, military, railroad systems, and policies on prisoners of war. Gradually, Seddon became one of Confederate president Jefferson Davis's closest advisers, and when Secretary of War George Wythe Randolph resigned, Davis chose Seddon to take Randolph's place.

As secretary of war, Seddon was particularly concerned with the Confederate effort in the western theater, because he did not believe that the generals there were as competent as those serving elsewhere. As a result, he convinced Davis to reorganize the Department of the West and appoint Joseph E. Johnston as its commander. Seddon subsequently tried to get Davis to remove Braxton Bragg from his command in the West, but Davis refused until Bragg was severely defeated at Chattanooga in November 1863.

In 1864, Seddon had to make hard decisions in response to numerous problems related to the decline in the Confederacy's fortunes. For example, in trying to acquire food for the Confederate army, he violated a Confederate law against trading cotton to the enemy. He also secretly supported Northern peace movements, trying to bring an end to the war before the South ran out of vital supplies. Nonetheless, as it became clear that the Confederacy was losing the war, Seddon received much of the blame. In February 1865 he finally resigned his post in anger, after the Confederate Congress demanded that Davis replace his cabinet members. Only afterward did Southerners begin to realize and publicly express the idea that Seddon had been doing the best job possible under the circumstances.

In May 1865 Seddon was arrested by Federal soldiers and imprisoned, first at Libby Prison in Richmond, Virginia, and then at Fort Pulaski, Georgia. After being released in December, he settled on his Virginia plantation and returned to practicing law. **See also** cabinet, Confederate.

Semmes, Raphael (1809–1877)

Confederate naval officer Raphael Semmes was charged with attacking enemy merchant vessels, a duty he accomplished with great success. As captain first of the CSS *Sumter* and then of the CSS *Alabama,* he destroyed sixty-four merchant vessels, captured another thirteen, and sank a U.S. Navy ironclad, the *Hatteras.* On the *Alabama* alone, Semmes was responsible for the burning and sinking of $4.5 million worth of shipping in the South Atlantic Ocean, the Gulf of Mexico, the Caribbean Sea, the Azores, and the waters off Newfoundland and South America.

Prior to the Civil War, Semmes served in the U.S. Navy. During the 1830s, he also practiced law in between his naval assignments, first in Ohio and then in Alabama. In the Mexican-American War (1846–1848) he served on four different ships and afterward wrote *Service Afloat and Ashore During the War with Mexico.* During the 1850s he had various assignments as a lighthouse inspector and member of the Lighthouse Board.

Semmes joined the Confederate navy as soon as Alabama seceded from the Union. Because of his lighthouse experience, Semmes was made chief of the Confederacy's Lighthouse Bureau. He was also given command of the *Sumter,* which he replaced with the *Alabama* after the *Sumter*'s boilers were damaged beyond repair.

Semmes advocated attacking U.S. merchant ships rather than the U.S. blockade fleet for two reasons. First, he knew that attacks on merchant ships would disrupt U.S. shipping; second, Semmes correctly suspected that U.S. warships would leave their posts to protect the merchant ships, thereby weakening the blockade.

Semmes's attacks ended in June 1864 just off the coast of Cherbourg, France, when the *Alabama* encountered the USS *Kearsarge,* one of several ships that had been hunting it. Captained by John A. Winslow, the *Kearsarge* sank the *Alabama* after seventy minutes of fierce fighting. Most of the *Alabama*'s crewmen, including Semmes, were rescued by a British yacht, the *Deerhound,* and taken to England. Once they arrived, British authorities, who were neutral throughout the conflict, refused to turn the crew over to the Union.

Semmes returned to Alabama in December 1864, whereupon he was promoted to rear admiral and placed in charge of the James River Squadron. Within a short time, though, he was ordered to destroy his fleet to prevent the Union from taking it. Jefferson Davis then asked Semmes to join him in Danville, Virginia, where the president made Semmes a brigadier general of artillery under Joseph E. Johnston in North Carolina. Shortly thereafter Johnston and Semmes were forced to surrender but were not held by Union forces. However, in December 1865 U.S. troops arrested Semmes and imprisoned him in Washington, D.C., for four months. After his release, Semmes held a series of jobs before returning to the practice of law in Alabama. He also wrote *Memoirs of Service Afloat During the War Between the States* (1869). **See also** *Alabama,* CSS; blockades and blockade runners; navies, Confederate and Union.

Seven Days' Battles

The Seven Days' Battles took place from June 25 to July 1, 1862, as part of the Peninsula Campaign, an attempt by the

Union to take the Confederate capital of Richmond, Virginia. At first it appeared that the Union campaign, which began in March 1862, would succeed. Then General Robert E. Lee took over the Confederacy's Army of Northern Virginia after its commander, Joseph Johnston, was wounded in another battle in the same campaign, the May 31–June 1 Battle of Seven Pines. Over a seven-day period Lee engaged Union forces at Mechanicsville (June 26), Gaines' Mill (June 27), Savage's Station (June 29), and Malvern Hill (July 1). Throughout this period, the commander of the Union forces, General George B. McClellan, gradually withdrew from the area, and by the last of the Seven Days' Battles McClellan's Peninsula Campaign had ended in a Union failure. In the end, there were 15,800 Union casualties and 20,100 Confederate casualties. **See also** Lee, Robert Edward; McClellan, George Brinton; Peninsula Campaign.

Seven Pines, Battle of (Battle of Fair Oaks)

Called the Battle of Fair Oaks by the Confederacy, the Battle of Seven Pines was one of a series of battles that took place on May 31–June 1, 1862. The Battle of Seven Pines, which resulted in five thousand Union casualties and sixty-one hundred Confederate casualties, was part of Union general George B. McClellan's Peninsula Campaign, an attempt to take the Confederate capital of Richmond, Virginia. The Battle of Seven Pines resulted, among other things, in General Robert E. Lee's taking command of the Army of Northern Virginia when General Joseph Johnston was wounded. Lee proved himself highly effective, and under his leadership in this and successive battles the Army of Northern Virginia was able to force the Union from the area. **See also** Johnston, Joseph Eggleston; Peninsula Campaign; Seven Days' Battles.

Seward, William Henry (1801–1872)

Antislavery activist and attorney William H. Seward served as U.S. secretary of state for both President Abraham Lincoln and his successor, Andrew Johnson. While in the Lincoln administration, Seward deftly handled an incident known as the *Trent* Affair that threatened to lead to war between the United States and Great Britain. Seward's diplomacy kept European nations from granting recognition to the Confederacy; he had less success, however, convincing England not to sell ships to the Confederacy.

Seward's first major political office was as governor of New York (1839–1843), and in 1849 he was elected to the U.S. Senate. While in Congress Seward often quarreled with members of his own political party, the Whigs, who wanted to compromise on various slavery-related issues. Therefore when the Republican Party was created with a strong antislavery platform, Seward not only joined the party but became one of its leaders.

When John Wilkes Booth planned the assassination of President Lincoln, he ordered his coconspirator Lewis Paine (also known as Lewis Powell) to kill Seward as part of the plot. Paine attacked and stabbed Seward, but his victim survived his wound and went on to serve in Andrew Johnson's administration through the end of Johnson's term in office. In 1867, Seward was instrumental in purchasing Alaska from Russia for a price of $7.2 million, an agreement that was then widely called "Seward's Folly." It was his last major political act. **See also** assassination of President Abraham Lincoln; Johnson, Andrew; *Trent* Affair.

sharpshooters

A sharpshooter (also called a sniper) is an expert marksman who typically fires on his target from a great distance and an unseen position. In the first year of the Civil

War, the U.S. government authorized the formation of an entire regiment of sharpshooters, under the supervision of expert marksman Hiram C. Berdan. Berdan held contests to find the best marksmen, requiring competitors to hit a ten-inch circle two hundred yards away ten times, and eventually created companies of sharpshooters from New York, New Hampshire, Maine, Vermont, Pennsylvania, Michigan, and Minnesota. The regiment formed from these companies was known as Berdan's Sharpshooters.

By the second year of the war, however, the Union had decided that having an entire regiment of sharpshooters was unnecessary. Instead, a small company of sharpshooters was attached to infantry regiments operating in areas where a sharpshooter's services would be helpful. The Confederacy made the same decision after it too formed an entire regiment of sharpshooters in 1862.

Sharpshooters targeted individual officers and soldiers both on and off the battlefield, sometimes shooting into enemy camps. Among their most common victims were signalmen, who were stationed in towers or on high ground in order to pass messages to other signalmen some distance away. Sharpshooters targeted the signalmen because of their importance to the enemy's communication system. **See also** communication systems.

Shenandoah Valley Campaigns

The Union fought many battles in attempts to gain and keep control of the Shenandoah Valley, one of the most fertile areas of Virginia, and as such a vital source of food for the Confederacy. There were two Shenandoah Valley Campaigns. The first, which took place from March to June 1862, is generally called Jackson's Valley Campaign, while the second, which took place from August 7, 1864, to March 2, 1865, is called Sheridan's Valley Campaign.

In the first campaign, Confederate general "Stonewall" Jackson led a force of about sixteen thousand soldiers against a combined Union force of approximately sixty-four thousand men, but despite being outnumbered he enjoyed a series of victories. These came as a result of his tricking the Union into thinking his troops were no longer in the valley by marching half of them out of the area and then secretly bringing them back by train. Eventually the Union had to send additional troops into the Shenandoah Valley—troops that were desperately needed to reinforce a Union campaign on the Virginia peninsula—but by the time they reached the area Jackson had moved his men elsewhere.

In the second campaign, Union major general Philip Sheridan led a new force, the Army of the Shenandoah, in a mission to destroy the Shenandoah Valley's agricultural productivity. As part of this campaign, Sheridan was also charged with finding and destroying the army of Confederate general Jubal Early, who Union leaders knew had a base somewhere in the valley. Over the course of the many battles in this campaign, including the Third Battle of Winchester (September 19), the Battle of Fisher's Hill (September 22), and the Battle of Cedar Creek (October 19), Sheridan succeeded in his goals. **See also** Early, Jubal A.; Jackson's Valley Campaign; Sheridan, Philip Henry.

Sheppard, William Ludwell (1833–1912)

William Ludwell Sheppard was a Confederate soldier who served in Virginia, first with the Richmond Howitzers and then with the topographical department of the Army of Northern Virginia. While he was performing his other duties, he was also producing sketches of various war scenes. Most of these sketches, however, were not reproduced until after the war. They include the illustrations for *Detailed Minu-*

tiae of Soldier Life in the Army of Northern Virginia by Carlton McCarthy and several prints of military engagements, such as *The Charge of the First Maryland Regiment at the Death of Ashby* and *Virginia 1864.* **See also** artists and artwork.

Sheridan, Philip Henry (1831–1888)

Philip H. Sheridan was one of the most successful U.S. cavalry leaders of the Civil War. As a graduate of the U.S. Military Academy who had served for several years on the American frontier, Sheridan entered the Civil War in 1862 as a colonel in the Second Michigan Cavalry. Within a few months he had been promoted to brigadier general in the Army of the Ohio, and he performed so well at the Battle of Stones River (December 1862–January 1863) that he was made a major general in the volunteer army. After several more battlefield successes, in 1864 Sheridan was placed in charge of the cavalry of the Army of the Potomac.

Sheridan then fought in the Battle of the Wilderness (May 1864) and led a cavalry raid in the Richmond, Virginia, area that resulted in the death of the foremost Confederate cavalry leader, General J.E.B. Stuart. After this Sheridan was placed in charge of the Army of the Shenandoah and led a campaign against Confederate forces in the Shenandoah Valley of Virginia. He was so successful in this regard that he was promoted to major general in the Regular Army. In 1865 Sheridan commanded the cavalry and an infantry corps at the siege of Petersburg and joined the Union pursuit of Robert E. Lee until the Confederate general surrendered his Army of Northern Virginia.

After the war, Sheridan continued to serve in the U.S. Army, and in 1867 he was given command of all U.S. military forces in Louisiana and Texas. At that time, the U.S. government was forcing these former Confederate states to accept certain Reconstruction policies, and in implementing them Sheridan was much more forceful than President Andrew Johnson wanted him to be. Therefore Johnson removed Sheridan from his command and sent him to serve in the West, where he fought in several battles against Native Americans. By 1885, Sheridan was made a full general of the U.S. Army. **See also** cavalry; Shenandoah Valley Campaigns; Stuart, James Ewell Brown.

Sherman, William Tecumseh (1820–1891)

Union general William T. Sherman commanded three Union armies in an invasion of Georgia in 1864, during which he captured the city of Atlanta and led sixty thousand men on a march from there across Georgia to the sea, devastating the state in the process. He then took his troops north through the Carolinas to Virginia to confront General Robert E. Lee's Army of Northern Virginia. As part of this campaign, he accepted the surrender of General Joseph Johnston and his force of twenty thousand Confederate soldiers.

A graduate of the U.S. Military Academy, Sherman did little during his early years in the military. In fact, even during the Mexican-American War (1846–1848) he served in an administrative position in California, and his superiors were not impressed with his work. In 1853 Sherman resigned from the U.S. Army to become the representative of a bank in California. Sherman was unsuccessful in banking and ended up $13,000 in debt. He tried to rejoin the U.S. Army, which refused to take him back, so Sherman took a job as the superintendent of a military academy in Louisiana. When Louisiana seceded, Sherman left this job to become a railroad executive in St. Louis, Missouri.

After the Civil War broke out, Sherman was allowed to rejoin the U.S. Army as a colonel, thanks to the influence of a

General William T. Sherman led his Union troops on a destructive march across Georgia.

brother who was a U.S. senator. By the First Battle of Bull Run in July 1861, Sherman was a brigadier general, and in October 1861 he was given command of the Army of the Cumberland in Kentucky. Shortly thereafter he experienced a mental breakdown, periodically becoming hysterical and experiencing attacks of paranoia in which he imagined his armies were surrounded by Confederate troops. As a result, he kept asking his superiors for more and more men, and eventually the secretary of the war went to check on him. After this visit, Sherman was sent home for an extended period of rest, and when he returned to duty he was placed under the supervision first of General Henry Halleck and then of General Ulysses S. Grant.

Sherman did extremely well under these two generals and experienced no recurrence of his mental problems. After the Battle of Shiloh in April 1862 he was promoted to major general and after Grant's 1862–1863 Vicksburg Campaign to brigadier general. Sherman subsequently commanded the Army of the Tennessee at the Battle of Chattanooga (November 1863). The following year he invaded Georgia.

After the war, many people encouraged Sherman to run for political office, but he refused. Instead he became the commanding general of the U.S. armies after Ulysses S. Grant became president in 1869. Sherman held this position until 1884. **See also** Carolinas Campaign; Grant, Ulysses S.; Halleck, Henry Wager; Johnston, Joseph Eggleston; Sherman's March to the Sea.

Sherman's March to the Sea

A military action known as Sherman's March to the Sea began on November 16, 1864, and is one of the most famous events of the Civil War. During this action, which was part of the Savannah Campaign (November–December 1864), Union general William T. Sherman led approximately sixty-two thousand men on a twenty-six-day, 250-mile march from Atlanta, Georgia, to Savannah, Georgia, near the Atlantic Ocean. When his troops left Atlanta, they did so in two columns to trick the enemy into thinking they were going in two separate directions, but instead they took a parallel route to the sea. As they marched, they foraged for food and wreaked havoc on the landscape, destroying rail lines, government buildings, and the farms, homes, and supplies of any Southerners who offered resistance. Their orders were to spare the property of Southerners who did not interfere with their progress, but many soldiers ignored this edict. Thus, as a result of the march, many innocent people suffered great losses. In fact, the damages were later valued at well over $100 million. **See also** Atlanta; Sherman, William Tecumseh.

Shiloh, Battle of (Battle of Pittsburg Landing)

Called the Battle of Pittsburg Landing by the Union but more commonly known by its Confederate name, the Battle of Shiloh took place in Tennessee on April 6–7, 1862, as part of a Union campaign to move troops up the Cumberland and Tennessee Rivers. The battle pitted the Union's Army of the Tennessee and Army of the Ohio, with a force of 65,085 commanded by Major General Ulysses S. Grant and Major General Don Carlos Buell, against the Confederacy's Army of Mississippi, with a force of 44,968 commanded by General Albert Sidney Johnston and General P.G.T. Beauregard. After losing several battles against the Union at the beginning of the campaign, the Confederates fell back to the town of Corinth, Mississippi, because it was served by several rail lines. At this point, Grant's Army of the Tennessee was at nearby Pittsburg Landing, having not yet been joined by Buell's Army of the Ohio. While waiting for this rendezvous, Grant failed to fortify his position, and he was unprepared when the Confederates attacked. As a result, he lost many men and nearly lost the battle. During the next day, however, the Union gained the advantage, aided by the arrival of Buell's troops and the establishment of defensive artillery. When General Beauregard realized that Grant's men had been reinforced, he went back to Corinth. During the two-day battle, there were more than thirteen thousand Union casualties and over ten thousand Confederate ones. Despite its higher losses, historians consider the Union the victor in this battle. **See also** Beauregard, Pierre Gustave Toutant; Grant, Ulysses S.; Johnston, Albert Sidney.

shoes

Shoes of the Civil War period could not hold up to the marching and other activities in which soldiers were forced to engage. This was because most shoes were made of leather, although manufacturers of footware increasingly incorporated rubber into their products during the 1860s. When shoes wore out, the Confederacy did not have the supplies or the funds to replace them. Meanwhile, the Union often had difficulty getting footwear to its troops. Because of these problems, soldiers often had to steal shoes from dead bodies or prisoners of war, and when these sources were not available they might wrap their feet in rags or cowhides or, lacking either of these, go barefoot. This made it difficult, if not impossible, for them to fight, particularly when there was frost on the ground. Consequently, soldiers marching through a town might loot stores in search of shoes. In fact, one of the reasons that the Battle of Gettysburg occurred at its particular location, as opposed to someplace else in Pennsylvania, was that Union and Confederate forces in the area had both heard that the town of Gettysburg had a warehouse filled with new shoes. **See also** uniforms and equipment.

slavery and slave life

Slavery was at the heart of long-standing disagreements between the North and South that culminated in the Civil War. The South's planters relied on slave labor. About one-fourth of all white Southerners were slave owners, and even those whites who did not own slaves often rented or borrowed them from those who did. Meanwhile, the Northern states, being industrial, had no such reliance on slavery, and as a result most had some type of emancipation legislation in place before the Civil War began.

There were over 3.5 million slaves in the South when the war broke out. Life as a slave at the outset of the Civil War varied depending on the slave owner's lifestyle and occupation. In 1860, most slave owners had only one or two slaves, who acted as household servants. These slaves generally had a much better life than slaves working on plantations. A plantation was a large farm with more than twenty slaves, who usually lived under crowded conditions and whose work was supervised by an overseer and/or slave driver.

A slave's quality of life also varied by region. The worst treatment of slaves generally occurred in the lower South, because the majority of the plantations in this region grew high-yield crops like cotton, tobacco, and sugar. Such crops required a massive amount of labor, and the policy in the lower South was to pay overseers and slave drivers according to crop production. Therefore these men had an incentive to work their slaves until they dropped, from sunup to sundown, without giving them time to build or maintain adequate shelters or to feed, clothe, and bathe themselves properly. Field slaves in the lower South (as opposed to house slaves, who worked in the owners' mansions doing domestic work) typically labored in large gangs, day after day. Under such circumstances these men (field slaves were usually men) had little chance of ever having wives or children. Slaves might show their objections to such treatment by openly disobeying their owners, but those who did so might be severely beaten or otherwise abused, perhaps to death (unless they were young, strong males, in which case their value was so high that they were less likely to be killed).

In contrast, slaves in the upper South generally did not have to endure the same hard physical labor as slaves in the lower South. This was because in the upper South the practice was to grow crops such as grains, which required less labor. Moreover, many plantation owners in the upper South did not employ overseers or slave drivers, and those who did so usually did not base their pay on crop production, reducing the incentive to overwork the slaves.

Even though daily life for slaves in the upper South was generally easier than it was for those in the lower South, many of them still had to deal with emotional cruelty stemming from the slave trade. Many slave owners in the upper South made a substantial part of their income by selling slaves to plantation owners in the lower South. As a result, between 1790 and 1860, over 2 million slaves in the upper South were forced to leave their parents, siblings, or other relatives to be sent to new owners in the lower South. Consequently, it was rare for any healthy male slave in the upper South to avoid this fate once he reached manhood. Moreover, because the slave trade was so profitable, female slaves were sometimes treated like brood mares, forced to produce a series of babies who would be sold as soon as they were old enough to leave their mothers. This also occurred in the lower South, where some slave owners had no compunction against raping the female slaves under their control. In fact, the impersonal relationship between owner and slaves on large plantations encouraged such abuse.

In all parts of the South, slaves were at the mercy of their owner's wishes, and they could not travel even a short distance without carrying a written pass provided by their owner. To ensure that no slave was traveling without permission, groups of white men on horseback patrolled the countryside checking passes, particularly during the night. In addition, most Southern states did not allow any freed slaves within their boundaries unless they had received their freedom only days before and could prove they were on their way north. Otherwise, any freed black who traveled in the South could be reenslaved. Most Southern states also passed restrictions regarding the right of a slave owner to free his slaves, so patrols could assume that any black they encountered belonged to someone and those without a pass were escapees.

Nonetheless, many slaves tried to escape their captivity, and various Northerners tried to help them. One of the most effective forms of helping fugitive slaves was the Underground Railroad, in which a network of escorts—called conductors—with access to hiding places spirited runaway slaves out of the South. Once in the North, however, a fugitive slave was not necessarily safe. Even during the first few months of the Civil War, the North honored the Fugitive Slave Act of 1850, which required that all runaway slaves be returned to their owners.

After the Civil War broke out, the number of runaway slaves increased because the army's need for able-bodied men made it difficult for Southerners to maintain their slave patrols and their plantation-management system of overseers and slave drivers. Many slaves took advantage of the distractions posed by the war to run away from their owners. Moreover, many of those slaves who remained in the South during the war aided the North. Sometimes they did this by working more slowly than usual or by feigning incompetence so that jobs were performed badly or not at all, in the process reducing agricultural productivity. Other times they helped the enemy by secretly providing soldiers with supplies or by passing them information as spies. Slaves who were owned by Confederate officers and accompanied their masters to the front lines were particularly effective in this regard, as were slaves who were forced to construct fortifications and field defenses. Slaves who were captured by the Union (whereupon they were called contraband) were given a chance to work for the Union army, either as laborers, servants, or soldiers. Thousands of former slaves eventually fought for the Union during the war, thereby helping to bring freedom to blacks throughout the South. **See also** black troops; contrabands of war; Underground Railroad.

This young boy and his sister were slaves until they were rescued by Union soldiers.

Smith, Edmund Kirby (1824–1893)

Confederate general E. Kirby Smith (changed to Kirby-Smith by his family after his death) was in charge of the Trans-Mississippi Department (all Confederate lands west of the Mississippi River) when it was cut off from the rest of the Confederacy (to the east) after the fall of Vicksburg, Mississippi, in July 1863. Therefore from this point forward, Smith had no access to Confederate supplies. Nonetheless, he managed to retain his control of the area until the very end of the war.

A graduate of the U.S. Military Academy and a veteran of the Mexican-American War (1846–1848) and several Indian campaigns on the American frontier, Smith joined the Confederate army in 1861 after his native state of Florida seceded from the Union. At the First Battle of Bull Run, where he served as a brigadier general, Smith was wounded but returned to duty in time to participate in several battles in Kentucky and Tennessee in 1862. In February 1863 Smith received command of the Trans-Mississippi Department. He surrendered his forces to the Union at Galveston, Texas, on June 2, 1865. After the war he became a school administrator, first as the headmaster of a military academy and then as a university president, and then was a professor of mathematics. **See also** armies, Confederate; theaters of war.

smuggling

Once the war began, the Confederacy forbade its citizens from doing business with the North. Therefore, Southerners who wanted goods that were only available in the North had to resort to smuggling, making trips into the North themselves or paying others to do so. For example, Southern photographer George Smith Cook routinely smuggled photographic chemicals and other supplies of his trade from the North into the South. During the first part of the war, before Southern products became scarce, some Northerners also resorted to smuggling in order to acquire cotton, tobacco, and alcohol from the South. **See also** cotton.

socializing with the enemy

Because Confederate and Union soldiers sometimes camped or served guard duty right near each other, there were opportunities for men to socialize with the enemy during times when there was no fighting going on. In fact, even during breaks in a major battle or after its conclusion, soldiers who were previously shooting at enemy counterparts might start talking, playing cards, drinking, or trading goods with them. Newspapers were among the most frequently traded items, probably because soldiers thought that supplying reading material to the enemy was a fairly harmless activity. Nonetheless, military law forbade all forms of fraternization with enemy soldiers, so the men who did so hid such behavior from their officers. Officers did, however, allow socializing with enemy civilians because this was sometimes a necessity in order to obtain food and supplies. In addition, soldiers were allowed to perform acts of kindness for men who were severely wounded and/or dying regardless of which side they were on. **See also** camps and camp life; civilians, war's impact on.

songs

There are hundreds of songs from the Civil War era. Many were rallying anthems for the troops, emphasizing the importance of the cause and the righteousness of the participants on either side. Among the best-known Northern songs of this type are "Battle Hymn of the Republic" (1862; lyrics by Julia Ward Howe and music by William Steffe), "Battle Cry of Freedom" (1862; lyrics and music by George F. Root), and "Rally Round the Cause, Boys" (1864; anonymous), which was derived from "Battle Cry of Freedom." In the South the most popular patriotic song was "Dixie," composed by Daniel Decatur Emmett in 1859.

Other Civil War songs were expressions of what ordinary soldiers were experiencing as a result of the conflict. One of the most prominent examples of this type of song is "Tenting Tonight on the Old Camp Ground." Composed by New Hampshire singer and lyricist Walter C.

Kittredge in 1863, it speaks of the "weary hearts" of soldiers who were "tired of war on the old camp ground" and were settling down for the night to sleep beside dead and dying comrades. For many years after the war, reunions and conventions of Union soldiers traditionally played this song as a way to memorialize those who had been killed on the battlefield.

Another Civil War song concerned with death was "All Quiet on the Potomac" (1861). The lyrics of this song were written by a Confederate soldier, Lamar Fontaine, who had just seen a comrade killed. The "quiet" in the title refers to the fact that the death was by sniper fire on a night following the First Battle of Bull Run when no fighting was taking place. John Hill Hewitt subsequently set Fontaine's poem to music, and it became popular in both the South and the North.

Also sentimental was "We Are Coming, Father Abraham," a call to arms whose lyrics were penned by James Sloan Gibbons, a Northern abolitionist and Quaker, in 1862. Set to music by Stephen Foster, it tells of men leaving their homes, livelihoods, and loved ones to help the Union take Richmond, Virginia (the Confederate capital), from "foul treason's savage group"; at such times, according to the song, "a farewell group stands weeping at every cottage door."

Stephen Foster subsequently wrote other Civil War songs, most notably "That's What's the Matter" (1862), "Was My Brother in the Battle?" (1862), and "Willie Has Gone to the War" (1863) with poet/lyricist George Cooper. However, the most prolific Civil War songwriter was George F. Root, whose works include not only "Battle Cry of Freedom" but also "Just Before the Battle, Mother," "Starved in Prison," and "The Vacant Chair," all written during the early 1860s. **See also** Root, George Frederick.

Sorrel, G. Moxley (1838–1901)

As chief of staff for Confederate brigadier general James Longstreet, G. Moxley Sorrel supervised the activities of Longstreet's spies and scouts. In October 1864 Sorrel became a brigadier general himself, which ended his association with Longstreet's spy network. However, after the war he wrote about Confederate espionage in his memoir, *Recollections of a Confederate Staff Officer.* **See also** Longstreet, James; spies.

South Carolina

South Carolina is the place where the Civil War officially began, at Fort Sumter (located on a man-made island in the middle of Charleston Harbor) on April 12, 1861. The state had seceded from the Union in December of the previous year. Once the war began, approximately sixty thousand South Carolinians became soldiers. Nearly one-fourth of these men were killed in various battles. In addition, South Carolina towns and farmlands suffered a great deal of wartime destruction, particularly during Union general William T. Sherman's march through the state in 1864.

During the Reconstruction period that followed the war, South Carolina was occupied by U.S. military forces, and the state government fell under the control of Radical Republicans. In 1868 they created a new constitution—as part of U.S. requirements regarding the state's readmission to the Union—that established certain civil rights for blacks. Despite these provisions, blacks continued to be treated badly throughout the state, and during the 1876 elections blacks were threatened with violence if they went to the polls. As a result, Democrat Wade Hampton, a former Civil War cavalry commander whose aim was to restore white supremacy in his state, was elected governor. South Carolina then came under the control of planters and others who had held sway prior to the Civil War. **See also** Carolinas Campaign; Fort Sumter; Hampton, Wade; Sherman, William Tecumseh.

spies

Both the Confederacy and the Union received a great deal of information about enemy battle plans and troop movements from spies. There were three basic types of spies. Some were enlisted men who were secretly sent to enemy cities—particularly Richmond, Virginia (the Confederate capital), and Washington, D.C. (the U.S. capital), which were only about one hundred miles apart—and other locations specifically to gather information. Others were residents of the North or South—male or female, white or black—who pretended to support the war efforts of their government while actually being sympathetic to the enemy. The remainder were Southerners living under Union occupation who managed to get information to Confederate agents.

Spies of the first type often adopted a variety of disguises to blend in to their surroundings. For example, in April 1861, Union spy Captain Peter Haggerty traveled through the streets of Baltimore pretending to be an organ grinder, complete with monkey. Another Union spy, Sarah Edmonds (aka Franklin Thompson), was a master of disguises. Her characters included a black man named Cuff (whom she created in part by coloring her skin with silver nitrate and wearing a black wig), an old black woman who was a laundress or a nursemaid, an overweight Irishwoman who peddled goods in Confederate army camps, and a young Southern white man.

In the Union, most spies worked for generals, although various efforts were made to create a national intelligence agency with a large network of spies. Allan Pinkerton's was the first such effort; his agency, which he called the Secret Service, disbanded in 1862. Around the same time, a spy named Lafayette Baker created the National Detectives in Washington, D.C., which reported to U.S. secretary of war Edwin Stanton.

Dissatisfied with the quantity and quality of information coming out of this agency, several generals established their own spy networks. For example, in 1862 Brigadier General James Garfield (who would later become U.S. president) trained several men to accurately estimate troop size and location and then sent them behind enemy lines as spies. That same year, Union brigadier general Grenville M. Dodge created the Corps of Scouts, an intelligence-gathering corps serving the Army of the Southwest. Dodge trained his spies so well that he was later asked to create a broader intelligence-gathering agency to serve General Ulysses S. Grant in the western theater; this agency ultimately had over one hundred spies, many of them Southerners sympathetic to the Union cause.

Similarly, in 1863, Union general Joseph Hooker of the Army of the Potomac created his own spy agency, the Bureau of Military Information, headed by Colonel George H. Sharpe (who was later promoted to general). This agency eventually served other commanding officers as well, although many high-level generals still preferred to rely on their own spies. Working for Sharpe were both government agents and civilians sympathetic to the Union. Among the latter was Samuel Ruth, who was in charge of the Confederacy's Richmond, Fredericksburg, and Potomac Railroad. In 1864 Ruth started supplying Sharpe with information regarding the Confederacy's use of the railroad to transport troops and supplies.

Also part of this spy network was Elizabeth Van Lew, who served as its Southern spymaster by coordinating the activities of various agents living in the South, including Ruth. Nicknamed "Crazy Bet" because she feigned mental illness, Van

Lew had a farm near Richmond, Virginia. She often brought food to Union prisoners held in Richmond, and because the guards thought her insane she had the opportunity to listen to them talk about Confederate plans. She then passed this and other information to Union officials. Van Lew's ruse was so convincing that her espionage activities were not discovered until after the war, at which point she was ostracized in the South.

Confederate generals also employed their own networks of spies. For example, Brigadier General James Longstreet had an extensive spy network supervised by his chief of staff, G. Moxley Sorrel, until Sorrel became a brigadier general himself in 1864. One of the spies in this network was Henry T. Harrison, who successfully adopted a Northern accent and used disguises to gather information behind enemy lines. In 1863 Longstreet loaned Harrison's services to General D.H. Hill in North Carolina, and later Longstreet sent Harrison to Washington, D.C., to learn about Union troop strength and movements in Maryland and Pennsylvania—information that proved vital to the Confederates in preparation for the Battle of Gettysburg.

General Joseph Hooker established the Bureau of Military Information, his own spy agency.

One of the most successful Confederate spies, however, was Rose O'Neal Greenhow, a Washington, D.C., socialite who led a vast ring of Confederate espionage agents under the supervision of Confederate general P.G.T. Beauregard's adjutant general Colonel Thomas Jordan. As the widow of a U.S. State Department official, Greenhow had many prominent friends in the U.S. government who unwittingly gave her vital information, and the members of her spy ring included people within the War Department, Navy Department, Adjutant General's Office, Military Affairs Committee, and Provost Marshal's Office. (Ironically, the Provost Marshal's Office, whose marshals were the chief military police officers of the army, was responsible for catching spies.)

Another successful Confederate spy was Belle Boyd. Whereas Greenhow convinced her fellow Northerners that she supported the Union, Boyd was a Southerner who was open about her support for the Confederacy. Nonetheless, she was able to charm or trick Union officers into giving her information, which she then smuggled to Confederate officers. Boyd was arrested several times for her espionage activities, but she was repeatedly released because she was a woman.

As Boyd's experience suggests, women who were caught spying rarely were punished as harshly as male spies were. When Union officers discovered that a particular woman was a Confederate spy, they generally did not arrest her until after they had given her several warnings to stop her activities, and even then she rarely served much time in prison. Therefore, it was not unusual for a female spy to continue her espionage work as soon as she was released, or even to gather intelligence from guards while she was in prison. The Confederacy, however, was not always as lenient. In 1863 Pauline Cushman, who engaged in espionage activities for the North while performing as an actress in Nashville, Tennessee, was convicted of treason and sentenced by the Confederacy to death by hanging. She escaped execution only because invading Union soldiers rescued her.

Both sides executed a number of male spies, and the first Civil War spy to be hanged for espionage was Timothy Webster. Webster was part of Allan Pinkerton's Union spy network, gathering information for George B. McClellan's Army of the Potomac. While operating in the South, Webster pretended to be a passionate secessionist who had come from the North to support the Confederate cause; he was so convincing in this story that eventually Confederate secretary of war Judah P. Benjamin hired Webster as a Confederate spy. In January 1862, however, Webster's true loyalties were exposed when a captured Union spy, John Scully, betrayed his colleague in an attempt to save himself from being hanged. Webster was executed on April 29, 1862, in Richmond, Virginia. In all, the Confederates executed more than sixty men and one woman for spying, while the Union executed approximately two dozen spies, all of them men. **See also** codes and ciphers; Edmonds, Sarah Emma; Greenhow, Rose O'Neal; Pinkerton, Allan; Van Lew, Elizabeth; Webster, Timothy.

Spotsylvania Campaign

The Spotsylvania Campaign was essentially a continuation of the Battle of the Wilderness, which was fought between the forces of Union general Ulysses S. Grant and those of Confederate general Robert E. Lee on May 5–7, 1864, in northern Virginia. After this battle, Grant pursued Lee and the two sides fought a series of engagements around Spotsylvania Court House, Virginia (about ten miles southwest of Fredericksburg), from May 8 to May 19. After the Battle of Spotsylvania on May 12, there was at least some fighting every day. On the Union side, approximately 100,000 men participated in these battles, and on the Confederate side approximately 52,000. Of these, about 18,000 Union soldiers and 12,000 Confederate ones, including cavalry commander J.E.B. Stuart, were killed. Eventually, Grant decided that he could not defeat the Confederates, and he withdrew from the area. **See also** Grant, Ulysses S.; Lee, Robert Edward; Stuart, James Ewell Brown; Wilderness, Battle of the.

Stanton, Edwin McMasters (1814–1869)

Edwin M. Stanton was President Abraham Lincoln's secretary of war throughout the Civil War, and after Lincoln was assassinated Stanton continued to serve as secretary of war under President Andrew Johnson. During both administrations, Stanton was known for speaking his mind. Under Lincoln, he criticized generals for not taking more aggressive actions to crush the Confederacy, and later Stanton fought with Johnson over how to deal with former Confederate states during Reconstruction.

Stanton began his professional career as an attorney in Ohio in 1836, then practiced in Pennsylvania from 1847 to 1856 before relocating to Washington, D.C. In December 1860 he became the U.S. attorney general under President James Buchanan. When Lincoln took office, Stanton became legal adviser to his secretary of war, Simon Cameron, and when Cameron resigned at the end of 1861 Stanton took his position.

Edwin Stanton served as secretary of war under President Lincoln.

After the war, Stanton dealt harshly with the people he believed were involved in Lincoln's assassination, overseeing their trials and presiding over the executions of those sentenced to hang. During Reconstruction, Stanton sided with Radical Republicans who wanted to punish the South, which put him at odds with Johnson, who favored leniency toward the South. When Johnson tried to fire Stanton because of their disagreements, Stanton's Radical Republican friends in Congress passed a law that barred presidents from firing their cabinet officers. Johnson fired Stanton anyway, and the House of Representatives impeached the president. When the Senate failed to remove Johnson from office, Stanton resigned and returned to practicing law. **See also** assassination of President Abraham Lincoln; cabinet, U.S.; Johnson, Andrew.

Stephens, Alexander Hamilton (1812–1883)

Alexander H. Stephens was vice president of the Confederate States of America (CSA) throughout the Civil War, and after the war he served as a U.S. congressman and as Georgia's governor. Trained as a lawyer, he was first elected to Congress in 1843 as a leader of the Whig Party. In 1855 he became a Democrat and continued to serve in Congress until 1859, when he decided to leave the U.S. House of Representatives.

During his time in the U.S. Congress, Stephens was in favor of maintaining the Union, and when Georgia was deciding whether to secede after Abraham Lincoln assumed the U.S. presidency in 1861, Stephens voted against secession. Nonetheless, the members of the Georgia state secession convention chose Stephens to be a delegate at the first Confederate convention, which took place in Montgomery, Alabama, in February 1861. There he helped write the Confederate Constitution and was chosen to be the CSA's provisional vice president; on November 6, 1861, the South elected him to be the permanent vice president of the Confederacy.

Stephens's time in office was difficult. He disagreed with many of the positions of President Jefferson Davis and was a forceful advocate for peace, so Davis and his other cabinet members gradually shut Stephens out of important policy discussions. In fact, some Confederates questioned Stephens's loyalty to the South. As a result of being either ignored or criticized, Stephens began to spend much of his time at home. However, he did participate in the unsuccessful Hampton Roads Peace Conference in February 1865.

On May 11,1865, Stephens was arrested by U.S. troops and imprisoned at Fort Warren in Boston Harbor until October 1865. Upon his release he began writing *A Constitutional View of the Late War*

Between the States, published as two volumes, one in 1868 and one in 1870. In 1882 he was elected governor of Georgia, but he fell ill and died after serving only a few months. **See also** cabinet, Confederate; Hampton Roads.

Stevens, Thaddeus (1792–1868)

Pennsylvania congressman Thaddeus Stevens was a leader of the Radical Republican faction in Congress during the Reconstruction era. As such, he was a champion of civil rights, insisting that before being readmitted to the Union former Confederate states must enact laws that promoted equality between blacks and whites. Prior to the war, beginning in 1816, Stevens practiced law in Pennsylvania, often volunteering his legal services to fugitive slaves. He was elected to the state legislature in 1833 and to the U.S. House of Representatives in 1849 as a member of the Whig Party. While in the House he opposed passage of the part of the Compromise of 1850 that allowed for the return of fugitive slaves to the South.

Reelected to Congress as a Republican in 1859, Stevens continued to press for the emancipation of all slaves, and he promoted the use of black troops during the Civil War. After the war he became an extremist even among the Radical Republicans. Stevens argued that the South was a conquered territory and therefore did not deserve the rights that states that had stayed in the Union enjoyed.

Consequently, as a member of Congress's joint Committee on Reconstruction he promoted military Reconstruction acts that dealt harshly with the South, and when President Andrew Johnson did not support firm measures to protect blacks' civil rights, Stevens introduced a resolution to have the president impeached. Stevens also unsuccessfully promoted the idea that the former Confederates who owned Southern plantations should be forced to turn over a portion of their lands to former slaves, with the rest being sold to pay off national war debts. Shortly before Stevens died in 1868, he asked to be buried in a black cemetery in Pennsylvania, and his wish was granted. **See also** political parties; Reconstruction.

Still, William (1821–1902)

The son of former slaves, abolitionist William Still was one of the most active members of the Underground Railroad, temporarily housing thousands of runaway slaves in his home in Philadelphia, Pennsylvania, during the 1840s and 1850s. Still kept complete records of his activities and later used them as the basis of a book, *The Underground Railroad* (1872). During the 1860s he was at the forefront of efforts to end segregation on his city's streetcars and was active in relief organizations dedicated to improving the lives of former slaves. In 1880 he established the first black division of the YMCA (Young Men's Christian Association). **See also** Underground Railroad.

Stones River, Battle of (Battle of Murfreesboro)

Called the Battle of Murfreesboro by Confederates, the Battle of Stones River was part of a Union campaign in Tennessee that took place in December 1862 and January 1863. This battle, which was considered a Union victory because the Southerners were eventually forced from the field, took place from December 31 to January 2 (with no fighting on New Year's Day) between approximately 44,000 Union soldiers of the Army of the Cumberland, commanded by General William Rosecrans, and 38,000 Confederate soldiers of the Army of Tennessee, commanded by General Braxton Bragg. The battle was notable for its fierceness. The Union had about 1,700 dead, 7,800 wounded, and 3,700 missing, while the Confederates had about 1,300 dead, 8,000 wounded, and 1,000 missing or captured. **See also** armies, Confederate; armies, Union; Bragg, Braxton.

Stowe, Harriet (Elizabeth) Beecher (1811–1896)

Harriet Beecher Stowe authored a novel, *Uncle Tom's Cabin; or, Life Among the Lowly* (1852), that so inflamed antislavery sentiments that historians believe it contributed to the start of the Civil War. A Congregationalist minister's daughter, Stowe was a teacher in Cincinnati, Ohio, during the early 1830s when she began writing stories for local publications. In 1836 she married minister Calvin Ellis Stowe, a religious scholar and professor who supported her work as a writer. She continued to produce stories and in 1843 her first book was published, *The Mayflower; or, Sketches of Scenes and Characters Among the Descendants of the Pilgrims.*

In 1850, after relocating to Brunswick, Maine, Stowe began writing an antislavery novel, working at night by candlelight once her six children were in bed. This work was published serially in the summer of 1851 as "Uncle Tom's Cabin: Life Among the Lowly" in the Washington, D.C., antislavery journal *National Era,* and then in March 1852 it was published in book form. The work immediately became a best-seller in the United States; translated into twenty-three languages, it became an international best-seller as well. However, Southerners criticized the work on the grounds that it was inaccurate, and in response Stowe published a collection of documents supporting the portrayal of slavery in her novel. Titled *A Key to "Uncle Tom's Cabin"* (1853), the book included slave narratives and newspaper stories that Stowe had gathered while preparing to write her novel. Stowe continued to write articles, stories, novels, and poems for the rest of her life, sometimes giving public readings of her works. **See also** abolitionists; *Uncle Tom's Cabin;* women, contributions of.

Strong, George Templeton (1820–1875)

George Templeton Strong is best known for his diary, *The Diary of George Templeton Strong.* Published in three volumes (edited by Allan Nevins) in 1952, with volume three reprinted in 1962 as *Diary of the Civil War, 1860–1865,* this work offers many insights into the thinking of Northerners before, during, and after the Civil War. Strong served as treasurer of the U.S. Sanitary Commission during the war, and as a politically active New York lawyer he managed to solicit $5 million in donations to this commission for the benefit of Civil War soldiers. His social position and fund-raising activities placed him in contact with many influential people, making his diary particularly valuable for the information it contains on notable personages. Strong began writing his diary in 1835 and continued it throughout the war, not only recording events and relating conversations but offering his own opinions on a variety of subjects related to the social and political issues of the time. **See also** letters and diaries; Sanitary Commission, U.S.

Stuart, James Ewell Brown ("Jeb") (1833–1864)

More commonly known as Jeb (for his initials, J.E.B.) Stuart, James E. Stuart was the foremost Confederate cavalry commander, skilled not only in leading his troops but in gathering information about the enemy's troops. In one particularly famous incident, he rode completely around the Union forces of General George McClellan during the Seven Days' Battles (June–July 1862) in order to determine the location of the Union's right flank and give this information to Confederate general Robert E. Lee.

A graduate of the U.S. Military Academy, Stuart served in one of the two first cavalry units established by the U.S. Army, the First Cavalry, prior to the Civil

War, and in 1859 he helped capture abolitionist John Brown as part of a force led by Robert E. Lee. When his native state of Virginia seceded, Stuart resigned from the U.S. Army to join the Confederate army as an infantry lieutenant, but within a short time he was made a cavalry captain. In this capacity, Stuart earned recognition for his bravery at the First Battle of Bull Run in July 1861, and by the end of the year he had been promoted to brigadier general in charge of the cavalry brigade of Lee's Army of Northern Virginia.

The following year Stuart was promoted to major general and placed in charge of a cavalry corps, which he led at the Second Battle of Bull Run in August 1862. Once again he rode completely around the Union forces, this time to raid enemy supplies. He returned to his camp with over twelve hundred Union horses, as well as several wagons and weapons. Stuart had many more successes in 1862, and in May 1863 he was given command of the Army of Northern Virginia's Second Army Corps during the Battle of Chancellorsville after its leader, "Stonewall" Jackson, had been mortally wounded.

After the Battle of Chancellorsville, Lee decided to take his army north into Pennsylvania. Along the way, Stuart's cavalry fought against Union cavalry in the Battle of Brandy Station near Culpeper, Virginia, on June 9, 1863. This battle involved more cavalry—from both the North and the South—than any other Civil War battle, with Stuart commanding six batteries of horse artillery and five brigades of cavalry to a Confederate victory. Afterward Stuart decided to lead his troops on a raid of Union supplies rather than obey Lee's orders to stay near the main army's right flank to act as a screen against Union forces. Stuart's raid took much longer than he anticipated and was far more exhausting than expected. As a result, his troops did not get to the Battle of Gettysburg un-

Confederate general Jeb Stuart leads his cavalry into battle in Culpeper, Virginia.

til the second day of the conflict, an error that earned Stuart a great deal of criticism among fellow Confederates.

Nonetheless, Stuart continued to conduct cavalry raids and gather information until the Battle of Yellow Tavern on May 11, 1864. This battle began as an extension of the Battle of Spotsylvania. During this engagement, Stuart noticed that a Union cavalry force, led by Philip Sheridan, had left the battlefield. He believed that Sheridan was going to raid Confederate supplies, so he gave chase, and during the resulting battle Stuart was mortally wounded and his cavalry defeated. **See also** cavalry; Chancellorsville, Battle of; Gettysburg, Battle of; Spotsylvania Campaign.

submarines

Submarines were first used to sink enemy ships during the Civil War. The South wanted to develop a reliable submarine that it could use to attack the Northern ships blockading Southern ports. To this end, the Confederacy eventually employed three submarines: the *Pioneer,* the *Pioneer II,* and the *Hunley.*

The *Pioneer,* whose construction was financed by Alabama businessman Horace L. Hunley in 1862, was thirty-four feet long, with a propeller that had to be hand-cranked by a three-man crew. It is unclear whether this vessel was ever sent to attack the enemy. According to some accounts, shortly after being built it was destroyed by Confederates who wanted to keep it out of enemy hands when New Orleans, where it was docked, was captured by the Union. According to other accounts, however, the submarine sank after leaving port on a mission to sink enemy warships.

In either case, the builders of the *Pioneer* immediately started work on the *Pioneer II,* a twenty-five-foot iron vessel whose propeller was intended to be cranked not by hand but by a battery-powered electric motor. Due to the Northern blockade, however, the builders had problems getting the necessary parts for the motor, so eventually they were forced to use a hand crank after all. This submarine sank near Mobile Bay, Alabama, while en route to attack enemy warships, but its crew of four survived.

The final Confederate submarine, the *Hunley,* was the first submarine to succeed in sinking an enemy vessel. With a propeller cranked by eight men, this vessel had a torpedo filled with ninety pounds of gunpowder, initially attached to a two-hundred-foot tow rope but later to a long rod, or spar. On the night of February 17, 1864, the *Hunley* struck the Union warship *Housatonic* with this torpedo and sank it. Unfortunately, the *Hunley* was damaged in the explosion and sank as well.

Although the Confederates were the first to use a submarine successfully against an enemy ship, they were not the first to use these vessels in war. During America's Revolutionary War (1775–1783), a crude wooden submarine was employed in an unsuccessful attempt to attach gunpowder to the underside of a British warship. During the nineteenth century, American inventor Robert Fulton (who built the first steamboat) built the submarine *Nautilus* for French ruler Napoléon Bonaparte, who also wanted to use such vessels to attach explosives to enemy warships. The *Nautilus* performed successfully in a test, sinking the ship *Dorothy,* but was never used in war. During the War of 1812, the United States commissioned David Bushnell to build another submarine for this same purpose, but its attempt to attach explosives to the hull of the HMS *Ramillies* off Connecticut failed. **See also** *Hunley,* CSS.

Sultana

The *Sultana* was a Confederate riverboat that was involved in a major maritime disaster. On April 10, 1865, the day after

Robert E. Lee had surrendered his Army of Northern Virginia, the Confederates released the paroled prisoners of war at Camp Fisk, a prison camp near Vicksburg, Mississippi. (These men had previously been transferred to Camp Fisk from other prisons, including the notorious prison known as Andersonville.) The Confederacy then arranged for these men, who numbered about two thousand, to travel north to Cairo, Illinois, aboard the Mississippi River steamboat *Sultana.* The riverboat, which was supposed to hold only 376 passengers, was also loaded with 300 civilian passengers plus numerous coffins holding dead Union soldiers. The resulting weight put a great strain on the *Sultana*'s steam boilers, and on April 26, when the vessel reached Memphis, Tennessee, workmen discovered that the boilers were leaking. They repaired them and sent the ship on its way. Two hours later, at 2 A.M. on the morning of April 27 when the *Sultana* was about ten miles north of Memphis, the boilers exploded and the vessel caught fire. Some of the boat's passengers were killed outright in the explosion, while others were scalded to death by the steam and hot water or burned to death in the flames. Of those passengers who survived the explosion, some ended up in the river, whether by accident or by choice, though not many of them could swim. A few, however, managed to jump onto a small island as the ship drifted along the river. Eventually about 785 passengers were pulled from the river, roughly 600 of those as the river's current was carrying them past Memphis, but about 200 later died in city hospitals. There were at least 1,700 deaths in all. **See also** Andersonville; prisons and prisoners of war.

Sumner, Charles (1811–1874)

Massachusetts senator Charles Sumner was a leading abolitionist prior to the Civil War and subsequently a major figure in Civil War and Reconstruction politics. Elected senator in 1852, he denounced a variety of legislative measures designed to compromise on the slavery issue, including the Kansas-Nebraska Act. In fact, in speaking out against this act Sumner was so insulting to colleagues who supported slavery that a congressman from South Carolina, Preston S. Brooks, attacked him with a cane. Sumner received such severe injuries from this beating that it took him three years to fully recover from it. After being named chairman of the Senate Foreign Relations Committee, Sumner was also involved in achieving a peaceful resolution to the *Trent* Affair of 1861, a dispute between Great Britain and the United States that threatened to lead to war. During the Civil War, Sumner continually prodded President Abraham Lincoln to free all slaves immediately, criticizing the president for allowing slavery to continue in the border states.

After the war, Sumner argued that the policies of Reconstruction were not aggressive enough to ensure blacks' civil rights. In particular, he wanted former Confederate states to be required to guarantee that blacks would have equal voting rights before they could be readmitted to the Union. In various debates over the next decade, he consistently took the position that blacks were completely equal to whites and should be treated as such. In 1874 he authored a civil rights act but died before it passed into law. **See also** civil rights, black; Kansas-Nebraska Act; Reconstruction.

surgery

Any soldier undergoing surgery during the Civil War was at great risk of developing a life-threatening infection, because surgeons rarely took the time to wash their hands or their surgical instruments prior to removing bullets or amputating shatterred limbs. To make matters worse, antibiotics, which might have fought infection, were unknown at the time.

Ironically, the most common reason for surgery was to reduce the risk of a deadly infection. Many surgeons routinely amputated injured limbs to prevent gangrene, a deadly infection caused by the bacterium clostridium. Once a wound developed gangrene, the tissue around the wound would die, and this dead tissue, if not removed, would then poison the victim's entire body. Sometimes the wound could be cleaned enough to stop the progression of the infection, but this was rare given physicians' attitudes and the skills and knowledge of the time. In fact, most physicians followed the common practice of amputating all injured limbs, whether or not they showed any evidence of gangrene, within two days, unless battlefield conditions made this impossible.

Amputation was performed quickly—sometimes in less than fifteen minutes—and often carelessly. A surgeon's tool for this operation was a saw, which was rarely cleaned between amputations. Also typically left unwashed was the table on which the patient was restrained, and by the end of the day the ground beside the table was often littered with amputated limbs. Given such horrible conditions, patients who knew that they were going to have a limb amputated usually screamed and struggled in an attempt to prevent the doctor from going ahead with the surgery, unless their senses had been dulled by the liquor, opium, or morphine usually given to them while they were awaiting treatment. During surgery, patients were usually sedated with chloroform, a general

A surgeon performs an amputation at a hospital tent in Gettysburg. Amputations were typically carried out with unclean implements, and many patients died from the procedure.

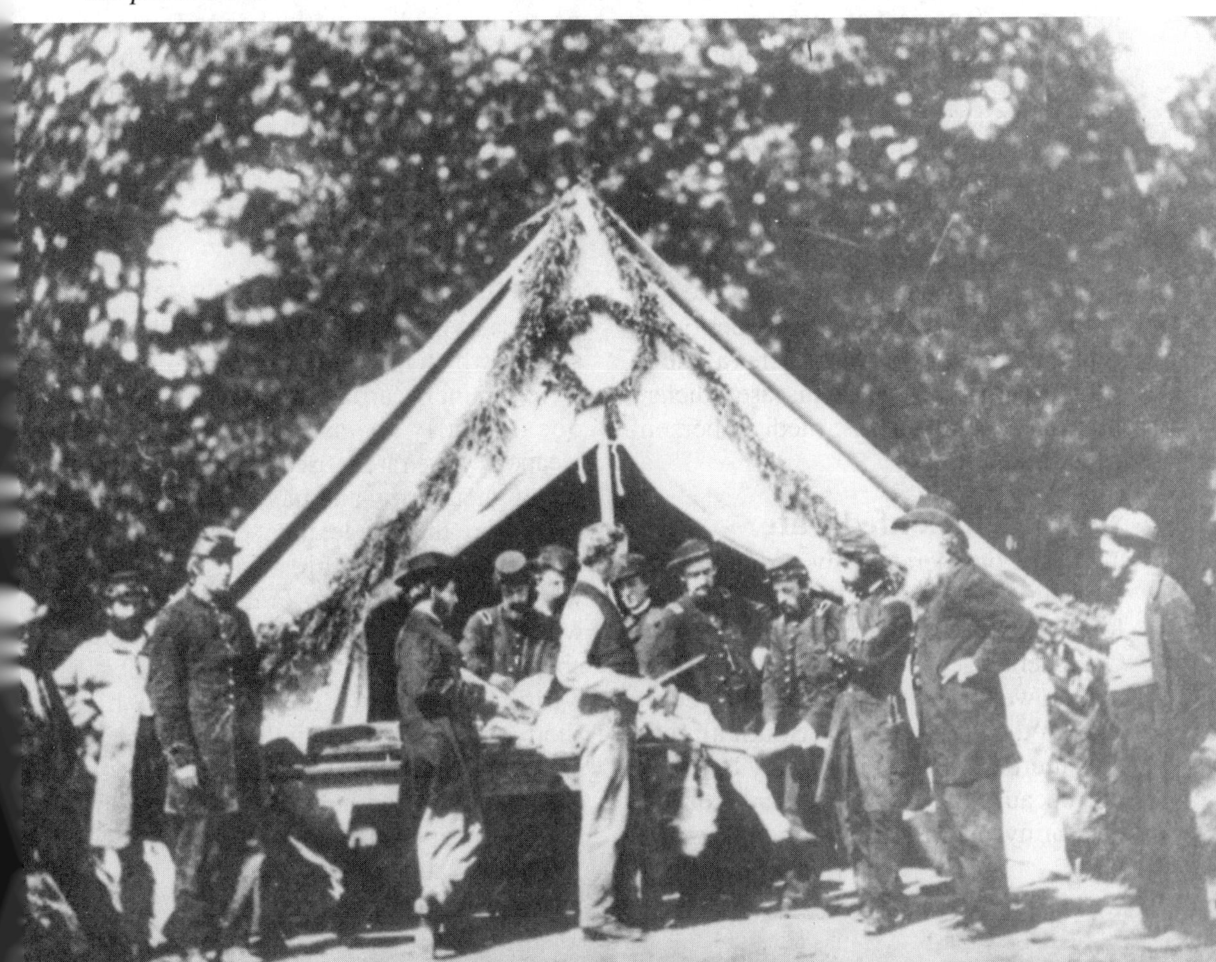

anesthetic administered on a cloth that was held under the patient's nose so that its fumes would be inhaled. In most cases the U.S. Medical Department could provide its physicians with enough chloroform to perform their surgeries, but Southern doctors often did not have chloroform and had to cut into patients who were conscious. Wounded soldiers who made it to the operating table still were often killed by the surgeon's attempt to remove the bullet. In fact, even a patient with a relatively minor wound might be killed by his surgeon because shortages of battlefield physicians often led to unqualified people being pressed into medical service. Statistics for surgery-related deaths among Confederate soldiers are unavailable. However, Union records show that out of 29,980 amputations reported by Federal surgeons during the war, 7,459 resulted in death. Of these, the most fatal amputations were those done at the hip joint; over 80 percent of such patients died during or after surgery. Amputations done at the knee joint resulted in a fatality rate of nearly 60 percent, while those done in the thigh had a fatality rate of about 55 percent. Shoulder-joint amputations killed about 30 percent of patients, and those in the upper arm nearly 25 percent. The least deadly amputations were those of the foot or toes (with a fatality rate of under 6 percent) and of the hand or fingers (a rate of about 3 percent). **See also** diseases, dietary illnesses, and infections; medical personnel and supplies.

surrender, Confederate

The last Confederate army surrendered to the Union on May 26, 1865, in New Orleans, Louisiana, under the direction of Confederate general Simon Bolivar Buckner. However, by this time many people in both the North and the South already considered the war over. They believed this because the most important Confederate army, the Army of Northern Virginia, led by General Robert E. Lee, had already surrendered to General Ulysses S. Grant on April 9, 1865, in Appomattox Courthouse, Virginia. **See also** Appomattox Campaign.

sutlers

Sutlers were the Civil War equivalent of traveling salesmen, following soldiers on the march in order to sell them goods they could not obtain from the army. These goods might include pies, cakes, and other bakery items; butter and milk; candy; tobacco; writing materials; newspapers and magazines; various types of clothing; and fresh and dried fruit. Some sutlers also sold alcohol, although this had to be done in secret because neither the U.S. nor the Confederate military allowed soldiers to buy or drink alcoholic beverages. Prices for all sutlers' wares were extremely high in comparison with those of town merchants, and instead of providing soldiers with change for their payments a sutler might offer him coupons that were good only for future purchases. As a result of such prices and practices, sutlers were often the targets of violent attacks by angry soldiers. **See also** camps and camp life.

swords, sabers, and bayonets

Swords (which had a straight blade) and sabers (which had a slightly curved blade) were routinely carried by cavalrymen, and occasionally by artillerymen. Such weapons were rarely used by infantrymen, although all army and navy officers typically wore them in leather scabbards during official ceremonies. Most swords, which might be single- or double-edged, were around thirty-six inches long and about one and a quarter inch wide. Sabers, which were single-edged, were a bit shorter than swords, with the shortest ones used by artillerymen.

Cavalry swords and sabers, which were typically kept in iron or steel scabbards, were primarily made in America (though often modeled after French styles) and were fairly plain and inexpensive. They had brass hilts and wooden grips that were wrapped with black leather held by twisted brass wire. (In the South, the grip might have oilcloth instead of leather, over which copper rather than brass wire was wound.) Swords used by officers were usually imported from Europe and might have silver or gold hilts decorated with jewels.

Bayonets were knives made to fit the muzzle of a rifle, but they could be removed for use in hand-to-hand combat. As with swords and sabers, there were various styles of Civil War bayonets, but essentially these fell into two categories: socket bayonets and sword bayonets. The main difference between these types of bayonets was length; sword bayonets, which had a grip just like that of a sword were longer than socket bayonets and therefore had to be used on shorter rifles. Another difference was that sword bayonets were attached to the rifle in a way that made them slightly easier to remove in the heat of battle. **See also** cavalry.

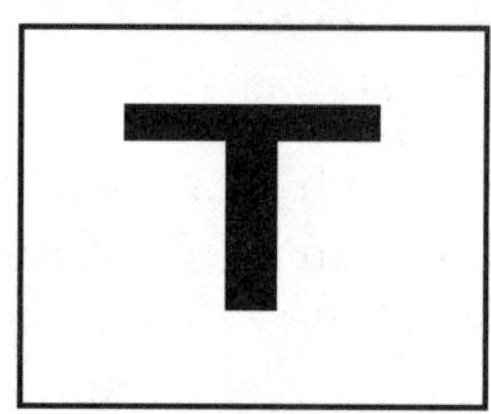

tactics, battle

At the beginning of the Civil War, commanders relied on battle tactics that had been developed in earlier wars. However, new technologies, such as steam engines and the telegraph, and new types of weapons had made these tactics obsolete, and gradually commanders realized that to prevail they had to change their approach to warfare. The Civil War, in fact, has often been called the first modern war.

In the infantry, commanders were accustomed to sending their soldiers charging toward the enemy to do hand-to-hand combat, because both sides had guns that were inaccurate beyond one hundred yards and took a long time to reload. After gun manufacturers developed weapons that could accurately and repeatedly hit targets from much farther away (250 yards to half a mile), Civil War commanders saw their troops struck down before they had gone more than a short distance. Indeed, some of the bloodiest battles of the war were the result of commanders continuing to rely on direct frontal infantry charges instead of adopting new tactics in which soldiers fired at the enemy from a distance while sheltered by strong field defenses and covering fire from artillery. However, commanders who refused to abandon the direct charge as a battle tactic did experiment with different formations in an attempt to reduce casualties. They also increased the density of formations so that even if a large number of their men were killed they would still have enough to continue the charge.

Cavalry commanders had to be even quicker to adapt their tactics because a shortage of trained horses and riders made large losses intolerable. Nonetheless, at the beginning of the war many cavalry commanders relied on the traditional cavalry charge, in which mounted soldiers rushed toward the enemy on horseback to hack at them with sabers and swords; the result was that many men had their horses shot out from under them. Consequently, cavalry commanders had to adopt dismounted tactics. Cavalrymen rode to within a safe distance of the enemy and then got off their horses to fight as infantrymen. Mounted cavalrymen could still be used, however, to conduct raids behind enemy lines and to scout enemy positions, because these situations required the speed and agility only a horse could provide and did not make the cavalryman an easy target.

In naval battles, commanders faced even greater challenges in figuring out which traditional battle tactics to keep and which to discard. At the beginning of the war, ship captains were still adjusting to the invention of steam propulsion systems that changed the manner and speed with which their vessels and the enemy's vessels moved. They also had to adapt their battle tactics to the fact that cannons had far greater range. Perhaps the most significant development to impact naval tactics was the invention of a new type of ship, the ironclad, whose sides were armored, making it more difficult for them to be pierced with shells or set on fire. Moreover, some of these vessels were fitted with revolving gun turrets. Given these innovations, in the beginning of the war ironclads typically won in battles against wooden warships. Eventually, however, the captains of wooden warships learned that by outfitting their ships with rams to which they could attach explosive devices, they might be able to go on the offensive, even against ironclads. **See also** artillery; cavalry; firearms; infantry, Confederate and Union; ironclads; navies, Confederate and Union.

Taney, Roger Brooke (1777–1864)

Roger Taney served as chief justice of the United States from 1836 to 1864, a period in which the U.S. Supreme Court made some critical decisions regarding U.S. banking, commerce, the economy, and slavery. The most significant in terms of Civil War politics was the 1857 *Dred Scott* decision, which was the outgrowth of a lawsuit from a slave who wanted to be declared a free man. The Supreme Court decided that no black man or woman could sue in a federal court because blacks were not U.S. citizens and that the Missouri Compromise, which prohibited slavery in certain U.S. territories, had been unconstitutional because, according to the U.S. Constitution, no man could have his property (e.g., slaves) taken from him without due process of the law.

A Maryland native, Taney came from a wealthy tobacco-growing family that owned slaves, although Taney freed them upon his father's death. He became a lawyer in 1799 and then served a one-year term in his state's House of Delegates before starting to practice law in Frederick, Maryland. From 1816 to 1821 he served in the Maryland Senate, and in 1827 he was named the Maryland attorney general. In 1831, Taney was appointed U.S. attorney general, and in this capacity he successfully fought against keeping the Bank of the United States as the central U.S. bank because it consistently abused its powers.

Because of Taney's strong stance against corrupt banking, in 1833 U.S. president Andrew Jackson appointed him to be the U.S. secretary of the treasury, but the Senate rejected this appointment. As a result, Taney went back to practicing law until 1836, when Jackson nominated him to be chief justice of the Supreme Court. Taney received the bulk of the criticism related to the Court's controversial *Dred Scott* decision. He was also criticized for speaking out against President Abraham Lincoln's decision at the beginning of the Civil War to suspend the writ of habeas corpus. Moreover, many Northerners objected to Taney's stance on the slavery issue. Although Taney personally abhorred slavery, he believed that states should have the right to decide for themselves how they would deal with the issue. **See also** *Dred Scott* decision; habeas corpus.

taxation

To help pay for the Civil War, the U.S. government on July 1, 1862, began taxing incomes of $600 to $10,000 at a rate of 3 percent. Incomes above $10,000 were taxed at 5 percent. As a result, taxation brought in about $2 million the first year. The second year the government increased the tax rates and implemented inheritance taxes and sales taxes on tobacco, liquor, and a variety of other goods and luxury items, including playing cards. This increased its revenue by taxation to about $20 million.

Shortly after the U.S. government imposed the first effective taxes on its citizens, the Confederacy instituted a property tax, but the amount it demanded was small (one-half of 1 percent of the property's assessed value, with an exemption for properties worth less than $500). In April 1863, the Confederacy decided to tax personal income and the profits from produce sales as well. Still, the amount of money that the Confederacy received from these taxes made up only 7 percent of its national income. **See also** economy, Southern vs. Northern.

Taylor, Richard (1826–1879)

The son of U.S. president Zachary Taylor, Confederate general Richard Taylor is perhaps best known for his 1879 book, *Destruction and Reconstruction,* which recounts the events of the Civil War and the subsequent Reconstruction period. As a young man Taylor studied military and literary history at Yale University. He then focused on running his own sugar plantation in Louisiana until that state seceded from the Union. In 1861 he joined the Ninth Louisiana Infantry as a colonel, and in 1862 he led troops under General "Stonewall" Jackson as a brigadier general in charge of the District of West Louisiana. In 1864 he fought against Union troops in the Red River Campaign, and in 1864–1865 he participated in several battles as a lieutenant general. He surrendered in Alabama in May 1865. **See also** Reconstruction.

Taylor, Susie King (1848–1912)

Susie King Taylor wrote *A Black Woman's Civil War,* the only published book written by a black Civil War nurse. In the book, published in 1902, Taylor tells about her experiences working as both a nurse and a laundress for the Thirty-third Colored Troops, which served primarily in South Carolina. **See also** medical personnel and supplies.

Tennessee

Tennessee was the last state to join the Confederacy, seceding from the Union on June 8, 1861. That it was late in making this decision is reflective of the fact that the state had both Union and Confederate sympathizers. During the war, Tennessee's proximity to the Union made it the site of many battles and campaigns, among the most significant of which were the Battle of Stones River (December 31, 1862–January 2, 1863) and the Franklin and Nashville Campaign (November–December 1864). The latter was a series of battles instigated by Confederate general John B. Hood. The Battle of Stones River was a fight between the Confederacy's Army of Tennessee and the Union's Army of the Cumberland. During this battle, Confederate cavalry commander Joseph Wheeler Jr. distinguished himself by leading eleven hundred of his men around the enemy's troops more than once in order to steal horses, destroy wagonloads of supplies, and take prisoners. **See also** Franklin and Nashville Campaign; Stones River, Battle of.

tents

Military camps typically consisted of rows of tents placed according to military unit and rank, with the tents of enlisted men located behind those of their commanding officers. These tents served as sleeping and living quarters for the soldiers, while other tents in camp were used as hospitals for the wounded or as kitchens for regimental cooks. Tents might also be used to keep certain types of supplies from being exposed to the weather.

A few different styles of living tents were used during the war. In the early months, most tents were of a type known as the Sibley. Named for army officer Henry Sibley, who designed the tent based on the structure of Plains Indian tepees, the Sibley tent was shaped like a cone, with a center height of twelve feet and a ground diameter of eighteen feet. Made of canvas, it had a wooden frame with a pole at the center and a vent hole at the top, as well as flaps in the lower canvas walls that could be opened to let in more air. The tent was intended to sleep twelve men, providing they pointed their feet toward the center, but in a crowded camp more than twenty men might be housed in each Sibley. As a result, the tents were often hot, sweaty, and smelly inside, even when the vents were open.

The Sibley was also difficult to transport, so within a short time both the Union and the Confederate armies abandoned this tent in favor of the more portable "A" tent, also known as the wedge tent. Its name comes from the fact that when looked at from one end, the tent was shaped like the letter "A." It was made by erecting two six-foot-tall poles six feet apart, then placing a horizontal pole atop these so that a piece of canvas could be draped over the horizontal pole and staked to the ground to create the shelter. These tents were intended to house four men, but as many as six were often assigned to each "A" tent.

By the end of the war, the preferred tent had changed again, from the "A" tent to the "dog" or "pup" tent. These were even more portable, because they were manufactured in halves. Two soldiers would pair up, each carrying one half of the

Union officers relax outside a Sibley tent (left) and an "A" tent (right). A black servant assists the officers.

tent's materials on a march, and when it was time to make camp they would work together to erect the structure, which could sleep only two. The tent was made with two 5 ½-foot-square pieces of canvas, one half with buttons and the other with buttonholes so that they could be buttoned together. Confederate soldiers were lucky to have even this meager accommodation by the end of the war. As canvas grew scarce, they resorted to sleeping under an oilskin cloth on a bed of leaves or grass or on bare ground, and sometimes even the oilskin cloth was not available.

Officers, however, whether Union or Confederate, always had the best available accommodations. They most typically used wall tents, peaked structures with four canvas walls. Also called hospital tents because tents of this design were often used to house wounded soldiers, these tents were big enough for furniture and tall enough so that people could comfortably stand inside. Many had wooden floors, which meant that they were not as damp as ordinary tents. Meanwhile, as the war progressed, Union soldiers were increasingly supplied with rubber or gutta-percha (a rubber-like substance) blankets, also called gumblankets, to protect them from damp ground.

Other types of tents might also have wooden floors during the winter. At this time of year, depending on the location, it was so difficult to travel that soldiers might stay in one place for weeks or months. On such occasions they had time to build log foundations for their tents, usually laying each foundation slightly below ground level. Depending on the amount of time and wood available, they might even build entire log cabins. Such structures might also be used as hospitals, although most physicians preferred to house their patients in tents because they believed that tents provided better air circulation than closed wooden buildings. **See also** camps and camp life.

Texas

Texas was a slave state prior to the war, but in early 1861 its governor, Sam Houston, tried to convince state legislators not to secede from the Union. When they ignored his recommendation, Houston refused to take the oath of allegiance to the Confederacy and left office. During the war, the main focus of military action in Texas was along the Gulf Coast, particularly at the port of Galveston. The Union initiated a blockade of this port on July 3, 1861, and in October 1862 it captured the city. However, it lost it again on January 1, 1863, after the Confederates launched an attack on Galveston using both land and sea forces. The Union never regained the city, making Galveston the only Southern port still under the control of the Confederacy at the end of the war.

Texas is also notable for contributing three regiments to a brigade in Robert E. Lee's Army of Northern Virginia. This brigade, which became known as Hood's Texas Brigade because its commander was General John Bell Hood, was one of the most distinguished fighting units of the war. However, it also experienced some of the heaviest losses. The brigade fought in thirty-eight military engagements, including the Battles of Gaines' Mill, Second Bull Run, Antietam, Gettysburg, Chickamauga, and the Battle of the Wilderness. As a result, of the more than 4,500 men who served with the unit, only 476 remained at the end of the war. In one eighty-three-day period alone (between the Battles of Gaines' Mill and Antietam), the Texas Brigade lost 1,780 men. **See also** blockades and blockade runners; Hood, John Bell.

theaters of war

Technically, the term *theater of war* is used to refer to the entire area (land, sea, and air) where a war takes place, and in the case of the Civil War, this would be all of America and its coastal waters. However, many people use the term *theater of war* to refer to Civil War "theaters of operation," which are specific areas within a theater of war where military operations take place. There were four such theaters: the Eastern Theater, the Western Theater, the Trans-Mississippi Theater, and the Coastal Theater.

The Eastern Theater was defined as anything east of the Appalachian Mountains. As such, it included the U.S. and Confederate capitals (Washington, D.C., and Richmond, Virginia, respectively), which were defended by the Army of the Potomac and the Army of Northern Virginia, respectively. The main battles in the Eastern Theater were the First Battle of Bull Run, the Second Battle of Bull Run, and the Battles of Antietam, Chancellorsville, and Gettysburg.

The Western Theater was generally defined as the area lying between the Appalachian Mountains and the Mississippi River. Many of the battles in this area involved land-sea attempts to capture strategically significant rivers, although it was the site of major land battles as well. The main battles in the Western Theater were the Battles of Shiloh, Chickamauga, Vicksburg, Atlanta, and Nashville.

The Trans-Mississippi Theater was defined as the area west of the Mississippi River. This included the states of Missouri and Kansas, both of which experienced heavy guerrilla activity. The main battles in the Trans-Mississippi Theater were the Battles of Wilson's Creek, Pea Ridge, and Mansfield.

The Coastal Theater, also known as the lower seaboard and gulf approach, was defined as the Atlantic coast from Virginia south to Florida and the coastline of the Gulf of Mexico. Most of the battles in this area involved attempts by one side or the other to take control of coastal forts. The most significant such attempt in the theater was the Confederate capture of Fort Sumter that began the Civil War. **See also** Fort Sumter; *individual battle entries.*

Thomas, George Henry (1816–1870)

Union general George H. Thomas earned the nickname "the Rock of Chickamauga" for his refusal to yield his troops' defensive position while under heavy fire in a September 1863 battle near Chickamauga Creek in Georgia. Thomas's action, which occurred after two days of fighting, allowed Union forces to retreat to Chattanooga, Tennessee, twelve miles to the south.

A veteran of the Mexican-American War (1846–1848), Thomas began the Civil War as a member of the Union's Second Cavalry, despite the fact that he had many relatives in the South. He fought in many battles of the Western Theater, first under General Don Carlos Buell and then under General William S. Rosecrans, and eventually achieved the rank of major general. Shortly after the Battle of Chickamauga, Thomas succeeded Rosecrans as the commander of the Army of the Cumberland. A year later, General William T. Sherman made Thomas his second-in-command for his Atlanta Campaign, charging Thomas with protecting the Tennessee cities of Chattanooga and Nashville against attacks by the Confederacy's Army of Tennessee, led by General John Bell Hood. As part of this defense, Thomas thoroughly defeated Hood's forces—the principal western army in the Confederacy—in the Battle of Nashville (December 1864), thereby earning himself a promotion to major general and an official commendation for his actions from the U.S. Congress.

From the war's end until 1869, Thomas was in charge of military affairs in Kentucky and Tennessee. He was then made the head of the Division of the Pacific on California's coast. However, he died about a year after moving to San Francisco to take this post. **See also** armies, Confederate; armies, Union; Chickamauga, Battle of.

Tompkins, Sally Louisa (1833–1916)

Also known as "Captain Sally," Sally L. Tompkins was the only woman ever commissioned as an officer in the Confederate army, holding the rank of captain in the cavalry. She served, however, not as a soldier but as a hospital nurse and administrator. Tompkins was living in Richmond, Virginia, in 1861 when Confederate president Jefferson Davis called on the citizens of Richmond to help provide medical care to wounded soldiers. In response, Tompkins convinced a local judge, John Robertson, to convert his home into a twenty-two-bed hospital and to allow her to run it. Shortly thereafter, Davis ordered all Southern hospitals to be placed under the administration of military personnel. Tompkins personally pleaded with the president to allow her to retain control over Robertson Hospital, and as a result—in order to accommodate her without reversing his own order—he awarded her a commission in the military on September 9, 1861.

Tompkins remained in charge of this facility until June 13, 1865, never receiving payment for her services. By that time, over a thousand patients had been treated at the hospital, yet only seventy-three died. Moreover, the Robertson Hospital returned a higher percentage of seriously wounded soldiers to battle than any other Confederate hospital.

After the war, Tompkins became involved in charity groups that served Confederate veterans. She was a member of the Daughters of the Confederacy and an honorary member of the R.E. Lee Camp of the Confederate Veterans. In 1905, in poor health and with little money, she was invited to spend the rest of her life in Richmond's Confederate Women's Home. After she died there in 1916, she was buried with military honors. **See also** medical facilities; medical personnel and supplies; women, contributions of.

Toombs, Robert A. (1810–1885)

A Georgia lawyer who was a U.S. senator just prior to the war, Robert A. Toombs served as the provisional Confederate secretary of state from February 21, 1861, to July 24, 1861. Toombs had been a candidate for the Confederate presidency but lost to Jefferson Davis, who then selected Toombs as his secretary of state. However, Toombs wanted to be more involved in the war, so he resigned from the Confederate cabinet in July 1861 to become a brigadier general in the Confederate army, even though he had no formal military training. He subsequently fought in the Peninsula Campaign, at the Second Battle of Bull Run, and at the Battle of Antietam, where he was wounded.

During his time as a general, Toombs often fought with his peers and was highly critical of anyone who had been educated at the U.S. Military Academy at West Point. This included Daniel H. Hill, his superior officer during the Seven Days' Battles. At that time Toombs challenged Hill to a duel over a petty quarrel and Hill declined, saying they should be concentrating on attacking the enemy.

After the Battle of Antietam, Toombs expected a promotion, and when he failed to get one he resigned from the Confederate army. Shortly thereafter he became a member of the Confederate Congress. There, he was a vocal critic of President Davis. In 1864 another critic of Davis, Confederate vice president Alexander H. Stephens, appointed Toombs to be the colonel of a Georgia regiment that was among those fighting (eventually without success) against Union general William T. Sherman's invasion of Georgia.

As soon as the war was over, Toombs fled to Paris, France. When he returned to the United States in 1867, he refused to take an oath of allegiance to the United States and was unapologetic about his role in the Civil War. As a result, he was banned for life from holding a national political office. **See also** cabinet, Confederate; Hill, Daniel Harvey; Stephens, Alexander Hamilton.

torpedoes

During the Civil War, explosive mines were called torpedoes, whether they were placed in the ground or under the water. On land, their typical use was to destroy fortifications; in the water, torpedoes were primarily used to prevent enemy ships from passing through a particular waterway. The placing of land torpedoes was typically under the control of engineers, although many other officers—particularly those trained in military schools—knew how to place them as well. To do this, they would order the digging of a vertical shaft that gradually sloped toward the structure to be destroyed and then turned into one or more horizontal shafts to house the torpedoes, which could then be placed directly underneath the target.

Naval torpedoes typically detonated upon impact with an enemy ship. To ensure that such an impact would occur, torpedoes were held either on or beneath the surface of the water, attached to wooden kegs, driftwood, buoys, or some other floating or anchored object. Alternatively, a torpedo might be attached to the tow line or spar (rod) of a ship or submarine, which would then ram or strike the torpedo against the targeted vessel. There were also naval torpedoes that used timers for detonation, or could be detonated by an observer who triggered the device, but these were far less common than impact torpedoes. **See also** Crater, Battle of the; *Hunley,* CSS; submarines.

transportation

Steam-powered locomotives and boats provided military leaders with faster transportation than they had enjoyed in previous wars, facilitating the movement of troops and supplies. However, the North had nearly three times the miles of railroad lines that the South had (by the end of the war, over twenty-five thousand as opposed to about nine thousand), because the North and South had different transportation priorities before the war. In the South, the main goal was to move cash crops from large plantations to ports, so rail lines were built only along these routes, and roads and canals were few. In the North, however, the priority had been to move both goods and passengers to and from a variety of locations, which necessitated extensive systems of rail lines, roads, and canals. After the war broke out, this transportation system enabled the North to move soldiers and military supplies from all parts of its lands to military bases in preparation for marches into the South. To further such efforts, in 1862 the U.S. Congress passed a law making it possible for the U.S. military to take over railroads whenever necessary to further the war effort.

A similar measure was not passed in the South until 1865, because it was not a priority. The Confederates relied mostly on horses, mules, and the vehicles these animals pulled to transport men and supplies. Although railroads were also used, sometimes to great effect, as the war went on the South increasingly lacked the supplies to repair rail lines. Roads fell into disrepair as well, so it was not always possible to travel by wagon—although as horses became scarce such travel became impractical anyway. There was also little money available in the South to clear blockages from waterways, except in places that the Confederate government deemed vital to military defense. All of these shortcomings had to be taken into account whenever military commanders of either side planned their campaigns. With careful thought, however, most were able to figure out ways to use available rail lines, roads, and other aspects of the

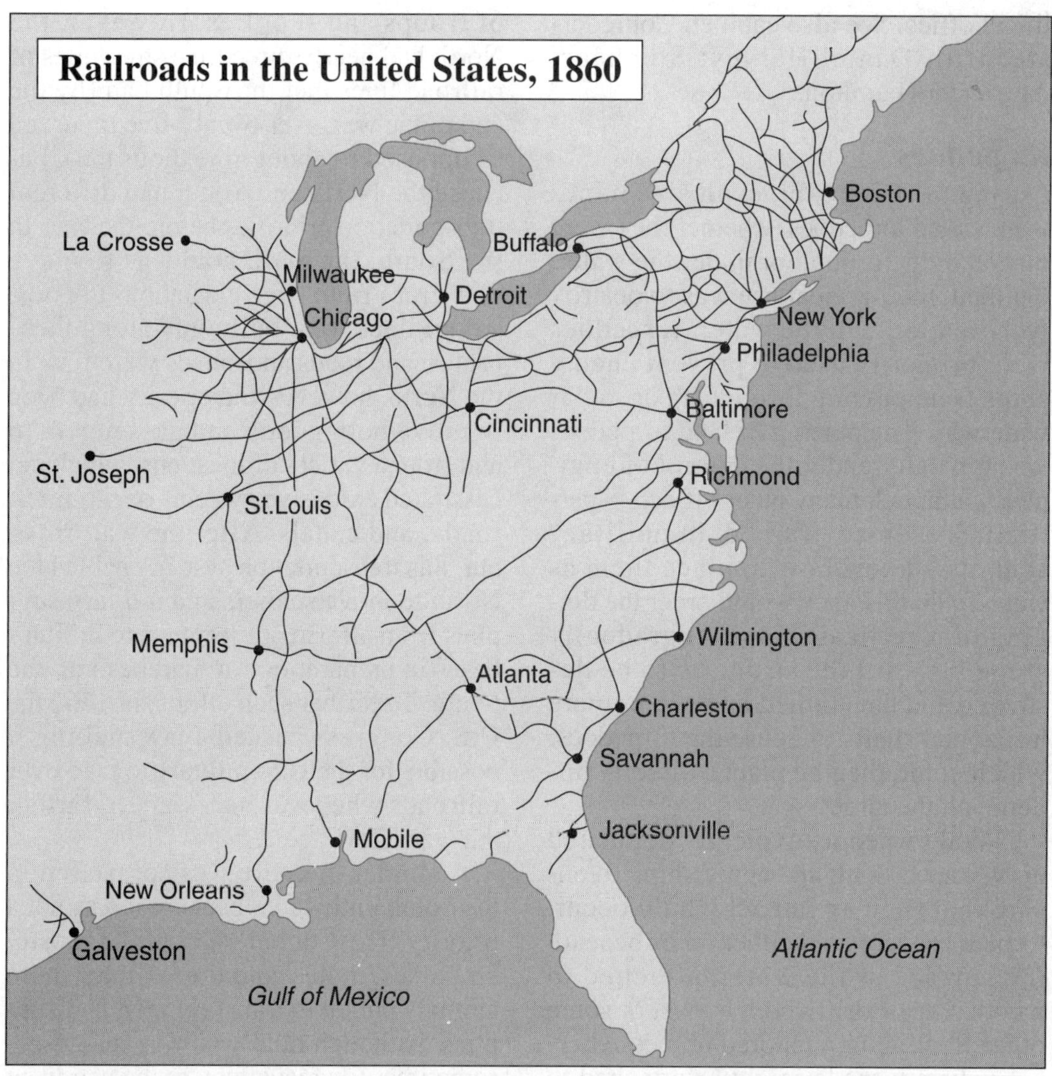

Southern transportation system to get troops and supplies where they wanted them, although delays in their arrival were not unusual. **See also** railroads.

Trenholm, George Alfred (1807–1876)

One of the wealthiest men in the South, South Carolina cotton merchant George A. Trenholm served as the Confederate secretary of the treasury from July 18, 1864, to April 27, 1865. He was highly experienced in financial matters, having worked for a South Carolina cotton-shipping company, John Fraser and Company, beginning in 1822 and been named the director of the Bank of Charleston (South Carolina) in 1836. Trenholm also served in his state legislature from 1852 to 1856. By 1860, he had become an owner of John Fraser and Company and expanded it to include branches in New York (where it was called Trenholm Brothers) and Liverpool, England (where it was Fraser, Trenholm & Co.).

When the war began, Trenholm built ships for the Confederacy without asking to be paid for them. He also used his own fleet of fifty ships as blockade runners. As secretary of the treasury, however, he was unsuccessful in acquiring foreign loans for the Confederacy. By the time he accepted the post the Confederacy was bankrupt, and there was nothing he could do to bring about its recovery. In fact, he spent so much of his personal fortune attempting to help the Confederacy that by the end of the war he was bankrupt as well. However, he was so resourceful that by 1874 he had rebuilt his fortune. **See also** blockades and blockade runners; cabinet, Confederate.

Trent Affair

The *Trent* Affair was an incident in 1861 that nearly led Great Britain to side with the Confederacy during the Civil War and declare war on the United States. In October 1861, Confederate president Jefferson Davis appointed two former U.S. senators, John Slidell of Louisiana and James M. Mason of Virginia, to become diplomatic agents of the Confederacy in establishing treaties with England and France, after first convincing the countries to recognize the Confederate government as an independent nation. To this end, the following month Slidell and Mason, traveling with two assistants, went to Havana, Cuba, on a blockade runner, the *Theodora,* and then booked passage from there to England on a British mail steamer, the *Trent.* In the meantime, a U.S. naval commander, Captain Charles Wilkes of the thirteen-gun warship *San Jacinto,* heard about the diplomats' intended voyage. Wilkes started looking for the *Trent,* and when he found it in the Old Bahama Channel three hundred miles east of Havana he fired a shot across its bow. The *Trent* then displayed its colors, showing that it was a British vessel and not a Confederate one, and kept going. Wilkes fired again. This time the *Trent* stopped and allowed itself to be boarded by several armed men from the *San Jacinto.* These men immediately declared the Confederate agents and their assistants to be prisoners of the U.S. government and forced them to board the *San Jacinto;* then they sent the *Trent* on its way.

The people of Great Britain expressed outrage over the incident, arguing that the United States had no right to interfere with the lawful progress of a British ship and its paying passengers, no matter what the politics of those passengers. It was only through the efforts of the U.S. minister to Great Britain, Charles Adams, that Britain was prevented from declaring war on the United States over Wilkes's unprovoked attack on a British ship. A skilled diplomat, Adams was able to convince the British that Wilkes and the men who boarded the *Trent* had been acting without orders from the U.S. government.

Nonetheless, the U.S. secretary of state, William Seward, officially apologized for the incident. He also assured the British government that the four Confederate diplomats had been well treated in prison (they were held at Fort Warren in Massachusetts), and promised that they would not only be released but safely transported to a meeting with British diplomats. Shortly thereafter, the Confederate diplomats were placed under British protection, with the British warning the United States to never again interfere with their ships. For some time afterward the Confederate government continued to hope that some lingering resentment toward the United States caused by the *Trent* Affair would lead Great Britain to support the Confederacy. Great Britain, however, quickly forgot the incident and maintained a position of neutrality in regard to the Civil War for the duration of the conflict. **See also** Adams, Charles Francis.

Truth, Sojourner (ca. 1797–1883)

Black religious leader Sojourner Truth was at the forefront of the abolitionist and women's rights movements. At the beginning of the Civil War, she was involved in efforts to establish and supply all-black volunteer regiments, and later during the war she worked to integrate public streetcars in the North. In 1864

President Abraham Lincoln personally thanked her for her efforts, and she was subsequently placed in charge of counseling former slaves for the National Freedmen's Relief Association.

A former slave originally named Isabella, Truth had a series of abusive masters during her childhood in New York, but eventually one of them, Isaac Van Wagener, freed her. By this time she had given birth to at least five children, one of whom had been sent south in bondage—an action that was then illegal under the laws of New York. Once Truth was free and New York had abolished slavery in 1827, she was able to sue in a court of law to get her son back. Two years later she became a domestic worker in New York City, supporting that child and another.

Around the same time, Truth became a missionary of the Retrenchment Society, an organization run by a religious zealot named Elijah Pierson. From childhood, Truth had claimed that she had heard voices which she believed came from God, and now she began sharing the words of God through street preaching. In 1843 she decided to spread her message outside of New York City. Taking the name Sojourner Truth, she began traveling from city to city, appearing at various camp meetings and churches in addition to continuing her street preaching. While in Northampton, Massachusetts, she met several abolitionists who convinced her to speak about abolitionism as well as religion. She did this at first throughout Massachusetts and then, in 1850, in the Midwest. The following year she also began speaking about women's rights. At all of her speaking engagements, she sold copies of a book, *The Narrative of Sojourner Truth,* which was the story of her life as narrated to Olive Gilbert.

After the war, Truth was active in programs that helped former slaves find places to live, advocating their migration to Kansas and Missouri for resettlement.

Sojourner Truth was an abolitionist leader and women's rights activist.

She was also involved in efforts to gain women the right to vote. She spent her last years in Battle Creek, Michigan. **See also** abolitionists; black troops.

Tubman, Harriet (ca. 1820–1913)

Before and during the Civil War, former slave Harriet Tubman helped hundreds of Southern slaves escape to freedom in the North via the Underground Railroad, a network of safe houses and hiding places run by people who opposed slavery. Tubman was born a slave on a Maryland plantation, where she was called Araminta and married a free black named John Tubman.

When her owner died in 1849 she escaped to Philadelphia, Pennsylvania, without her husband, who refused to leave Maryland. She then worked with others to organize the Underground Railroad, initially using it to rescue her relatives from slavery.

Over the next three years, from 1849 to 1852, Tubman made eleven trips to the South as a "conductor" of the "railroad," leading several dozen slaves north. She also provided information to abolitionist John Brown that helped him in his efforts to take over Harpers Ferry, Virginia, as a base for freed slaves. In 1852 Tubman moved to Canada, but when the Civil War broke out she resumed her Underground Railroad activities, making nineteen more trips to escort slaves fleeing to the North. She also worked as a Union nurse and scout in Georgia, North Carolina, South Carolina, and Florida. In addition, she was involved in intelligence work, spying on Confederates for the Union either alone or as the leader of a corps of black troops, and inspiring slave uprisings in various locations. In South Carolina, Tubman was responsible for encouraging over eight hundred slaves to fight for or escape to freedom.

After the war, Tubman established a facility in Auburn, New York, to house ill and elderly blacks. She was also involved in efforts to help newly freed slaves build new lives. In her later years, she contributed to the women's rights movement as well. **See also** Underground Railroad.

Turner, Nat (1800–1831)

In August 1831, slave Nat Turner led a slave revolt that succeeded in the short term but ultimately resulted in harsher laws restricting the activities of blacks. Turner's mother had been brought to the Virginia plantation where he was born after being captured by slave traders in Africa. She raised Turner with a deep hatred of slavery, but she also encouraged him to get an education. Consequently, he convinced his master's sons to teach him how to read, and he studied the Bible whenever he was not working in the fields. In his early twenties, his master sold him to a local farmer, and shortly thereafter Turner decided that God wanted him to lead a slave rebellion; this belief intensified after he was sold again in 1831. When Turner witnessed an eclipse of the sun that summer, he took it as a sign that it was time for him to act. He developed a plan to take over an armory in the nearby town of Jerusalem and use its weapons to arm his fellow slaves.

On August 21, 1831, in the middle of the night, Turner and seven other slaves attacked and killed Turner's new owner, Joseph Travis, and his family. The group then began traveling to Jerusalem, and along the way they gathered about seventy-five other slaves as followers and killed nearly sixty whites. Before they could reach Jerusalem, however, they were stopped by a state militia of nearly five thousand men. This force killed most of the rebellious slaves, as well as some innocent ones who happened to be nearby, and captured others. Turner escaped this attack, but he was caught six weeks later and eventually executed by hanging. After this, Southern whites decided that the subservience and peacefulness of blacks could no longer be taken for granted, and they enacted laws to make it more difficult for blacks to rebel in the future. For example, state laws made it much more difficult or even impossible for slaves to gather in groups, travel without being accompanied by their masters, or learn to read. **See also** slavery and slave life.

Uncle Tom's Cabin

Published in March 1852, the antislavery novel *Uncle Tom's Cabin* by Harriet Beecher Stowe influenced public opinion on the slavery issue, not only in the United States but abroad. President Abraham Lincoln checked the book out of the Library of Congress right before writing his Emancipation Proclamation, and the prime minister of Great Britain, Lord Palmerston, claimed to have read the novel three times. In fact, some historians believe that the book's popularity among the British was one reason why England did not offer diplomatic recognition to the Confederacy during the Civil War.

The novel, which Stowe later said she wrote by candlelight after her six children were in bed, was first published in serialized form, appearing as "Uncle Tom's Cabin: Life Among the Lowly" in the Washington, D.C., antislavery journal *National Era,* beginning in June 1851. The book version sold 5,000 copies within two days of its March 1852 publication. Two months later, 50,000 copies had been sold, and within a year there had been 300,000 copies sold in the United States and over 1 million in England. By the end of 1862, 2 million copies of the book had been sold in America, with some of those sales in the South. However, Confederate officials considered the novel so inflammatory that they made its ownership illegal.

The plot of *Uncle Tom's Cabin* was designed to appeal to the sentiments of a white, Christian audience. Its main character is Uncle Tom, a Christian slave who maintains his faith despite being sold over and over again. He is eventually beaten to death, but even while he is dying he prays that his master will repent his evil ways and be forgiven by God. In contrast to the evil slave owner, Simon Legree, is Little Eva, a white girl who is so good to her slaves that when she dies they weep for her.

After the book was published, many men in the South who owned slaves complained about the way *Uncle Tom's Cabin* depicted male slaveholders, and some of them accused the author of creating a false picture of the South in order to promote abolitionism. In response, in 1853 Stowe published *A Key to "Uncle Tom's Cabin,"* which was a collection of documents supporting the accuracy of her portrayal of slavery. These documents included slave narratives and newspaper stories that she had gathered while researching her story.

Stowe's work brought slave abuses to light. However, her novel also inspired the creation of traveling minstrel shows, also called "Tom shows," in which some of the events in the novel were acted out. During subsequent civil rights movements, these shows—and Stowe's novel as well—were criticized for perpetuating certain stereotypes about blacks, particularly the notions that they were always passive and eager to please whites. In fact, in the twentieth century "Uncle Tom" came to refer to a black person who would do anything to please whites, even at the cost of his or her own interests. **See also** Stowe, Harriet (Elizabeth) Beecher.

Underground Railroad

The Underground Railroad was a network of individuals willing to help fugitive slaves escape from the South to the North or to Canada. The first part of its name came from the fact that one meaning of "underground" is "done in secret"; since helping runaway slaves was against the law (with penalties ranging from fines to imprisonment), it was vital for members of the network to keep their activities to themselves. The second part of the name was related to the railroad terminology that the network used as code words for various aspects of its operations, most of which took place under the cover of darkness. Runaway slaves, for example, were referred to as "passengers," safe houses where they could hide were referred to as "stations," and people who guided runaways from one station to the next were "conductors."

Between the 1790s and 1860, there were at least thirty-two hundred such conductors, some white and some free blacks. One of the best-known conductors was Harriet Tubman, a former slave who led more than two hundred runaways to freedom. Another was John Fairfield, who had come from a family of slave owners and pretended to be one himself in order to transport fugitive slaves. Fairfield typically turned over fugitives wanting to go on to Canada to the care of a Quaker named Levi Coffin, who was eventually responsible for taking more than three thousand runaway slaves over the border. Information about the early activities of the Underground Railroad is vague, but beginning in 1850 the network provided aid to at least one thousand escaped slaves a year. **See also** Tubman, Harriet.

uniforms and equipment

At the beginning of the Civil War, uniforms varied greatly because soldiers supplied their own. Some men wore state militia uniforms; others wore uniforms designed for their volunteer regiments. For example, the Zouaves, who adopted the clothing styles of French troops in Africa, wore pants with legs that ballooned outward. A New York regiment called the Highlanders wore plaid, while an Irish regiment from Mobile, Alabama, wore green. Several regiments in both the North and the South wore red shirts, and one Tennessee company dressed entirely in yellow. These bright colors, however, quickly proved impractical in the field because they made men easier targets. Consequently, by the end of 1861 both sides had adopted muted colors: blue for the Union and gray for the Confederacy.

In the North, soldiers were issued machine-made uniforms at first, but as the clothes wore out the men were expected to replace them at their own expense according to a dress code. The standard attire for a Union infantryman was a dark blue short jacket or long coat and shirt and a pair of light blue pants, all made of wool. Beneath the pants the soldiers wore long underwear, called drawers. They also wore wool socks, heavy black shoes, and their choice of several types of hats, all of which had some kind of brim to protect their face from the sun. The most common hat was the forage cap, also known as the kepi, which had a flat top and a visor. Union cavalrymen and artillerymen had a similar uniform, although they wore boots instead of shoes and had a shorter jacket for greater ease of movement on horseback or while handling cannons. In addition, the trousers of cavalrymen were reinforced in the seat and inner thighs so they would not wear out from rubbing against the leather saddle.

The caps of Union cavalry officers were embroidered in yellow with a picture of two crossed sabers, while infantry officers had a blue bugle and artillery officers two red crossed cannons. Enlisted men had sabers, bugles, or cannons as well, but their insignias were brass rather than embroidered. The uniform buttons of enlisted men were stamped with an eagle, while officers' buttons were marked with an *I*, *C*, or *A* for infantry, cavalry, or artillery, and both soldiers and officers had additional markings indicating their regiment and company. (Each Union regiment had an identifying number, each company an identifying letter.) Commissioned officers also had an insignia denoting their rank on their shoulders, while noncommissioned officers had one on their sleeves.

In the South, uniforms were initially provided by the soldier himself, with each man being given a $50 clothing allowance. (Sometimes this money was paid to the states rather than to individual volunteer soldiers.) These clothes might be either homemade or purchased from manufacturers familiar with the Confederate dress code, although this code was often followed only loosely. However, the clothes that the soldiers provided were typically of inferior quality, so in October 1862 the Confederacy decided to provide soldiers

Union officers and enlisted men pose together in their dark blue uniforms.

with uniforms, usually manufactured from imported gray cloth. Confederate cavalrymen, however, wore a variety of shades of both blue and gray, trimmed their uniforms in gold and scarlet, and might wear plumed hats.

In general, Southern infantrymen wore a uniform much like that of their Northern counterparts, except that their shirts were white and made of cotton rather than wool and their coats—long at the beginning of the war, short later—were gray. Their trousers were supposed to be light blue, with officers having a red stripe down the leg to denote rank, but most soldiers wore gray trousers instead because they associated blue with the Union. After 1863, it became difficult to obtain gray cloth from abroad, or even the standard commercial dye used to color it, because of the Northern blockade of Confederate ports, so the Confederacy turned to a homemade dye made of walnut shells soaked in rusty water. However, the resulting solution produced a cloth that was a muddy yellow color, called butternut, rather than gray. This dye was also sometimes used to change the color of captured Union uniforms so that they could be worn by Confederates.

The equipment of Union and Confederate soldiers varied according to what they were willing to carry with them on long marches. Generally, however, soldiers carried anywhere from thirty to fifty pounds of gear, including weapons and ammunition. Most had two blankets (one wool and one rubber, for warmth and dryness, respectively), a canteen (metal covered with canvas for Union soldiers, wooden for Confederate ones), a knapsack for personal possessions, and a haversack (a type of bag) for food. By the midpoint of the war, each soldier might also carry half of a two-person tent called a pup tent, which was designed to be divided into two parts for easier transport. **See also** camps and camp life; food; tents; weapons.

Union

The Union was a term used for the United States of America prior to and during the Civil War. At the beginning of 1860, there were thirty-four states in the Union, but by mid-1861 eleven had seceded. At this point what had once been the United States was divided into two nations, the Union with twenty-three states and about 22 million people and the Confederacy with eleven states and about 9 million people. The Union entered the war with a fully functioning government and military, whereas the Confederacy had to create these entities.

The Union had another distinct advantage over the Confederacy: Prior to the war the North had developed its industrial strength, whereas the South had focused on agricultural concerns. Therefore, once the war broke out, the Union was able to manufacture thirty times more firearms than the Confederacy, and it had far more iron, steel, copper, and coal. The Union also had nearly three times the miles of railroad lines, and its ports were much larger than the Confederacy's. **See also** Confederate States of America; industry and technology; railroads.

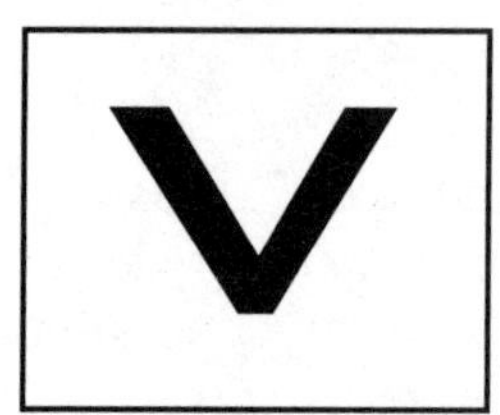

Van Lew, Elizabeth ("Crazy Bet") (1818–1900)

A Union spy known as Crazy Bet because she feigned mental illness as part of her cover, abolitionist Elizabeth Van Lew lived in the Confederate capital of Richmond, Virginia. There, she brought food from her family farm to Union prisoners and used the opportunity to engage their guards in conversation to glean information about Confederate plans. She passed this and other information to Union officials via fellow spies whose work she oversaw as the network's spymaster. Van Lew's spies included Martin M. Lipscomb, a merchant who provided supplics to the Confederate armies and therefore knew troop locations; Philip Cashmeyer, who worked for Confederate general John Henry Winder as a counterintelligence agent; and Samuel Ruth, the supervisor of a Richmond railroad who not only passed on information for Van Lew but used his position to cause delays in the delivery of vital supplies to Confederate troops.

Another spy in the network was Mary Elizabeth Bowser, a black woman who had been Van Lew's slave when Van Lew was a child. Van Lew later freed Bowser and sent her north for an education, but Bowser returned to the South when the war began to spy for Van Lew, pretending to be a slave so she could work in the Confederate White House. In 1865, Van Lew helped Bowser escape north once again after the Confederates became suspicious that someone in the executive mansion was passing information to the Union. However, the two women made it look as though Bowser had escaped not because she was a spy but because she was a slave wanting her freedom, and no one suspected Van Lew's involvement.

Van Lew also helped Union prisoners of war escape. On one occasion, for example, she provided some prisoners with the equipment they needed to tunnel out of jail, and over one hundred of them fled captivity. She then hid them on her farm until they could sneak out of Richmond.

After the war, Southerners learned of Van Lew's espionage activities, refused to patronize her farm, and drove her into bankruptcy. In 1869 she asked President Ulysses S. Grant, formerly a Union general, for help, and he placed her in charge of the Richmond post office. **See also** spies; Winder, John; women, contributions of.

veterans

After the Civil War, its veterans had to deal with physical disabilities and infirmities caused by war wounds and diseases. They also had to cope with life back among their loved ones, which might require them to repress horrible memories of what they had experienced in combat. However, Northern veterans returned home to find a booming economy and many job opportunities; in contrast, veterans from the South often found their homes, farms, and towns destroyed and the Southern economy devastated. As a result, many Southern veterans faced extreme poverty. Even more severely impacted were the 186,000 black Union veterans who headed south intending to live and work in the region they had once called home. Despite the Northern victory, these individuals still had to deal with racism and oppression by whites unwilling to accept them as equals.

The Union did provide some monetary compensation to its veterans. Upon leaving the army at the end of the Civil War, each soldier received a payment averaging $250. In addition, beginning in 1861 a soldier who had to be released from service because of a debilitating injury or illness would receive a pension based on rank, with a former officer receiving $30 a month and a former private $8. In 1864 the U.S. government provided additional payments for certain injuries. For example, a man would receive an additional $20 a month if he had lost both feet in the war, or $25 for losing both hands. Widows and orphans could also receive payments based on their losses. Given all of these payments, in 1866 the government spent $15.5 million on its veterans, and this amount continued to increase as additional laws to benefit veterans enacted over the next decade broadened the definition of disability.

To further help those with serious war-related disabilities, shortly after the war the U.S. government established nursing care facilities for disabled veterans and orphanages for the children of those killed in battle who had no other family members to care for them. Beginning in 1863, the government also implemented the practice of putting disabled soldiers to work in appropriate noncombat jobs as part of the U.S. Invalid Corps, renamed the Veteran Reserve Corps in 1864. These jobs fell into two categories: guard duty and hospital work. Approximately sixty thousand Union soldiers served in this capacity between 1863 and 1866, when the corps was disbanded. In 1864 the Confederacy established a similar corps that lasted only a year, because by then the Confederate government had ceased to exist. In contrast to Union veterans, former Confederate soldiers received no monetary compensation or health care benefits after the war.

Following the war, Union veterans as well as Confederate ones also had the opportunity to join veterans groups that offered them emotional support and fellowship. Many such groups existed, but the most prominent were the United Confederate Veterans (UCV) organization in the South and the Grand Army of the Republic (GAR) in the North. The UCV was established in 1889 by a group of former Confederate soldiers, and in 1899 it published a twelve-volume work, *Confederate Military History,* to present a Southern view of the war. The GAR was established in 1865 by former Union general John A. Logan, who served as its commander in chief for several years. In this capacity, he established Memorial Day (then called Decoration Day) in 1868, asking all members of the GAR to honor those who had died in the Civil War by putting flowers on their graves every May 30. These and other veterans' organizations tried to influence government policies related to veterans in the years after the war, as well as providing opportunities for veterans, and later for their descendants, to socialize with one another and share information about the war. **See also** Logan, John Alexander.

Vicksburg Campaign

The Vicksburg Campaign was a Union attempt from November 1862 to July 1863 to use land-based forces to capture Vicksburg, Mississippi, after bombardment from ships sailing up the Mississippi River failed to force the city's surrender. Located at a strategically significant site (on the Mississippi River about halfway between the cities of Memphis, Tennessee, and New Orleans, Louisiana), the city was served by rail lines for the Southern Railroad of Mississippi and the Mississippi Central Railroad and had active riverboat wharves. To protect these assets, the Confederacy fortified Vicksburg with seven artillery batteries on high ground and nearly thirty thousand Confederate soldiers.

The Vicksburg Campaign assault was under the command of General Ulysses S. Grant, who began leading an army of approximately thirty thousand men toward the city from Tennessee in early November 1862. At the same time, Grant ordered Major General William T. Sherman to take a force of thirty-two thousand men down the Yazoo River to rendezvous with him at a point west of Vicksburg for a combined attack. This plan failed when Grant's supply depot and a key rail line were attacked by Confederate cavalry while he was en route to Vicksburg. As a result, he no longer had adequate supplies to go on, and Sherman's forces decided to attack Vicksburg without Grant's. After three days, Sherman withdrew from the area in defeat.

Over the next several months, Grant came up with several other plans for getting his troops to Vicksburg. Some were abandoned before being tried, while others were tried and failed. Finally Grant came up with a successful approach, diverting the enemy with a cavalry attack while he ferried his men across the Mississippi River at a point south of Vicksburg. He then marched his troops far to the east of the city to cut its rail and communication lines.

As Grant marched his troops east rather than north toward Vicksburg, the Confederates thought that he was abandoning his plan to attack the city and were therefore slow in countering his moves. Consequently, Grant not only succeeded in cutting the rail and telegraph lines but also was able to drive nearby Confederate troops, led by General John C. Pemberton, back to Vicksburg. Grant then attacked and laid siege to the city, establishing field defenses around Vicksburg and moving additional soldiers into the area.

By the end of May 1863 there were fifty thousand Union soldiers surrounding Vicksburg, and by the middle of June there were a total of seventy-seven thousand. In addition, Grant established a defensive line of approximately thirty-four thousand men at a point fifteen miles east of Vicksburg to prevent the Confederacy from mounting an attack on his forces from that direction. Seeing that such an attack was impossible, Confederate general Joseph E. Johnston tried to draw Grant out of the area by launching attacks elsewhere, but this approach failed. Finally, Pemberton was forced to surrender Vicksburg on July 4, 1863. With this surrender, the Union not only captured the city but gained thousands of arms and prisoners of war. **See also** Grant, Ulysses S.; Johnston, Joseph Eggleston; Pemberton, John Clifford; Sherman, William Tecumseh.

Virginia

The state of Virginia was the scene of many of the key battles of the Civil War, largely because the Confederacy had chosen the city of Richmond, Virginia, as its capital. However, Virginia had only reluctantly joined the Confederacy. In its initial vote on secession in January 1861, state leaders decided two to one against leaving the Union. Then U.S. president Abraham Lincoln demanded that Virginia furnish troops for an invasion of the South intended to stop the secession movement even before the North had officially declared war on the South. Virginia opposed what it considered an act of aggression, and in April 1861 its leaders voted two to one in favor of secession. From that point on, the state was the main focus of Union strategy.

The state's Army of Northern Virginia also possessed some of the most experienced soldiers and officers of the war—such as Robert E. Lee and Jeb Stuart. In fact, this army was so completely associated with the fortunes of the Confederacy that when its commander, Robert E. Lee, surrendered the army in April 1865 the Civil War was considered over, even though a few other Confederate armies had yet to give up the fight. **See also** armies, Confederate; Lee, Robert Edward.

Virginia Military Institute

Many Confederate officers received their military training at the Virginia Military Institute. Located in the town of Lexington in Virginia's Shenandoah Valley, this school was founded in November 1839 as a place to train young men to act as guards for an arsenal on the site. The institute gradually began to train soldiers for other types of military duties as well, although it did not intend for them to serve in the professional army. Instead, the purpose of the institute was to create citizen soldiers who would serve in times of emergency.

By the time of the Civil War, however, there were nearly 350 graduates of the institute, and of these, roughly 300 were sent to Richmond, Virginia, to help train and drill other soldiers. Approximately 1,200 students were enrolled at the institute when the war broke out, and about 800 more enrolled during the war. Three of these roughly 2,000 students eventually became major generals in the Confederate army and 17 became brigadier generals, with many of the rest becoming other ranks of officers. In addition, a group of 247 cadets from the school distinguished themselves at the Battle of New Market, fought in the Shenandoah Valley on May 15, 1864, by making a heroic charge at the Union forces of Major General Franz Sigel. Ten of the men were killed outright or died later of battle wounds, and about 45 were injured.

The following month, on June 12, 1864, Union forces led by Major General David Hunter looted and set fire to the Virginia Military Institute in retaliation for Confederate guerrilla activity in the Shenandoah Valley. A little more than a year later, however, the institute had been rebuilt and was once again admitting students. After the war, the state of Virginia pressed the U.S. government to compensate the Virginia Military Institute for the losses it incurred as a result of Hunter's attack and theft of institute property, and in 1916 the U.S. government paid the school $100,000. **See also** military schools, bias against.

volunteers

During the Civil War, approximately 2.2 million men fought for the Union and between 750,000 and 1.25 million men fought for the Confederacy. Of these, the majority were volunteers, even after the South initiated conscription (also known as the draft) in 1862 and the North in 1863. One reason for the preponderance of volunteers, aside from patriotism, was the fact that volunteers often received cash for volunteering, whereas men who were drafted did not.

The U.S. government made a concerted effort to keep the volunteer army separate from the Regular Army, although some officers from the Regular Army were sent to train soldiers in the volunteer army. Volunteer regiments were typically raised by individual states, in accordance with calls for volunteers that were issued by U.S. president Abraham Lincoln. Lincoln's initial call, on the day after the Confederates took Fort Sumter in April 1861, was for seventy-five thousand volunteers. Shortly thereafter he called for over forty-two thousand more, and in July 1861 he called for an additional 1 million spread out over three years. A year later, in July 1862, he called for 300,000 more volunteers.

Men in New York line up to answer the call for volunteers to serve in the Union army.

In both the North and the South, there were many complaints from professional soldiers regarding the inexperience, poor training, and lack of discipline of volunteers as compared to professional soldiers. In response, many volunteer soldiers complained about the rigidity of professional soldiers, suggesting that men who had been trained in traditional military schools were unable to adapt to the new types of warfare seen on Civil War battlefields. Indeed, there were many changes in battle tactics during the war, and in some cases professional soldiers had more trouble than civilian soldiers did in substituting new techniques for old. Nonetheless, the U.S. and Confederate governments implemented more rigid training techniques for volunteers, drilling them extensively and providing them with numerous military training manuals to study; as a result, the volunteer army eventually became as capable as the Regular Army. **See also** conscription; infantry, Confederate and Union; military schools, bias against.

Walker, Mary Edwards (1832–1919)

Known for dressing in men's clothing (though she did not pretend to be a man), Mary E. Walker was one of the very few women who worked as a physician at the time of the Civil War. Due to the encouragement of her father, a New York physician who supported women's rights, she was granted entrance to Syracuse Medical College, the only U.S. university to allow women students to pursue medical studies on an equal basis with men, and graduated in 1855.

Walker, in partnership with her husband who was also a physician, had briefly practiced medicine in Rome, New York. When the Civil War began, Walker tried to enlist in the Union army but was rejected. She then volunteered as a medical officer, becoming the first female surgeon in the U.S. military. At first she worked in Washington, D.C., but later she became a field surgeon on the front lines, working on men wounded in the Battles of Fredericksburg, Chattanooga, and Chickamauga. In September 1863 she became the assistant surgeon of the Army of the Cumberland, at which point she began wearing a Union officer's uniform.

A short time later Walker was made the assistant surgeon of the Fifty-second Ohio Infantry, and apparently the Union War Department asked her to do some intelligence work as well. She frequently crossed enemy lines, supposedly to treat civilian patients, and was captured as a spy by the Confederacy near Chattanooga, Tennessee. She was then imprisoned in Castle Thunder Prison in Richmond, Virginia. Four months later she was released in a prisoner exchange.

After the war, Walker devoted her time to a variety of social causes, particularly women's rights, as a writer and lecturer.

Mary Edwards Walker poses with the Medal of Honor she earned as a Civil War physician.

On November 11, 1865, U.S. president Andrew Johnson officially awarded Walker a Congressional Medal of Honor for her services during the Civil War, making her the only woman so honored. However, in 1917 Congress asked her to give the medal back because she had not been in actual combat. (A military board rescinded hundreds of medals at that time for the same reason after changing the rules for awarding Medals of Honor.) Walker, then eighty-five years old, refused to return her medal, and fifty-eight years later Congress decided it had been wrong in rescinding the honor. The U.S. government then reawarded the Congressional Medal of Honor to Walker posthumously. **See also** Congressional Medal of Honor; medical personnel and supplies; spies.

Washington, D.C.

As the U.S. capital, Washington, D.C., was well fortified, but unlike the Confederate capital of Richmond, Virginia (which had its own White House), it was never attacked by enemy forces, although in July 1864 a Confederate army led by General Jubal Early came close to the outskirts of the city. In addition, the Confederates did try to blockade the city's access to Chesapeake Bay and the Potomac River in May and June 1861, but the Union eventually drove them off.

Washington, D.C., was the site of sixteen general hospitals, only six of which had existed at the start of the war, and seven more were located just outside the capital in Alexandria, Virginia. Washington, D.C., had several U.S. military prisons as well. The two main prisons in the capital were Carroll Prison and the Old Capitol Prison, which held a combined total of 2,763 prisoners at their peak. Both were seriously overcrowded; their combined maximum capacity was only 1,500 prisoners. During the war, more than 457 prisoners died while incarcerated in these two facilities and 16 managed to escape from them. **See also** Richmond, Virginia.

Waud, Alfred and William (1828–1891; 1830–1878)

Alfred and William Waud were two brothers from England who worked as book illustrators in the United States just prior to the Civil War. The *New York Illustrated News* hired Alfred Waud to cover the war in 1861, while *Frank Leslie's Illustrated News* hired William Waud as an artist-correspondent in late 1860. In 1862, both men went to work for *Harper's Weekly.* Alfred Waud primarily covered the activities of the Army of the Potomac, while William Waud spent most of his time with Confederate forces in South Carolina. Both men continued producing sketches in the years after the war. **See also** artists and artwork.

weapons

Civil War soldiers used a variety of weapons, including firearms, artillery pieces, explosive devices, swords, sabers, knives, and bayonets. Some of these weapons were made in the United States, others in Europe. The Union purchased at least 4 million rifles and muskets from both domestic and foreign manufacturers and more than ten thousand artillery pieces during the war. The U.S. Ordnance Department also purchased nearly 525,000 sabers, swords, lances, and cutlasses. There is only one record of Confederate weaponry purchases, covering transactions in 1863. Known as the Gorgas Report because it was prepared by Josiah Gorgas, the Confederate chief of ordnance, it indicates that the Confederate army bought over 323,000 infantry arms, 34,000 cavalry arms, and 1,300 field artillery pieces that year—a large number of weapons given that the Confederacy was having severe financial problems by this time. **See also** ammunition; artillery; firearms; swords, sabers, and bayonets; torpedoes.

Webster, Timothy (1822–1862)

Timothy Webster is generally regarded as the most successful Union spy operating between 1860 and 1862. However, he also holds the distinction of being the first Civil War spy to be hanged for espionage, as well as the first American spy to be executed since the British killed Nathan Hale in 1776.

Born in England, Webster immigrated to America in 1830, living in Princeton, New Jersey, until becoming a New York City policeman in 1853. The following year he was hired by Allan Pinkerton to join the Pinkerton Detective Agency, then specializing in protecting railroads from theft. In February 1861, Webster was sent to Baltimore, Maryland, to investigate rumors of an impending attack on a railroad. Instead, he learned about a plan to assassinate president-elect Abraham Lincoln. Webster reported this to Pinkerton, who then took steps to foil the plan.

When the Civil War broke out, Pinkerton recruited Webster to become part of a Union spy network under General George B. McClellan of the Army of the Potomac. Webster's first wartime assignment, in the spring of 1861, was to gather information about the condition of the Confederate armies in Kentucky and Tennessee. To do this, be pretended to be a passionate secessionist who had come from the North to support the Confederate cause, and he was so convincing that Confederate officers gave him a tour of their camps. Webster used the same ruse on his next assignment, which was to gather information on Confederate operatives in Baltimore during the summer of 1861.

At a meeting of these operatives, one of them accused Webster of working for Pinkerton, having seen him entering Pinkerton's Washington, D.C., office. Webster's denial of this charge was so passionate that the group believed he had been wrongly accused. They then invited him to join a secret society, the Knights of Liberty, that was planning to attack Washington, D.C., with thousands of armed men. After Webster notified Pinkerton about these plans, Union soldiers captured the leaders of the Knights of Liberty during one of their meetings. Webster was present at this meeting as well, but he pretended to escape, and his true loyalties were not revealed.

In fact, Webster was still so convincing as a Confederate sympathizer that shortly thereafter he was arrested as a Confederate spy by another of Pinkerton's agents, who did not know that Webster was in Pinkerton's employ. Webster used this mistake to enhance his reputation as a Confederate spy, staging a dramatic escape from federal custody. A few months after this, Webster received a pass from the Confederate government that allowed him to travel throughout the South without being questioned regarding his activities.

With this pass, Webster made several trips to Richmond, Virginia, to gather information in the Confederate capital. While on one of these trips in the fall of 1861, he rescued two women and three children who had fallen into the Potomac River. This act not only made him a hero in the South but provided him with intelligence information, because one of the women had unknowingly dropped a bundle containing information that had been gathered by a Confederate spy working in the U.S. Provost Marshal's Office. After Webster found this bundle and gave it to Pinkerton, the man was quickly arrested. Meanwhile, Confederate secretary of war Judah P. Benjamin honored Webster for his heroics by making him a Confederate spy—without knowing that Webster was actually working for the Union.

Because of his status as a "double agent," Webster was able to aid in catching many Confederate spies working in Washington, D.C. However, Webster's swim in the Potomac had resulted in a decline in his health, and in January 1862 he fell seriously ill while in Richmond, Virginia. Unable to get word back to Pinkerton, he was considered missing by his spy network, and after a short time fellow spies John Scully and Pryce Lewis were sent to locate him. They found Webster in a hotel room, but shortly after leaving his side they were recognized as being Union spies and arrested. To save himself from hanging, Scully told his captors that Webster had been spying for the Union, and Confederate spycatcher John Winder immediately ordered Webster's arrest.

Webster was quickly tried and sentenced to hang. His execution was carried out on April 29, 1862, in Richmond, Virginia. Webster's body was buried there until 1877, when Pinkerton arranged for it to be moved to Onarga, Illinois, where Webster's widow lived. **See also** Pinkerton, Allan; spies; Winder, John.

Welles, Gideon (1802–1878)

Gideon Welles served Presidents Lincoln and Johnson in succession as U.S. secretary of the navy from March 7, 1861, to March 3, 1869. After becoming secretary of the navy, Welles and his assistant, Gustavus Fox, oversaw the construction of many new ships, particularly ironclads; recruited new sailors and officers to replace those who had left to join the Confederacy; and supervised the blockading of Southern ports. Prior to the war, Welles held a variety of jobs, including newspaper editor, state controller, postmaster, Connecticut legislator, and head of the U.S. Navy's Bureau of Provisions and Clothing. In 1856 he founded a Republican newspaper, the *Hartford Evening Press*, and after leaving the U.S. cabinet in 1869 he returned to his writing, producing magazine articles and a book titled *Lincoln and Seward* (1874). In 1911 his diary was published posthumously as *Diary of Gideon Welles,* providing many details about the people and events associated with Welles's cabinet career. **See also** blockades and blockade runners; Fox, Gustavus Vasa; ironclads; navies, Confederate and Union.

West, the

Because it was so geographically distant from the battlefields of the South, the West did not figure prominently in the Civil War, except as a haven for deserting soldiers. The West did play a role in the political disputes that led up to the conflict, however, since one of the main disagreements between North and South was whether western territories should be open to slavery either before or after they became states. In particular, Southerners in Congress violently opposed California's admission into the Union as a free state, but in the end they gave in as part of the Compromise of 1850, which allowed western territories to vote on whether they would permit slavery within their borders.

The West also played a role in postwar politics concerning newly emancipated blacks. In the South, blacks were subject to discrimination and violence in the years after the war, and in the North many whites were not enthusiastic about the influx of black workers who threatened their jobs. Therefore, many whites throughout the country suggested that blacks be sent to African American colonies either in a foreign country, such as Liberia, or in the West, and groups were formed to support various colonization plans. As a result of such efforts, between 1866 and 1899 more than 145,000 blacks settled across the West—except for Texas, which had been a part of the Confederacy and where racist sentiment continued to be strong. **See also** California; colonization movement; Compromise of 1850.

West Point

West Point is the common name for the U.S. Military Academy located at West Point, New York, about fifty miles north of New York City. Many of the commissioned officers on both sides in the Civil

War had been trained at West Point, including Ulysses S. Grant, William T. Sherman, Robert E. Lee, Thomas "Stonewall" Jackson, and James Longstreet. Confederate president Jefferson Davis was a graduate of West Point as well. In fact, Southerners made up over half of every prewar class at the academy.

The school was opened on July 4, 1802, as a training center for military engineers who would serve in the U.S. Army Corps of Engineers. Ten years later, on April 29, 1812, an act of Congress turned the engineering school into a four-year military academy for 250 students, or cadets, with military officers as instructors. West Point's goal then was to teach its corps of cadets how to be good officers in the U.S. Army; when cadets graduated they would be given a commission as a second lieutenant in the army. Highly selective, West Point accepted only young men who had achieved high scores on academic tests and who had been recommended by either a member of Congress or some other person of political influence. **See also** engineers; military schools, bias against.

Wheeler, Joseph (1836–1906)

Also known as "Fighting Joe," Confederate general Joseph Wheeler fought in a total of 127 battles during the Civil War. During these battles he was wounded three times, and on sixteen occasions his horse was shot out from under him. Wheeler also made a major contribution to military training, publishing a manual for cavalrymen, *Cavalry Tactics,* in 1863.

Born in Georgia but raised primarily in Connecticut, Wheeler served as a second lieutenant in a U.S. mounted-rifle regiment in New Mexico Territory prior to the Civil War. In 1861 he left the U.S. Army to become a first lieutenant of artillery in the Confederate army, and within a year he was the colonel of the Nineteenth Alabama Infantry, which he led during the Battle of Shiloh in April 1862. Wheeler was then made chief of the cavalry in the Army of Mississippi, commanded by General Braxton Bragg.

Wheeler remained with the Confederate cavalry until the war's end. In October 1862 he was promoted to brigadier general, and in January 1863 to major general. By May 1864 he was the top cavalry leader in the Confederacy. Although he had fought with distinction in numerous battles in Mississippi, Tennessee, and Kentucky, he became particularly famous for his activities during the Union's campaign against Atlanta, Georgia, in the summer and fall of 1864. Specifically, he led his men on raids of supplies intended for Union general William T. Sherman's troops and offered the only serious resistance to Sherman's troops on their march through Georgia. At the end of the war, Wheeler was a lieutenant general commanding the cavalry of General Joseph Johnston's army in North Carolina.

After the war, Wheeler was briefly imprisoned by the U.S. government at Fort Delaware. He then settled in Alabama, where he practiced law and became a plantation owner. In 1881 he began the first of eight terms in the U.S. House of Representatives. He returned to the U.S. Army, however, to serve in the cavalry during the Spanish-American War as a major general of volunteers, and he subsequently served in the same capacity in the Philippines. When he finally retired from the military, Wheeler was a brigadier general in the U.S. Army. **See also** armies, Confederate; Bragg, Braxton; cavalry.

Whitman, Walt (1819–1892)

American poet, journalist, and essayist Walt Whitman had a long career and produced numerous works, but in terms of the Civil War his most significant contribution was two volumes of Civil War poetry, *Drum-Taps* (1865) and *Sequel to Drum-Taps* (1866), and an elegy to Abraham Lincoln, "O Captain! My Captain!," which

Poet Walt Whitman served as a nursing aide during the Civil War.

became one of Whitman's most popular poems. (A second elegy to Lincoln, "When Lilacs Last in the Dooryard Bloom'd," was published in *Sequel to Drum-Taps.*) Whitman's Civil War poems show the range of emotions associated with the conflict, from patriotism and elation to horror over the great suffering caused by war. Whitman also described the horrors of war in prose pieces that were published in an 1882–1883 collection of his writings titled *Specimen Days.*

Whitman began his career as an apprentice printer at the age of twelve. Over the next few years he worked not only as a printer but as a teacher and journalist in New York. In 1842 he became a newspaper editor. By 1848 he had become involved with what eventually became the Free-Soil Party, and his connection to this antislavery group eventually cost him two editing jobs. Consequently, from 1850 to 1855 he worked in building construction and real estate while continuing to write. He self-published his first book of poetry, *Leaves of Grass,* in 1855. He self-published a second edition in 1856 with additions and revisions, and in 1860 a Boston publisher put out a third and greatly expanded edition.

When the Civil War broke out, Whitman's brother, George Washington Whitman, volunteered for the Union army and was subsequently wounded in the Battle of Fredericksburg. When Whitman heard about this he went looking for his brother, and after he found him was relieved to learn that the wounds were not serious. However, during his search he saw many other men in bad condition, suffering in understaffed military hospitals in Washington, D.C. Troubled by the lack of help for these soldiers, Whitman decided to volunteer as a nursing aide, a position he held from 1862 to 1865. At the same time he worked in the Washington paymaster's office for a meager salary. In 1865 he took a job as a clerk in the Department of the Interior, but soon lost that job and went to work in the attorney general's office, a position he held until 1874. Meanwhile, other editions of his *Leaves of Grass* continued to appear until his death in 1892. By this time, he had earned enough money from his poetry to be able to devote his time entirely to his writing. **See also** Fredericksburg, Battle of; literature, Civil War; poetry, Civil War.

Whittier, John Greenleaf (1807–1892)

Abolitionist John Greenleaf Whittier, a member of the Quaker faith, was a poet who used his writing as a way to express his political views. A friend of prominent abolitionist William Lloyd Garrison, he worked as a journalist while writing poetry from 1826 to 1832. During this period, he edited several newspapers and magazines, including a Whig Party journal called the *New England Weekly Review.* His poetry, however, was not receiving the acclaim he had hoped for, and he decided that God was punishing him for caring more about himself than about others. As a result, he put aside his poetry to devote himself to abolitionism, writing persuasive pamphlets in support of the cause. He also became a lobbyist for antislavery legislation. Whittier continued to be devoted to abolitionist causes until 1842, at which time he turned his attention to broader humanitarian causes. At the same time, he returned to writing poetry; in fact, he would eventually be remembered more for his literary works than for his abolitionism. **See also** poetry, Civil War; Quakers.

Wigfall, Louis Trezevant (1816–1874)

South Carolina politician Louis T. Wigfall served in the U.S. Senate from 1859 to 1861 and in the Confederate Senate from 1862 to 1865. Although his only military experience was as a young man, when he served for a short time as a colonel in the state militia, Wigfall also briefly commanded Confederate troops at the outset of the war, first as a colonel and then as a brigadier general.

Wigfall first became involved in politics in 1844, when he was made a delegate to the South Carolina Democratic Convention. There, he argued in favor of secession, because he believed that the North would never respect South Carolina's right to support slavery. Wigfall is therefore credited with being the first South Carolina politician to suggest that the state leave the Union, sixteen years before it actually did so.

In 1846 Wigfall moved his family—which included a wife and three children—to Texas to escape financial and personal problems in his native state. Once in Texas he established a new law practice and continued to speak in favor of every state's right to secede from the Union if it did not agree with U.S. government policies. In 1850, after becoming a state legislator, he spoke out against the Compromise of 1850 and those in the U.S. Congress who had supported it, particularly the U.S. senator from Texas, Sam Houston. (As a result of Wigfall's efforts, the Texas legislature officially censured Houston.) In 1857 Wigfall was elected to the state senate and in 1859 to the U.S. Senate.

As a Southern senator known for his violent verbal outbursts, Wigfall was immediately labeled a fire-eater, a term used to refer to pro-slavery extremists who would rather destroy the Union than give up the right of a state to decide for itself whether or not its citizens could own slaves. Wigfall continually supported secession and opposed any compromise measures; in fact, he was instrumental in preventing the passage of the Crittenden Compromise, which historians think might have averted or at least delayed the Civil War. He was equally successful in preventing the passage of a homesteading act, out of fear that such legislation did not provide settlers with enough land to create plantations large enough to encourage slavery. He also helped write the Southern Manifesto, a document that called for the creation of a confederacy of Southern states.

When the first shot of the Civil War was fired by Confederates at Fort Sumter, Wigfall immediately gained notoriety by delivering the terms of surrender to the Federal soldiers under siege at the fort, though he had not been authorized to do so. After supporting Jefferson Davis's election as the Confederate president, Wigfall became one of Davis's assistants and a member of the Confederate Congress. In July 1861 he was given command of a Texas battalion near Richmond, Virginia.

From this point on, his relationship with Davis deteriorated, as Wigfall repeatedly disagreed with the president regarding which commanders in the Confederate army deserved which rank. In December 1861 Wigfall resigned his command but remained in the Confederate Congress, where at first he supported the president's actions but then began to criticize them. For example, while Wigfall supported Davis's position that conscription was necessary in order to provide the Confederacy with enough soldiers, he disagreed with most of Davis's military strategies, believing Generals Robert E. Lee and James Longstreet to be better suited to command the Confederate armies. In fact, in January 1865 Wigfall persuaded the Confederate Congress to name Robert E. Lee the general in chief of the Confederacy.

As it became clear that the war was a lost cause, Wigfall publicly blamed Davis for the defeat. Wigfall went to England as soon as he heard of the Confederacy's surrender, and there he tried to convince Great Britain to declare war on the United States. Six years later, in 1872, he returned to Texas, where he died in 1874. **See also** Compromise of 1850; Crittenden Compromise; fire-eater.

Wilderness, Battle of the

The Battle of the Wilderness was fought between the Union forces of General Ulysses S. Grant and the Confederate forces of General Robert E. Lee on May 5–7, 1864, in an area of northern Virginia in Orange and Spotsylvania Counties known as the Wilderness because of its thick woods. Grant had over 120,000 men, with at least that many reserve forces in the area, while Lee had only 65,000 and very limited reserves. Moreover, due to a shortage of horses, the Confederate cavalry had to fight almost completely as infantry—the first of several times this occurred during the war. During the battle, Confederate general James Longstreet was accidentally shot by his own soldiers, who mistook him for a Union soldier as he rode past their hiding place in dense forest. Otherwise, however, the Confederate troops performed well despite the fact that they were greatly outnumbered. At the end of the second day of battle, the total casualties were approximately eight thousand to ten thousand Confederate soldiers, as opposed to nearly eighteen thousand Union soldiers, and the Confederates had captured two Union brigadier generals in addition to hundreds of other soldiers and officers. Grant then decided to move his forces away from the Wilderness and headed toward Richmond, Virginia. **See also** Grant, Ulysses S.; Lee, Robert Edward; Longstreet, James.

Wilmot Proviso

The Wilmot Proviso was a piece of legislation introduced in the U.S. Congress by Representative David Wilmot of Pennsylvania in 1846. Attached to a bill providing money for the purchase of Mexican-held lands as part of the peace settlement for the Mexican-American War (1846–1848), the proviso stated that slavery would be banned in these territories once they became part of the United States. The U.S. House of Representatives narrowly passed the Wilmot Proviso but the Senate rejected it several times, and finally the legislation died. However, politicians continued to debate whether slavery should be allowed in U.S. territories right until the outbreak of the Civil War. **See also** Compromise of 1850.

Winder, John (1800–1865)

As provost marshal of Richmond, Virginia, whose job was to catch Union spies, John Winder is known for being one of the most incompetent officers of the Civil War. He caught very few spies, and even when he did it was usually because of the spies' own mistakes. In fact, at least one spy was operating out of Winder's own office. Moreover, Winder could be bribed to provide a Confederate travel pass—a requirement for anyone wanting to travel throughout Confederate lands—in exchange for money, gifts, or favors. Several Union spies later reported that they got their passes by paying Winder $100 or more.

Prior to the war, Winder was an instructor at the U.S. Military Academy, having graduated there himself in 1820, but even after many years in the U.S. Army he had failed to rise above the rank of major. Therefore, he did not hesitate to join the newly formed Confederacy when Confederate president Jefferson Davis, one of his former students, asked him to serve as the provost marshal of Richmond. Winder did a poor job from the beginning, particularly in regard to hiring the agents who worked under him. The agents were largely disreputable men who often openly drank on duty. In fact, one of these men, supposed spycatcher Philip Cashmeyer, was actually a part of a network of Union spies headed by a local woman, Elizabeth Van Lew, whom Winder failed to recognize as a Union agent. Winder unwittingly made it easier for such people to get information on Confederate troop movements by posting on a wall in his office the names and sizes of all Confederate regiments in his area.

The Confederacy finally recognized Winder's incompetence and transferred him to another job, that of supervising the distribution of supplies to prisoners of war. At the same time, he was promoted to the rank of brigadier general. But Winder proved incompetent at this assignment as well, often failing to send supplies where they were needed. Winder often complained of being overworked and fatigued, and when he died in 1865 his physician cited these two conditions as the reason for his death. **See also** spies; Van Lew, Elizabeth.

Wirz, Henry (Heinrich Hermann) (1823–1865)

Confederate captain Henry Wirz was the only soldier, Confederate or Union, to be tried and executed for war crimes once the Civil War was over. Born in Switzerland, he claimed to be a physician when he immigrated to America sometime before the Civil War but appears to have had no medical training. For most of the war he served as a sergeant in the Fourth Louisiana Infantry, but on March 27, 1864, he was sent to Andersonville, a prison camp in Georgia, to manage its day-to-day activities. Wirz was later blamed for the prison's deplorable living conditions, although many of Andersonville's problems had been created by his superiors. Near the war's end, Wirz was arrested at Andersonville and brought to trial in Washington, D.C., where he was hanged on November 10, 1865. Transcripts of his trial were then published by the U.S. government as a means of keeping alive anti-Southern sentiments after the war. **See also** Andersonville; executions; prisons and prisoners of war.

women, contributions of

Women from both the North and the South made many contributions to the war effort. Some donated handmade goods to the military, while others volunteered their time in charity efforts to support the war and its soldiers. Still others took up jobs traditionally performed by men, because during the war there were not enough male workers outside of the military. For example, most workers in ordnance laboratories and factories (places that developed and manufactured ammunition) were women, as were many telegraph operators. Women also served as doctors or nurses on the battlefield or as spies behind enemy lines.

In the South, where clothing and other supplies became scarce as the war progressed, many women sewed or knitted clothing and other items for soldiers. One of the most industrious knitters during the war was reputed to be Mary Custis Lee, the wife of Confederate general Robert E. Lee. By May 1864, with the help of her three grown daughters, she had made over four hundred pairs of socks for Confederate soldiers, many in her husband's Army of Northern Virginia.

Other women contributed their nursing rather than sewing skills. By some estimates, more than three thousand women served as nurses, either official or unofficial, during the Civil War. In the South, where the majority of battles took place, many women entered nursing out of necessity when wounded soldiers showed up on their doorsteps. Their informal, temporary field hospitals were known as wayside hospitals, and although these facilities did not have the physicians and medical supplies of the formal, big-city Northern and Southern hospitals, they still might treat hundreds of soldiers. A wayside hospital near High Point, North Carolina, for example, served 5,795 Confederate soldiers between September 1863 and May 1865.

A few women also served as hospital administrators. For example, after Confederate president Jefferson Davis called on citizens in Richmond, Virginia, to create private hospitals to care for soldiers wounded in the 1861 First Battle of Bull Run, Sally L. Tompkins convinced a local judge, John Robertson, to convert his home into the twenty-two-bed Robertson Hospital, which she would manage. She remained in charge of this facility throughout the war, even after Davis instituted a requirement that all Confederate hospitals be run by military officers. (In order to retain Tompkins as the hospital's administrator, Davis made her a cavalry captain; she was the only woman ever commissioned as a Confederate army officer.)

Even though most Northern women lived far from the war's battlefields, they too contributed nursing care to soldiers. One prominent Civil War nurse was Mary Ann Bickerdyke, who served under Union general Ulysses S. Grant as the head of nursing, hospital, and welfare services for his western armies during the Civil War. She followed his soldiers from conflict to conflict, establishing field hospitals as needed. Near the end of the war, she did the same for General William Tecumseh Sherman, accompanying his forces on their march from Atlanta, Georgia, to the sea. Between 1861 and 1865, Bickerdyke provided nursing care on at least nineteen battlefields.

Perhaps the most prominent Civil War nurse was Clara Barton, the founder of the American Red Cross. She nursed wounded soldiers who were sent to Washington, D.C., to recuperate, organized an agency whose purpose was to ensure that medical supplies reached wounded soldiers on the battlefield, and was involved in fundraising activities in New England that helped send nurses, including herself, to the front lines.

Barton and Bickerdyke were professional nurses, but others took up nursing simply because they were already on the front lines and wanted to help. These women were the officers' wives who accompanied their husbands to military camps and provided various volunteer services, including cooking, washing dishes and clothes, sewing, and tending to the wounded. Sometimes called "daughters of the regiment," they generally were kept far from the fighting, although some women did end up in the thick of combat. For example, Marie Tebe, whose husband was with the 27th and then the 114th Pennsylvania Infantry, was reportedly in heavy action at least thirteen times and tended to the wounded at the Battle of Chancellorsville even during a barrage from enemy artillery.

A few Northern women were full-fledged physicians rather than nurses, although female doctors were a rarity in the nineteenth century. For example, Mary Edwards Walker, a graduate of Syracuse Medical College in New York, tried to enlist in the Union army immediately after the Civil War began. When she was denied a commission, she volunteered her medical services without pay, thereby becoming the first female surgeon in the U.S. Army. She is also the only female veteran ever to receive a Congressional Medal of Honor for her services. After a short stint at a hospital in Washington, D.C., Walker spent two

A soldier poses with his family in front of their tent. Wives traveling with military units performed various chores to help the soldiers.

years as a battlefield surgeon, administering to Union soldiers during such conflicts as the Battle of Fredericksburg and the Battle of Chickamauga.

Other female physicians served out of political activism. Specifically, in April 1861 Drs. Elizabeth and Emily Blackwell held public meetings at their New York Infirmary, a hospital staffed entirely by women, where they encouraged ninety-one women to sign a letter demanding that the government create a soldiers' relief organization. This eventually led to the establishment of the U.S. Sanitary Commission on June 9, 1861, which was charged with overseeing all army hospitals.

The South had its political activists as well. Some, like the Blackwells, were dedicated to improving the treatment of wounded soldiers. Others were concerned with improving conditions for all Southerners. Approximately one thousand women marched in front of the governor's house in Richmond, Virginia, on April 2, 1862, to protest the high prices and meager supplies of food in the South.

Southern women also took a stand against the occupation of their lands by Union soldiers. In particular, after the Union forces of Major General Benjamin F. Butler occupied New Orleans, Louisiana, in April 1862, the women of the city insulted or even spat on the soldiers they saw in the street. One woman even dumped a chamber pot filled with human excrement on the head of Captain David Farragut from her second-story window. Others sang Confederate songs in the street. The only way that Butler could stop this abuse was by issuing General Order 28 on May 15, 1862—also known as the Woman's Order—decreeing that any woman caught repeatedly insulting a Union soldier by word, gesture, or other means would be thereafter treated as though she were the town prostitute. In other words, the woman would be derided with vulgar comments and obscene gestures in return for her behavior, and if she continued it she might be fined or imprisoned.

Even before the war broke out, women in both the North and the South expressed their political views on issues related to the conflict, especially slavery. To this end, many women produced books and articles that argued in favor of giving slaves their freedom. For example, Harriet Beecher Stowe's antislavery novel *Uncle Tom's Cabin* and former slave Sojourner Truth's memoir *The Narrative of Sojourner Truth* both increased opposition to slavery just prior to the Civil War.

Meanwhile, other women took a hands-on approach to helping slaves, opening their homes to those escaping from the South to the North both before and during the war. Former slave Harriet Tubman created a network of such "safe houses" called the Underground Railroad that helped hundreds of slaves escape to freedom. Tubman also encouraged over eight hundred slaves in South Carolina to fight for or escape to freedom, and she did some spying for the Union as well.

Female spies served both the North and the South during the Civil War. Among the most prominent were Confederate spies Belle Boyd and Rose O'Neal Greenhow and Union spy Elizabeth Van Lew. Pauline Cushman, an actress in Nashville, Tennessee, also spied for the North until she was captured, tried for treason, and sentenced to hang in 1863. She was rescued before her execution by invading Union soldiers.

In addition to participating in covert activities, women also fought the enemy openly. At least 750 women were involved in battlefield conflicts. A few women found themselves in the thick of combat after becoming "daughters of the regiment." For example, Kady Brownell carried the U.S. flag into battle for her husband's military unit, the Fifth Rhode Island Infantry. Bridget Devens became known as "Michigan Bridget" for serving as flagbearer for the First Michigan Cavalry, in which her husband was a private.

Most women who wanted to fight, however, disguised themselves as male soldiers or sailors, since neither the Union nor the Confederacy allowed women to enlist in the military. By some estimates, there were approximately four hundred disguised women, although only about one hundred cases have been documented. One such case was an unidentified woman who was discovered in male clothing among the dead at Gettysburg in July 1863. Another female soldier whose gender was discovered after her death was Sarah Rosetta Wakeman, who enlisted in the U.S. Army disguised as a man and served with the 153rd New York Regiment. The woman with the most documented period of service, though, was Jennie Hodgers, a young Irishwoman who spent three years with the Ninety-fifth Illinois Infantry Regiment as Albert Cashier. Hodgers was able to conceal her identity for so long because she never needed medical care. As a result, she was able to fight in approximately forty battles and campaigns, including the Vicksburg Campaign. (The name Albert Cashier appears on a Civil War monument there.) After the war, Hodgers continued to masquerade as a man, working as a farmhand in Illinois, until a doctor discovered her true gender while treating her for a broken leg in 1911.

Some female soldiers did not continue their deceptions after the war, however, instead deciding to share their experiences in writing. Among these was Sarah Emma Edmonds, who enlisted in 1861 as a male nurse under the name Franklin Thompson but a year later became a spy for the Union. More commonly, though, women writers told about more ordinary wartime experiences. For example, Mary Boykin Chesnut, a Southern officer's wife, wrote about what she saw in military camps and the Confederate capital, and abolitionist Fanny Kemble, author of *Journal of a Residence on a Georgian Plantation* (1863), shared her experiences as a Southern plantation owner's wife. Other women writers produced patriotic articles and editorials for newspapers and magazines during the war. Of these, among the most prominent was Mary Abigail Dodge, who wrote under the pen name Gail Hamilton. In her 1863 *Atlantic Monthly* article "A Call to My Country," she exhorted Northern women to support their soldiers' efforts in order to keep the men's morale high.

After the war, women continued to write articles and books about their war-related experiences and views. For example, in 1868 Mary Todd Lincoln's former seamstress, Elizabeth Keckley, published *Behind the Scenes, or Thirty Years a Slave and Four in the White House,* in which she told what it was like to work for the Lincolns during the war. In 1887, Mary Livermore published *My Story of the War: A Woman's Narrative* to share her experiences working with relief agencies to deliver supplies to soldiers on the front lines and to improve living conditions in military camps and hospitals. Livermore remained politically active after the war, as did many other women who were involved in political activism during the Civil War. For example, Sojourner Truth participated in postwar programs that helped former slaves find places to live and later joined efforts to gain women the right to vote. Harriet Tubman and many other prominent Civil War activists also became involved in the woman's suffrage movement, as well as efforts to improve the lives of emancipated slaves. **See also** Barton, Clarissa (Clara) Harlowe; Bickerdyke, Mary Ann; Boyd, Belle; Chesnut, Mary Boykin; Greenhow, Rose O'Neal; Livermore, Mary; Stowe, Harriet (Elizabeth) Beecher; Truth, Sojourner; Tubman, Harriet; Van Lew, Elizabeth; Walker, Mary Edwards.

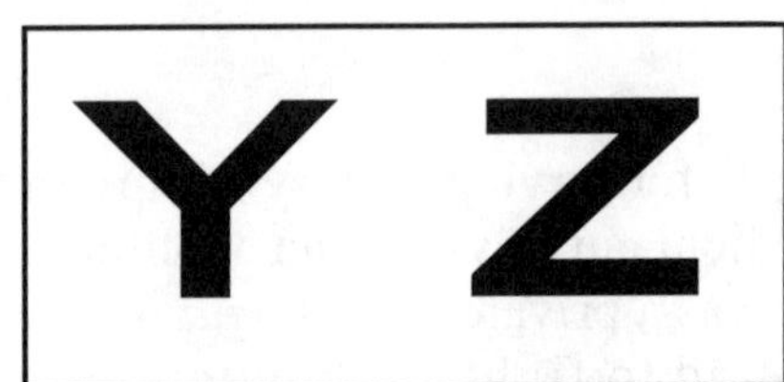

Yancey, William Lowndes (1814–1863)

As an Alabama state senator and then a U.S. congressman during the 1840s, William L. Yancey argued passionately in favor of Southern secession. In fact, his belief in secession was so strong that in 1846 he resigned his seat in Congress because he was unwilling to support the prevailing notion that various compromises were necessary to keep the Union together. After leaving Congress, he gave a series of speeches promoting states' rights in general and Southern rights in particular, and throughout the 1850s he repeatedly argued both in favor of secession and against abolitionism, sometimes getting into brawls over his views. (Historians believe that Yancey's passion about these issues stemmed in large part from the dislike he had for his stepfather, a New York abolitionist and minister named Nathan Beman who often spoke ill of Yancey's deceased father, who was a Georgia slaveholder.)

In January 1861 Yancey was an active participant in the state convention at which Alabama voted to leave the Union. However, because of his volatile personality and relatively radical political views, the Confederacy did not want to include him in its new national government, and when Yancey pressured Confederate president Jefferson Davis for a position, Davis sent him overseas as a Confederate diplomat. Yancey's job was to convince the British and French to grant the Confederacy diplomatic recognition, but his temperament and persuasive skills were not up to the task. Nonetheless, while Yancey was abroad he was elected to the Alabama Confederate Congress, and he returned to the South to take office in April 1862. From the outset Yancey criticized the way Davis was running the Confederacy and fought with fellow politicians, both verbally and physically. Even though he was generally disliked, Yancey did succeed in convincing his peers that the Confederacy should not have a centralized government but instead should let each state handle its own issues through state supreme court rulings and state legislation. In June 1863, Yancey retired from public life due to poor health, and the following month he died of kidney failure. **See also** Davis, Jefferson.

Yorktown, Battle of

The Battle of Yorktown took place around Yorktown, Virginia, in April 1862 after Union troops led by General George B. McClellan spotted Confederate troops across the Warwick River. Although the Confederates were seriously outnumbered and outgunned, their commander, General John B. Magruder, managed to fool McClellan into thinking he had more firepower than he did by constructing fake cannons out of logs (later called Quaker cannons) and displaying his troops as though he had men to spare. As a result, even though the two groups exchanged fire, McClellan decided not to mount a serious attack until he had received reinforcements, and this allowed Magruder to receive reinforcements as well. Even with additional men, however, the Confederates were still in a weak position, so as McClellan readied for a major battle Magruder secretly led his men away. By the time the Union attacked on May 4, 1862, the Confederate camp was deserted. **See also** Magruder, John Bankhead; McClellan, George Brinton; Quakers.

Zouaves

During the Civil War, some volunteer regiments adopted the flamboyant uniforms worn during the Franco-Austrian War (1859) by the Zouaves, or French African troops. American soldiers who adopted these uniforms—which typically featured ballooned trousers, short coats, and wrapped-cloth headdresses—called themselves Zouaves as well. Most Zouave units were among the Northern forces, with the largest coming from New York, but the South also had Zouave units. However, as the war progressed, Southern soldiers no longer had the money or supplies to replace damaged Zouave uniforms, and gradually their Zouave units disappeared. **See also** uniforms and equipment.

APPENDIX

Casualty Figures

The following casualty figures for many of the most significant Civil War battles are approximate and rounded to the nearest ten. Confederate statistics are far less reliable than Union figures due to lost or destroyed records (and, toward the end of the war, to the fact that the Confederates stopped compiling casualty reports).

Battle or Campaign	Losses
Antietam	Confederate: 1,550 dead, 7,750 wounded, 1,020 missing Union: 2,110 dead, 9,550 wounded, 750 missing
Appomattox	Confederate: 28,000 dead or missing, 30,000 captured Union: 9,000 dead or missing
Atlanta	Confederate: 3,040 dead, 18,950 wounded, 12,980 missing or captured Union: 4,420 dead, 22,820 wounded, 4,440 missing or captured
Ball's Bluff	Confederate: 150 dead Union: 920 dead, 700 captured
Brandy Station	Confederate: 50 dead, 130 missing Union: 1,650 dead
(First) Bull Run	Confederate: 390 dead, 1,580 wounded, 10 missing Union: 460 dead, 1,120 wounded, 1,310 missing
(Second) Bull Run	Confederate: 1,500 dead, 7,300 missing or wounded Union: 1,750 dead, 8,500 wounded, 4,200 missing
Chancellorsville	Confederate: 1,670 dead, 9,080 wounded, 2,020 missing Union: 1,600 dead, 9,760 wounded, 5,920 missing
Chattanooga	Confederate: 360 dead, 2,180 wounded, 4,200 missing or captured Union: 750 dead, 4,700 wounded, 350 missing or captured

Battle or Campaign	Losses
Chickamauga	Confederate: 2,310 dead, 14,680 wounded, 1,470 missing Union: 1,660 dead, 9,750 wounded, 4,740 missing
Franklin & Nashville	Confederate: 13,800 dead Union: 3,000 dead
Fredericksburg	Confederate: 5,500 dead, wounded, or missing Union: 1,280 dead, 11,370 wounded or missing
Gettysburg	Confederate: 28,000 dead, wounded, or missing Union: 3,070 dead, 14,500 wounded, 5,430 missing
Petersburg	Confederate: Unknown Union: 1,690 dead, 8,510 wounded, 1,190 missing
Red River (two campaigns)	Confederate: 5,200 dead, wounded, or missing Union: 4,200 dead, wounded, or missing
Seven Days'	Confederate: 20,100 dead, wounded, or missing Union: 15,800 dead, wounded, or missing
Seven Pines	Confederate: 6,100 dead, wounded, or missing Union: 5,000 dead, wounded, or missing
Shiloh	Confederate: Over 10,000 dead, wounded, or missing Union: 1,750 dead, 8,400 wounded, 2,880 missing
Spotsylvania	Confederate: 9,000–12,000 dead Union: 2,730 dead, 13,420 wounded, 2,260 missing
Wilderness	Confederate: 8,000–10,000 dead Union: 2,300 dead, 12,000 wounded, 3,400 missing

CHRONOLOGY

1860

November 6
Abraham Lincoln is elected U.S. president.

December 20
South Carolina secedes from the Union.

1861

January 9
Mississippi secedes.

January 10
Florida secedes.

January 11
Alabama secedes.

January 19
Georgia secedes.

January 26
Louisiana secedes.

January 29
Kansas joins the Union as a free state.

February 1
Texas secedes.

February 4
The seceded states hold a convention in Montgomery, Alabama, to officially establish the Confederate States of America (CSA), electing provisional leaders and drafting a constitution.

March 4
Lincoln is inaugurated U.S. president.

April 12
Confederate forces fire on the U.S. garrison at Fort Sumter, South Carolina, thereby starting the Civil War.

April 17
Virginia secedes, adding an important federal arsenal (Harpers Ferry) and naval base (Norfolk) to the Confederacy.

May 6
Arkansas secedes.

May 20
The Provisional Confederate Congress relocates the Confederate capital from Montgomery, Alabama, to Richmond, Virginia; North Carolina secedes.

June 8
Tennessee secedes.

September 3
Confederate troops invade Kentucky, a border state that had previously declared itself neutral.

November 8
A U.S. Navy vessel attacks a British ship, HMS *Trent,* and takes into custody two Confederate diplomats on their way to Europe; this incident, known as the *Trent* Affair, nearly draws England into America's Civil War.

November 28
The Confederacy claims that Missouri has seceded, based on a vote by state legislators; however, the Union remains in control of the state.

December 10
The Confederacy claims that Kentucky has seceded, based on a vote by state legislators; however, the Union remains in control of most of the state.

1862

February 6
The Union capture of Fort Henry, Tennessee, makes it possible for U.S. forces

to use the Tennessee River to penetrate deep into the South.

February 22
Jefferson Davis is inaugurated, having been voted C.S.A. president after serving provisionally in the position from the beginning of the Confederacy.

March 8–9
The first combat between two ironclads, the CSS *Virginia* and the USS *Monitor,* takes place.

April 16
Lincoln officially ends slavery in Washington, D.C.

April 29
Union spy Timothy Webster becomes the first American spy to be executed since the Revolutionary War, when Confederate officials hang him in Richmond, Virginia.

May 20
The U.S. Congress passes the Homestead Act, whereby its citizens are encouraged to settle U.S. territories.

June 19
The U.S. government officially prohibits slavery in U.S. territories.

August 25
The U.S. government begins establishing black regiments (although their commanding officers are white).

September 22
Lincoln issues the Preliminary Emancipation Proclamation, warning Southern states that unless they return to the Union by January 1, 1863, their slaves will be declared free.

September 24
Lincoln suspends habeas corpus, allowing the U.S. government to detain citizens indefinitely without due process of law.

1863

March 3
Lincoln establishes the first federal conscription law, permitting the U.S. government to draft soldiers into the army against their will.

March 6
The first of several Northern antidraft riots occurs in Detroit, Michigan, during which blacks are targeted for attack.

April 2
Serious food shortages in the South lead to a riot in Richmond, Virginia, during which many stores are looted.

May 1
The Confederacy gives its military the authority to execute white Union officers captured while commanding black regiments.

June 20
West Virginia is admitted to the Union.

July 4
Vicksburg, Mississippi, and nearby Port Hudson, Louisiana, are captured by the Union, thereby cutting off the Trans-Mississippi Department from the rest of the Confederacy.

July 13–17
A major draft riot occurs in New York City.

August 21–22
Confederate guerrillas led by William Quantrill kill more than 150 antislavery settlers in Lawrence, Kansas.

September 9
The Union takes control of Chattanooga, Tennessee, formerly a Confederate stronghold significant for its proximity to the North.

November 19
Lincoln delivers the Gettysburg Address.

December 8
Lincoln issues the Proclamation of Amnesty and Reconstruction, offering conditions under which Southern states and secessionists can return to the Union.

1864

February 27
The Confederate prison camp known as Andersonville, located in Georgia, begins to house prisoners; after the war its commander will be tried and executed on criminal charges for the facility's inhumane conditions.

March 9
Ulysses S. Grant becomes general in chief of all U.S. armies.

June 19
The highly successful Confederate raider CSS *Alabama* is attacked and sunk off the coast of France.

September 2
Sherman takes the Confederate city of Atlanta, Georgia.

November 8
Lincoln is reelected U.S. president.

November 16
Sherman begins his twenty-six-day march across Georgia to the sea.

December 21
Union forces take Savannah, Georgia.

1865

February 3
The unsuccessful Hampton Roads Peace Conference takes place between U.S. and Confederate officials, including Lincoln and Confederate vice president Alexander H. Stephens.

March 3
The U.S. government creates the Bureau of Refugees, Freedmen, and Abandoned Lands to provide aid to freedmen.

March 13
Davis authorizes the use of blacks as Confederate soldiers.

April 2
The Confederates begin to abandon Richmond.

April 9
Confederate general Robert E. Lee surrenders his Army of Northern Virginia at Appomattox, thereby ending Southern hopes of victory in the Civil War.

April 14
Lincoln is shot at Ford's Theater and dies the next day.

April 26
Lincoln's assassin, John Wilkes Booth, is killed by Federal troops.

May 10
Federal troops capture Davis in Georgia and kill Confederate guerrilla William Quantrill in Kentucky.

May 29
Lincoln's successor, Andrew Johnson, pardons most former Confederates.

December 18
The Thirteenth Amendment to the U.S. Constitution, whereby slavery is officially abolished throughout the United States, is ratified.

FOR FURTHER RESEARCH

Edward Porter Alexander, *Fighting for the Confederacy: The Personal Recollections of General Edward Porter Alexander.* Ed. Gary W. Gallagher. Chapel Hill: University of North Carolina Press, 1989.

Mark M. Boatner III, *The Civil War Dictionary.* Vintage Civil War Library Edition. New York: Random House, 1991.

Gabor S. Boritt, ed., *Why the Confederacy Lost.* New York: Oxford University Press, 1992.

Alice E. Carter and Richard Jensen, *The Civil War on the Web: A Guide to the Very Best Sites.* Wilmington, DE: Scholarly Resources, 2003.

Catherine Clinton and Nina Silber, eds., *Divided Houses: Gender and the Civil War.* New York: Oxford University Press, 1992.

Robert Cowley, ed., *With My Face to the Enemy: Perspectives on the Civil War.* New York: G.P. Putnam's Sons, 2001.

Marilyn Mayer Culpepper, *All Things Altered: Women in the Wake of Civil War and Reconstruction.* Jefferson, NC: McFarland, 2002.

———, *Trials and Triumphs: Women of the American Civil War.* East Lansing: Michigan State University Press, 1991.

Charles E. Dornbusch, ed., *Military Bibliography of the Civil War.* 4 vols. New York: New York Public Library, 1987.

Editors of Time-Life Books, *Echoes of Glory: Illustrated Atlas of the Civil War.* Alexandria, VA: Time-Life, 1991.

David J. Eicher, *The Civil War in Books: An Analytical Bibliography.* Foreword by Gary W. Gallagher. Urbana: University of Illinois Press, 1997.

John Hope Franklin, *Reconstruction After the Civil War.* Chicago: University of Chicago Press, 1994.

Gary W. Gallagher and Alan T. Nolan, eds., *The Myth of the Lost Cause and Civil War History.* Bloomington: Indiana University Press, 2000.

Joseph T. Glatthaar, *Forged in Battle: The Civil War Alliance of Black Soldiers and White Officers.* Baton Rouge: Louisiana State University Press, 2000.

Ulysses S. Grant, *The Civil War Memoirs of Ulysses S. Grant.* Ed. Brian M. Thomsen. New York: Forge, 2002.

Herman Hattaway and Archer Jones, *How the North Won: A Military History of the Civil War.* Urbana: University of Illinois Press, 1991.

John T. Hubbell, *Battles Lost and Won: Essays from Civil War History.* Westport, CT: Greenwood, 1975.

Earl B. McElfresh, *Maps and Mapmakers of the Civil War.* Foreword by Stephen W. Sears. New York: Harry N. Abrams, 1999.

Phillip S. Paludan, *A People's Contest: The Union and the Civil War, 1861–1865.* 2nd ed. Lawrence: University of Kansas Press, 1996.

Robert Gould Shaw, *Blue-Eyed Child of Fortune: The Civil War Letters of Colonel Robert Gould Shaw.* Ed. Russell Duncan. Athens: University of Georgia Press, 1992.

William Tecumseh Sherman, *Memoirs of General W.T. Sherman.* New York: Library of America, 1990.

Jean Edward Smith, *Grant.* New York: Simon & Schuster, 2001.

Allen W. Trelease, *Reconstruction: The Great Experiment.* New York: Harper & Row, 1971.

———, *White Terror: The Ku Klux Klan Conspiracy and Southern Reconstruction.* Baton Rouge: Louisiana State University Press, 1995.

WORKS CONSULTED

Books

Stephen V. Ash, *When the Yankees Came: Conflict and Chaos in the Occupied South, 1861–1865.* Chapel Hill: University of North Carolina Press, 1995.

Ronald H. Bailey and the Editors of Time-Life Books, *The Bloodiest Day: The Battle of Antietam.* The Civil War series. Alexandria, VA: Time-Life, 1984.

Ambrose Bierce, *Ambrose Bierce's Civil War.* Ed. William McCann. New York: Random House, 1996.

Steven A. Channing and the Editors of Time-Life Books, *Confederate Ordeal: The Southern Home Front.* The Civil War series. Alexandria, VA: Time-Life, 1984.

Champ Clark and the Editors of Time-Life Books, *The Assassination: Death of the President.* The Civil War series. Alexandria, VA: Time-Life, 1985.

———, *Gettysburg: The Confederate High Tide.* The Civil War series. Alexandria, VA: Time-Life, 1987.

Robert F. Curden, *The Gray and the Black: The Confederate Debate on Emancipation.* Baton Rouge: Louisiana State University Press, 1972.

Richard N. Current et al., eds., *The Confederacy.* Selections from the four-volume Simon & Schuster *Encyclopedia of the Confederacy.* New York: Macmillan Reference USA, 1993.

William C. Davis, *The Battlefields of the Civil War.* Rebels and Yankees series. London: Salamander, 1999.

———, *The Commanders of the Civil War.* Rebels and Yankees series. London: Salamander, 1999.

———, *The Fighting Men of the Civil War.* Rebels and Yankees series. London: Salamander, 1999

William C. Davis and the Editors of Time-Life Books, *Brother Against Brother: The War Begins.* The Civil War series. Alexandria, VA: Time-Life, 1983.

———, *First Blood: Fort Sumter to Bull Run.* The Civil War series. Alexandria, VA: Time-Life, 1983.

Dictionary of the Civil War. London: Brockhampton, 1997.

David Herbert Donald, Jean H. Baker, and Michael F. Holt, *The Civil War and Reconstruction.* New York: Norton, 2001.

Editors of Time-Life Books, *The Blockade: Runners and Raiders.* The Civil War series. Alexandria, VA: Time-Life, 1983.

———, *Lee Takes Command: From Seven Days to Second Bull Run.* The Civil War series. Alexandria, VA: Time-Life, 1984.

———, *Spies, Scouts, and Raiders: Irregular Operations.* The Civil War series. Alexandria, VA: Time-Life, 1986.

Shelby Foote, *The Civil War: A Narrative.* New York: Vintage, 1986.

Gary W. Gallagher, *The Confederate War.* Cambridge, MA: Harvard University Press, 1997.

Webb Garrison, *Civil War Curiosities: Strange Stories, Oddities, Events, and Coincidences.* Nashville, TN: Rutledge Hill, 1994.

Michael Golay, *Generals of the Civil War.* New York: Barnes & Noble, 1997.

Laurence M. Hauptman, *Between Two Fires: American Indians in the Civil War.* New York: Free Press Paperbacks/Simon & Schuster, 1995.

David S. Heidler and Jeanne T. Heidler, eds., *Encyclopedia of the American Civil War: A Political, Social, and Military History.* Santa Barbara, CA: ABC-CLIO, 2000.

John T. Hubbell and James W. Geary, eds., Jon L. Wakelyn, advisory ed., *Biographical Dictionary of the Union: Northern Leaders of the Civil War.* Westport, CT: Greenwood, 1995.

August V. Kautz, *The 1865 Customs of Service for Officers of the Army.* Mechanicsburg, PA: Stackpole, 2002.

Angus Konstam, gen. ed., *The Civil War: A Visual Encyclopedia.* London: PRC, 2001.

Jerry Korn and the Editors of Time-Life Books, *Pursuit to Appomattox: The Last Battles.* The Civil War series. Alexandria, VA: Time-Life, 1987.

———, *War on the Mississippi: Grant's Vicksburg Campaign.* The Civil War series. Alexandria, VA: Time-Life, 1985.

E.B. Long and Barbara Long, *The Civil War Day by Day.* New York: Doubleday, 1971.

David Madden, ed., *Beyond the Battlefield: The Ordinary Life and Extraordinary Times of the Civil War Soldier.* New York: Touchstone/Simon & Schuster, 2000.

James M. McPherson, *Battle Cry of Freedom: The Civil War Era.* New York: Oxford University Press, 1988.

———, *Ordeal by Fire: The Civil War and Reconstruction.* New York: Knopf, 2000.

James M. McPherson, ed., *The Atlas of the Civil War.* New York: Macmillan, 1994.

James M. McPherson and William J. Cooper Jr., eds., *Writing the Civil War: The Quest to Understand.* Columbia: University of South Carolina Press, 1998.

David Nevin and the Editors of Time-Life Books, *Sherman's March: Atlanta to the Sea.* The Civil War series. Alexandria, VA: Time-Life, 1986.

James I. Robertson Jr. and the Editors of Time-Life Books, *Tenting Tonight: The Soldier's Life.* The Civil War series. Alexandria, VA: Time-Life, 1984.

Theodore F. Rodenbough, Robert S. Lanier, and Henry W. Elson, *The Photographic History of the Civil War.* 3 vols. New York: Portland House/Random House, 1997.

Kenneth M. Stampp, ed, *The Causes of the Civil War.* New York: Touchstone/Simon & Schuster, 1991.

The Timechart History of the Civil War. Ann Arbor, MI: Lowe & B. Hould/Borders, 2001.

Noah Andre Trudeau, *Like Men of War: Black Troops in the Civil War, 1862–1865.* Boston: Back Bay/Little, Brown, 1998.

Margaret E. Wagner, Gary W. Gallagher, and Paul Finkelman, eds., *The Library of Congress Civil War Desk Reference.* New York: Simon & Schuster, 2002.

Jon L. Wakelyn, *Biographical Dictionary of the Confederacy.* Westport, CT: Greenwood, 1977.

Geoffrey C. Ward, with Ric Burns and Ken Burns, *The Civil War: An Illustrated History.* New York: Borzoi/Knopf, 1990.

William Watson, *Life in the Confederate Army: Being the Observations and Experiences of an Alien in the South During the American Civil War.* Baton Rouge: Louisiana State University Press, 1995.

Emmy E. Werner, *Reluctant Witnesses: Children's Voices from the Civil War.* Boulder, CO: Westview, 1998.

Jerry D. Wert, *A Brotherhood of Valor: The Common Soldiers of the Stonewall Brigade, C.S.A., and the Iron Brigade, U.S.A.* New York: Touchstone/Simon & Schuster, 2000.

Steven E. Woodworth, ed., *The American Civil War: A Handbook of Literature and Research.* Westport, CT: Greenwood, 1995.

Periodicals

Andrew Curry, "The Better Angels: Why Are We Still Fighting over Who Was Right and Who Was Wrong in the Civil War?" *U.S. News & World Report,* September 30, 2002.

Louis A. Garavaglia, "Sherman's March and the Georgia Arsenals," *North and South,* vol. 6, no. 1, December 2002.

Mike Woshner, "Men and Matériel: Rubber and Gutta Percha Goods Used During the War Included Everything from Blankets to Pontoons," *America's Civil War,* January 2003.

Websites

American Academy of Arts & Sciences Web Site, "Occasional Papers Synopsis; War with Iraq: Costs, Consequences, and Alternatives," (includes costs of all of America's wars for purposes of comparison), www.amacad.org.

Black History (subsections cover the Freedmen's Bureau, Redemption, Reconstruction, *Uncle Tom's Cabin,* and many other topics), www.africana.com.

The Civil War (including pages on history, biography, chronology, and miscellaneous facts), www.civilwarhome.com.

The Civil War in Miniature: Civil War Terminology, maintained by Roger L. Curry, http://civilwarmini.com.

The Freedmen's Bureau Online, http://freedmensbureau.com.

"Mary Edwards Walker: Civil War Doctor" by the St. Lawrence County, NY, Branch of the American Association of University Women, www.northnet.org.

Songs of the Civil War, www.fortunecity.com.

Virtual American Biographies. www.famousamericans.net. (Can also be accessed through http://virtualology.com).

INDEX

PICTURE CREDITS

Cover photo: © Geoffrey Clements/CORBIS
© Bettmann/CORBIS, 147, 158, 226, 298, 303
© CORBIS, 76, 195, 212, 223, 293
Corel Corporation, 254
Courtesy of the Lincoln Museum, Fort Wayne, Indiana, 50, 145
Dover, 55, 140, 292
Hulton/Archive by Getty Images, 23, 79, 87, 106, 117, 132, 162, 242, 247, 257, 266, 275, 282
Library of Congress, 16, 19, 27, 30, 35, 43, 72, 93, 110, 122, 129, 135, 171, 176, 179, 185, 204, 233, 240, 261
© Medford Historical Society Collection/CORBIS, 286
National Archives, 60, 67, 100, 127, 153, 169, 181, 190, 209, 263, 269
National Portrait Gallery, Smithsonian Institution, 57
North Wind Picture Archives, 11, 95, 120, 219

ABOUT THE AUTHOR

Patricia D. Netzley is the author of more than thirty nonfiction books on a wide range of topics. Her works include *The Encyclopedia of Special Effects* (Oryx Press Hardback, 1999; Facts On File Paperback, 2001); *The Encyclopedia of Women's Travel and Exploration* (Oryx Press, 2001); *Environmental Literature: An Encyclopedia of Works, Authors, and Themes* (ABC-CLIO, 1999); and *Social Protest Literature: An Encyclopedia of Works, Characters, Authors, and Themes* (ABC-CLIO, 1999). Netzley also writes novels for children and young adults. She has three teenagers of her own: Matthew, Sarah, and Jacob.

ABOUT THE CONSULTING EDITOR

Kenneth W. Osborne received his doctorate from Providence College. A member of the history department at Roger Williams University in Providence, Rhode Island, Dr. Osborne conducts research on U.S. military history and teaches courses on the American Civil War.

pleasantness of the memory almost startled him. The Paula of his memory was somehow different from the Paula of today—more fresh, more excited, less tired. And himself—the self he saw in those Sunday walks had the world by the tail, or thought he did. Back in those days there hadn't been enough hard knocks to take the wind out of his sails.

But he closed the diary. He was still happy, wasn't he? And so was Paula, he thought. Perhaps happy in a more mellow, less excited sort of way, but they were still happy, weren't they? Oh, the responsibility of four children (one just becoming a teenager) took its toll, as did the job and the other burdens. And there really wasn't time for Sunday walks any more or for the deep personal communication that went with them. But they were still reasonably happy. And those old romantic things could always be brought back into their lives, couldn't they? After the children were raised? After he got the promotion at work? After the new wing on the house was finished?

Bill tossed the old diary back onto the shelf and turned to leave the room. Then he turned back. There was a sweetness and an excitement in just reading those pages. He wanted to have it again. He picked the book up and read through it once more—this time slowly, in deep thought.

It was an hour later when he closed the diary again. His eyes were blurred by tears. He was ready now to admit to himself that their marriage had lost some of its romance and communication, and that their lives had lost a corresponding amount of joy.

He felt that he stood at a crossroads. He could shrug off the feeling, put the book back on the shelf, and succumb to the notion that the closeness and excitement of years ago was impossible now. Or he could call a baby sitter, sweep Paula off her feet and out of the door, drive across town to that little park by their old apartment, and spend the evening not only reminiscing but *planning* how to bring it all back.

Somehow, Bill couldn't escape the feeling that on his simple decision of what to do hung the eternal future of a marriage and a family.